Women in Magazines

Women have been important contributors to and readers of magazines since the development of the periodical press in the nineteenth century. By the mid-twentieth century, millions of women read the weeklies and monthlies that focused on supposedly 'feminine concerns' of the home, family and appearance. In the decades that followed, feminist scholars criticised such publications as at best conservative and at worst regressive in their treatment of gender norms and ideals. However, this perspective obscures the heterogeneity of the magazine industry itself and women's experiences of it, both as readers and as journalists. This collection explores such diversity, highlighting the differing and at times contradictory images and understandings of women in a range of magazines and women's contributions to magazines in a number of contexts from late nineteenth century publications to twenty-first century titles in Britain, North America, continental Europe and Australia.

Rachel Ritchie is an Associate Research Fellow at Brunel University London.

Sue Hawkins teaches nineteenth-century British social history at Kingston University London.

Nicola Phillips is a Gender Historian and Co-Director of the Bedford Centre for the History of Women and the MA in Public History at Royal Holloway, University of London.

S. Jay Kleinberg is a Professor Emerita at Brunel University London and Chair of the Society for the History of Women in the Americas.

Routledge Research in Gender and History

1 **The Women's Movement and Women's Employment in Nineteenth Century Britain**
Ellen Jordan

2 **Gender, Sexuality and Colonial Modernities**
Edited by Antoinette Burton

3 **Women's Suffrage in the British Empire**
Citizenship, Nation and Race
Edited by Ian Christopher Fletcher, Laura E. Nym Mayhall and Philippa Levine

4 **Women, Educational Policy-Making and Administration in England**
Authoritative Women Since 1800
Edited by Joyce Goodman and Sylvia Harrop

5 **Women, Gender and Labour Migration**
Historical and Global Perspectives
Edited by Pamela Sharpe

6 **Women, Accounting, and Narrative**
Keeping Books in Eighteenth-Century England
Rebecca Elisabeth Connor

7 **The Educated Woman**
Minds, Bodies, and Women's Higher Education in Britain, Germany, and Spain, 1865–1914
Katharina Rowold

8 **Political Women**
The Women's Movement, Political Institutions, the Battle for Women's Suffrage and the ERA
Alana S. Jeydel

9 **Women, Education, and Agency, 1600–2000**
Edited by Jean Spence, Sarah Jane Aiston, Maureen M. Meikle

10 **Gender, Migration and the Public Sphere, 1850–2005**
Edited by Marlou Schrover and Eileen Janes Yeo

11 **Across the Religious Divide: Women, Property, and Law in the Wider Mediterranean (ca. 1300–1800)**
Jutta Gisela Sperling and Shona Kelly Wray

12 **Gender, Power, and Military Occupations**
Asia Pacific and the Middle East since 1945
Edited by Christine de Matos and Rowena Ward

13 **The Schooling of Girls in Britain and Ireland, 1800–1900**
Jane McDermid

14 **Gender in Late Medieval and Early Modern Europe**
Edited by Marianna G. Muravyeva and Raisa Maria Toivo

15 **The Political Worlds of Women**
Gender and Politics in Nineteenth Century Britain
Sarah Richardson

16 **Men After War**
Edited by Stephen McVeigh and Nicola Cooper

17 **Female Agency in the Urban Economy**
Gender in European Towns, 1640–1830
Edited by Deborah Simonton and Anne Montenach

18 **Women and the Media**
Feminism and Femininity in Britain, 1900 to the Present
Edited by Maggie Andrews and Sallie McNamara

19 **Gender in Urban Europe**
Sites of Political Activity and Citizenship, 1750–1900
Edited by Krista Cowman, Nina Javette Koefoed and Åsa Karlsson Sjögren

20 **Women and the Reinvention of the Political**
Feminism in Italy, 1968–1983
Maud Anne Bracke

21 **Women in Higher Education, 1850–1970**
International Perspectives
Edited by E. Lisa Panayotidis and Paul Stortz

22 **Gendering the Settler State**
White Women, Race, Liberalism and Empire in Rhodesia, 1950–1980
Kate Law

23 **Women in Magazines**
Research, Representation, Production and Consumption
Edited by Rachel Ritchie, Sue Hawkins, Nicola Phillips and S. Jay Kleinberg

Women in Magazines
Research, Representation,
Production and Consumption

**Edited by Rachel Ritchie, Sue Hawkins,
Nicola Phillips and S. Jay Kleinberg**

LONDON AND NEW YORK

First published 2016 by Routledge

2 Park Square, Milton Park, Abingdon, Oxfordshire OX14 4RN
52 Vanderbilt Avenue, New York, NY 10017

Routledge is an imprint of the Taylor & Francis Group, an informa business

First issued in paperback 2019

Copyright © 2016 Taylor & Francis

The right of the editors to be identified as the authors of the editorial material, and of the authors for their individual chapters, has been asserted in accordance with sections 77 and 78 of the Copyright, Designs and Patents Act 1988.

All rights reserved. No part of this book may be reprinted or reproduced or utilised in any form or by any electronic, mechanical, or other means, now known or hereafter invented, including photocopying and recording, or in any information storage or retrieval system, without permission in writing from the publishers.

Notice:
Product or corporate names may be trademarks or registered trademarks, and are used only for identification and explanation without intent to infringe.

Library of Congress Cataloging-in-Publication Data
Names: Ritchie, Rachel, editor of compilation. | Hawkins, Sue, 1956– editor of compilation. | Phillips, Nicola (Nicola Jane) editor of compilation. | Kleinberg, S. J., editor of compilation.
Title: Women in magazines : research, representation, production and consumption / edited by Rachel Ritchie, Sue Hawkins, Nicola Phillips and S. Jay Kleinberg.
Description: New York : Routledge, 2016. | Series: Routledge research in gender and history ; 23 | Includes bibliographical references and index.
Identifiers: LCCN 2015041768 (print) | LCCN 2016000526 (ebook) | ISBN 9781138824027 (alk. paper) | ISBN 781315741727 (ebk) | ISBN 9781315741727 ()
Subjects: LCSH: Women's periodicals—History. | Women—Periodicals—History. | Women and literature—History.
Classification: LCC PN4835.5 W66 2016 (print) | LCC PN4835.5 (ebook) | DDC 050.82—dc23
LC record available at http://lccn.loc.gov/2015041768

ISBN: 978-1-138-82402-7 (hbk)
ISBN: 978-0-367-26379-9 (pbk)

Typeset in Sabon
by Apex CoVantage, LLC

Contents

List of Figures   x

Introduction   1
RACHEL RITCHIE, SUE HAWKINS, NICOLA PHILLIPS AND S. JAY KLEINBERG

PART I
Thinking About Women's Magazines

1 Fragmentation and Inclusivity: Methods for Working with Girls' and Women's Magazines   25
PENNY TINKLER

2 Landscape for a Good Woman's Weekly: Finding Magazines in Post-war British History and Culture   40
TRACEY LOUGHRAN

PART II
Ideals of Femininity and Negotiating Gender Norms

3 Gender, Reproduction and the Fight for Free Love in the Late Nineteenth-Century Periodical Press   55
SARAH JONES

4 Inter-war Czech Women's Magazines: Constructing Gender, Consumer Culture and Identity in Central Europe   66
KARLA HUEBNER

5 Make Any Occasion a Special Event: Hospitality, Domesticity and Female Cordial Consumption in Magazine Advertising, 1950–1969   81
ROCHELLE PEREIRA-ALVARES

6 Righting Women in the 1960s: Gender, Power and
Conservatism in the Pages of *The New Guard*   92
SINEAD MCENEANEY

PART III
Women, Magazines and Employment

7 Getting a Living, Getting a Life: Leonora Eyles,
Employment and Agony, 1925–1930   107
FIONA HACKNEY

8 'Corresponding with Men': Exploring the Significance
of Constance Maynard's Magazine Writing, 1913–1920   125
GRETCHEN GALBRAITH

9 The Married Woman Worker in *Chatelaine*
Magazine, 1948–1964   137
HELEN GLEW

10 Nanny Knows Best?: Tensions in Nanny Employment
in Early and Mid-Twentieth-Century British Childcare
Magazines   148
KATHERINE HOLDEN

PART IV
Young Women in Magazines

11 The American Girl: Ideas of Nationalism and
Sexuality as Promoted in the *Ladies' Home Journal*
during the Early Twentieth Century   165
CHEYANNE CORTEZ

12 A Taste of *Honey*: Get-Ahead Femininity in 1960s Britain   183
FAN CARTER

PART V
Women's Bodies from Second Wave Feminism
to the Twenty-First Century

13 Popular Feminism and the Second Wave: Women's
Liberation, Sexual Liberation and *Cleo* Magazine   201
MEGAN LE MASURIER

14 How *Ladies' Home Journal* Covered Second
   Wave Health, 1969–1975   214
   AMANDA HINNANT

15 *Beauty Trade* and the Rise of American Black
   Hair Magazines   228
   CARINA SPAULDING

   Contributors   241
   Bibliography   248
   Index   261

Figures

1.1 'This cigarette business!' Cover and featured article. © The British Library Board. *Girls' Favourite*, 4 December 1926, 409. — 35
1.2 'This cigarette business!' Cover and featured article. © The British Library Board. *Girls' Favourite*, 4 December 1926, 411. — 35
4.1 Front cover of *Moderní dívka*, 5 March 1926 (possible misprint for April). — 70
4.2 Front cover of *List paní a dívek* ('Pražanka'), 9 December 1925. — 71
4.3 Front cover of *Eva*, 1 February 1929. — 73
5.1 'How about stepping in this evening?' Hiram Walker advertisement, *Gourmet*, March 1956, 69. — 86
5.2 McMullen's Cordial Casuals/Hiram Walker advertisement, *Sports Illustrated*, 4 April 1960, 11. — 88
7.1 (Margaret) Leonora Eyles (née Pitcairn) (Mrs D.L. Murray), photograph by Howard Coster, 1934 © National Portrait Gallery, London. — 109
10.1 'Over the Teacups', reproduced courtesy of *Nursery World*. — 151
10.2 Illustration for the article 'Mother and/or Nanny' in *Nursery World* by Phyllis Hostler, December 1956. Reproduced courtesy of *Nursery World*. — 156
10.3 Illustration for the article 'Mother and/or Nanny' in *Nursery World* by Phyllis Hostler, December 1956. Reproduced courtesy of *Nursery World*. — 156
11.1 Charles Dana Gibson, 'Mr Gibson's American Girl', *Ladies' Home Journal*, February 1903. — 168
12.1 *Honey*, June 1965, with kind permission of © Time Inc., UK Ltd and The British Library. — 188

Introduction

Rachel Ritchie, Sue Hawkins,
Nicola Phillips and S. Jay Kleinberg

In December 2012, the British magazine *Woman's Weekly* celebrated one hundred years of publication by including a reproduction of its first issue within the pages of its centenary edition. Around the same time, the publishers of US *Vogue* launched their much-anticipated digitised archive, containing every page of every issue since the magazine began in 1892. These events marked major milestones for two of the longest-running titles for women on either side of the Atlantic. They also served as a reminder of the history behind these publications. The very form of the magazine obscures the past of these and other well-known women's journals around the world; the periodical exists in the continual present, whether that is weekly, monthly or even quarterly in nature.

These landmarks for *Woman's Weekly* and *Vogue* prompted the editors of this collection to bring together an international group of scholars interested in magazines in the present, but more particularly in the past, at an interdisciplinary conference held at Kingston University, London, in June 2012. Our focus then and now was the gendered dynamic of many such publications, both in their depictions of women within their pages and women's roles in making and reading them. Our deliberately ambiguous *Women in Magazines* title, also used as the name of the conference, reflects this broad remit. It is not simply about women's magazines, although they are an important genre. Rather, contributors explore the position of women *in* magazines, the rich and varied history of how they have been represented in periodicals, involved in their production and held the dominant position in consuming them.

For many of the eighty-plus researchers who presented papers at Kingston University, there was palpable relief at being able to talk about their findings without having to spend half of their allocated time explaining the validity of periodicals as historical evidence. This allowed us to go deeper and further with our analysis than is usually permitted in conference papers. Doing so further highlighted the fruitfulness of magazines as a source and sent us away invigorated, with an even greater commitment to pursuing this field of enquiry. A mailing list and two further international conferences, one in the US and one in the UK, have followed.

A primary goal of this collection is to demonstrate this validity to a wider audience by showcasing the usefulness of magazines as an historical source. Individually and collectively, those papers selected for inclusion reveal the breadth and depth of insight that the study of magazines can yield. Some of our authors are magazine specialists. Others use periodicals as part of a range of resources to research a wide variety of topics, such as women's employment or popular understandings of feminism. Whichever the writer's stance, these case studies add to our understandings of individual publications, magazines as a cultural form and the workings of the periodical press. This is important because, as Sammye Johnson notes in her assessment of the relationship between academic scholarship and the magazine industry in the twenty-first century, 'research about [. . .] magazine professionals has been neglected. But so has magazine research in general'. This is despite 'the thousands of magazines—past and present—available for us to study'.[1] Chapters in this collection also offer important contributions to other academic debates, from the attitudes of free-love advocates in the late nineteenth century to racialised notions of beauty in the late twentieth and early twenty-first centuries. Taken together, they provide a wide-ranging historical perspective on the relationship between women and magazines: representations of women in magazines, women as contributors to and creators of magazines and women as readers of magazines in the long twentieth century (the 1890s to early 2000s).

A second aim of the collection is to highlight the tensions and paradoxes that both characterise the relationship between women and magazines and are inherent within the publications themselves. While there is great variety in terms of each author's area of focus, underlying the entire collection is a strong commitment to exploring the diverse and often conflicting evidence that emerges from such studies (at times even within a single issue of one title). There is a clear recognition within the chapters and across the collection as a whole of the complexities and ambiguities contained within these publications. This is in part about the composite nature of magazines. Three distinct elements make up every issue of a publication: editorial content, advertising and reader input. These elements involve the staff (writers, freelancers and those involved in the production process), numerous advertisers and readers, including those who wrote into the magazine or appeared in its features. There are disparities and tensions between these groups (between different types of content, for example, such as advice columns compared to fiction) as well as within them (such as conflicting messages from advertisers for rival products). This internal heterogeneity, in addition to differences between titles or across issues, helps to explain the paradoxes and tensions within magazines.[2]

Concomitant with this recognition of ambiguity and complexity, authors explore the opportunities that magazines presented to women (as readers and as contributors) as well as their limitations. This attitude and approach, acknowledging the positive attributes of the genre, has not always been apparent in scholarship on the women's periodical press. Many second wave feminist writers condemned contemporary women's periodicals as perpetuating narrowly defined, socially acceptable gender roles and encouraging conformity to these norms. In *The Feminine Mystique* (1963), Betty Friedan was highly critical of the post-war women's press despite (or perhaps because of) having worked as a freelance journalist for such publications. After outlining the editorial contents of a 1960 issue of *McCall's*, for instance, she stated:

> The image of woman that emerges from this big, pretty magazine is young and frivolous, almost childlike; fluffy and feminine; passive; gaily content in a world of bedroom and kitchen, sex, babies, and home [. . .] where is the world of thought and ideas, the life of the mind and spirit? In the magazine image, women do no work except housework and work to keep their bodies beautiful and to get and keep a man [. . .]. And this was no anomaly of a single issue of a single women's magazine.[3]

Even magazines that seemed to offer a different model of femininity were subject to academic censure. Writing thirty years after Friedan, feminist literary scholar Ellen McCracken argues that 'At first glance, *Cosmopolitan* seems to contradict the traditionally accepted ideals of female beauty and fashion [. . .] [its cover photograph] presents women with an ideal image of their future selves [. . .] at the other end of the social spectrum from that of the affluent *Vogue* or *Bazaar* cover.'[4] At the same time, however, McCracken deplores *Cosmopolitan* as offering only 'a pseudo-sexual liberation': a commercially successful, 'modified version of liberation' that reflects a male stereotype of women's desirability.[5]

Yet while some feminist writers were critical, their interest acknowledged the importance of women's magazines as a cultural product. Prior to the feminist resurgence of the late 1960s and 1970s (of which Friedan was an early forerunner), there had been very little academic attention paid to women's magazines. There were some exceptions. In the seminal 1966 article on 'the cult of True Womanhood', for example, Barbara Welter drew her evidence from US women's magazines published between 1820 and 1860.[6] However, writing about the British context, Cynthia White observed in 1970 that there was a lack of sociological and historical work about such publications: 'apart from one short literary study of women's periodicals in the period 1700–1760, no history of the women's press exists, and the state of the magazine industry in contemporary Britain has been similarly neglected'.[7] This was despite an enormous post-war boom in the popularity of women's magazines; for much of the 1950s and 1960s, the combined sales of the three best-selling publications alone reached over six million copies per week.[8] White's *Women's Magazines 1693–1968* entered this relative vacuum as the first major survey of the women's periodical press in Britain, with some consideration of the US market too.

The huge contrast between the circulation figures for women's magazines and the low level of scholarly interest indicates just how little consideration was given to the industry and women's history prior to second wave feminism. This is in part symptomatic of academic neglect of magazines *per se*, as already noted. However, it also reflects widespread disregard of, and disdain for, cultural forms associated with women. In the preface to her 1996 investigation of the nineteenth-century British women's press, Margaret Beetham notes how '[a]s a clever middle-class girl I was taught that I should despise women's magazines as silly if not pernicious'.[9] This attitude is discussed by Tracey Loughran in this collection, too.

Richard Hoggart's influential *The Uses of Literacy* (1957) was a rare exception. Hoggart examined changes in British working-class cultures between the 1930s and 1950s. He was particularly interested in how these shifts were 'being encouraged by mass publications'—and he rightly included women's magazines in that category.[10] Hoggart's concern for what he regarded as authentic working-class ways of life led to some defence of some older titles. When discussing their fictional stories, for instance, he argued that '[T]here is no virtue in merely laughing at them: we need to appreciate first that they may in all their triteness speak for a solid and relevant way of life.' Even so, value judgements abound; he went on to say '[t]he world these stories present is a limited and simple one [. . .]. It is often a childish and garish world.'[11] Moreover, when it came to the higher circulation cross-class magazines for women, Hoggart believed that their smarter presentation extended to a slicker attitude: '[this] change is not always for the good', with a greater emphasis on shallow materialism and 'kittenish domesticity'—an assessment that echoed the negative critique by later feminists.[12]

Hoggart subsequently established the innovative Centre for Contemporary Cultural Studies at the University of Birmingham (UK) to pioneer research into mass popular culture.[13] Janice Winship is one of a number of scholars looking at women's magazines who has been based at the Centre over the years. Her publications, notably *Inside Women's Magazines* (1987b), bring together the twin strands of cultural analysis and feminism.[14] Crucially, Winship recognised the possible pleasures of magazine reading. While not refuting all the criticism levied at the periodical press by other feminist scholars, she discusses the allure that magazines offered readers, evocatively comparing them to the consumption of chocolate.[15]

Winship is part of an important scholarly shift that took place following the 1980s. Along with others, her work challenged the casual dismissal of forms of media associated with women—romantic fiction and soap operas as well as magazines—as trivial, ephemeral and insignificant. This in turn formed part of a wider move to seriously study aspects of women's lives either ignored or belittled by historians and other scholars in the past.[16]

Moreover, Winship's willingness to propose a more complex reading of magazines and their content signified an important change in tone. By the 1990s, some strong criticism continued to appear, as is apparent in the earlier quotation about *Cosmopolitan* from McCracken, but scholarship offering increasingly nuanced interpretations became more widespread.

Historical work on women's magazines contributed significantly to this shift. At times, this involved a revision of earlier claims. Notably, Joanne Meyerowitz's 1993 study disputed Friedan's assertions about US women's magazines in the 1950s, showing her account was 'only one piece of the postwar cultural puzzle'. Rather than being monolithic, the publications that Meyerowitz looked at embraced a range of viewpoints: '[a]ll of the magazines sampled advocated both the domestic and the non-domestic, sometimes in the same sentence'.[17] In the same piece, Meyerowitz reflects on a change in attitude:

> For Betty Friedan and for some historians, popular magazines represented a repressive force, imposing damaging images on vulnerable American women. Many historians today adopt a different approach in which mass culture is neither monolithic nor unrelentingly repressive. In this view, mass culture is rife with contradictions, ambivalence, and competing voices. We no longer assume that any text has a single, fixed meaning for all readers, and we sometimes find within the mass media subversive, as well as repressive, potential.[18]

Writing a year later, Jennifer Scanlon's assessment of the US market-leader, *The Ladies' Home Journal,* in the early twentieth century illuminates Meyerowitz's statement. Scanlon argues that the publication 'alternately and at times even simultaneously acknowledged and neglected, celebrated and decried, promoted and impeded social changes and their accompanying conflicts'. Furthermore, she continues with the claim that *The Ladies' Home Journal* 'offered clear and limited cultural definitions of womanhood, but it also recognised and gave voice to women's own concerns—and in doing so the *Journal* helped sow the seeds for women's later demands for autonomy and self-definition.'[19]

Meyerowitz and Scanlon were not alone. From the 1980s onwards, there was an expansion in historical scholarship on magazines that drew attention to both the socio-cultural pressures placed on women and fissures within these expectations.[20] This research highlighted the dominant ideologies surrounding gender while also revealing resistance to, subversion of or departure from such norms and ideals. By emphasising the multiplicity, ambiguities and paradoxes within the texts, this body of work played an important role in revising attitudes towards the periodical press.

At the same time, this historical work also greatly added to understandings about women's lives in the past. Meyerowitz's study, for instance, has been instrumental in challenging perceptions of the 1950s as a universally repressive time for women. To give another example from an earlier period, Beetham uncovered rafts of reader correspondence enquiring about opportunities for paid work, demonstrating just how wide the gulf could be between the Victorian 'Angel in the House' domestic ideology and the lived experiences of even many middle-class women. Her findings undermined some previously widespread assumptions about nineteenth-century society and culture.[21]

In the twenty-first century, new scholarship continues to demonstrate the usefulness of magazines as historical sources. Recent analyses of 1950s women's magazines in the UK have added to the ongoing revisionist debate, which Meyerowitz's findings over twenty years ago helped to generate, about women's lives in this decade.[22] To pick another example which demonstrates that magazines and their contents can add to understandings of the past, historians have used publications targeting young British women to more fully explore discourses surrounding female health and reproduction at the turn of the twentieth century. In one case, this focus on magazines followed an earlier examination of evidence from the government and industrial health agencies, signalling the extent to which such publications have gained legitimacy as a historical source.[23]

One final example underscores the extent to which historical scholarship can simultaneously enhance knowledge about magazines and understandings of the past more widely. Noliwe Rooks' research on African American women's magazines from the 1890s onwards is significant in part because it restores 'lost' publications, editors, writers and, indeed, readers to the canon of women's magazines. Yet there are wider implications too. As she states,

> [T]hese magazines represent source material about the lives, thoughts, and political leanings of African American women. At the same time, the location of the magazines in areas of the United States that often go unremarked in African American publishing history helps to broaden our understanding of African American life and activity in those regions in particular, as well as in the United States in general.[24]

Likewise the chapters in this collection are not just of interest to magazine scholars; they contribute to other historical debates, as the second part of the Introduction now outlines.

WOMEN IN MAGAZINES: THE COLLECTION

One goal of the collection is to demonstrate the usefulness of magazines as historical sources and another is to highlight tensions and paradoxes within the relationship between women and such publications. A third is to bring together studies by scholars working in different fields. As the examples already cited demonstrate, academics from a variety of disciplines, including history, sociology, cultural studies and literary studies, have contributed to the literature on women and periodicals. Even former journalists and magazine practitioners offer different disciplinary perspectives. Friedan was a journalist at the time of writing *The Feminine Mystique* but had done postgraduate research in psychology.[25] Marjorie Ferguson had been a senior editor on a British women's weekly before moving into academia and producing the sociological *Forever Feminine: Women's Magazines and the Cult of Femininity*. Former Hearst publisher, Brian Braithwaite, wrote *Women's Magazines: The First 300 Years*.[26]

In the twenty-first century, scholarship on magazines continues to be a multi-disciplinary affair. Those in the design field, for instance, offer alternative approaches to magazine material. They do not focus solely on appearance but often emphasise visual aspects of the magazine, as in Marie-Louise Bowallius' investigation of the use of colour in the US publication *Woman's Home Companion*, and Alice Beard's study of fashion imagery in the British title *Nova*.[27] These are characteristics that researchers from other disciplines tend to neglect, but the findings of design scholars provide encouragement to consider image as well as text, layout as well as content—the more holistic approach that Penny Tinkler calls for in her opening chapter here.

As the example of design indicates, the diverse mix of academic backgrounds is a strength of the scholarship, generating different insights. However, notwithstanding widespread talk of interdisciplinarity within academic circles, subject boundaries continue to prevail. As a result, those concerned with magazines may be unfamiliar with or even unaware of relevant work produced in other areas. In an effort to counter such divisions, and to showcase just how wide the interest in the topic is, this collection brings together scholars from a range of disciplines, including American Studies, art history, design, history, journalism, media and communication studies and sociology.

The collection likewise covers a broad geographical area. With some exceptions, such as White's *Women's Magazines 1693–1968* and Jeremy Aynsley's more recent co-edited design history collections, the literature tends to focus on single nations, and particularly the UK and the US.[28] This volume adds three valuable new case studies to the pool of English-language scholarship on magazines outside the Anglo-American periodicals market.[29] The contributions looking at inter-war Czechoslovakia (Karla Huebner), mid-century Canada (Helen Glew) and late twentieth-century Australia (Megan Le Masurier) highlight shared tropes and discourses as well as circumstances and debates unique to the specific country or region. They sit alongside chapters about the UK and the US and allow readers to make international comparisons.

Together the fifteen contributors provide a diverse range of case studies that are relevant to an audience as varied as they are. This mirrors the sheer breadth of subject matter encompassed by the terms 'magazines' and 'magazine industry'. There are, of course, different types of periodical; there is, for instance, a growing body of literature exploring men's magazines that complements research into women and magazines.[30] There are also different approaches: Joke Hermes explored reader reception, while more recently Anna Gough-Yates (who did her PhD at Birmingham's Centre for Contemporary Cultural Studies, or CCCS) has written about the business side of the women's periodical press.[31] Even within the women's magazines market there are sub-genres and different categories. Both Tinkler and Angela McRobbie (also formerly of CCCS), for example, have written extensively about magazines specifically appealing to girls and young women.[32]

The chapters here draw upon a wide variety of periodicals. Some are mass-market women's magazines: *Chatelaine* (Canada—Glew), *Cleo* (Australia—Masurier), *Honey* (UK—Fan Carter) and *The Ladies' Home Journal* (US—Cheyanne Cortez and Amanda Hinnant).[33] Others are less well known and long out-of-print: *Moderní dívka* (*Modern Girl*), *Pražanka* (*Prague Woman*) and *Eva* from Czechoslovakia (Huebner) and *Modern Woman* and *Miss Modern* from the UK (Fiona Hackney and Tinkler, respectively).

The collection also features periodicals from outside the canon of women's magazines, reflecting our broad women *in* magazines remit. This extends from publications associated with leisure (*Gourmet* and *Sports Illustrated* in Rochelle Pereira-Alvares' chapter) to those concerned with particular careers (childcare, as in Katherine Holden's contribution about *Nursery World* and *Norland Quarterly*). Political journals appear, too. Hackney examines the left-wing *Lansbury's Labour Weekly* and Sinead McEneaney explores the right-wing *The New Guard* (the former from inter-war Britain and the latter 1960s America). Others investigate niche titles that focused on specific topics, ranging from a late nineteenth-century British publication about 'free love' (*The Adult*—Sarah Jones), to an early twentieth-century transatlantic religion and philosophy journal (*The Hibbert*—Gretchen Galbraith), to a late twentieth-century US Black hair care magazine (*Beauty Trade*—Carina Spaulding). Both individually and collectively, the fifteen chapters highlight the multiple and diverse relationships between women and magazines.

PART I: THINKING ABOUT WOMEN'S MAGAZINES

Part I features two reflective pieces that inspire readers to think in new ways about magazines, how we select them and what we do with them. The first is Tinkler's chapter, 'Fragmentation and Inclusivity: Methods for Working with Girls' and Women's Magazines', which builds upon her keynote lecture at the original 2012 conference in Kingston. Then, as now, Tinkler challenges scholars interested in magazines in the past to reconsider how we work with them. She offers two innovative models for others to use. One involves mapping periodical provision around a chosen title either laterally (investigating what comparable publications existed during the period of interest) or longitudinally (its forerunners and successors). The other is an holistic approach to magazine content. Rather than cherry-picking content or considering only one aspect of a magazine, the holistic approach that Tinkler puts forward involves looking at different types of content as well as how content is presented, integrating text, visuals and layout.

While Tinkler concentrates on how researchers use magazines, the section's second chapter focuses on how we think about them. In 'Landscape for a Good Woman's Weekly: Finding Magazines in Post-war British History and Culture', Loughran calls for us to reflect on attitudes towards periodicals and their audiences, thinking more imaginatively about the role of magazines in the lives of their readers and more critically about their place in the cultural imagination. Like Tinkler, Loughran uses mapping. She begins by tracing fragments of references to post-war British women's magazines in other cultural sources from the same period, then plots the standpoints of contemporary cultural theorists and second wave feminists.

Both Loughran and Tinkler situate periodicals in their historical context. Loughran explores depictions of magazines across 1950s and 60s British culture more widely, whereas Tinkler contextualises by comparing the title *Modern Girl* with similar publications from inter-war and post-war periods. Tinkler specifically discusses magazines for girls and young women, providing an interesting background to Carter's later chapter on 'teens and twenties' title *Honey* (1960–1986). Tinkler's contribution also illuminates some of the issues raised here in the Introduction. For example, the benefits of considering visuals as well as text (and how they interact), pioneered by many design historians, is clearly apparent in her investigation of the varied depictions of smoking, which she uses to illustrate the advantages of the holistic model that she proposes. In the same case study, Tinkler also highlights the many 'voices' within a magazine, which are a result of their composite nature. Loughran's chapter likewise develops points from this Introduction. She discusses the opprobrium towards women's magazines in cultural studies and second wave feminist scholarship as well as in post-war British culture more widely. These negative attitudes manifest themselves in two of the chapter's key themes: magazines as a sign firstly of consumerism and individualism and secondly of class and educational difference.

Class is important in later chapters too, as is the 'heterosexual career' *leitmotif* that Tinkler draws attention to. Both contributions are starting-points for further discussion and research. We hope that others will utilise the models proposed, particularly as the two chapters clearly show the rich, complex picture that emerges when disparate evidence is pieced together— whether that be across different sources, longitudinally or laterally between different magazines or even within a single issue of a title.

PART II: IDEALS OF FEMININITY AND NEGOTIATING GENDER NORMS

Complexity, along with ambiguity, characterises the magazines discussed in Part II as well. The four chapters presented in this section on the ideals of femininity and negotiating gender norms examine popular and political magazines in Czechoslovakia, the UK and the US in the late nineteenth and twentieth centuries. The authors interrogate how editorial viewpoints and advertisers reflected or challenged contemporary values of women's roles, demonstrating the ways in which the representations of women and the arguments about their roles accepted or refuted contemporary gender norms. In some cases, the journals used depictions of women in a seemingly conventional mode which actually subverted contemporary gender ideology. In other instances, they used them to support a product or a political ideal.

The periodicals reviewed here run the gamut of political perspectives, from the advocates of free love in *fin de siècle* Britain to the young supporters of conservative Republicans in the US in the 1960s. Jones' analysis of the Legitimation League's London-based Journal, *The Adult*, published between 1897 and 1899, demonstrates that the supposedly radical men who favoured free love without regard to monogamous marriage did not extend their beliefs to include women. These self-declared sexual radicals maintained socially conservative views opposing comparable sexual freedom for women based upon their purported inferiority and responsibilities as mothers. They upheld a highly gendered stance that subordinated women by privileging male sexual freedom to have sexual relations outside marriage. Free love feminists used the pages of *The Adult* to counter the double standard that limited free sexual expression to men. Instead they asserted that their roles as mothers meant they should be free to choose their mates in a Darwinian fashion in order to advance the species by producing strong healthy children.

The arguments in this journal provided a foretaste of the free love arguments swirling around the radical movements of the 1960s, where some of the same gender issues arose and helped produce second wave feminism. Not all politically active women of this period, however, challenged gender roles so directly. Indeed, the women of the radical right frequently rejected second wave feminism with its advocacy of, amongst other things, the legalisation of abortion and overt challenges to the gender status quo. As McEneaney argues in 'Righting Women in the 1960s: Gender, Power and Conservatism in the Pages of *The New Guard*', this periodical published by the Young Americans for Freedom (YAF) provided an opportunity for women to acquire visibility in a male-dominated organisation. This distinguished YAF from the Civil Rights Movement and the New Left, both of which had very active female participants but less of an overt commitment to their politicisation or leadership. She explores how female members of YAF utilised contemporary ideals of femininity as a means of obtaining visibility and standing within the organisation.

Huebner expands our understanding of women's magazines through her exploration of the little-studied women's journals produced in interwar Czechoslovakia's First Republic. She explores the differences between

Czech and Slovak periodicals, taking account of the differences in literacy between the highly urbanised Czechs and the more rural Slovaks. She finds that the Czech-language women's magazines of this era featured young women as symbols of modernity and sophistication. Slovak journals of the same period rejected this symbolism by clothing women in folk costumes as markers of national identity and pride. She concludes that the major consumer magazines of inter-war Czechoslovakia excluded Slovakian women from their pages and thus from their vision of the First Republic.

In 'Make any Occasion a Special Event: Hospitality, Domesticity and Female Cordial Consumption, 1950–1969', Pereira-Alvares investigates how the distilled spirits industry manipulated images of women in advertisements in mainstream lifestyle and gourmet periodicals of the 1950s and 1960s. In order to support sales to the potentially lucrative new market of middle- and upper-class white women, the distillers sought to moralise female alcohol consumption by linking it to domesticity and fashion. Since the US had only repealed Prohibition in the 1930s as a means of stimulating the economy, there was still widespread ambivalence about women's drinking. Many women's magazines, for example, still did not accept advertising copy depicting alcoholic beverages. The distilled spirits industry only repealed its ban on the portrayal of women in alcoholic beverage advertising in 1958. Following this revocation, Hiram Walker began marketing cordials, brightly coloured liqueurs, in a highly gendered fashion. Their advertisements relied upon stylised images of women as perfect hostesses and housewives incorporating cordials into their hospitality, even though they did not show women actually drinking them for another decade.

All the articles in this section demonstrate how highly politicised the norms of femininity were in periodicals in Europe and the US. The magazines studied here were places in which women's roles were argued about and also often stylised in an effort to support the sale of consumer items. They were sites of contestation over those roles or subversion of them. The style of representation could reinforce stereotypes and a particular view of the nation and women's role within it. Authors, editors and advertisers might have different understandings of appropriate behaviour for women, and these differences shaped the depictions of femininity that they shared on the pages of these publications.

PART III: WOMEN, MAGAZINES AND EMPLOYMENT

The third section, 'Women, Magazines and Employment', continues this emphasis on the complexities and ambiguities inherent within magazines, again demonstrating the extent to which they could both reinforce and refute gender norms. Despite the frequent focus on magazines as a medium for culturally reinforcing women's roles as wife, mother and homemaker, scholars adopting more holistic methods of analysis have here highlighted the many ways in which magazines contributed to debates about working women and provided practical advice. If the 'messages' they conveyed overall were sometimes contradictory, magazines nevertheless enabled both single and married women to discuss the challenges they faced when seeking, keeping and balancing work with home life. Glew analyses the often competing discourses in editorials, feature articles, advice columns, correspondence pages, fiction and advertising of *Chatelaine* (1948–64), the first Canadian produced magazine aimed specifically at women. While some UK magazines like *Good Housekeeping* ceased discussing wives' work in the early 1950s, *Chatelaine* began cautiously addressing the issue in editorials. In 1958 it issued a special supplement urging husbands and wives to view their employed work equally seriously, and by the 1960s, the magazine was confidently supporting married women's work despite printing fictional stories of damaged marriages repaired only by a wife's return to domesticity and advertisements almost universally aimed at the housewife.

The authors in this section have also ranged well beyond the canon of popular women's periodicals to provide valuable insights into links between women's marital status and their personal and professional relationships, both within and outside the home. Galbraith and Hackney illustrate how two women whose lives spanned both Victorian and Modern generations wrote for a broad range of magazines aimed at men and women in order to debate and disseminate their passionately held political and religious beliefs. As Galbraith reveals, Constance Maynard (1849–1935) cried when she was appointed the first Head of Westfield College for women because she knew it meant renouncing love and marriage to follow her professional and spiritual vocation. She attempted to refuse the distinction between motherhood and single professional woman by trying to adopt a young girl and felt frustrated at her academic seclusion from the world. After her retirement she found new social and mental freedom in writing for intellectual and philosophical journals, such as *The Hibbert*, which enabled her to engage with male contributors on equal terms and become, in her own eyes, a thinker of the world.

Leonora Eyles (1889–1960) was a committed Christian Socialist and feminist whose writing crossed many genres, including journalism, fiction and sociological texts. This, Hackney argues, enabled her to adapt and convey her ideas to a wider and more diverse readership. Eyles' output is a reflection of the ability of magazines to inform and entertain, as she turned to popular media, most notably as an agony aunt for *Modern Woman* and, later, *Woman's Own*. As a socialist writing for *Lansbury's Labour Weekly*, Eyles engaged in class consciousness-raising to stir both poor working men and women to action. As an agony aunt for *Modern Woman*, she dispensed advice based on her personal experience of marriage and work to solve romantic as well as career and employment problems for women. Yet as an individual she feared she had not really succeeded at either.

Holden takes a different approach by comparing specialist and professional publications *Nursery World* and *Norland Quarterly*, both of which functioned as discussion fora for often fraught working and emotional relationships between mothers and nannies in the first half of the twentieth century. Her analysis of the letters pages demonstrates that contributors' dissonant voices reflected conflicts surrounding social position, marital status and divergent child-rearing practices. At the same time, this correspondence reveals the mutual dependence between mothers, often engaged in philanthropic or social duties, and the trained nannies or 'lady nurses' they employed. It also reveals the tensions between gendered ideas of 'natural' maternal love and the 'expert' knowledge gained by professionally acquired skills. The status of expert advice is a common theme in several of these chapters, although experts espoused different attitudes towards women's employment. While post-war childcare experts in Britain advised mothers to take on the main responsibility for their children's health and emotional welfare, increasing demand for general 'mother's helps' instead of trained nannies, Canadian experts advocated part-time work to enable wives to balance 'self-fulfilment' with family commitments.

For anyone researching women's employment in the early to mid-twentieth century, magazines serve as a valuable source for recapturing the voices of 'ordinary' working women and for assessing shifts in attitudes towards single and married women's work. In these chapters, it is noticeable that readers, female journalists, editors and publishers responded to economic and demographic change. Hackney demonstrates how *Modern Woman* targeted the rising number of young 'business girls' working in offices and factories as symbols of desirable modern freedoms in the 1920s, but during the economic crisis of the 1930s, Eyles supported both poor working wives and untrained middle-class married women struggling to make ends meet. *Chatelaine* rarely covered married women workers until printing an editorial on the issue in 1950. This may have been a response to a rise in the numbers of working wives but perhaps equally to the over 500 letters generated by a provocative piece presenting negative views of non-working wives. The editor's stance was equivocal, which may have reflected anxiety over which view to hold but also guaranteed more debate and a wider readership, thus suggesting that commercial imperatives were also an important consideration in magazines' desire to engage more with working wives.

PART IV: YOUNG WOMEN IN MAGAZINES

Part IV of the collection focuses on depictions of young women in magazines from two very different periods. In the first chapter in this section, Cortez investigates the way the *Ladies' Home Journal*, the most popular women's magazine in the US, was used by its editor to promulgate ideas of nationalism and sexuality at a time in US history when national identity was in something of crisis. This is followed by Carter's analysis of *Honey*, a UK magazine from a completely different era, the swinging sixties, and its promotion of a new way of life for young women as Britain emerged out of post-war austerity.

In 'The American Girl: Ideas of Nationalism and Sexuality as promoted in the *Ladies' Home Journal*', Cortez focuses on the powerful image of the American Girl, which pervaded mass culture in the US at the turn of the twentieth century, and its use by the *Journal*'s editor Edward Bok to promote the 'ideal' woman to protect the 'American' race. As Cortez explains, the American Girl was single, middle class and beautiful, but most important of all she was white. Her rise to national prominence was prompted by a growing fear among the indigent white population of the 'other' at a time when America was experiencing heightened levels of immigration from southern and eastern Catholic Europe. The American Girl, Cortez claims, was a construct designed to unite the nation's majority against this threat to the bloodline and democracy established by the Founding Fathers.

In contrast to the ambiguity emphasised in other chapters, Cortez's contribution highlights the extent to which this title, under Bok's singular editorship, promoted strong and unambiguous messages about the nation and US society. Through the *Journal*, Bok offered his readers the latest news, information and entertainment, but also developed a relationship with them built on trust. As Cortez argues, the *Journal*'s Girl was a friend, sister and daughter, but was also an aspirational role model on which the country's future could be constructed. However it was only aspirational for one section of American society. There were no African American women in its pages in the early twentieth century, conveying the message clearly that such women were not the future of this great nation, airbrushed from the public consciousness, invisible as both readers and consumers. This exclusion continued throughout the twentieth century, as Spaulding notes in her later contribution about Black hair magazines.

Carter takes us into new territory as she explores the impact of *Honey*, a magazine launched in the early 1960s specifically targeted at a new market for advertisers: the teen young woman. In contrast to Cortez's focus on the messages for young women about national unity and racial purity in *Ladies' Home Journal*, Carter draws attention to the strength of the relationship between editorial and commercial interests. According to Carter, *Honey* was a pioneer of a new type of magazine, targeting young, single women and their new-found disposable income. It promoted the new freedoms which were opening up for young women in early 1960s Britain, presenting to them a world of mass consumption based on the newest fashions and leisure activities. The magazine's target demographic carried strong echoes of the earlier American girl ideal in *Ladies' Home Journal*: the young, single, aspirational woman. Until later in the decade, she was white too. But whereas the *Journal* was promoting conformity, *Honey* was promoting rebellion, if only in the mildest form. Nevertheless, it is interesting to consider the two side by side, noting how many similarities exist—if not in language then certainly in their repeated focus on how to deal with the opposite sex.

The young women pursued by *Honey*, and represented within its pages, were mobile, ambitious and dedicated to fashion. They were also the same young women who feminists, such as Friedan, claimed were under the influence of the consumer market, infantilised and trivialised by it. While acknowledging the role of advertisers in determining how the new 'young woman' should behave and look, and the part played by *Honey* and other similar titles in promoting such messages, Carter argues that such magazines also opened up narratives which had previously gone unheard. *Honey*'s representation of young women and their lives in the 1960s resonated with its readers and challenged them to aspire to the dreams depicted within its pages. The *Honey* in Carter's chapter might appear to be superficial and perhaps focused rather too much on appearance, but it could not be accused, by Friedan or other feminists, of depicting womanhood as only glorified through domesticity and motherhood. The *Honey* girls are far from this stereotype.

PART V: WOMEN'S BODIES FROM SECOND WAVE FEMINISM TO THE TWENTY-FIRST CENTURY

The book's final section, 'Women's Bodies from Second Wave Feminism to the Twenty-First Century', contains three chapters in which the imagined physical form of the presumed female reader is central to the magazine's content. In 'How *Ladies' Home Journal* Covered Second Wave Health, 1969–1975', Hinnant compares and contrasts discussion of central themes in the women's health movement as represented in its own publications with the presentation of the same issues in the mass-circulation *Ladies' Home Journal*. Core topics included sexism in medicine and pharmaceuticals, and women's reproductive capacities, including contraception, abortion and childbirth. As Hinnant notes, this concern is in some ways at odds with the wider feminist disavowal of women's sexual difference. At the same time, however, by striving to make women better informed about their own bodies and health, attention to such issues could encourage liberated self-determination.

The theme of liberation is apparent in Le Masurier's chapter about women's sexual bodies in the Australian monthly *Cleo* (sex and reproduction remaining connected but no longer so intrinsically intertwined for many women by the late 1960s). In 'Popular Feminism and the Second Wave: Women's Liberation, Sexual Liberation and *Cleo* Magazine', Le Masurier—like other contributors to this collection—accentuates the plurality of voices contained within one publication. We even see how readers could assume very different standpoints on the same issue. Amongst the voices in this 'demotic babble', there was acknowledgement of the differences in women's sexuality, including discussion of homosexuality. This is notable, disrupting the overwhelming emphasis on 'the heterosexual career' (to use Tinkler's phrase) in the mainstream women's magazine market throughout the twentieth century and still today.

This example and others from Le Masurier demonstrates the potential of even popular commercial magazines to be inclusive and provide a forum for women whose voices may be silenced or shamed elsewhere. This potential is also evident in the section's third chapter, '*Beauty Trade* and the Rise of American Black Hair Magazines'. In this piece, Spaulding shows how these specialised publications, which developed from the 1970s, catered to an audience of Black women who remained excluded from US national beauty culture because of their race. Although separated by the best part of a century, this marginalisation echoes the discourses surrounding the American Girl, as discussed by Cortez.

As well as sharing a focus on women's bodies, the chapters which form Part V illustrate the ways in which the industrial and production context shapes magazine content too. These influences are central to Anna Gough-Yates' informative *Understanding Women's Magazines: Publishing, Markets and Readership* (2003) but remain underexplored areas of study.[34] Le Masurier and Hinnant refer to specific behind-the-scenes events that influenced what appeared on the publications' pages (consciousness-raising style editorial meetings and a sit-in demonstration respectively), whereas Spaulding outlines the broader business climate that was integral to the development of titles such as *Beauty Trade*. The economics of the publishing market were not the sole contextual factor driving the growth of the Black hair magazine genre. As Spaulding also demonstrates, the Civil Rights and Black Power movements were fundamental to their emergence as well. Furthermore, she firmly positions *Beauty Trade* and counterparts within the fight for racial equality, presenting them as a form of activism, an example of consumer citizenship in action.

Le Masurier and Hinnant similarly situate *Cleo* and *Ladies' Home Journal* in relation to a social movement: in these cases, second wave feminism. Their contributions join a growing body of literature examining and at times re-examining the relationship between the women's periodical press and feminism in the 1960s and 70s. Work by Laurel Forster, Gough-Yates and Scanlon, for instance, not only complicates our understanding of this relationship but also provides insights into the multiple versions of feminism in circulation during the final third of the twentieth century.[35] Our authors likewise add to awareness about different styles of feminism. Le Masurier's discussion of 'popular feminism' reveals the links between magazine content and key feminist debates, such as the nature of female orgasm, and the dissension, with readers and experts offering varied views and experiences. Hinnant too charts overlap along with points of departure in health coverage provided by *Ladies' Home Journal* and the women's health literature, accentuating the extent to which the magazine's 'therapeutic feminism' stance remained largely focused on an individual level rather than proposing the more collective or systemic changes that characterised the demands of feminists in the women's health movement.

CONCLUSION

Taken together, these chapters clearly show that the relationship between women and magazines is characterised by ambiguity and tensions. Even if a particular contributor or advertiser had a specific version of womanhood that they wished to promote, a particular title rarely, if ever, promulgated a single, unified vision. There were simply too many voices, even within one issue of a specific title. These voices fall into three categories: the staff, the advertisers and the readers. Across the chapters, there are numerous examples of tensions between these elements. Pereira-Alvares, for instance, notes that the Hiram Walker Distillery's desire to promote their cordials to women jarred against continued ambivalence towards female alcohol consumption amongst magazine owners (and the public at large). Carter points out that the publisher's strategy of 'group' buying for advertisers resulted in *Honey* containing some rather odd advertisements for products of little interest to its intended readership and would ultimately contribute to the title's closure. Glew also comments on the disconnect which could occur between editorial and advertising content, arguing that while *Chatelaine*'s writers were attuned to growing presence of married women in the workforce, advertisers largely relied on what were increasingly anachronistic images of domesticated womanhood. The two visions sat uneasily together on the magazine's pages.

A number of contributors discuss women who contributed content to magazines. Hackney and Galbraith extensively explore the intersection of employment, professional roles and personal identity in relation to two specific women writers (Eyles and Maynard). However, comparable themes are apparent in the chapters by Jones, McEneaney and Le Masurier, who also talk about women who wrote for magazines. Similarly, Carter highlights the significance of Audrey Slaughter's tenure as editor of *Honey*—an early position in an influential publishing career (it is also notable that Slaughter's step-daughter is the indomitable editor of US *Vogue*, Anna Wintour). In all these cases, working for or contributing to a publication allowed these women to share their vision with a wider public. From a commitment to greater sexual freedom for women to right wing political campaigning, writing for such publications gave these women a forum in which to express their views.

Readers also often expressed their views on the pages of magazines. Attention to this third element within publications is another theme across several chapters. Readers were not simply passive consumers of these publications and their contents. Rather there was a reciprocal, albeit unbalanced, relationship between them and the publisher. As Hackney, Cortez and Spaulding allude to, there was an issue of trust between the two; without this, a title would not flourish. Furthermore, while we must remain alert to questions about authenticity and remember that such correspondence was selected, edited and mediated, chapters here by Hackney, Holden and Le Masurier demonstrate the usefulness of reader correspondence as a historical source. Holden, for instance, reveals the rich insights that can be garnered from careful reading of letters pages. All three indicate that magazines provided a virtual community long before the advent of the digital world.

The findings drawn from such correspondence underline the extent to which magazines are fora of differing voices, with readers offering contrary viewpoints on topics as disparate as childcare practices and oral sex. These chapters also show that the letters page could be a space for dissension from the status quo, whether that be disrupting hierarchical class relationships (Holden) or rebelling against sexual mores (Le Masurier). Such examples provide an important counterpoint to the chapters in which we see magazines conveying a strong message, as in Huebner's and Cortez's pieces about national identity. They are a reminder that for every advertiser or publisher trying to mould readers to their desired image of womanhood, there may be a reader voicing resistance—that is to say nothing of those who may have resisted without expressing it.

It is an asset of this collection that the chapters showcase such variety, from the singular vision of Bok in the early twentieth-century *Ladies' Home Journal* to the 'demotic babble' of *Cleo* many decades later. We are willing to embrace such breadth along with all the conflicts and contradictions that it entails. This stance reflects our position in the scholarship on women and magazines. Building upon other historical scholarship on the subject, we recognise the heterogeneity within magazines, let alone between them. They were—and remain—cacophonous, filled with often irreconcilable paradoxes. Despite, or perhaps because of, this complexity, they remain under-utilised historical sources. The fifteen chapters here highlight their value in this respect, adding to our understanding of racial and ethnic identities, second wave feminism and married women's employment, to name but three topics. In doing so, the chapters aptly demonstrate the ambiguities and tensions that characterise the shifting and capricious relationship between women and magazines.

NOTES

1 Sammye Johnson, 'Why should they care?,' *Journalism Studies* 8 (2007): 525.
2 This is explored by Penny Tinkler's chapter in this collection. See also: Margaret Beetham, *A Magazine of Her Own? Domesticity and Desire in the Woman's Magazine, 1800–1914* (London: Routledge, 1996), 12; Rachel Ritchie, ' "Beauty isn't all a matter of looking glamorous": Attitudes to glamour and beauty in 1950s women's magazines,' *Women's History Review* 23

Introduction 19

(2014): 732; Penny Tinkler, *Constructing Girlhood: Popular Magazines for Girls Growing Up in England, 1920–1950* (London: Taylor and Francis, 1995), 186.
3 Betty Friedan, *The Feminine Mystique* (New York: Norton, 1963), 30–1. For details of her time as a freelance journalist, see Daniel Horowtiz, *Betty Friedan and the Making of the Feminine Mystique: The American Left, the Cold War, and Modern Feminism* (Amherst: University of Massachusetts Press, 1998), 180–96.
4 Ellen McCracken, *Decoding Women's Magazines: From Mademoiselle to Ms* (London: Palgrave Macmillan, 1993), 158.
5 McCracken, *Decoding Women's Magazines*, 159.
6 Barbara Welter, 'The cult of true womanhood: 1820–1860,' *American Quarterly* 18 (1966): 151–74.
7 Cynthia White, *Women's Magazines 1693–1968* (London: Michael Joseph, 1970), 17–18.
8 These were *Woman*, *Woman's Own* and *Woman's Weekly*. White, *Women's Magazines*, Appendix IV.
9 Beetham, *A Magazine of Her Own?*, viii.
10 Richard Hoggart, *The Uses of Literacy* (Penguin: London, 1958), 9.
11 Hoggart, *Uses of Literacy*, 129.
12 Hoggart, *Uses of Literacy*, 131.
13 'About CCCS: history and project,' University of Birmingham website, accessed 22 July 2015, http://www.birmingham.ac.uk/schools/historycultures/departments/history/research/projects/cccs/about.aspx.
14 For example, see: Janice Winship, *Inside Women's Magazines* (London: Rivers Oram Press, 1987); Janice Winship, '"A girl needs to get street-wise": Magazines for the 1980s,' *Feminist Review* 20 (1987): 25–46. Examples of publications about women and magazines written by other one-time CCCS members include: Anna Gough-Yates, *Understanding Women's Magazines: Publishing, Markets and Readerships* (London: Routledge, 2003); Angela McRobbie, author of works including *Feminism and Youth Culture: From Jackie to Just Seventeen* (Basingstoke: Macmillan, 1991); Trevor Millum, *Images of Woman: Advertising in Women's Magazines* (London: Chatto and Windus, 1975).
15 Winship, *Inside Women's Magazines*, 53.
16 For examples, see: Ien Ang, *Watching 'Dallas': Soap Opera and the Melodramatic Imagination* (London: Methuen, 1985); Christine Geraghty, *Women and Soap Opera: A Study of Prime Time Soaps* (Cambridge: Polity Press, 1991); Janice A. Radway, *Reading the Romance: Women, Patriarchy, and Popular Literature* (Chapel Hill: University of North Carolina Press, 1991).
17 Joanne Meyerowitz, 'Beyond *The Feminine Mystique*: A reassessment of postwar mass culture, 1946–1958,' *Journal of American History* 79 (1993): 1458. The article was reprinted in *Not June Cleaver: Women and Gender in Postwar Americas, 1946–1960*, ed. Joanne Meyerowitz (Philadelphia: Temple University Press, 1994), 229–62.
18 Meyerowitz, 'Beyond *The Feminine Mystique*,' 1457.
19 Jennifer Scanlon, *Inarticulate Longings: The Ladies' Home Journal, Gender, and the Promises of Consumer Culture* (New York: Routledge, 1995), 2. Until May 1927, the magazine's title was *The Ladies' Home Journal*. From the June 1927 issue onwards, it was *Ladies' Home Journal*. References in this collection vary accordingly.
20 For other examples, see Beetham, *A Magazine of Her Own?*; Ros Ballaster, Margaret Beetham, Elizabeth Fraser and Sandra Hebron, *Women's*

Worlds: Ideology, Femininity and the Woman's Magazine (Basingstoke: Palgrave Macmillan, 1991); Helen Damon-Moore, Magazines for the Millions: Gender and Commerce in the Ladies' Home Journal and the Saturday Evening Post, 1880–1910 (Albany: SUNY Press, 1994); Amy Erdman Farrell, Yours in Sisterhood: Ms Magazine and the Promise of Popular Feminism (Chapel Hill: University of North Carolina Press, 1998); Ellen Gruber Garvey, The Adman in the Parlor: Magazines and the Gendering of Consumer Culture, 1880s to 1910s (Oxford: Oxford University Press, 1996); Kathryn Shevelow, Women and Print Culture: The Construction of Femininity in the Early Periodical (London: Routledge, 1989); Tinkler, Constructing Girlhood; Mary Ellen Zuckerman, A History of Popular Women's Magazines in the United States, 1792–1995 (Westport, CT: Greenwood Press, 1998). Nor was this limited to work on women's magazines. For an example of historical scholarship on magazines more generally, see: John Tebbel and Mary Ellen Zuckerman, The Magazine in America, 1741–1990 (Oxford: Oxford University Press, 1991).
21 See, for example, Beetham, A Magazine of Her Own?, 139–41.
22 Penny Tinkler, ' "Are you really living?" If not, "GET WITH IT!" The teenage self and lifestyle in young women's magazines, Britain 1957–70,' Cultural and Social History 11 (2014): 597–619; Ritchie, 'Beauty isn't all a matter of looking glamorous,' 723–43; Rachel Ritchie, 'Women and Woman: Representations of youthful femininity in the "world's greatest weekly for women", 1954–1969,' in Women and the Media: Feminism and Femininity in Britain, 1900 to the Present, ed. Maggie Andrews and Sallie McNamara (Routledge: London, 2014), 143–55.
23 Vicky Long and Hilary Marland, 'From danger and motherhood to health and beauty: Health advice for the factory girl in early twentieth-century Britain,' Twentieth Century British History 20 (2009): 454–81; Alisa Webb, 'Constructing the gendered body: Girls, health, beauty, advice, and the Girls' Best Friend, 1898–1899,' Women's History Review 15 (2006): 253–75.
24 Noliwe M. Rooks, Ladies' Pages: African American Women's Magazines and the Culture That Made Them (New Brunswick: Rutgers University Press, 2004), 24.
25 Horowitz, Betty Friedan and the Making of the Feminine Mystique, 69–102.
26 Marjorie Ferguson, Forever Feminine: Women's Magazines and the Cult of Femininity (London: Heinemann, 1983); Brian Braithwaite, Women's Magazines: The First 300 Years (London: Peter Owen, 1995).
27 Jeremey Aynsley has co-edited two useful collections on design and magazines: Jeremy Aynsley and Kate Forde, ed., Design and the Modern Magazine (Manchester: Manchester University Press, 2007); Jeremy Aynsley and Francesca Berry, ed., 'Special Issue: Publishing the modern home: Magazines and the domestic interior 1870–1965,' Journal of Design History 18 (2005). Marie-Louise Bowallius, 'Advertising and the use of colour in Woman's Home Companion, 1923–33,' in Design and the Modern Magazine, ed. Aynsley and Forde, 18–36 (Manchester: Manchester University Press, 2007); Alice Beard, 'Put in just for pictures: Fashion editorial and the composite image in Nova 1965–1975,' Fashion Theory: Journal of Dress, Body and Culture 1 (2002): 247–60. Fiona Hackney is a design historian whose work does not focus solely on magazine visuals. As well as her chapter in this collection, see Fiona Hackney, ' "Use your hands for happiness": Home craft and make-do-and-mend in British women's magazines in the 1920s and 1930s,' Journal of Design History 19 (2006): 23–38; Fiona Hackney, 'Making modern woman, stitch by stitch: Dressmaking in women's magazines in Britain, 1919–1939,' in The Culture of Sewing: Gender, Consumption and Home Dressmaking, ed. Barbara Burman (Oxford: Berg, 1999), 73–95.

28 White, *Women's Magazines*; Aynsley and Forde, eds., *Design and the Modern Magazine*; Aynsley and Berry, eds., 'Special Issue' *Journal of Design History* 18 (2005).

29 For a selection of scholarship about women and magazines outside of the US and UK, see: Lynne Attwood, *Creating the New Soviet Woman: Women's Magazines as Engineers of Female Identity, 1922–1953* (Basingstoke: Macmillan, 1999); Caitriona Clear, *Women's Voices in Ireland: Women's Magazines in the 1950s and 60s* (Bloomsbury: London, 2015); Annabelle Cone and Dawn Marley, eds., *The Francophone Women's Magazine: Inside and Outside France* (New Orleans: University Press of the South, 2010); Faye Hammill and Michelle Smith, *Magazines, Travel, and Middlebrow Culture: Canadian Periodicals in English and French, 1925–1960* (Detroit: Wayne State University Press, 2015); Valerie J. Korinek, *Roughing It in the Suburbs: Reading Chatelaine Magazine in the Fifties and Sixties* (Toronto: University of Toronto Press, 2000); Iona Macintyre, *Women and Print Culture in Post-Independence Buenos Aires* (Woodbridge: Tamesis Books, 2010); Rachel Mesch, *Having It All in the Belle Epoque: How French Women's Magazines Invented the Modern Woman* (Stanford: Stanford University Press, 2013); Susan Sheridan, Lyndall Ryan, Barbara Baird and Kate Borrett, *Who Was That Woman? The Australian Women's Weekly in the Postwar Years* (Sydney: University of New South Wales Press, 2002); Loubna H. Skalli, *Through a Local Prism: Gender, Globalization, and Identity in Moroccan Women's Magazines* (Lanham, MD: Lexington Books, 2006); Susan Weiner, *Enfants Terribles: Youth and Femininity in the Mass Media in France, 1945–1968* (London: Johns Hopkins University Press, 2001); Ulrike Wöhr, Barbara Hamill Sato and Suzuki Sadmi, eds., *Gender and Modernity: Rereading Japanese Women's Magazines* (Kyoto: International Research Center for Japanese Studies, 2000).

30 For examples of scholarship on men's magazines, see: Bethan Benwell, ed., *Masculinity and Men's Lifestyle Magazines* (Oxford: Blackwell, 2003); Ben Crewe, *Representing Men: Cultural Production and Producers in the Men's Magazine Market* (Berg: Oxford, 2003); David M. Earle, *All Man!: Hemingway, 1950s Men's Magazines, and the Masculine Persona* (Kent, OH: Kent State University Press, 2009); Tonia Fondermann, *The Medial Mirror: Female Representations in Men's and Women's Magazines* (Norderstedt, Germany: GRIN Verlag, 2002); Peter Jackson, Nick Stevenson and Kate Brooks, eds., *Making Sense of Men's Magazines* (London: Polity, 2001); Frank Mort, *Cultures of Consumption: Masculinities and Social Space in Late-Twentieth Century Britain* (London: Routledge, 1996); Bill Osgerby, *Playboys in Paradise: Masculinity, Youth and Leisure-Style in Modern America* (Oxford: Berg, 2001).

31 Joke Hermes, *Reading Women's Magazines: An Analysis of Everyday Media Use* (Cambridge: Polity Press, 1995); Gough-Yates, *Understanding Women's Magazines*.

32 For example, see: Angela McRobbie, '*More!*: New sexualities in girls' and women's magazines,' in *Back to Reality? Social Experience and Cultural Studies*, ed. Angela McRobbie (Manchester: Manchester University Press, 1997), 190–209; McRobbie, *Feminism and Youth Culture*; Penny Tinkler, 'Red tips for red lips: Advertising cigarettes for young women in Britain, 1920–70,' *Women's History Review* 10 (2001): 249–70; Penny Tinkler, 'Rebellion, modernity and romance: Smoking as a gendered practice in popular young women's magazines, Britain 1918–1939,' *Women's Studies International Forum* 24 (2001): 111–22; Tinkler, *Constructing Girlhood*.

33 As noted, until May 1927, the magazine's title was *The Ladies' Home Journal*. From the June 1927 issue onwards, it was *Ladies' Home Journal*. References throughout the rest of this collection vary accordingly.
34 Anna Gough-Yates, *Understanding Women's Magazines: Publishing, Markets and Readerships* (London: Routledge, 2003).
35 Laurel Forster, 'Printing liberation: The women's movement and magazines in the 1970's,' in *British Culture and Society in the 1970s: The Lost Decade*, ed. Laurel Forster and Sue Harper (Cambridge: Cambridge Scholars Publishing, 2010), 93–106; Anna Gough-Yates, '"A shock to the system": Feminist interventions in youth subculture—the adventures of Shocking Pink,' *Contemporary British History* 26 (2012): 375–403; Jennifer Scanlon, *Bad Girls Go Everywhere: The Life of Helen Gurley Brown* (New York: Oxford University Press, 2009).

Part I

Thinking About Women's Magazines

1 Fragmentation and Inclusivity
Methods for Working with Girls' and Women's Magazines

Penny Tinkler

We currently have a fragmented picture of how to address historical questions using girls' and women's magazines. Though much has been written about the history of these papers—their production, content, readers/consumers—how researchers work with them is rarely tackled directly and in detail in historical studies. Magazine research methods are typically embedded in discussions of findings and they have to be teased out by the interested reader. This chapter aims to counter this tendency and encourage greater reflection on, and more overt discussion of, our research practices.

Magazine methods typically involve working *around* magazines and working *with* them. In this chapter I focus on working *with* magazines, but ways of working around them are also relevant. Working around magazines embraces the processes of producing them, including the roles of publishers, editors, advertisers, illustrators, designers and so on, as well as the practices of consumption and reading, including what sense people make of magazines. The production and consumption of magazines can be a focus in themselves, but they are also elements of contextual research. Contextual research includes the broader socio-economic, political and cultural contexts and, depending on research questions, the study of potential and actual readers and of editors and publishers. It bridges working around magazines and working with them. Contextual research is an important element in the magazine researcher's toolkit, and it informs the discussion of methods for working with magazines that are the focus of this chapter.

It is not just historians who work with girls' and women's magazines; these periodicals also attract attention from scholars in media and cultural studies, sociology and psychology.[1] In general, historical approaches tend to be distinctive from those of other social science disciplines. Whereas historians are typically attentive to temporally specific social and cultural contexts, other social scientists usually study the present and assume context or address it in general terms. The latter also tend to work with magazines to identify dominant meanings by tracing patterns and trends (using, for example, quantitative content analysis, thematic and discourse studies), often relating these to broader discourses. Sometimes they study the mechanisms through which magazines construct meaning (using semiotic analysis, for instance). Historians draw on social science insights into how meanings are constructed in print media, and they often identify and explore key themes in magazines, but typically they are also interested in particularities.

Girls' and women's magazines are complex cultural products. They are part of the periodical industry and designed in relation to one another.[2] Their content is diverse in format and incorporates different contributors. They are the product of negotiation, typically between publishers, editors, advertisers and readers. Their pages harbour diversity, inconsistency, contradiction and tension.[3] For all these reasons it is helpful to have a methodology for working with magazines that is inclusive rather than fragmentary.

An inclusive research strategy is also important because researchers are often tempted to isolate a title from the field of periodicals within which it has been shaped and encountered or to focus on parts of magazines. The latter is particularly likely where historians dip into magazines for examples to bolster or illustrate an argument; this 'cherry picking' produces a decontextualised and often skewed impression of how particular topics are represented in magazines. But even where magazines are the focus of study, it is easy to lose sight—often quite literally—of their complexity and of how visual, textual and material features work together. This can result from our choice of methods and analytic strategies, for example, a preoccupation with textual features and the marginalisation of visual elements or a focus on tracing key themes across several issues. Fragmentation also arises from practical constraints. Historians are lucky if they have their own copies of magazines. Often we rely on a combination of notes and photocopies or scans made from archival volumes of magazines. Digitisation is expanding access to women's magazines but this also contributes to fragmentation in two main ways. First, search facilities encourage a decontextualised selection of magazine extracts. Second, digitisation transforms a three-dimensional object—a magazine—into a two-dimensional image, thereby creating a disjuncture between what we are researching and the version of it that we can work with. The digitisation process reinforces a preoccupation with the visual and obscures the material and tactile aspects of what it means to read a magazine.[4]

In this chapter I present two ways of working inclusively with magazines and address each in turn: first, mapping the field of periodical publishing in which individual titles are located; second, adopting a holistic approach to magazine content.

MAPPING PERIODICAL PROVISION

There are two dimensions to mapping periodical provision: a lateral dimension and a longitudinal one. The lateral dimension is the range of magazines published for a particular constituency at a specific point in time, whilst the longitudinal one considers the forerunners and successors of the magazines that are the focus of the research. I start by explaining why lateral mapping is important and how to do it. Lateral mapping can be particularly useful for exploring the construction of difference, and I demonstrate this with reference to the meaning and significance of age in British magazines for girls and young women in the period 1920–40. Following this I discuss the significance of longitudinal mapping and use the example of mid-twentieth century provision for 'teenagers' to illustrate how this technique can be illuminating of social and cultural change.

LATERAL MAPPING

Lateral mapping is an important aspect of magazine research. It prompts questions about how publishers and editors view girls and women: who do they think wants a magazine? What kind of content do they think these intended readers want or need and why? Who is not provided for and why? How are groups of readers differentiated from one another and on what basis? These questions are important because popular magazines help construct particular versions of what it means to be a girl or woman, and these constructions contribute to wider discourses on girlhood and womanhood. Lateral mapping is also helpful for thinking about readers. Familiarity with the range of magazines on sale at a particular historical juncture sheds light on aspects of readers' experiences, specifically what options girls and women were presented with and what can be learnt from their consumer choices. In practical terms, thinking about provision is important for contextualising individual titles and for evaluating the significance of what is included in a particular magazine or group of titles.

It is often possible to use secondary sources to map a field and to locate individual papers or clusters of them within this broader terrain. It is, however, difficult to appreciate the look, content and feel of different magazines from second-hand written descriptions and visual fragments. Moreover, if we rely only on academic accounts of magazines, it is hard to appreciate the choices readers made when they selected one magazine in preference to another and the experiences that different magazines offered them. For all these reasons it can be productive to see for ourselves the range of girls'/women's magazines published in a particular period. Sometimes research necessitates a detailed study of a range of magazines, but often a scan of provision is sufficient. Four practices are key to scanning provision: first, identification of a paper's intended reader using its title, cover image and manner of address; second, description of the magazine's contents, particularly the proportion of space and emphasis given to fiction, articles, fashion, personal and consumer guidance, advertising and editorials; third, assessment of the use in magazines of visual material (illustrations, photographs) and colour; fourth, noting how often a magazine was published, its size and cost.

Lateral mapping of provision for girls and young women in the period 1920–40 reveals how publishers constructed a market of 'girl readers'.[5] It contributes to understanding the meaning and significance of age, cross-cut by gender, in a period characterised by increased attention to young people and attempts to organise, regulate and protect them.[6] By 1920, most publishers in Britain had segmented the 'girl' market and acknowledged two categories of readers/consumers—the schoolgirl and the working girl. This differentiation was apparent from magazine content, titles and the figures that appeared on magazine covers. Schoolgirl papers generally targeted readers aged ten to fourteen or fifteen years, although a few magazines for mainly middle-class readers, such as the *Girl's Own Paper*, also addressed older schoolgirls.[7] School fiction and schoolgirl heroines reinforced the notion of a schoolgirl identity; the emphasis was on fun, girlfriends and, in some papers, also hobbies, sports and other leisure activities.

Working girls' papers targeted young women aged fifteen to twenty years. Readers were assumed to have traded full-time schooling for paid employment, to have grown out of tomboyish romps and to have replaced girlfriends with boyfriends. Paid work was presented in the editorials, features and fiction as key to the reader's identity. The working girl was expected to aspire to marriage and motherhood, but this was not presented as her current reality (though there were occasional features on wives). These magazines were differentiated by the intended reader's type of employment and spending power, which correlated crudely with social class. Weekly 'mill-girl' papers targeted working-class girls in mills, factories and domestic service, while weekly business girls' papers addressed upper-working-class and lower-middle-class young women—'modern girls'—in sales and clerical work. The monthly *Miss Modern* (1930–40) targeted middle-class young women with a fairly high degree of disposable income working in retail and clerical work, also the lower professions.

The process of lateral mapping reveals the principles underlying inter-war provision for young women, namely that reader identities were constructed along two axes that gave meaning to age: occupation (school, paid work) and the 'heterosexual career'.[8] The 'heterosexual career' was informed by understandings of adolescent development, principally whether girls were deemed to be too young to be interested in boys or at an age where this interest was expected to be paramount as a prelude to marriage and motherhood. The heterosexual career shaped all aspects of magazine provision explicitly or implicitly; it not only determined what was represented, but also how. Although the category of 'girls' embraced a diversity of experience, 'girls' were clearly differentiated from 'women' by the fact that they were usually assumed to be unmarried, even if on the brink of marriage.

Lateral mapping also reveals the instability of a commercial identity for young wage-earning women in the inter-war years. This is evidenced by the amalgamation of most of the weekly working girls' papers into women's romance magazines. These amalgamations were a rationalisation exercise, but they also signal that publishers did not regard the identities of young wage-earning women as particularly distinctive pre-1940. Although the reader's status as a paid worker was distinct from that of the wife and mother who typically did not engage in full-time paid work, her perceived preoccupation with romance and heterosexual fulfilment through marriage was seen to overlap sufficiently with that of older and married women so that a separate magazine was not deemed essential. The middle-class monthly, *Miss Modern*, was an exception. Launched in 1930, *Miss Modern* folded in 1940 seemingly only because of paper shortages caused by the Second World War. It is tempting to conclude that, unlike the papers that relied on working-class readers, *Miss Modern* did target a group of readers who wanted a youth-oriented magazine and who could afford to pay for it. Moreover, the paper's success in securing advertising revenue suggests that readers also bought the goods that were promoted in its pages.

LONGITUDINAL MAPPING

The story of *Miss Modern* is part of another development in periodical history—the emergence in the mid-twentieth century of 'teen' magazines. Here we shift attention from lateral to longitudinal mapping because the latter helps generate the bigger picture necessary to evaluate the relationship between youth, consumerism and periodical publishing. Locating 'teen' magazines within a longitudinal framework facilitates engagement with debates about when a modern teenage identity emerged, defined largely by leisure, style and consumption: were teenagers a 1950s' phenomenon, or did the inter-war years witness the 'birth of the teenager' or elements of teenage lifestyles?[9] Longitudinal mapping raises questions about how to interpret the identification by publishers of new groups of readers. How significant was a new manner of address, i.e., were post-war 'teens' different from inter-war 'working girls'? Did social and cultural changes create new groups of potential readers in terms of consumer power and common interests, or were publishers suddenly aware of pre-existing groups of potential readers previously not catered for, and, if so, why?

From the mid-1940s publishers started targeting girls in their 'teens'. *Mayfair* (1946–1950) proclaimed itself 'Britain's first teenage magazine', and like *Heiress* (1947–1956), another middle-class monthly, it presented a distinctive youth identity for a relatively exclusive group of affluent readers.[10] A few years later 'Teen page' was introduced into the weekly *Woman* magazine (1949–1951), and in the 1950s several weekly papers were launched for working-class young women in their teens and early twenties, including *Marilyn* (1955–1965), *Valentine* (1957–1974) and *Roxy* (1958–1963). *Valentine*, for example, described its 'keynotes' as romance, youth and excitement; amidst romance fiction and music features it presented advice on dress for 'the teenage purse'.[11]

At first glance, provision for teenagers seems consistent with claims that the post-war period witnessed the emergence of a new and distinctive 'teenage' identity. However, longitudinal mapping of magazines for young women complicates this picture; it provides a more nuanced understanding of perceptions of young women mid-century and puts the 'teenager' into historical perspective. Indeed, despite post-war reference to a new group of young people—teenagers—publishers did not construct a modern 'teenage' identity for most girls until the late 1950s (affluent young women were an exception). *Honey*, launched in 1960, was the first broad appeal magazine that visibly and successfully targeted a modern teenager with distinctive leisure, consumption and style.

The label 'teenager' needs to be approached cautiously; this becomes clear as we look longitudinally at the use of the term in periodical publishing. 'Teenagers' were targeted by some British magazines as soon as the Second World War ended, which is too early for a distinctive post-war youth identity to have emerged; 'teenager' was simply a new name for girls aged fifteen to twenty. For instance, *Woman*'s 'Miss Teenagers' were 'under-twenties'; the teenager was not defined by a distinctive relationship to consumer culture but by her 'special job' of growing up.[12] Mid-1950s' romance comics, such as *Marilyn*, also initially lacked a modern notion of a teenager. The popularity of early marriages in the 1950s prompted publishers to cater for young workers and young wives together, suggesting their interests could be conflated.[13] It was not until the late 1950s that the teenaged worker emerged as the principal intended reader of romance comics with distinctive teen interests. Whereas publishers found it relatively easy to combine the interests of young and older women in the inter-war years through to the mid-1950s, by 1960 this was no longer possible as a distinctive teenage identity was firmly established for young women across the social-class spectrum.

Reinforcing the point that there was very little novelty in periodical publishing for young women until the late 1950s, longitudinal mapping reveals important continuities between the content of early 1950s 'teen' magazines and those for inter-war working girls. For example, paid work and romance were dominant themes in post-war provision for teenage girls, but these themes were also central to inter-war working girls' magazines. Consumption was prominent in post-war magazines, but it was also a feature of middle-class working girls' papers. It was particularly prominent in *Miss Modern*, which featured thirteen pages of advertisements in its October 1930 issue; in many respects *Miss Modern* seems the prototype for post-war monthly teen magazines. There were also differences, but these were not notable until the late 1950s. The most visible and distinctively youthful feature to emerge in the late 1950s was a heavy emphasis on pop music; this became one of the hallmarks of provision for the modern teenager.[14]

Longitudinal mapping also reveals that publishers struggled to make a consumer-oriented teenage identity a viable commercial category until the 1960s. Middle-class monthlies may have heralded a teenage consumer in the 1940s, but they were premature because the category was too exclusive. *Mayfair*'s editor promised to introduce readers to 'reliable manufacturers', and in 1949 she proudly announced the magazine's success in persuading retailers to cater for the 'junior miss'.[15] But as Cynthia White explains, the market for this 'junior glossy' for the daughters of the wealthy was too small to tempt advertisers.[16] As late as 1960 many advertisers remained unsure about the viability of the teenage consumer.[17] When the monthly *Honey* magazine was launched, prompted by Mark Abrams' market research on teenage consumers, it struggled initially to attract advertising revenue.[18]

Posing questions about the field of periodical publishing can help researchers maintain a critical perspective on the particular magazines they work with. Both longitudinal and lateral mapping are inclusive approaches; they keep the bigger picture in mind. The bigger picture is key to another central feature of working with magazines, the analysis of their content; this is the focus of the second part of this chapter.

A HOLISTIC APPROACH TO MAGAZINE CONTENT

A holistic approach involves engaging with the different types of content within a magazine and how they are presented, particularly the relationship between text, images and design features. Textual and visual methods, such as semiotics, can be incorporated into this approach. The rest of the chapter explains why a holistic approach is useful before outlining its three key features. This is followed by a demonstration of how this approach sheds light on representations of smoking in inter-war business girls' magazines.

A holistic approach is useful because magazines are 'composite', 'hybrid' or 'heterogeneous' in form; they are composed of different types of content: fiction, features, editorials, advertisements, pictures and so on.[19] This composite form is integrated according to editorial policies and objectives, and it is managed through design practices which include layout, the positioning and style of captions and the use of images and colour. Magazines are not, however, necessarily coherent or tidy, in part because of their composite form. Their pages often harbour diversity, inconsistency, contradiction and tension. They also mediate competing objectives (for instance, providing satisfaction and generating need[20]) and different interests and viewpoints (those of publishers, editors, readers, advertisers). Adding to this complexity, magazines simultaneously promote femininity as natural and as something that needs to be achieved.[21] Their constructions of femininity maintain continuity but they also respond to social and cultural change.[22]

A holistic approach is necessary for understanding the production of magazines and what editors tried to achieve. It is also essential for thinking about readers' experiences. For example, one of the advantages of studying advertising in magazines is that it can be viewed in context; this provides insights into how advertising is framed and encountered by readers.

A holistic approach exposes *some* of the meaning-making opportunities afforded by magazines which are typically more diverse and subtle than identified by focusing only on prominent features in isolation from, rather than in dialogue with, one another. Magazines offer multiple interpretations, which may be deliberate or accidental.[23] 'Preferred readings', for instance, may be reinforced or become ambiguous or undermined when considered within the broader magazine environment.[24] Of course, the magazine experience is not just about reading and looking, but the interplay of these and how people engage with magazines as material objects in their everyday lives.[25] It is easy when doing research to forget the embodied experiences and range of things people do with magazines. This can be difficult to study historically, but a holistic approach helps keep the reader in mind because it prompts us to engage with the material and multi-sensory dimensions of how people experience representation and magazines.

A holistic approach has three main features, which I discuss in turn: tracing the threads in themes; reflecting on the impression created by magazine content; attending to the different 'voices' that emerge. These three features bring into focus the visual, material and phonic qualities of magazines. First, working holistically involves tracing the threads that make up themes, rather than focusing solely on the bright beads of high-profile features that initially draw the eye. For example, a holistic approach to research on friendship would consider articles that directly discuss it, also references to it in fiction and problem pages, the use of the language of friendship in editorials and images of girls together in fiction, features and advertising. How magazines represent a theme is often a combination of explicit coverage as well as dispersed appearances in text and images. Additionally, where advertising is a prominent feature of a magazine, there can be related editorials, or 'tie ins'. There is sometimes a tendency to pluck details out of magazines, especially in research that mines them for specific information. In doing this, the researcher risks losing sight of how different elements work within the context of a magazine and the complexity of how a theme is presented.

The second feature of a holistic approach entails reflection on the impression created by magazine content. This works at two inter-related levels: individual features and the magazine as a whole. It is tempting to equate pictures and not words with the visual, but words are visual elements too; editorial decisions about typefaces demonstrate appreciation of the visuality of the written word.[26] The impression conveyed by any one feature, for instance a problem page, cannot be assessed by focusing only on the text; the feature's size and the use of imagery, colour and captions are all integral to its possible meanings and effects, as is print quality. Editors consciously used different types of imagery to create different impressions, although intentions should not be conflated with effects. For example, inter-war reliance on sketches was often driven by cost, but there were also other considerations. Illustrations sometimes offered more scope than photos for producing highly stylised images, including representations of fashionably dressed women; in fiction, sketches facilitated graphic if unrealistic representations of the drama. Photos were, however, deployed as evidence of the authenticity of the editorial team or readers, and high quality photos were used in elite magazines, such as *Vogue*, to convey modernity. Interwar advertising exhibited similar patterns: photos were used as scientific evidence while drawings engaged with the intended reader's dreams and aspirations.[27] The impression created by the magazine as a whole also needs attention because the meanings and effects of individual features are shaped by their relationship to the rest of the magazine. This is often deliberately fostered by design elements such as colour or stylistic features, for example, repeated use of particular images to establish visual links relating disparate elements throughout a paper.[28]

Attention to the different 'voices' in a magazine is the third feature of a holistic approach. Magazines are not only composite in visual/textual form, they also expose 'readers' to a plurality of voices, for instance those of agony aunts, the editor, fiction writers, advertisers, readers. A holistic approach attends to these voices and how they are constructed, managed and put to work by editors singly and in combination.[29] For instance, working girls' magazines often used fictional male advisors to introduce a masculine voice and perspective. The use of this voice could have worked in several ways simultaneously: to add status to the viewpoint conveyed or to enable the editor to introduce, but also distance themselves from, controversial or unpopular advice.

The benefits of working holistically can be appreciated by examining examples of inter-war representations of young women smoking.[30] In 1880 tobacco consumption was widely regarded as a masculine practice, and women rarely smoked in public. In the 1920s smoking amongst upper-class and middle-class women became more visible in everyday life and in the media; the most talked-about smokers were modern young women, usually Society girls and middle-class young workers. Women's magazines contributed to the increased visibility of smoking, though there were distinctive class dimensions to this. Women's smoking featured routinely in affluent women's magazines, such as *Vogue*, and more tentatively in magazines targeting middle-class women, including the weekly business girls' papers such as *Girls' Friend* and *Girls' Favourite*, which addressed upper-working-class and lower-middle-class young workers. It was not, however, present in inter-war magazines that exclusively targeted working-class women, probably because women's smoking continued to have associations with prostitution.

A holistic approach exposes nuances in how business girls' magazines responded to the practice of women smoking, providing insight into the ways that cultural and social changes were mediated. While it is tempting to interpret all seemingly positive signs of smoking as an endorsement of the practice, a holistic approach enables a more subtle evaluation of the significance of what is featured. It reveals contradictions that are suggestive of ambivalence. Close scrutiny of business girls' papers also suggests that representations of smoking did not always or only present a particular position on smoking. Inconsistencies are not *always* signs of ambivalence, nor are reinforcements necessarily evidence of deliberate promotion; smoking was often included to serve other purposes, in other words, it was a device. Magazines are visual and textual objects that were designed with deliberation; a host of decisions were made by editors and other contributors about how to achieve a particular look and present magazine content in ways that were accessible and attractive to readers.

Smoking practices served as devices in several ways: semiotic, aesthetic and dramatic; understanding this is key to ascertaining the salience of what is featured in magazines. They were semiotic in that smoking served as textual and visual shorthand for feminine modernity. For example, in one fiction series the significance of the cigarette as a symbol of modernity was evident in the use of smoke from the protagonist's cigarette to form the phrase 'modern girl' in the story's title.[31] In another series, the story's opening lines declared that the fictional heroine, Barbara, was 'a modern girl' who smoked: 'Barbara had been sitting on the edge of the table, swinging her legs. She took the cigarette from her lips [. . .]'.[32] As in other stories where the cigarette was merely symbolic of modernity, after the initial description of the heroine smoking in a way that suggested it was commonplace, there was no further reference to the practice. Smoking also served, often simultaneously, as an aesthetic device; cigarettes in holders were used to enhance the graceful lines of a female figure, to produce an elongated and streamlined modern look or to create a smoky haze that gave a couple privacy.

Cigarettes were also deployed as dramatic devices that facilitated storytelling. In the mid-1920s, depictions of women smoking were sufficiently novel as to facilitate narrative action—they were mildly shocking—but they were also becoming established as facilitators of heterosexual romance. The following extract demonstrates both dramatic uses. Daisy's smoking was dramatically shocking, a sign that she was modern and worldly wise, but it was also a means to bring her physically close to a young man who was disapproving of her modernity.

> He rose and handed her his case. She took a cigarette and slipped it between her lips, waiting for him to give her a light. For a moment he hesitated, for there was something in the way her soft, red lips closed round the cigarette that covered him with confusion. [. . .] He lighted a match and held it to her cigarette, and again he noticed how red and curved were her lips.[33]

This smoking ritual was presented as a means of fostering romance and arousing passion: the lighting of the cigarette brought the couple close together; the cigarette highlighted the sensuality of the woman's lips which were then illuminated by the flame from the match.

A holistic approach discourages the decontextualisation and over-interpretation of *individual* textual and visual representations. Tracing the threads across an issue, researchers are better equipped to identify and evaluate how smoking is presented. In business girls' papers, women's smoking was frequently embraced as an aspect of feminine modernity in fiction and articles; there were no cigarette advertisements probably because these papers were too small in circulation to attract tobacco advertisers. However, a holistic approach reveals inconsistencies and contradictions in the representation of smoking, suggesting ambivalence about the practice. It shows that in the 1920s cigarettes were still associated principally with men, and that women's smoking was widely seen as a challenge to traditional gender hierarchies. Working holistically does, however, take us further than this, to demonstrate the complexities of how smoking was managed. This also exposes the opportunities for readers to generate multiple understandings of the practice.

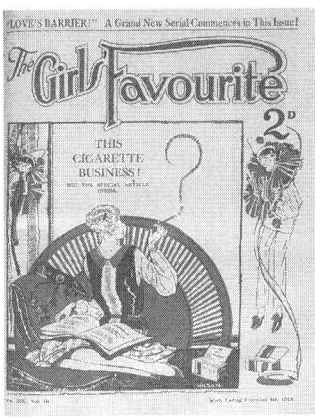

Figure 1.1 'This cigarette business!' Cover and featured article. © The British Library Board. *Girls' Favourite*, 4 December 1926, 409.

Figure 1.2 'This cigarette business!' Cover and featured article. © The British Library Board. *Girls' Favourite*, 4 December 1926, 411.

A 1926 issue of *Girls' Favourite* provides an example of how ambivalence was conveyed through contradictions in the representation of smoking (see Figures 1.1 and 1.2). The blue and green front cover is the first point in the thread on smoking; it creates a generally positive impression of smoking even though on close inspection there are counter signs of unease with the practice. It is dominated by a sketch of an attractive young woman holding, daintily, a cigarette in a holder; the text refers to a 'special article' on 'This cigarette business!' The decision to publicise the topic on the cover indicates that the editor thought smoking would interest readers but also that the magazine was generally positive towards women who smoked. For aesthetic and commercial reasons it would be odd to have an unattractive woman featured on the cover, but there was no need for the smoking article to be given high visibility if the editor detested the practice. Ambivalence is suggested, however, in the exclamation mark in the article's title and in the question mark formed from the cigarette smoke. It also emerges from the shocked expressions of the clowns on either side of the seated young woman, though their disapproval is relegated to the margins of the image. It is important not to over analyse these details because of the aesthetic priorities of the illustrator, but it seems significant that the central figure corresponds to a historically specific intended reader with fashionable clothes and hairstyle, while the clowns are mildly amusing and lacking historical specificity, which suggests their views may be old-fashioned.

Contradictions are amplified when we turn to the inside of the magazine. The page featuring the cigarette article visually reinforces the positive first impression created by the cover because of the inclusion of a sketch featuring another attractive smoker. However, the text contradicts the image. The special article is a diatribe against women smoking which articulates the feared significance of smoking for gender identity and gender relations; it contradicts the notion, seen elsewhere in business girls' papers, that smoking could facilitate heterosexual relations. The author details the ways in which smoking killed romance by arguing that women who smoked lost their femininity and their distinctiveness from men, which was the foundation of gender relations, romance and marriage:

> [H]ow can he get the proper atmosphere when, on bending to extract the kiss that seals the bargain, he finds that her waving locks are perfumed with stale smoke instead of the sweet, subtle perfume that he has been given to expect, and that her answering kiss might be that of his best boy chum for fragrance?[34]

In overblown terms the author proceeds to describe the results of women smoking, revealing the association between smoking and masculinity: 'she might soon grow into a mannish, nicotine-stained and perfumed travesty of her former dear little self, lolling inelegantly on chair-arms, viewing the world through a cloud of smoke and cynical remarks. She might even—terrible thought—call me "old thing!" '[35]

The tension within the article between words and images conveys ambivalence. Though the speaker is critical of the smoker, the accompanying illustration softens the effect of the text and suggests that the magazine is not supporting the speaker's views, merely providing a platform for them. Interestingly, the critique of the smoker is delivered by an unnamed male outsider. The masculine voice allows objections to women smoking to be displaced onto a man. This could add to the status of the objections to women smoking, given that readers were assumed to be preoccupied with finding a husband and therefore eager to discover a male point-of-view. However, the voice of an unnamed man is also, potentially, a critic who can be ignored, especially given a hint of irony in the presentation of his exaggerated fears. Like the clowns on the front page, he can be brushed aside as out of date and out of touch. The complex ways in which smoking was represented, as shown in this example from *Girls' Favourite*, provides insights into how editors managed different viewpoints in their efforts to broach topical issues in ways that entertained readers and avoided alienating them.

CONCLUSION

To work effectively *with* magazines, scholars need a research strategy that is inclusive rather than fragmentary. Fragmentary practices are, however, commonplace, though not always transparent in historical research because of a tendency to embed rather than explicate our methods. They result from the researchers' choice of method and analytical strategies, from practical constraints and sometimes from pragmatic selections or 'cherry picking' to illustrate a point or argument. Fragmentary practices limit what we can learn from working with girls' and women's magazines. They tend to isolate publications from the field of periodicals past and present and to splinter and over simplify magazine content. An inclusive research strategy counters this reductive tendency; at its core is a holistic approach to magazine content. A holistic approach is essential to engage with the composite character of magazines and how diverse elements are integrated; design features and materiality are aspects of this integration.

Tracing the threads of themes, reflecting on impression and attending to the interplay of 'voices', a holistic approach exposes the subtleties, inconsistencies and tensions that result from the composite form of magazines and the diverse interests and standpoints that are represented, and sometimes explicitly managed, within them. It safeguards against misinterpreting the salience of individual features or images, instead engaging with the broader textual, visual, material and phonic contexts within which these are embedded, encountered by readers and rendered meaningful in multiple ways. An inclusive strategy also involves mapping periodical provision both laterally and longitudinally. Such mapping reveals why and how particular titles are distinctive and the options available to consumers/readers. It illuminates shifts in the construction of readers and the identity of magazines, enabling researchers to engage in debates about social and cultural change. This chapter introduces and champions an inclusive approach to working with magazines. In doing this it challenges fragmentary research practices and encourages historians to be more open and reflexive about how they use magazines to learn about the past.

NOTES

1 Notable examples include: Janice Winship, *Inside Women's Magazines* (London: Pandora, 1987b); Angela McRobbie, '*Jackie* magazine: Romantic individualism and the teenage girl,' in *Feminism and Youth Culture*, ed. Angela McRobbie (London: Macmillan, 1991), 81–134; Marjorie Ferguson, *Forever Feminine: Women's Magazines and the Cult of Femininity* (London: Heinemann, 1983).
2 For example, Cynthia White, *Women's Magazines 1693–1968* (London: Michael Joseph, 1970); Kristine Moruzi, *Constructing Girlhood Through the Periodical Press, 1850–1915* (Farnham: Ashgate, 2012), 2. White dates the women's periodical industry from 1875, White, *Women's Magazines*, 56.
3 See, for example: Jeremy Aynsley and Kate Forde, eds., *Design and the Modern Magazine* (Manchester: Manchester University Press, 2007); Ros Ballaster et al., *Women's Worlds: Ideology, Femininity and the Woman's Magazine* (London: Macmillan, 1991); Margaret Beetham, *A Magazine of Her Own* (London: Routledge, 1996); Fiona Hackney, ' "They opened up a whole new world": Feminine modernity and the feminine imagination in women's magazines, 1919–1939' (PhD diss., Falmouth University, 2010); Moruzi, *Constructing Girlhood*; Rachel Ritchie, ' "Beauty isn't all a matter of looking glamorous": Attitudes to glamour and beauty in 1950s women's magazines,' *Women's History Review* 23 (2014): 723–43; Jennifer Scanlon, *Inarticulate Longings: The Ladies' Home Journal, Gender, and the Promises of Consumer Culture* (London: Routledge, 1995); Penny Tinkler, *Constructing Girlhood: Popular Magazines for Girls Growing Up in England 1920–50* (London: Taylor & Francis, 1995a).
4 On material transformations generated by hardcopy archiving practices: Margaret Beetham, 'Open and closed: The periodical as a publishing genre,' *Victorian Periodicals Review* 22 (1989): 96.
5 Tinkler, *Constructing Girlhood*, chapter three.
6 Penny Tinkler, 'Youth,' in *Twentieth-Century Britain: Economic, Cultural and Social Change*, ed. Francesca Carnevali and Julie-Marie Strange (Harlow: Pearson, 2007), 214–30; John Davis, *Youth and the Condition of Britain: Images of Adolescent Conflict* (London: Athlone, 1990).
7 Between 1918 and 1947 the majority of children received only an elementary education up to fourteen years. A minority of working-class, and most middle-class, children received post-fourteen education in secondary schools. See Tinkler, *Constructing Girlhood*, 21–2.
8 Tinkler, *Constructing Girlhood*, 3, 72–6.
9 For an overview see Tinkler, 'Youth,' 227. Penny Tinkler, ' "A material girl?" Adolescent girls and their magazines, 1920–58,' in *All the World and Her Husband: Women in Twentieth-Century Consumer Culture*, ed. Maggie Andrews and Mary M. Talbot, London: Cassell, 2000, 97–112.

10 'The importance of being teenage,' *Mayfair*, Winter 1949, 2–3.
11 'A letter from your editor,' *Valentine*, 31 August 1957, 19.
12 Carol Graham, 'Teen page,' *Woman*, 2 July 1949, 14–15.
13 Interview Patricia Lamburn, 23 July 1985. Lamburn was the editor of girls' and women's magazines from the 1960s to the 1990s.
14 Tinkler, 'Material girl,' 106–7.
15 *Mayfair*, September 1946, 2; 'The importance of being teenage,' Winter 1949, 2–3.
16 White, *Women's Magazines*, 187.
17 See Fan Carter 'A taste of *Honey*: Get-ahead femininity in 1960s Britain' elsewhere in this volume, for a discussion of *Honey*'s attempts to attract advertising copy. Penny Tinkler, ' "Are you really living?" If not, "GET WITH IT!": The teenage self and lifestyle in young women's magazines, Britain 1957–70,' *Cultural and Social History* 11 (2014): 597–620.
18 Interview Patricia Lamburn; Mark Abrams, *Teenage Consumer II* (London: Exchange Press, 1961).
19 Aynsley and Forde, *Design and the Modern Magazine*, 2; Hackney, 'They opened up a whole new world,' 26; Beetham, *A Magazine of Her Own*, 1.
20 Scanlon, *Inarticulate Longings*.
21 Beetham, *A Magazine of Her Own*, 1.
22 See note 3.
23 Ballaster et al., *Women's Worlds*, 7.
24 Stuart Hall, 'Encoding/decoding,' in *Culture, Media and Language: Working papers in Cultural Studies*, ed. Stuart Hall et al. (London: Hutchinson, 1980).
25 Joke Hermes, *Reading Women's Magazines. An Analysis of Everyday Media Use* (Oxford: Blackwell, 1995).
26 Jeremy Aynsley, 'Fashioning graphics in the 1920s: Typefaces, magazines and fashion,' in *Design and the Modern Magazine*, ed. Aynsley and Forde, 37–55.
27 Hackney, 'They opened up a whole new world,' 148; Marie-Louise Bowallius, 'Advertising and the use of colour in *Woman's Home Companion*, 1923–33,' in Aynsley and Forde, *Design and the Modern Magazine*, 18–36.
28 Hackney, 'They opened up a whole new world,' 60.
29 Dependence on advertising revenue meant editors often had little control over voices used in advertisements.
30 Penny Tinkler, *Smoke Signals: Women, Smoking and Visual Culture in Britain* (Oxford: Berg, 2006); Penny Tinkler, ' "Red tips for hot lips": Advertising cigarettes for young women in Britain, 1920–70,' *Women's History Review* 10 (2001): 249–72.
31 William E. Groves, 'A modern girl,' *Girls' Friend*, 23 May 1925, 6.
32 Effie Scott, 'Barbara: A modern girl,' *Girls' Friend*, 21 March 1925, 1. See also *Girls' Friend*, 4 July 1925, 7.
33 Violet Craufurd, 'That dreadful Miss Cardew!,' *Girls' Friend*, 16 May 1925, 8.
34 'This cigarette business!,' *Girls' Favourite*, 4 December 1926, 411.
35 'This cigarette business!,' *Girls' Favourite*, 4 December 1926, 411.

2 Landscape for a Good Woman's Weekly
Finding Magazines in Post-war British History and Culture

Tracey Loughran

In *Landscape for a Good Woman* (1986), Carolyn Steedman recalls a childhood dream. An unidentified woman hurries along a wide road, occasionally turning back to shake her finger at the young Carolyn. The woman's appearance is vividly described: 'She wore the New Look, a coat of beige gabardine which fell in two swaying, graceful pleats from her waist at the back (the swaying must have come from very high heels, but I didn't notice her shoes), a hat tipped forward from hair swept up.'[1]

In the early 1950s of Steedman's dream, when clothes rationing had only just ended, a New Look skirt symbolised unspeakable opulence. For Steedman's mother, a working-class woman living in social housing in south London, the New Look was much-desired and unobtainable, the stuff of dreams; it is not surprising that it found its way into her daughter's psychic landscape. Steedman's description of the dream-woman consists of the type of details usually noticed and immediately forgotten—a particular fashion, a certain garment, colours and fabrics, the way clothes affect deportment. To linger on these details, to accord them significance in the interpretation of dreams or the world around, is to risk accusations of triviality, superficiality and vanity. Historically, these accusations have been levelled at women rather than men, as though fashion and its fripperies are essentially feminine concerns. Moreover, they are the concerns of a particular type of woman: beautiful but empty-headed, as superficial and vain and ultimately trivial as fashion itself. Advertising a concern with appearance risks a particularly gendered opprobrium.

Within the web of cultural and historical meanings Steedman traces, the New Look is more than just a style of dress. It is a symbol of a desire, of the yearning of the dispossessed for material things. This is a desire which has been refused meaning by the dominant culture and by existing traditions of working-class history and biography. Steedman's achievement in *Landscape for a Good Woman* is the counter-refusal of the conventional interpretative devices available to explain her mother's longings. The 'landscape' of the title refers to, among other things, the space in cultural criticism which Steedman forces open to accommodate the story of her mother's life, and her creation of alternative historical, social, political and psychological contexts to explain the longings of women like her mother. Steedman's purpose is 'to admit [her mother's] desire for the things of the earth to political reality and psychological validity', and to insist that these desires stemmed from a sense of material want as important to 1950s working-class experience as unionisation and autodidacticism.[2] The desire for a New Look skirt must be historicised and politicised, and this also means understanding it as a desire rooted in the lived experiences of working-class women. For women excluded from political and social power, who have only their bodies and their labour, clothes, shoes and make-up are not fripperies, but 'material stepping-stones' to a different, better place in the world.[3]

As with women's clothes, women's magazines have often been treated as trivial and irrelevant to the 'real' business of history. This is partly because magazines are disposable and therefore inherently ephemeral. Often even their readers do not attribute much importance to magazines. They are designed to be picked up, leafed through and thrown away. But women's magazines are historically important because they have formed part of everyday life for so many women. In the 1960s, weekly sales of women's magazines in the UK reached 12.1 million copies per week. It was estimated that five out of six women saw at least one women's magazine every week.[4] Because women's magazines define their readership in terms of gender, they have also reflected and sometimes helped to shape wider changes in women's social and political roles.[5] Perhaps paradoxically, it is because women's magazines are such a powerful symbol of mass culture that they have been belittled and maligned as cultural forms, marginalised within 'mainstream' (non-women's) British history and stigmatised by influential traditions of cultural criticism, including feminist scholarship.

In this chapter, I trace some of the ways in which women's magazines and their readers were depicted within British culture in the 1960s and then consider how the persistent and pervasive cultural denigration of magazines was reflected within cultural studies and feminist scholarship on magazines.[6] I aim to encourage others to reflect critically on assumptions about the status of magazines and their readers. How do these opinions mirror certain attitudes towards class, gender and education which shaped and continue to exert influence on the disciplines many of us work within? At the same time, early cultural studies and feminist scholarship took an uncompromising stance on the importance of class and/or collective action, which has perhaps faded out of more recent scholarship on women's magazines. I argue that by thinking against the dominant forms of historical understanding of women's magazines, we can think more imaginatively and productively about the meaning of magazines in readers' lives. What place did the cultural form of women's magazines hold in the collective imagination? What can this tell us about prevalent attitudes towards class and gender in postwar British culture?

Women's magazines are usually associated with the private sphere, but they also occupied public space. They were visible on news-stands and in the public places where women might spend time sitting around: laundrettes, common rooms and the waiting rooms of doctors' and dentists' surgeries, family planning clinics and hospitals. Authors who referred to them expected even those who did not buy or read women's magazines to be familiar with the kind of material they contained. In Anthony Burgess' comic novel *Inside Mr Enderby* (1963), the guileless Enderby embarks on his first reading of women's magazines at the behest of a potential new employer:

> He was shocked and touched by letters sent to Millicent Goodheart, a blue-haired lady with sharp red talons and a gentle smile: 'He said it was artificial respiration, but now I find I am to have his child'; 'I have only been married three months but I have fallen in love with my husband's father'.[7]

The humour depends on Burgess' assumption that readers will recognise the familiar tropes of the agony column. As this example suggests, because magazines were a continuous, ever-present part of the background of everyday life, they are also found in the background of other cultural artefacts, such as books, films, television and music. The fragmented references in these forms allow us to reconstruct the role of women's magazines in the cultural imagination, and so provide a 'landscape' for women's magazines within British history and culture.

This is a different way of thinking about the history of women's magazines, which I hope subsequent scholars will further develop. There is a large body of scholarship on the historical development of magazines, constructions of femininity within these magazines and (to a lesser extent) the roles of these magazines in women's lives. This literature overlaps with cultural histories, which use women's magazines as source material to understand their main subjects. We know a fair amount about the history *of* women's magazines, and the history of women *in* magazines, but we know less about the place of women's magazines in the cultural imagination—their part in the mass of narratives, ideas and symbols out of, or against which, people create a sense of their identities. These narratives, ideas and symbols have their origins in the 'real' social world, but they are also part of a shared imaginative world which enables people 'to locate themselves imaginatively within their complexly structured social worlds'.[8] If we can understand more fully the symbolic importance of magazines as a cultural form, then we can make more informed intuitive leaps about the role of magazines in readers' lives.

In this chapter, I focus on the interlinked themes of gender, class and education in novels, films and cultural and feminist scholarship, as these are the most prominent themes in the 'fragments' I have amassed so far. But this is only the starting point of a possible new direction in the history of magazines. Like magazines and their readers, our identities are multiple and kaleidoscopic. If others take up this call to pursue this new direction, our collective action can produce a richer and more densely populated 'landscape' for women's magazines, populated with figures of different races, sexualities and ages, as well as people of different classes, educational statuses and life experiences.

CONSUMERISM, CLASS AND DIFFERENCE

In the cultural traces of women's magazines I have uncovered, two themes recur: the status of magazines as emblems of empty consumerism and selfish individualism and as markers of class and educational difference. This characterisation of magazines tells us about wider perceptions of femininity and about the class dimensions of the persistent denigration of women and their interests as represented by these magazines. A good example of the first kind of placing of women's magazines is the film *Darling* (dir. John Schlesinger, 1965), which stars Julie Christie as the amoral model Diana Scott, who sleeps and dances her way through the Carnaby-tian world of swinging London. The film is framed by the device of Christie's character giving an interview to a female journalist for a women's magazine. This device highlights the disjunction between Scott's self-serving justification of her actions, delivered in the familiar banal language of celebrity interviews, and the appalling and destructive behaviour witnessed by the audience. It therefore highlights the superficiality of women's magazines and their collusion in the creation of an alluring but ultimately damaging dream-world.

Women's magazines are associated with unsavoury desires. Indulgence in magazines indicates hopeless solipsism. In Elizabeth Taylor's *Mrs Palfrey at the Claremont* (1971), the superficial and quasi-sexual allure of women's magazines reflects the personality of Ludo's mother, portrayed as a slattern who lives with her lover. When she is ill in bed, surrounded by 'screwed-up tissues and discarded hot water bottles', 'sticky bottles and smeared glasses' and the remnants of 'a gin-and-french', her son sits by her bedside reading her *Woman's Own* to pass the time.[9] Later, when her lover has left and the hard-up Ludo is supporting her financially, he notes her purchases of 'a large box of chocolate mints, both *Vogue* and *Harper's*, and [. . .] what looked like a new sweater'.[10] This selfish impecuniousness is presented as a particularly feminine form of decadence.

When magazines are mentioned in the context of male desire, other kinds of solitary pleasures are hinted at. In Stan Barstow's *A Kind of Loving* (1960), the main character Vic comments approvingly that one woman 'looks a real picture, just like somebody in one of them glossy women's mags'.[11] But as he lusts after another woman, he muses, 'Once I'd have given anything just to be with her like this, but now I want her like I want the bints in the magazines. It's not really her I want at all, if you see what I mean.'[12] To scholars of magazines, women's magazines are an entirely different genre to pornographic magazines, with different aims and audiences.

However, in Barstow's depiction of courtship and sexuality, the glossy allure of magazines and the dreams they sell slides into the sordid desires of pornography, which Vic acknowledges as unreal and dissatisfying. The categories which we impose on our subjects for the purposes of scholarship do not always reflect the messiness of the associations which inhabit the cultural imagination and which also surface, as we will see later, in some cultural scholarship.

The portrayal of magazines as superficial and destructive symbols of consumerism overlaps with their use to mark class and educational difference. In novels, magazines are read by those who lack the intellectual wherewithal for more cerebral pursuits. This is not just an expression of class snobbery but a way of signalling the existence of more valuable pursuits, aspirations and ways of being. In *A Kind of Loving*, Vic scorns the 'common' interests of his wife, Ingrid:

> Good heavens, no, she says, she can't read books. She gets three magazines a week and can hardly get through them for watching telly. 'Telly.' I don't like that word somehow. It always reminds me of fat ignorant pigs of people swilling stout and cackling like hens at the sort of jokes they put on them coloured seaside postcards [. . .]. So I just go on holding the book and say nothing. There's something just in the feel of a book, I always think; something solid that's here to stay. Not like television, switched on and off like a tap. I think it's a pity she doesn't read because it means we shan't ever be able to talk about the books we've both read and recommend them to one another.[13]

Vic is a trained draughtsman from a working-class background whose slow ascent up the class ladder is threatened by his marriage to Ingrid, from a similar but more affluent class background. Ingrid's enjoyment of television and magazines is seen by Vic as a sign of her vacuity and inferiority. Barstow, the grammar school-educated son of a coal-miner, contrasts the solidity of masculine working-class traditions and self-improvement with the flashy and disposable pleasures of the modern age, coded as feminine and lower middle class through their association with Ingrid. Vic asserts his own value at least partly through the denigration of his wife.

In other types of novel, the working-class readers of women's magazines are pitted against the middle-class female producers of magazines. In *Inside Mr Enderby* (1963), Vesta Bainbridge, the 'Features Editress [sic]' of *Fem*, is an immaculately coiffed and costumed vision of 'slender and sheer-hosed glamour'. She is the polar opposite of her readers, who have 'an aura of back kitchens about them, tea served to shirt-sleeved men doing their pools [a form of betting on association football], the telly flicking and shouting in the background'.[14] To Vesta, these are women of limited vocabulary, who 'cannot bear too much reality', and want '[t]he mystery of the stars [. . .] especially if seen from the garden of a council house'.[15]

Doris Lessing sets up a similar scenario in *The Golden Notebook* (1962), but is more sympathetic to journalists and readers and more conscious of the potential tensions (of class, education and aspirations) between producers and consumers. Ella works for *Women at Home*, a magazine aimed at working-class women, replying privately to the hundreds of letters sent in by depressed women. She is appalled by the 'hundreds and thousands of people, all over the country, simmering away in misery and no one cares'.[16] This genuine compassion co-exists with submerged disdain for the magazine's readers, women who strive for status through the adoption of bourgeois styles, but never get it quite right.[17] Ella also feels guilty at her own complicity in hoodwinking readers into this kind of behaviour. Her shame is sharpest when she visits the home of her married lover and sees his wife's copies of *Women at Home* on the kitchen table:

> Ella felt she had been delivered a direct blow; but told herself that after all she worked for this nasty snobbish magazine, and what right had she to sneer at people who read it? [. . .] But it was no use; there was a small television set in the corner of the kitchen, and she imagined the wife sitting here, night after night, reading *Women at Home* or looking at the television set and listening for the children upstairs.[18]

Ella recoils from the readers of *Women at Home* partly because she fears becoming like them: unhappy, isolated and trapped. This is the life she is trying to escape, but her independence is bought at the expense of these women—stay-at-home wives whose husbands are unfaithful with women like Ella and who are encouraged to busy themselves with 'pointless' domesticity by the women who produce magazines. Ella does not like this type of journalism, but it comes easily to her, and she fears that this is because she is, at heart, no different from these housewives. The world of women's magazines, 'coy, little-womanish, snobbish', is too close for comfort, too easy to slip into, and must be rejected.[19] In *The Golden Notebook*, ultimately magazines represent the constraints of conventional femininity rather than lack of moral, social or intellectual worth. Ella's involvement in the world of women's magazines despite her recoil from their contents and readers reflects the difficulty of finding alternative ways of being a woman at this point in time.

WOMEN'S MAGAZINES, CULTURAL STUDIES AND SECOND WAVE FEMINISM

The two earliest traditions of scholarship on mass-market women's magazines, the critiques formulated by early British cultural studies and second wave feminism, developed out of movements which also sought alternative ways of being. Both traditions continue to exert a great deal of influence on different strands of modern British history. The mode of cultural analysis which emerged out of the work of Richard Hoggart, Raymond Williams and E. P. Thompson in the late 1950s and early 1960s shaped the approaches of a whole generation of post-war British historians to class and culture. These thinkers insisted on the existence, dignity and value of a distinct working-class culture which they saw as under threat from new forms of mass culture. The salvation of the working classes lay in education (all three men worked in adult education). Women were often neglected in this form of cultural analysis.

A partial exception to this rule is Richard Hoggart's *The Uses of Literacy* (1957), which devoted considerable space to magazines. Hoggart was sympathetic to 'older magazines' in the tradition of *Peg's Paper* (a magazine aimed at working-class girls in their teen years), which he believed reflected 'solid and relevant' forms of ordinary working-class life.[20] However, he denounced 'newer' glossy publications, which he saw as obsessed with 'money-prestige', public personalities and 'kittenish domesticity'.[21] In Hoggart's view, these magazines catered for short attention spans and presented fragmented oddities which aimed only to entertain, not to challenge, engage or enrich the reader. They offered 'a slick and hollow puppet-world' of '"dolly-mixtures" pleasures'.[22] Mass publications catered to the lowest common denominator in order to increase their profit margins, and in so doing 'culturally robbed' the working class and stopped them looking 'outwards and upwards' to more satisfying forms of culture and ways of life.[23]

In Britain, the second wave feminist movement developed out of Marxist socialism, and so it is unsurprising that initial feminist critiques of women's magazines had much in common with Hoggart's analysis. Socialist-feminist critiques saw women's magazines as repressive agents of socialisation which furthered commercial and patriarchal interests by confirming women 'in their traditional role of docile homemaker, serene, selfless guardian of the hearth and family'.[24] Second wave feminists highlighted the status of women's magazines as consumer commodities which encouraged women to accept their subordination rather than participate in political struggle. In both these traditions, the stigmatisation of women's magazines is bound up with assumptions about class, gender and culture: about who represents and speaks for women and the working classes, the moral and political inferiority of particular forms of cultural consumption and how marginalised groups should understand their position in the world and work to change it.

The early cultural studies were concerned with class rather than gender, and for the most part second wave feminists focused on sex rather than class, but both traditions came to broadly similar conclusions about women's magazines. Both viewed women's magazines as expressions of capitalist consumer culture which lacked the moral and political value of more 'authentic' cultural forms. In arguing that magazines foster false consciousness, they simultaneously assumed the power of magazines, the uncritical responses of readers and the lack of agency of readers (the working class and/or women). The magazine reader was implicitly contrasted with a superior fully conscious agent who held the same position as the author: in one case the educated worker, in the other the feminist activist. Finally, authors in both traditions most often spoke from outside the position they addressed, by virtue of their status as an author and therefore an 'authority' if nothing else, but did not acknowledge their exteriority. Hoggart claimed some kind of solidarity with workers through his working-class origins, while second wave feminists claimed the 'we' of shared female experience. Ultimately, although both forms of scholarship claimed to speak for the subordinated and dispossessed, they replicated the messages of dominant cultural forms and therefore unwittingly reinforced elements of existing power relations. In culture and cultural criticism alike, working-class female readers were placed beyond the grace of the sanctioned rescuers of their class and their sex.

More recent historical scholarship acknowledges the normative ideological functions of women's magazines and the commercial imperatives which drive their production, but also draws out the positive roles magazines can play in women's lives. Women's magazines are not perfect, but they nevertheless constitute a form of female culture which offers readers 'a privileged space, or world, within which to construct and explore the female self'.[25] Janice Winship argues that in everyday life, women tend to be isolated from each other and their concerns perceived as secondary to those of men. In their magazines, at least, women are placed centre stage and their everyday activities taken seriously. She concludes that 'the "woman's world" which women's magazines represent is created precisely because it does not exist outside their pages'.[26]

A similar line of argument is pursued by Naomi Wolf's *The Beauty Myth* (1991), which maintains that no matter how apparently trivial some of the content or how misogynist some of the advertising, women's magazines are important and valued to their readers because they represent women's mass culture. Wolf asks,

> Where else do women get to feel positively or even negatively connected with millions of women worldwide? The images in women's magazines constitute the only cultural female experience that can begin to gesture at the breadth of solidarity possible among women, a solidarity as wide as half the human race.[27]

Women's magazines reflect the contradictions of female subjectivity but can also provide a way into understanding women's experiences, hopes and aspirations. Magazines help women to imagine different ways of being. Their promise of the perfect self may be false, but it glitters: sometimes, what we need is the not-real, the ability to see into worlds which are not our own. Some novels hint at the ways magazines can shape these dreams. In Angela Carter's *The Magic Toyshop* (1967), the recently orphaned teenage narrator considers running away. She could 'get a job and live by myself in a bed-sitting room, like the girls in stories in magazines':

> Brewing Nescafé on her own gas-ring and buying solitary quarter pounds of cheese for herself; and painting one wall geranium red and another cornflower blue and the others white, as she wanted to do at home but her mother would not let her.[28]

This is a flight of fancy, but it is also a remarkably prosaic dream. It speaks partly to the inability of younger people to choose their own ways of life but also to the limits of imagination under certain conditions. The dreamer does not own this room for herself, and it does not even need to have a view: just walls of the colour she chooses. When a bed-sitting room is a symbol of freedom, the narrowness of a person's world is the problem which needs to be examined, not the magazines which give shape and colour to the dreams of escape.

The older traditions of scholarship simultaneously denied the worth of the kinds of aspirations symbolised by and found within magazines and refused to acknowledge that their readers had any 'real' freedom to choose. Early cultural theorists and second wave feminists alike saw magazines as blinding women to the real conditions of their lives and preventing them from challenging the status quo. Hoggart was particularly saddened by the 'younger working-class women who feel smarter and want, understandably, to remain smarter than their mothers', and who bought the newer women's magazines. The most damning element of enjoyment of these magazines was that they sold a 'vision of life' informed by middle-class tastes rather than authentic working-class culture. He mocked these aspirations by reciting snippets from typical articles: ' "You can do wonders with a bit of cretonne"; "How I glamorise my bedroom by the Honorable . . . "; "A new way of arranging Birthday Cards" '. Without pausing for breath, Hoggart slides into a denunciation of 'pin-up photography' (the same shift Vic makes in *A Kind of Loving*). The implication is that the desire of working-class women for nicer homes is another unreal and pathetic kind of lust.[29]

The feminist writer Elizabeth Wilson also identifies women's magazines with pornography, but from the standpoint of the (guilty?) user. She describes fashion magazines as provoking a 'distinct erotic thrill' which is 'never fully satisfied' by their contents. She is in thrall to the 'magical thinking' of these magazines and at the same time exhausted by the desires they provoke and can never fulfil. She describes this as 'the pornography of narcissism'.[30] Although this is not a positive assessment of magazines, it is sympathetic to their readers, who include Wilson. This contrasts with Germaine Greer's 'othering' of magazine readers. In *The Female Eunuch* (1970), Greer quotes a letter sent to the *Woman* agony aunt Evelyn Home from a jealous husband as well as Home's reply (make your wife feel special and then she will not stray). Greer explains that,

People who buy books may laugh at such views, dismiss them as typical of a certain civilisation, but this is to set aside the fact that the moral attitudes of a concept like 'Evelyn Home' [. . .] are computer-proven to be the ones that the great majority of female readers find acceptable.[31]

The unthinking separation of magazine readers from 'people who buy books' underlines Greer's conviction of the truth of this division, which assumes that moral values and intelligence are aligned with reading habits. This is a judgment about class and education as much as gender. It is exactly the same kind of attitude which led author Margaret Drabble's mother to despise 'those for whom the word "book" meant "magazine"'.[32]

The newer scholarship on women's magazines tries to take dreams and aspirations seriously. It may not always succeed in this aim, but it makes a deliberate effort in this direction where older critiques did not. This newer scholarship reinstates the reader's agency and argues that she actively produces meaning from what she reads.[33] It does not dismiss the hopes, fears and values of magazine readers as these older traditions sometimes did. At the same time, some of the important concerns of the older traditions seem to be slipping out of view. The attitudes of early cultural theorists towards class were sometimes value-laden and oppressive, but they did acknowledge the importance of class in people's lives. Second wave feminists sometimes unreflexively censured the habits and beliefs of women who were not like them, but they also demonstrated that women's capacity for meaningful action in the world cannot be separated from how they live out femininity on a day-to-day basis. Today, the concept of class has lost its position as the dominant category of analysis in historical scholarship and it is sometimes claimed that we are all classless now; women's studies departments have closed, gender history has superseded women's history and many women argue that feminism is no longer necessary.[34] These are important losses.

CONCLUSION: IMAGINING NEW HISTORIES OF WOMEN'S MAGAZINES

It is essential that we recognise that women do make choices, even if we do not agree with those choices, and that we realise that imagination and dreams are also the stuff of history. But the danger of history which emphasises agency and self-fashioning is that we lose sight of the structural determinants which shape and limit the capacity for agency and set boundaries on the kinds of selves we can imagine. Jill Julius Matthews argues that women's history 'can be asked to speak in two directions': 'outwards, to the malestream [sic] of traditional history', or 'inwards, to the creation of a new feminine subjectivity'. In the first approach, we lose sense of women's agency and individuality, and in the second, it is easy to reduce history to 'a timeless saga of individual consciousness'. What is needed is an integration of the two directions, 'a balancing of the social and the personal, of politics and pleasure, of structure and subjectivity'.[35] How can we achieve this kind of history for women's magazines, a form of female mass culture which has refused the dominant interpretative strategies of historical and cultural scholarship?

The placing of women's magazines in *Landscape for a Good Woman* suggests one possible answer to this question. Steedman treats women's magazines as both representations of the consumer society from which women like her mother are excluded and as agents which help these women to understand the possible modes of access to that world. She portrays magazines as products which seem to understand the terms of working-class women's exclusion from the material world and which offer guidance on gaining admittance to it. They are aspirational *and* practical, and not to be condemned. From her mother's magazines, the young Carolyn learns 'how the goods of that world of privilege might be appropriated, with the cut and fall of a skirt, a good winter coat, with leather shoes, a certain voice; but above all with clothes, the best boundary between you and a cold world'.[36] Steedman reflects that women's magazines also helped her mother to act in defiance of the world around her. She encouraged her daughters to 'walk round to the post-box with our dressing gowns on and our hair in rollers' partly because 'the women's magazines told her that a certain physical licence, a defiance of the narrow conventions, was the provenance of people like Mrs Simpson, and the women whose nails she later manicured'.[37]

It is even arguable that the new consumer journalism played a part in leading Carolyn herself to a different type of life. She passed the eleven-plus exam to gain a place at a grammar school and her mother saw this cleverness as evidence that the girl would get on and marry well. But it is partly because 'the Sunday colour supplements were full of pictures of student life' that Carolyn's mother 'came to see a university as offering the same arena of advantage as the good job had earlier done'.[38] Steedman insists that her identity is a product of a lucky accident, her birth in the historical moment of the formation of the welfare state. The 1944 Education Act determines her future in many ways: the eleven-plus, her entry to grammar school and then to Sussex University. However, the state can only provide opportunities. It requires family and cultural influence for individuals to take advantage of them. For working-class children, going to university often depends on parental acceptance of this as a legitimate goal. What if we take an intuitive leap and bring the role of magazines in Steedman's life into sharper focus than in *Landscape for a Good Woman*? What if it was the convergence of her mother's desire for material things, supported within the pages of women's magazines, with the cultural and intellectual aspirations pushed by the Sunday supplements, which helped to create and to legitimise in Steedman and her mother the desire for a university education? If so, magazines provided a form of aspiration which helped to create the conditions under which Steedman could eventually write and publish *Landscape for a Good Woman*.

This is a potential history of women's magazines which has not been told, for which there has been no space in British history and culture. The landscape for a woman's weekly which I have started to explore here suggests that in the post-war period, women's magazines were associated with marginality, superficiality and class difference. In fiction and film, magazines were throwaway symbols of aspirant femininity. This aspiration was perceived as purely material and therefore shallow: comfort and luxury coded by the home-owning classes as soft and feminine. Elsewhere, magazines symbolised the lower class and educational status of their female readers. The persistent use of women's magazines in this way is of a piece with their symbolic status in influential traditions of scholarship. The women's magazine is marginalised and denigrated because it is associated with the kind of femininity which working-class autodidacts and middle-class feminists alike have sought to escape.

It is perhaps because of this denigration that although we have many other histories of women's magazines, we do not yet have a history of their place in culture. But one of the most consistent lessons of the past half-century of historical writing is that the most productive histories are often written from the margins. Finding women's magazines in British history and culture may enable us to find a new place for these magazines in our mental landscapes, one which, with Steedman, does not ignore or trivialise women's desires but understands this trivialisation as itself a form of ignorance about the realities of class and gender. In turn, this may help us to create new histories of femininity, desire and class which do not apologise for women's mass culture. The 'real' history is not elsewhere.

NOTES

1 Carolyn Steedman, *Landscape for a Good Woman* (London: Virago, 1986), 128.
2 Steedman, *Landscape for a Good Woman*, 109.
3 Steedman, *Landscape for a Good Woman*, 15, 89.
4 Cynthia White, *Women's Magazines 1693–1968* (London: Michael Joseph, 1970), 216.
5 Ros Ballaster et al., *Women's Worlds: Ideology, Femininity and the Woman's Magazine* (Houndmills: Macmillan, 1991), 109.
6 I use 'I' throughout this chapter, as one of the arguments I later develop rests on the view that authors are present in their texts, and that assuming a position of scholarly objectivity hides subject positions and creates 'blind spots' in the scholarship. I do not wish to hide my own subject position, especially as I move into speculative and exploratory territory towards the end of the chapter.
7 Anthony Burgess, *Inside Mr Enderby* (Harmondsworth: Penguin, 1966), 87.
8 Graham Dawson, *Soldier Heroes: British Adventure, Empire and the Imagining of Masculinities* (Routledge: London and New York, 1994), 22.

9. Elizabeth Taylor, *Mrs Palfrey at the Claremont* (London: Virago, 1982), 109.
10. Taylor, *Mrs Palfrey at the Claremont*, 169.
11. Stan Barstow, *A Kind of Loving* (Cardigan: Parthian, 2010), 12.
12. Barstow, *A Kind of Loving*, 181.
13. Barstow, *A Kind of Loving*, 128.
14. Burgess, *Inside Mr Enderby*, 56, 70.
15. Burgess, *Inside Mr Enderby*, 61, 63.
16. Doris Lessing, *The Golden Notebook* (London: Harper Perennial, 2007), 165.
17. Lessing, *Golden Notebook*, 171.
18. Lessing, *Golden Notebook*, 204.
19. Lessing, *Golden Notebook*, 170.
20. Richard Hoggart, *The Uses of Literacy* (Harmondsworth: Pelican, 1958), 96–102.
21. Hoggart, *Uses of Literacy*, 103.
22. Hoggart, *Uses of Literacy*, 164–5.
23. Hoggart, *Uses of Literacy*, 195–201.
24. Carolyn Faulder, 'Women's magazines,' in *Is This Your Life? Images of Women in the Media*, ed. Josephine King and Mary Stott (London: Virago, 1977), 173.
25. Ballaster et al., *Women's Worlds*, 176.
26. Janice Winship, *Inside Women's Magazines* (London: Pandora, 1987), 7.
27. Naomi Wolf, *The Beauty Myth: How Images of Beauty are Used Against Women* (London: Vintage, 1991), 77.
28. Angela Carter, *The Magic Toyshop* (London: Virago, 1981), 78.
29. Hoggart, *Uses of Literacy*, 175.
30. Elizabeth Wilson, *Mirror Writing: An Autobiography* (London: Virago, 1982), 18.
31. Germaine Greer, *The Female Eunuch* (London: Flamingo, 2003), 176–7.
32. Margaret Drabble, *The Pattern in the Carpet: A Personal History With Jigsaws* (London: Atlantic Books, 2010), 191.
33. Penny Tinkler, *Constructing Girlhood: Popular Magazines for Girls Growing Up in England, 1920–1950* (London: Taylor and Francis, 1995a), 6–7.
34. For reflections on the fading of 'class' within historical scholarship, see Selina Todd, 'History from below: Modern British scholarship,' *The Many-Headed Monster*, accessed 3 October 2014, http://manyheadedmonster.wordpress.com/2013/08/23/selina-todd-history-from-below-modern-british-scholarship/. For debates on the comparative value of women's versus gender history, see *Gender and History* 1 (1989). Although this discussion is more than twenty years old, the same issues are still at stake.
35. Jill Julius Matthews, 'They had such a lot of fun: The Women's League of Health and Beauty between the wars,' *History Workshop Journal* 30 (1990): 37.
36. Steedman, *Landscape for a Good Woman*, 38.
37. Steedman, *Landscape for a Good Woman*, 92–3.
38. Steedman, *Landscape for a Good Woman*, 43.

Part II
Ideals of Femininity and Negotiating Gender Norms

3 Gender, Reproduction and the Fight for Free Love in the Late Nineteenth-Century Periodical Press

Sarah Jones

In the late 1890s in the UK, within the context of an astounding increase in the publication of periodicals, newspapers and reviews, the Legitimation League began to publish their journal, *The Adult*.[1] The London-based journal, published monthly between 1897 and 1899, was dedicated to debating the question of freedom in relationships between men and women, and was almost unique in Britain at this time in its focus on 'free love'. Some of the key problems facing those debating what a meaningful free love relationship might look like were questions of reproduction. For some, the assumptions that women would take prime responsibility for the care of a child and the belief that a woman's physical and emotional constitution meant that her very 'essence was reproductive' were inherently problematic, since they rendered complete sexual equality and freedom difficult.[2] While men, it was assumed, could continue their free love lives unburdened by parenthood, women had to find a way to balance sexual freedom with both reproduction and their subsequent 'natural responsibility' for their children. In this view, female free lovers were declared inferior to their male counterparts, restricted by their physical and mental capacity for motherhood. Some feminist free lovers countered this argument with a eugenic view that emphasised the importance of female sexual choice and positive pre-natal influence, placing reproductive free love advocating women at the heart of their campaigns for reform. This chapter will explore the debates around the problem posed by reproduction to the politics of free love as represented in the pages of the League's magazine.

Between the end of 1897 and the summer of 1898, an array of authors in *The Adult* participated in the discussion of reproduction and its relationship to free love. Within the context of the vibrant and vigorous nineteenth-century periodical press, which Angelique Richardson has argued 'had achieved a place of unprecedented importance in national social, political, and intellectual debate' by the *fin de siècle*, *The Adult* provided a rhetorical space in which to debate the issue of reproduction as part of deliberations of radical sexual reform.[3] Although the journal's title and its provocative subtitles, such as 'A crusade against sex-enslavement', appeared to present a cohesive set of concerns, encounters between authors highlight a diversity of views. Despite the fact that we know little about readership and circulation, a study of this type of publication is informative as it reveals the gendered fault lines, key concerns, areas of disagreement and development of thought that characterised debates about free love.[4] Supporting the assertion of literary scholars Laurel Brake and Julie F. Codell that 'nineteenth-century periodicals were not normally univocal' and claims by historians of the late nineteenth century that the periodical press 'was a critical cultural site for the representation of competing gender ideologies', this study of *The Adult* recognises the diverse and often contradictory voices that used the journal as a space in which to negotiate disparate views on provocative issues like gender, race and sexual freedom under the banner of free love.[5] Research to date has tended, like the contemporary mainstream press, to use the term 'free love' loosely to discuss a broad range of what were considered to be unorthodox or transgressive sexual and marital behaviours. Exploring free love through this unique magazine, characterised by heterogeneous and often conflicting views, thus offers a new insight into the complexity and sophistication of a concept often taken for granted or ignored in the existing scholarship on *fin de siècle* sex radicalism.

The journal, due to its particular form, introduces multiple voices that indicate the wide-ranging and conflicting perspectives on the issues about gender and reproduction that lay at the heart of free love discussion. This chapter focuses on the interventions of League president Lillian Harman and British editor Henry Seymour. Harman was an American anarchist and free love advocate who had been imprisoned at sixteen for participating in an unsanctioned marriage. Seymour was an important individualist, an anarchist who had established the first English-language anarchist periodical in Britain in 1885. They were two of the most dominant and outspoken authors on opposing sides of the debate.[6] An exploration of the contributions of these particular authors shows the key issues at stake in free love discussions. It draws together contemporary fears about human degeneration, the rights and roles of women in society and the desire to radically overhaul contemporary attitudes towards sex. The sophisticated dialogue occurring around reproduction here demonstrates in microcosm the instability of ideas about gender that were positioned at the heart of free love debate. As the analysis of the League's magazine in this chapter will show, authors with opposing viewpoints on 'The Woman Question' manipulated or reinterpreted gendered ideas about the female body and its reproductive function to support their different aims.

HENRY SEYMOUR, SEXUAL INEQUALITY AND THE REPRODUCTIVE DOUBLE STANDARD

Assumptions about the centrality of women's reproductive role and the belief in fixed biological sex difference structured the free love politics of individual writers. Some authors in *The Adult* had grave concerns about the ability of women to achieve a level of sexual freedom equal to that of men, as women were seen as unable to continue living a free love 'lifestyle' after the birth of a child. Unlike men, who it was assumed bore little responsibility for their offspring, the free loving mother would be burdened by her 'natural' responsibility towards her children. These ideas were based on a set of assumptions about the biology and psychology of the reproductive woman and the negative impact of child-bearing on women's physical and mental abilities.[7] Reflecting on a 'reproductive double standard' present in the late nineteenth century that viewed the male reproductive apparatus as a source of power but the female equivalent as a physical handicap convinced some authors that sexual inequality—even in a free love system—was biologically fixed and thus fundamentally natural.[8]

This viewpoint allowed writers to maintain a set of free love beliefs that challenged monogamous sexual customs while upholding a gender status quo that sustained the social and sexual subordination of women and privileged male sexual expression. Such a perspective shows how radicals struggled to reconcile their ideas about maternity, children and the position and role of women in society alongside their radical sexual views. An analysis of the contributions of the journal's second editor, Henry Seymour, provides an insight into the way that concerns about women and their reproductive function were used as a key point around which to negotiate different free love political beliefs.

Henry Seymour linked the fact that women, and not men, bore children to his conviction that women were the physically and mentally inferior sex and thus naturally subject to male authority. For Seymour the idea that 'woman [was] naturally inferior, in her locomotive and mental systems, to man' explained her 'natural subjectivity', and he argued that 'no social rectification of the natural inequality can ever make possible an equality of the sexes unless by some revolutionary process of sexual inversion men take to bearing half the babies'.[9] While Seymour did not provide particular scientific rationale for his deductions, he clearly linked woman's perceived inferior position to her physical reproductive role. He questioned the very possibility of sexual emancipation of women in these terms: 'Is she really physically constructed so as to enjoy an equality of liberty with man? Does not the maternal function at once condemn her to an inferior plane of freedom?'[10] As Cynthia Eagle Russet has shown, there was a double standard surrounding reproduction present in the late nineteenth century that viewed the female reproductive system as a source of physical deficiency.[11] This was linked to evolutionary ideas surrounding sexual selection by contemporary writers, such as Patrick Geddes and J. Arthur Thompson, that argued that women and men evolved differently, as women needing to preserve energy for reproduction became 'fragilely attractive', while men, unburdened, grew to be 'muscular and courageous.'[12] 'Nature', Russet states, 'had decreed a secondary role for women.'[13] Broadly reflecting this view, Seymour viewed women as inherently and ineradicably different and inferior to men due to her physical role in the human reproductive cycle. This was a sentiment echoed by a number of writers in the journal, including Herbert Edwards, who claimed that 'man has a physiological advantage, which must for ever place him in a position of greater sexual freedom than the woman' due to the fact he was not called upon to bear children.[14]

Like widespread scientific texts of the nineteenth century that emphasised the mental and physical inferiority of women, many male writers in *The Adult* stressed women's apparent intellectual mediocrity, her social and financial vulnerability and her utter dependence on men.[15] This rhetorical tactic provided them with an apparently solid, biological standpoint that legitimated their reservations about the implementation of increased sexual freedom for women. In this instance, by establishing female mental and physical inferiority as a biological 'fact', Seymour was able to argue for a new moral and ethical code that considered sexual freedom for men but continued to subordinate women in social and sexual terms. While Seymour acknowledged the mistreatment of women in contemporary marriage and challenged traditional monogamous customs that he argued fell 'so very short of the ideal', he did not advocate a system of total sexual equality due to his concerns that under freedom woman would 'be doomed [. . .] to go to the dogs'.[16] As historian Joanne Passet has noted, writers like Seymour had 'a vision of a new world order in which patriarchy remained intact'.[17] While he sought to change the way that people thought about sex and marriage, his reforms did not advocate change to an extent that would allow women any increased sexual freedom. For Seymour, the reproductive function of women was too dangerous, and indeed too debilitating, to allow women to experience the same sexual freedom as men in a free love system.

LILLIAN HARMAN, FREE-LOVE FEMINISM AND ANARCHIST EUGENICS

The journal, however, was characterised by diverse voices and offered writers with opposing views a rhetorical space in which to challenge these ideas. Free love feminists countered assertions of female physical inferiority with their own particular eugenic narrative that glorified women's reproductive power. In this view, allowing women free sexual choice, regardless of marital status and based solely on individual desire, ensured they would produce strong, healthy, free children. Far from representing an obstacle, to these women reproduction signified the potential power of women to become harbingers of sexual equality and racial improvement in a free love system. Writers such as Lillian Harman and Dora Kerr used the idea that free women would produce stronger, healthier children than women held within the confines of monogamous marriage to heavily criticise contemporary marriage customs from a racial vantage point. This allowed them to emphasise the importance of free female sexual choice.[18]

Although scholars have discussed the ways in which Darwinian evolutionary theory was used to reinforce traditional gender roles, in the case of the free love feminists in *The Adult,* emerging ideas about the importance of female sexual choice meant these writers were able to position women, and not men, at the heart of their free love political beliefs.[19] Contributing to a journal, a form of publication recognised in research to date as distinctively characterised by heterogeneous voices, offered these writers an opportunity to argue that racial progress could be ensured not by controlling individual female sexuality, but by letting women be free to choose their sexual partners and to change them at will.[20] As historian Lucy Bland has noted, many feminists of the period exploited the idea of 'woman as mother' to empower women and to advocate increased female sexual choice from a vantage point of scientific, racialised superiority.[21] Although advocating a radical sexual view, free love feminists employed the same rhetorical tactic to challenge a notion of free love that left patriarchy intact. An examination of the writings of Legitimation League president Lillian Harman shows how these writers countered the views of authors like Henry Seymour to place female sexual freedom and the power of motherhood at the heart of campaigns for sexual reform.

Contributors like Lillian Harman allied with the North American free love movement and *The Adult's* radical American 'sister' paper, *Lucifer, the Light-Bearer,* which forcefully employed a eugenic discourse to defend a woman's right to control and dictate maternity in a free love system.[22] Harman was a proponent of a system (as Hal Sears has termed it) of 'anarchist free love eugenics'.[23] This system of beliefs attacked monogamous customs, rejected the necessity of state or church sanction of unions and emphasised the right of the individual to free choice. It was favoured by many of the most prominent names in American free love politics, including Angela and Ezra Heywood, and Harman's father, Moses.[24] Moses Harman had argued in editorials, for example, that monogamous marriage customs had 'filled the prisons and asylums and so-called civilised lands with the degenerate products [. . .] of ignorant, haphazard, reckless generation'.[25] That the American free love traditions of which the Heywoods and the Harmans were a part were heavily linked to eugenic thought is clear. Indeed it was prominent free lover (and *Adult* contributor) Moses Harman who published the first periodical dedicated to eugenics in the United States—the *American Journal of Eugenics,* which ran from 1907 until 1910—as the direct successor to *Lucifer, the Light-Bearer.*[26]

Lillian Harman believed that racial decline had been caused by reproduction that was the product of the 'inharmony, degradation and cruelty' of monogamous relationships.[27] Children born out of such miserable unions, the 'offspring of the "submitting" slave mother', were inevitably seen to be detrimental to racial advancement.[28] She based her eugenic theories on a stark and unforgiving portrayal of contemporary marriage in which insatiable men and passive, sexually apathetic women were forced, via the confines of monogamy, to continue one-sided and coercive sexual relationships.[29] The enslaved woman in this arrangement, compelled into motherhood, thus perpetuated the mode of her enslavement by continuing to produce slavish children. An editorial in *Lucifer, the Light-Bearer*, for instance, stated, 'the enslavement of woman in these relations reacts upon the race as a whole—thereby incarnating and perpetuating slavery for *all*, except the prenatally and postnatally favoured few'.[30]

Rather than the traditional morality of the monogamous home keeping degeneration at bay, this narrative described the impact of the characteristically subordinate mother and unrelenting father on their children in harsh terms: 'The unwelcome, deserted children, which in themselves are a terrible indictment of present society are the fruit of the ignorance and weakness of their mothers, of the criminal carelessness and conscienceless insistence of their fathers.'[31] To counter this retrogression, Harman argued for a more dynamic system of relationships based on free individual choice. Rather than being tied to one partner for life as in monogamous marriage, Harman called for 'freedom to learn what is best for us [. . .] freedom to profit by our failures, as well as by our successes'.[32] Although she did not rule out monogamy or any other kind of relationship, she emphasised the necessity of less rigid and less permanent relationship structures. Giving the individual freedom to choose and change a partner at will, she believed, would stop the degradation caused by the 'disgust, aversion, [and] rape' of monogamy and benefit from the 'harmony of feeling, and unison of desire' seen to characterise free love relations.[33]

Her criticism of enforced lifelong monogamy and her advocacy of individual freedom of choice allowed Harman to draw from a dynamic interpretation of mate selection theories to support her free love beliefs. Influenced by popular evolutionary ideas that permeated the public sphere, Harman argued that allowing a woman to be free to choose her reproductive partner, regardless of her marital status, would ensure that she picked the most suitable genetic mate.[34] For Harman, monogamous marriage represented the perversion of nature, as it placed unnatural restrictions on women's sexuality. She presented legal marriage as being a bar to human evolution and free love as the most progressive sexual option. She argued in her presidential address to the Legitimation League in 1898, later published in *The Adult*, 'Marriage is a woman's worst enemy, and is therefore the enemy of the race.'[35] Reasoning that 'so long as we have legally enforced prostitution and rape [. . .] as now, there can be little progress', Harman sought to undermine conventional sanctioned marriage by showing it to be retrogressive and racially damaging.[36]

Demonstrating also her belief in ideas about positive prenatal influence, which stressed that the emotional state of the parent influenced the condition of the children produced, she asserted that the adoption of anarchist free love eugenic beliefs would put an end to the production of the weak, unhappy children of 'enforced' and unhappy monogamous unions.[37] By rejecting the perceived hypocrisy of contemporary monogamous marriage and turning to a system of free love that emphasised the importance of individual free female sexual choice, Harman believed that important racial improvements could be made. Employing these anarchistic eugenic views she stated her belief, for example, that 'Only from free, self-respecting mothers can the highest type of children be born.'[38] By rejecting orthodox marriage and the lack of female sexual control this implied, she sought to improve racial health and allow children to be well born through a system of free sexual selection and positive prenatal influence. Thus in this American free love view, brought to Britain by radical writers like Harman in *The Adult*, the dynamics of private life, particularly in the realm of female sexuality and motherhood, had the potential to address pressing public problems by combatting degeneration and racial decline.

Drawing from popular evolutionary theories, such as Darwin's theory of sexual selection, which stressed the importance of female sexual choice, Harman advocated free love from an evolutionary and eugenic vantage point. Her free love politics promised to improve the race by producing healthier and happier children outside of the artificial and unethical confines of enforced, limiting monogamy and the conventional nuclear family.[39] Harman relied less on particular scientific theory and more generally on persuasive evolutionary rhetoric to make her case for the eugenic power of free love.[40] She asserted that 'happily for the higher development of the race', the children of free love advocate women would 'imbibe the spirit of their free mother, and will be happy, healthy, and independent—in marked contrast to the offspring of the "submitting" slave mother'.[41]

Echoing the use of Darwinian evolutionary ideas by free love feminists such as Victoria Woodhull and Lois Waisbrooker in the United States, feminist writers like Harman sought to use the malleable and gendered nature of evolutionary theories and the open platform of the periodical press to advocate her particular free love ideas.[42] Whereas monogamy relied on 'the insistence of men and the submission of women', for example, a free love feminist would 'sustain only the relations which she herself desires, will be happy in the love of her lover, and tenacious of her own self-respect'.[43] By asserting that her free love system heralded a move towards racial progress as it allowed women to exercise free sexual choice, Harman posited the reproductive free love advocate woman as a key player in keeping racial decay at bay. In post-Darwinian Britain, which George Robb has argued was characterised by fears of racial degeneration and social decline, this would have been a powerful rhetorical and ideological tool.[44]

Demonstrating the disparity of ideas about female sexuality and gender at the heart of free love debates in *fin de siècle* Britain, this viewpoint put Harman's free love beliefs in direct opposition to writers like Seymour in her own intellectual circles who saw the maternal function as limiting for women. Far from rendering women dependent and vulnerable, Harman's eugenic narrative, which drew from ideas about the nature of evolution, the potential power of the maternal female body and anxieties about racial degeneration, countered Seymour's assertion of female inferiority and placed the powerful reproductive woman at the forefront of campaigns for the advancement of the race and as the driving force behind her free love politics.[45] Employing the influential rhetoric of progress versus decline, which would have been a powerful tactic in the context of a racially anxious metropole, Harman both confronted the perceived injustices experienced by women in monogamous marriage and battled against writers within her own free love circles who attempted to use biological narratives to prioritise male sexual freedom and advocate the continued subordination of women.[46]

CONCLUSION

The complexity and disparity of the discussion of reproduction in *The Adult* has significant implications for the way that we understand free love in Britain at the end of the nineteenth century. By examining free love through journals, characterised by diverse and often contradictory voices, we are able to see the complexity and sophistication of a concept often misunderstood, misrepresented or ignored in accounts of the period. The investigation of the disputes surrounding reproduction and female sexuality presented here also highlights the tension surrounding gender that lay at the heart of debates about free love occurring in Britain. While male free love advocates emphasised female inferiority and vulnerability and debated their free love politics around maintaining male domination, radical women used their female reproductive capacities to present themselves as champions of progressive social and racial change.

A consideration of the implicit gender questions in deliberations over reproduction in the journal shifts the portrayal of free love from an indistinct set of radical sexual behaviours and beliefs to a more sophisticated negotiation of some of the most vibrant and topical debates of the time, engaging with questions about gender, sexuality and the rights and roles of women in late nineteenth-century society. These negotiations drew from important contemporary issues about race, science and evolution which demonstrate that sex radicals appropriated and manipulated powerful contemporary concerns in different ways to posit their own often conflicting beliefs as logical, moral and progressive. *The Adult* played a crucial role in these debates, as its form offered writers a unique space in which to discuss their different and often contradictory views on sex, gender and motherhood. The structure of the journal thus offers us a unique and important opportunity to examine the heterogeneous voices and gendered debate at the heart of free love campaigns in late nineteenth-century Britain.

NOTES

1. *The Adult* was first published in June 1897 by the London-based University of Watford Press and ceased publication in March 1899. For a brief overview of the rise and fall of the journal, see Anne Humpherys, 'The Journal that did: Form and content in *The Adult* (1897–1899),' *Media History* 9 (2003): 63–78; Patricia Anderson, 'Free love and free thought: *The Adult* 1897–1899,' *Media History* 1 (1993): 179–81; Edward Royle, *Radicals, Secularists and Republicans: Popular Freethought in Britain, 1866–1915* (Manchester: Manchester University Press, 1980). *The Adult* is discussed in the context of an explosion of periodical publishing in Anne Humpherys, 'The journals that did: Writing about sex in the late 1890s,' *Interdisciplinary Studies in the Long Nineteenth Century* 3 (2006): 1–19.
2. Discussion of the idea that women's essence was reproductive as found in scientific texts can be found in Cynthia Eagle Russet, *Sexual Science: The Victorian Construction of Motherhood* (Cambridge, MA: Harvard University Press, 1989), 43.
3. Angelique Richardson, 'Eugenics and freedom at the *fin de siècle*,' in *Culture and Science in the Nineteenth-Century Media*, ed. Louise Henson et al. (Aldershot: Ashgate, 2004), 275.
4. *The Adult* had a number of different subtitles during its run, including 'The journal of sex' (November/December 1897) and 'A journal for the free discussion of tabooed topics' (October 1897).
5. Laurel Brake and Julie F. Codell, eds., *Encounters in the Victorian Press: Editors, Authors, Readers* (Basingstoke: Palgrave MacMillan, 2005), 5; Hilary Fraser, Stephanie Green and Judith Johnson, *Gender and the Victorian Periodical* (Cambridge: Cambridge University Press, 2008), i.
6. Henry Seymour became the second editor of *The Adult* in 1898 following founding editor George Bedborough's arrest on obscenity charges. For information on Seymour, see Hermia Oliver, *The International Anarchist Movement in Late Victorian London* (London: Croom Helm, 1983). Lillian Harman was an American anarchist and journal editor, and became president of the Legitimation League in 1897. See Joanne Passet, *Sex Radicals and the Quest for Women's Equality* (Urbana: University of Illinois Press, 2003).
7. On the way science was used to legitimate ideas about sexual difference, see Ornella Moscucci, *The Science of Woman: Gynaecology and Gender in England, 1800–1929* (Cambridge: Cambridge University Press, 1993).
8. Russet, *Sexual Science*, 30–1.
9. Henry Seymour, 'The question of children: A symposium,' *The Adult* 2 (1898): 166.
10. Seymour, 'The question of children,' 166.
11. Russet, *Sexual Science,* 30–1.
12. Russet, *Sexual Science*, 12.
13. Russet, *Sexual Science*, 12.
14. Herbert Edwards, 'The question of children,' *The Adult* 2 (1898): 67.
15. Lucy Bland, *Banishing the Beast: Feminism, Sex and Morality* (London: Tauris Parke, 2002), 73–4. Bland discusses the construction of the idea of mentally and physically inferior women in popular nineteenth-century scientific texts, including the commonplace comparison of women and the 'lower races'.
16. Henry Seymour, 'The poetry of the passions,' *The Adult* 1 (1897): 90.
17. Passet, *Sex Radicals*, 4.

18 Canadian sex radical Dora Kerr also wrote under the name Dora Forster. Forster's involvement in sex radical circles on both sides of the Atlantic is discussed in Angus McLaren, 'Sex radicalism in the Canadian Pacific Northwest, 1890–1920,' *Journal of the History of Sexuality* 2 (1992): 527–46.
19 For anti-feminist interpretations of Darwin, see Wendy Hayden, *Evolutionary Rhetoric: Sex, Science, and Free Love in Nineteenth-Century Feminism* (Carbondale: Southern Illinois University Press, 2013), 59–61; Richardson, *Love and Eugenics*, 78. Richardson argues that while Darwin's *Origin of Species* questioned traditional values and attitudes towards women, his *Descent of Man* endorsed many. The appropriation of Darwinian evolutionary theories in American free love rhetoric is detailed in Jesse Battan, ' "Sexual selection" and the social revolution: Anarchist eugenics and radical Darwinism in the United States, 1850–1910' in *Darwin in Atlantic Cultures: Evolutionary Visions of Race, Gender and Sexuality*, ed. Jeannette Eileen Jones and Patrick B. Sharp (New York: Routledge, 2010), 33–52.
20 On the heterogeneity of periodicals, see Margaret Beetham and Kay Boardman, eds., *Victorian Women's Magazines: An Anthology* (Manchester: Manchester University Press, 2001), 4; Barbara Green, 'The feminist periodical press: Women, periodical studies and modernity,' *Literature Compass* 6 (2009): 191–205.
21 Bland, *Banishing the Beast*, 70.
22 The relationship between *The Adult* and *Lucifer* is a rich and interesting one that has not been examined in depth by historians. They shared authors, advertised each other's work and acted as international distributors for each other. Hal Sears, in the index to his seminal work on the American free love movement *The Sex Radicals: Free Love in High Victorian America* (Lawrence, KS: Regents Press, 1977), lists *The Adult* as 'The English equivalent of *Lucifer*'. The dialogue between free love movements in America and Britain has not been explored in existing scholarship, but will be discussed in my forthcoming PhD thesis.
23 For a discussion of the formation and application of free love eugenic ideas in American free love movements, see Sears, *Sex Radicals*, 121.
24 Sears, *Sex Radicals*, 11.
25 Moses Harman, 'Yesterday, tomorrow, today,' *The American Journal of Eugenics* 1 (1907): 29.
26 Moses Harman's subtle shift from simple advocacy of women's sexual emancipation towards a more eugenic understanding of free love is discussed in Passet, *Sex Radicals*.
27 Lillian Harman, 'Some problems of social freedom,' *The Adult Extra* 2 (1898): 11.
28 Lillian Harman, 'Pen points,' *The Adult* 2 (1898): 96.
29 Harman, 'Pen points,' 96.
30 'The university magazine on the American movement,' *Lucifer, the Light-Bearer* 1 (1897): 188–9.
31 Lillian Harman, 'Eve and her Eden,' *The Adult* 2 (1898): 32.
32 Harman, 'Problems of social freedom,' 9.
33 Harman, 'Eve and her Eden,' 34.
34 Wendy Hayden, '(R)Evolutionary rhetoric: Science and sexuality in nineteenth-century free love discourse,' *Rhetoric Review* 29 (2010): 119–20.
35 Harman, 'Some problems of social freedom,' 11.
36 Harman, 'Some problems of social freedom,' 11.
37 Jesse Battan has examined ideas about prenatal influence and the impact of Lamarckian thought on Free Love politics in ' "Socialism will cure all but an

unhappy marriage": Free love and the American left, 1850–1910,' in *Meetings and Alcôves: The Left and Sexuality in Europe and the United States since 1850*, ed. Jesse Battan, Thomas Bouchet and Tania Régin (Dijon: Editions Universitaires de Dijon, 2004), 29–46.
38 Harman, 'Pen points,' 96.
39 George Robb has discussed the eugenic ideas of sex radicals and has highlighted their belief in the importance of mutual sexual pleasure in 'Race motherhood: moral eugenics vs. progressive eugenics, 1880–1920,' in *Maternal Instincts: Visions of Motherhood and Sexuality in Britain, 1875–1925*, ed. Claudia Nelson and Ann Sumner Holmes (Basingstoke: Macmillan, 1997), 58–75.
40 This was a tactic employed by many American free lovers. See Hayden, '(R)Evolutionary rhetoric,' 116.
41 Harman, 'Pen points,' 96.
42 Hayden, '(R)Evolutionary rhetoric,' 116.
43 Harman, 'Pen points,' 96.
44 George Robb, 'The way of all flesh,' *Journal of the History of Sexuality* 6 (1996): 602.
45 For links between ideas about maternal power and free love, see Passet, *Sex Radicals*, 153. Passet argues that, despite advocating freer sexual relationships, most free lovers did not question prevailing domestic systems and saw maternity as the inevitable outcome of female sexuality. George Robb makes a similar point, and states that for free lovers, 'Freedom from babies was unthinkable.' Robb, 'The way of all flesh,' 602.
46 For a discussion of the powerful influence of ideas surrounding degeneration, evolution and the concept of progress, see Peter Bowler, *The Invention of Progress: The Victorians and the Past* (Oxford: Basil Blackwell, 1989).

4 Inter-war Czech Women's Magazines
Constructing Gender, Consumer Culture and Identity in Central Europe

Karla Huebner

English-language scholarship on women's magazines focuses predominantly, and unsurprisingly, on English-language magazines. Significant attention has also been paid to Weimar-era German women's magazines.[1] Much of the existing scholarship, however, has involved sifting magazines for data rather than examining individual publications or groups of publications to gain an accurate picture of their purposes, roles and histories. Such data extraction is perhaps most characteristic of sociological approaches, although it also has its uses in broader historical and visual culture studies.[2] Readers of such studies need, however, to have a clear sense of the nature of the periodicals used, and this is especially important when the periodicals originate in less familiar historical periods or geographic regions. This chapter introduces just such a set of magazines: those produced in Bohemia during the inter-war Czechoslovak First Republic.

Czechoslovakia, founded in 1918 as part of the dismantling of Austria-Hungary, was a site of considerable optimism during the 1920s, particularly in regard to democracy and women's rights. Widespread acceptance of female higher education and political equality in the Czech (though to a lesser extent the Slovak) lands suggests that neither older feminists nor 1920s-style 'New Women' provoked the serious anxiety in their compatriots so often found in France and Germany, where such women were often seen as a threat to masculinity and the nation. Scholars agree that resistance to nineteenth-century Czech feminism was weak, perhaps because Czech feminists linked their cause to Czech nationalism. Feminism was less developed in nineteenth-century Slovakia, but there, too, emphasis was placed on women's role as nurturers of nationhood.[3] The highly literate and industrialised regions of Bohemia and Moravia produced numerous periodicals for women, from the explicitly feminist and political to the purely fashion-oriented, while in Slovakia, the history of women's magazines began with Terézia Medvecká Vansová's *Dennica* (*The Diary*, 1898–1914), which was founded to encourage education and Slovak nationalism among women.[4] As yet, little scholarship has been published in any language on Czechoslovakia's women's magazines. For example, a recent book surveying twentieth-century Czech media simply notes that an increased emphasis on women's magazines reflected the strengthening of women's role in society.⁵ However, women's newspapers and magazines provide intriguing insights not only into local concerns relating to politics, pleasure and identity but also provide a useful comparative to similar magazines produced during the same period in the UK, the US and Germany. Thus, this chapter considers both what women's magazines were like in inter-war Czechoslovakia and some of the ways that Czech and Czechoslovak women were imagined and pictured in periodicals designed for their own consumption. It analyses these images of women as symbolic of a modernity that was intended to be simultaneously international and Czechoslovak.

THE CZECHOSLOVAK CONTEXT

Czechoslovakia in the 1920s was an energetic new state formed from parts of the former Austria-Hungary; Bohemia, Moravia and Silesia had been ruled by Austria, while Slovakia and Sub-Carpathian Ruthenia had been part of Hungary. The First Republic, later idealised as a golden age, lasted from 1918 to 1938. It was a parliamentary democracy with strong political ties to France, the United Kingdom and the United States.⁶ Pre-independence Czech political parties had mostly endorsed women's suffrage. Particular support had come from philosopher and first president Tomáš Garrigue Masaryk, whose American wife Charlotte was an active feminist and whose surname, Garrigue, he had taken upon their marriage.⁷ At the country's founding, women achieved the vote and constitutional promises of legal equality. By 1929, *Revue Française de Prague*, published by the local Alliance Française, noted that some western feminists even considered Czechoslovakia a 'paradise of the modern woman'.⁸

Yet while the First Republic was a relatively successful democracy during its twenty-year existence, the Masaryk and Beneš governments never succeeded in creating the gender-equal state guaranteed in the constitution. Feminists and legal scholars strove to revise inherited and patriarchal Austrian and Hungarian legal codes relating to family law but could not come to a consensus. Indeed, while inter-war Czechs generally believed that women had a right to intellectual and political equality, women's rights in practice, as was the case elsewhere in Europe and the Americas, remained subordinate to the rights of family and nation and did not take precedence over essentialised concepts of womanhood. Legally, a woman was female first, a citizen second.⁹

During the First Republic, however, Czechs were only one ethnic group—albeit the dominant one—in a country that was also home to many Slovaks, Germans, Ruthenians (Rusyns) and members of other ethnicities. Literacy and educated women were far more typical of the industrialised Czech- and German-speaking western areas (Bohemia, Moravia, Silesia) than of Slovakia or Ruthenia. In 1918 these various ethnicities found themselves to be citizens of Czechoslovakia. However, ethnic or national identity remained important. The Czechs felt strongly that their culture had been subjugated by the Germans since the Battle of White Mountain in 1620, and this belief was a major reason for uniting Slovakia with the Czech lands in 1918. Germans had to be outnumbered by Slavs. The new regime tried to foster a new 'Czechoslovak' ideology in which Czechs and Slovaks constituted a single state-forming Czechoslovak nation. In reality, things were not that simple, as examination of Czech women's magazines will show.

Historically, women's magazines have been part of a woman-centered discourse with an important role in the construction and expression of gendered and class identity. Inter-war Czechoslovakia was no exception, and its periodicals also helped construct and express nationality and modernity. The periodicals focused on here were mainstream middle-class publications, although each occupied a specific social niche. Published in Czech, they were accessible to Slovaks and may have been intended to be more Czechoslovak than narrowly Czech, especially given that there seem to have been few specifically Slovak women's magazines. Germans and Ruthenians were unlikely to read these magazines, as German-speakers could read periodicals from Germany and Austria while remote and impoverished Ruthenia was only marginally literate.[10]

It was among the urban Czechs of Bohemia and Moravia, therefore, that the New Woman was most evident during the 1920s. Modern, urban Slovak women were fewer in number and less visible in the media. In fact, while some of the periodicals published in Czechoslovakia during the 1920s and early 1930s used many photographs of modern women, these pictures were often of foreign origin. Czech periodicals depicted their own New Women more often through drawings, sketches and cartoons than via photography, although photographs of prominent Czech and Slovak women show that their appearance was generally quite up-to-date, for example, short-haired and wearing skirts well above the ankle. Whether photographic or sketched, visual images were a potent means of imagining Czechoslovak women's liveliness, fashion-consciousness and physical fitness.[11] This was the case for general interest and men's magazines as well as those intended specifically for women, but was more true for Czech-language publications than Slovak-language ones because the latter showed less interest in imagery that was not ethnically specific.[12]

Prior to independence, feminism, fashion, religion and politics were major categories in Czech women's periodicals. Due to the strong nineteenth-century Czech feminist movement, various feminist magazines and newspapers existed at the beginning of the twentieth century, including *Ženské listy* (*Women's Pages*, 1873–1926), *Ženský obzor* (*Women's Horizon*, 1900–41), *Ženská revue* (*Women's Revue*, 1905–18) and several called *Vesna* (*Springtime*), which were mostly published by the feminist Vesna organisation. Early twentieth-century fashion periodicals included *Dámské modní listy* (*Ladies' Fashion Pages*, 1901–24) and *Dámský modní obzor* (*Ladies' Fashion Horizon*, 1911–13). The difference in phrasing here between feminism's '*ženy*' (women) and fashion's '*dámy*' (ladies) is comparable to English usage, in which 'women' are universal and inclusive, whereas 'ladies' are refined and (historically, at least) of high social status.

Also akin to British and North American practice, many religious periodicals were produced for women, such as the Catholic periodical *Ženský časopis Eva* (*Women's Magazine Eva*). Finally, the various political parties often published periodicals specifically for women, frequently in the form of newspapers rather than magazines. All of these categories remained significant during the inter-war period, but while religious and political women's periodicals continued relatively unchanged, feminist periodicals languished. Feminism in the First Republic, as elsewhere, stagnated partially due to its very successes; major goals like suffrage had been achieved and new goals were not yet fully formulated. Meanwhile, newer women's magazines aimed at a broad audience took the stage and to some extent replaced or developed from the dedicated fashion magazines. Around the same time, some of the older general interest magazines, such as the venerable *Světozor* (*World Horizon*, publication resumed 1904), grew less male-centered.

THREE CONSUMER MAGAZINES

This chapter will now focus on three mainstream consumer oriented women's publications, all founded in the 1920s, two of which continued through the 1930s and into the 1940s. They were chosen for their intended wide circulation, their related yet distinct target audiences and their availability at the National Library in Prague. Issues from the 1920s and early 1930s were examined cover to cover with the goal of assessing their overall character, including design choices, types of articles, visuals and advertising, and in order to relate them to other periodicals of their time.

The glossy black-and-white magazine *Moderní dívka* (*Modern Girl*, founded in October 1924) stressed fashion and preparing young women for love and marriage. It appears to have had a target audience in the fifteen to twenty-five age range, judging by its stress on young middle-class women's activities (dance, foreign language acquisition) and hopes of romance. Costing 3.50 Kč per issue or 40 Kč per year, its relatively static imagery centred on smartly dressed women. Its readers either were Czech or read Czech; however, in its second year its subtitle inclusively stressed that it was for Czecho*slovak* girls. *Moderní dívka* was laid out appealingly with graceful typography and generous but not excessive white space. It combined photography with elegantly drawn illustrations. Yet its visual style had more ties to the previous decade than to the cleaner, more Bauhaus-like, designs that would soon become typical of the most up-to-date Czech magazine layouts.

Moderní dívka was not a long-lived publication, but the reason for its demise probably lays less in its layout than in the fact that just after its founding in November 1924 readers discovered what became a far more

Figure 4.1 Front cover of *Moderní dívka*, 5 March 1926 (possible misprint for April).

successful periodical, the weekly paper *List paní a dívek* (*Women and Girls' Page*, popularly known as *Pražanka* or *Prague Woman*). Produced on newsprint and costing 1 Kč per issue or 13 Kč quarterly within Czechoslovakia, Austria, Yugoslavia and Poland (26 Kč quarterly farther afield), this periodical became perhaps the most widely circulated and best-known women's

Figure 4.2 Front cover of *List paní a dívek* ('Pražanka'), 9 December 1925.

publication of the period in Czechoslovakia. Targeting bourgeois women of childbearing age, visually it emphasised fashion and imagery of small children. Its text included both cultural and practical topics. Initially printed in black and white, it added red at the end of its first year. During the second year it occasionally even experimented with four-colour printing, although the results were not always impressive given its poor quality paper. Its initial layout style was busier and far less elegant than that of *Moderní dívka*, which may have assured readers that it offered good value with lots of content.

From 1925 to 1943, *Pražanka* added a regional edition called *Moravenka* (*Moravian Woman*), and from 1930 to 1935 it also appeared as *Slovenka* (*Slovak Woman*). These regional versions appear different mainly in their mastheads. *Slovenka*'s text was in Czech rather than Slovak, and its advertisements were largely for Prague businesses. This prompts us to ask why the publishers changed the title if women in Moravia and Slovakia were content to read a magazine from Prague with advertisements listing one Prague address after another? Why bother even to suggest that the audience was Moravian or Slovak women? In the case of *Moravenka*, it should be noted that while Moravian women, like Prague women, spoke predominantly Czech and German, Moravian regional identity was (and remains) strong. A periodical named *Pražanka* would have been an annoying reminder that Bohemia's Prague was the capital, not Moravia's Brno. As for *Slovenka*, while any literate Slovak could read Czech, the regional target audience may have been a mix of Czechs posted to eastern civil service posts and Czechophile Slovaks—Slovaks who bought into the Czechoslovak idea rather than Slovak nationalism.

The third magazine considered here, the handsomely produced twice-monthly *Eva*, made its debut in December 1928. Printed in up to four colours—though mainly black and white—on semi-glossy paper, and initially costing 4 Kč per issue, *Eva* presented articles on culture, fashion, decor and fitness accompanied by a well-designed mix of photography and illustration. Somewhat like the publications of the German Ullstein house during the same period, *Eva* represented the modern Czech woman as short-haired, active and young—a rational and thrifty but well-dressed and fun-loving working woman. Health, exercise and dance were constants for *Eva*; children were not.

A charming example of *Eva*'s view of the modern girl can be seen in Ondřej Sekora's cartoon of a young woman's New Year's resolutions for 1929. In the full-page cartoon, the heroine first vows to dress inexpensively, then to cook at home every day. She continues her list with plans to clean house, to mend all of Daddy's clothes, to learn something serious, to refrain from squandering money on trivialities like fashion and jewelry and finally to go to bed early and get up early—but *today* she's going to dress up and go live it up with her top-hatted beau.[13] *Eva*'s mix of photography (often of American women, French fashions or exotic peoples but also of Czech women writers and performers) and lively, often colourful illustrations thus created a look that was contemporary and sophisticated. Its modern woman was both visibly and invisibly international, since the editorial intent was clearly to suggest that the domestic readership partook of this international modernity.

Eva continued publication until 1943, but the worldwide Great Depression made itself felt in Czechoslovakia and economic pressures were clearly a factor in the scaling back of its use of colour printing. In its second year (1929–30), its price had dropped to 3 Kč and in its third year covers

Figure 4.3 Front cover of *Eva*, 1 February 1929.

temporarily went to a highly standardised layout in which only the woman's face and the accent colour changed from one issue to the next. Few inside pages boasted an accent colour and four-colour printing became minimal, about two pages per issue. By the mid-1930s, however, lavish colour had returned. While like its readers the magazine had undergone hard times, the less affluent as well as the well-heeled clearly felt it provided good entertainment value. As with the movies, *Eva* provided an appealing escape into a world of luxury and intelligent, healthy fun, and it made clear that at least some of the pleasures chronicled were available to the average or upwardly mobile reader.

While *Moderní dívka* was clearly targeted at the not-yet married, *Eva* perhaps aimed more at childless young working women, and *Pražanka* at women who probably already had children, all three of these consumer periodicals covered many of the same major topics. Each gave significant coverage to fashion and provided articles on topics deemed to be of special interest to women, such as needlecrafts, fitness and social dance. All included literature, with *Pražanka* and *Eva* offering serialised novels such as *Babiola* by actress and writer Olga Scheinpflugová, which featured in *Eva*'s first issues. All covered film, though *Eva* was strongest of the three in its coverage of individual films, plays, operas and the arts in general. None were overtly political, but *Pražanka* and *Eva* included some coverage of current events and major political figures or their wives. In 1929, for example, *Eva* showed the wife of Foreign Minister (later second president) Edvard Beneš modeling an evening gown of ivory crepe-satin.[14]

As befitted their perhaps younger readerships, *Eva* and *Moderní dívka* enthusiastically promoted dance, especially during the winter ball season.[15] *Moderní dívka*'s dance coverage contained romantic pictures of couples and hailed the advent of new dances, including the foxtrot, tango and *paso doble*. It considered such topics as dance music and how to dress for ball season in articles entitled 'Dance and its magic' and 'Toward an esthetic of modern dance'.[16] In contrast, the profusely illustrated *Eva* used relatively few photographs or drawings of twosomes dancing, instead providing fashion coverage of ball gowns. It did not avoid imagery of couples on the dance floor, but the percentage of them in the magazine's overall pictorial content was far lower. *Eva* promoted modern dance and revues as well as more traditional social dances. For example, during the 1930 ball season it inquired 'What do you think, is there to be found a woman who doesn't love dance?' Yet this query was not illustrated by a couple but with photos of two modern dancers, one shown topless.[17] While *Moderní dívka*'s articles discussed modern dance, the magazine did not illustrate it in any significant way. *Eva*, however, made frequent use of photos of female modern dancers, and the Laban-trained dancer, Milča Mayerová, proselytised modern dance in the magazine's pages.[18] *Pražanka* also occasionally advertised lessons in 'physical harmony' by Dalcroze student Mary Kyselková, but focused far less on dance than *Eva* or *Moderní dívka*.

All three magazines showed interest in women's achievements outside the home, with *Eva* giving perhaps the most space to such topics. Both feminist periodicals and consumer magazines noted that Czech women were becoming not only artists, writers, composers and office workers but also pilots, motorcyclists and racing car drivers. *Eva* featured one-page photo essays on women from around the world in unusual fields of endeavor and included a page on women and work in each issue.[19] Although to today's eye *Eva* looks quite traditional, with its ongoing coverage of classic women's magazine topics such as textile crafts, domestic arts and especially fashion, the magazine gave strong support for basic feminist goals. Still, *Eva*'s heavy coverage of fashion earned it a critique from the political magazine *Fronta*, which gibed that the publishing house of Melantrich used its pages to promote snobbery and teach Czechoslovak women how to mix cocktails.[20] Yet only explicitly feminist and leftist magazines focused more intently on women's work, education and political lives than on combinations of fashion, domesticity and pleasure.

The magazines varied in their coverage of domesticity and well-being. *Pražanka* featured cooking suggestions in each issue, as well as information on health. *Eva*, on the other hand, included more photos of food and drink in its sparser coverage of culinary matters and covered health mainly in relation to sport and fitness.[21] *Moderní dívka* largely ignored food but gradually and timidly began to support women's fitness beyond the time-honored areas of dance and Sokol gymnastic exercise.[22] Of the three, only *Pražanka* emphasised childrearing.

All included advertising. *Pražanka* had the largest concentration of advertisements, largely for practical items. *Eva* had the next largest, often for more discretionary purchases. *Moderní dívka* had very few—another possible reason that the magazine did not last long. *Pražanka*'s ads were scattered throughout, whereas *Moderní dívka* and *Eva* placed theirs discreetly at the front and back. Common to all three, unsurprisingly, were ads for soaps, hair and skin care products and books. *Moderní dívka*'s genteel young readers were offered dance classes and books on piano technique and marriage. Advertisements in the pages of *Eva* and *Pražanka*, on the other hand, offered a wide range of goods and services, from the purely practical (doctors, steam laundries, bouillon cubes, water heaters, inexpensive feathers for bedding) to the useful but potentially luxurious (coffee, tea, stockings, underwear, coats, bathing suits, beauty salons, sewing machines and typewriters) to decidedly big ticket items (furniture, refrigerators, automobiles).

On the whole, while each of the three had its own distinct personality, they were not so unalike that they could not appeal to the same woman at different points in her life. These Czech-based consumer periodicals were thus in theory Czechoslovak, not narrowly Czech, but were published in the Czech language and focused on town-dwellers' rather than rural-dwellers' interests. Urban Slovak readers might choose to identify with the fashionable modern women shown in these Czech magazines, but for rural Slovaks, *Moderní dívka*'s or *Eva*'s imagery would have functioned primarily as fantasy. In predominantly rural regions, most women's clothing would have had more in common with that shown in *Eva*'s March 1930 anthropological photo spread 'How women of various nations dress' than with recent fashion.[23] Slovak periodicals, in fact, still emphasised folk costume as a marker of identity and pride, whereas the unstated message from Czech consumer periodicals after about 1925 was that folk costume was charming but not modern. Folk costume did not appear at all in *Eva*'s playful one-page pictorial history of clothing from Creation to the present.[24] While the more down-to-earth *Lada* fashion magazine included occasional advertisements from a company offering 'original' regional costume, it also included advertisements for hair care that showed an old-fashioned looking woman with hair past her feet.[25] Such advertisements suggested the era of the nineteenth-century Czech National Awakening, not the late 1920s.

It is important, therefore, to note not only what was shown in these mainstream Czech women's magazines, but also what was ignored and left out. In what has been called a 'multinational nation-state',[26] where the dominant Czechs espoused an ideology of Czechoslovakism, Czech periodicals made few gestures towards actual Czechoslovakism (such as publication in both Czech and Slovak). Not only did 'Czech' evidently equal 'Czechoslovak' for editors and publishers, but while internationalist and focusing on depictions of women of generic European heritage (modern but not readily identifiable as Czech, French, English, Danish, American, etc.), these magazines avoided any recognition that the First Republic included Germans, Hungarians, Roma or other minorities.

The magazines discussed here particularly emphasised imagery of young women, who could be taken as representing the energetic young state as well as mere human youthfulness. Images of young women consequently stressed attractiveness, modernity and competence. However, images of older women also appeared with some frequency. These typically represented either solid, often feminist, respectability and achievement or, occasionally, the labouring classes. This was similar to imagery of women in non-gender-oriented periodicals, except that in the latter, older women sometimes represented backwardness and images of young women sometimes referred to prostitution. Not surprisingly, magazines expressly for women avoided unsympathetic portrayals of women, although their texts could discuss women's problems.

CONCLUSION

The existence of numerous and varied Czech-language periodicals for women during the First Republic—only a few of which have been covered here—shows that magazine publishers perceived Czech and Czechoslovak women as eager to read about culture, politics, practical matters and women's achievements as well as wanting visuals of fashion, film and the world at large. Furthermore, the fact that the majority of First Republic Czech imagery—especially, but not only, in women's magazines—showed young Czech women as modern, well-dressed and competent suggests that Czechs not only valued modernity strongly but expressed it in part through pictures of women. These women were represented without markers of ethnic specificity: urban and internationalist, they could be read as modern and cosmopolitan. This was a major change from the early 1920s, when Czech periodicals had still stressed Czechness and Slavic identity. It also contrasted with imagery in Slovak periodicals, which continued to place more emphasis on markers of ethnic specificity in order to emphasise Slovak pride. In addition to revealing an urban middle-class Czech vision of Czechoslovakism, this difference between Czech and Slovak imagery in the late 1920s and early 1930s also related to Slovakia's later developing sense of national identity and perhaps also to a growing awareness among Slovaks of their cultural difference from the more dominant, better educated Czechs.

While the First Republic's magazines had distinct personalities and each promoted its own vision of the country's women, readers made their purchasing decisions in an environment teeming with periodicals of nearly every possible kind—both for women and for a general audience—and showed that a relatively small country with several major languages could support an active and diverse woman-focused press. Such magazines therefore constitute a rich lode for researchers studying gender, media, consumer culture and identity in inter-war Europe. They reveal how editors, authors and in turn readers collaborated in the construction of twentieth-century middle-class femininities. They also show the important role of consumer magazines in spreading a modern design aesthetic. As well as being a valuable resource for scholars of inter-war Czechoslovakia, these magazines can also provide material for scholars in other fields, offering bountiful evidence of Czech fascination with modernity and international economic and cultural connections (consumption of Hollywood films, Frigidaire refrigerators and French fashion, exploration of new dances and foreign sports). Although women's magazines from Central Europe have been a neglected resource for historians, their texts and visual images formed part of a woman-centered discourse that reveals many different facets of femininity, women's opportunities and identities. Focusing on one of Europe's smaller, less-studied countries thus proffers a useful perspective for the study of women's history, consumer culture and modernity.

NOTES

1 Scholars of the Weimar Republic regularly use women's magazines in their research. This is now expanding to include studies of earlier German women's magazines. For an example, see Beth Muellner, 'The photographic enactment of the early new woman in 1890s German women's bicycling magazines,' *Women in German Yearbook* 22 (2006): 167–88.
2 A JSTOR search for articles with 'women's magazines' in the title turned up examples of data-driven use of women's magazines including Nancy Berns, '"My problem and how I solved it": Domestic violence in women's magazines,' *Sociological Quarterly* 40 (1999): 85–108; Francesca M. Cancian and Steven L. Gordon, 'Changing emotion norms in marriage: Love and anger in

US women's magazines since 1900,' *Gender and Society* 2 (1988): 308–42; Mary G. Hatch and David L. Hatch, 'Problems of married working women as presented by three popular working women's magazines,' *Social Forces* 37 (1958): 148–53. Studies paying close attention to the magazines themselves were Jeffrey A. Auerbach, 'What they read: Mid-nineteenth century English women's magazines and the emergence of a consumer culture,' *Victorian Periodicals Review* 30 (1997): 121–40; Kay Boardman, 'The ideology of domesticity: The regulation of the household economy in Victorian women's magazines,' *Victorian Periodicals Review* 33 (2000): 150–64. Somewhere in the middle were such articles as Fiona Hackney, '"Use your hands for happiness": Home craft and make-do-and-mend in British women's magazines in the 1920s and 1930s,' *Journal of Design History* 19 (2006): 23–38; Kathryn Keller, 'Nurture and work in the middle class: Imagery from women's magazines,' *International Journal of Politics, Culture, and Society* 5 (1992): 577–600.

3 English-language scholarship on late Imperial Czech feminism includes: Katherine David, 'Czech feminists and nationalism in the late Hapsburg monarchy: "the first in Austria,"' *Journal of Women's History* 3 (1991): 26–45; Karen Johnson Freeze, 'Medical education for women in Austria: A study in the politics of the Czech women's movement in the 1890s,' in *Women, State and Party in Eastern Europe*, ed. Sharon L. Wolchik and Alfred G. Meyer (Durham, NC: Duke University Press, 1985), 51–63; Iveta Jusová, 'Fin-de-siècle feminisms: the development of feminist narratives within the discourses of British imperialism and Czech nationalism' (PhD diss., Miami University, 2000); Jitka Malečková, 'The emancipation of women for the benefit of the nation: The Czech women's movement,' in *Women's Emancipation Movements in the Nineteeth Century: A European Perspective*, ed. Bianka Petrow-Ennker and Sylvia Paletschek (Stanford: Stanford University Press, 2004), 167–88. On Slovak women during the same period, see Norma Rudinsky, *Incipient Feminists: Women Writers in the Slovak National Revival* (Columbus, OH: Slavica, 1991) and Nora Weber, 'Feminism, patriarchy, nationalism, and women in "fin-de-siecle" Slovakia,' *Nationalities Papers* 25 (1997): 35–65. On women in the First Republic, see Karla Huebner, 'Girl, trampka, or žába? The Czechoslovak New Woman,' in *The New Woman International: Representations in Photography and Film from the 1870s through the 1960s*, ed. Elizabeth Otto and Vanessa Rocco (Ann Arbor: University of Michigan Press, 2011), 231–51; Melissa Feinberg, *Elusive Equality: Gender, Citizenship, and the Limits of Democracy in Czechoslovakia, 1918–1950* (Pittsburgh: University of Pittsburgh Press, 2006); Bruce M. Garver, 'Women in the first Czechoslovak republic,' in *Women, State and Party*, ed. Wolchik and Meyer, 64–81.

4 Vansová's struggle to promulgate *Dennica* as a magazine specifically for women is discussed in Rudinsky, *Incipient Feminists*, 90–100 and Weber, 'Feminism, patriarchy,' 50–2.

5 Jakub Končelík, Pavel Večeřa and Petr Orság, *Dějiny českých médií 20. století* (Prague: Portál, 2010), 55.

6 Some useful general resources on early Czechoslovakia include Hugh Agnew, *The Czechs and the Lands of the Bohemian Crown* (Stanford: Hoover Institution Press, 2004); Petr Cornej and Jiří Pokorny, *A Brief History of the Czech Lands to 2000* (Prague: Prah Press, 2000); Stanislav J. Kirschbaum, *A History of Slovakia: The Struggle for Survival* (New York: St. Martin's Griffin, 1995); Derek Sayer, *The Coasts of Bohemia: A Czech History* (Princeton: Princeton University Press, 1998); Peter A. Toma and Dušan Kováč, *Slovakia*

from Samo to Dzurinda (Stanford: Hoover Institution Press, 2001); Victor S. Mamatey and Radomír Luža, ed., *A History of the Czechoslovak Republic, 1918–1948* (Princeton: Princeton University Press, 1973); Věra Olivová, *The Doomed Democracy: Czechoslovakia in a Disrupted Europe, 1914–38*, trans. George Theiner (Montreal: McGill-Queen's University Press, 1972).

7 See Marie Neudorfl, 'Masaryk and the women's question,' in *Thinker and Politician*, vol. 1 of *T. G. Masaryk (1850–1937)*, ed. Stanley B. Winters (New York: St. Martin's, 1990), 258–82.

8 *Europe Centrale*, 24 August 1929, quoted in XXX [pseud.], 'Le féminisme en Tchécoslovaquie,' *Revue Française de Prague* 8 (1929): 410. Francophile Czechoslovakia boasted an astonishing seventy-two Alliance Française chapters in 1938: Georges Pistorius, *Destin de la Culture Française dans une Démocratie Populaire: La Présence Française en Tchécoslovaquie* (Paris: Les isles d'or, 1957), 26.

9 On the political and legal situation of inter-war Czech women, see Feinberg, *Elusive Equality*.

10 The literacy rate in Ruthenia gradually rose from 22 per cent in 1910 to about 58 per cent by 1930. Paul Robert Magocsi, *The Shaping of a National Identity: Subcarpathian Rus', 1848–1948* (Cambridge, MA: Harvard University Press, 1978), 15–16.

11 I explore this split in visual imagery in Huebner, 'Girl, trampka, or žába?' and Huebner, 'Sketching the Czechoslovak New Woman,' *Paper Presented at the Annual Midwest Slavic Association Conference*, Columbus, OH, 15–17 April 2011.

12 Regarding imagery of women and ethnicity in Czech and Slovak periodicals for both men and women, see Karla Huebner, 'Otherness in first republic Czechoslovak representations of women,' in *Competing Eyes: Visual Encounters with Alterity in Central and Eastern Europe*, ed. Dagnosław Demski, Ildikó Sz. Kristóf and Kamila Baraniecka-Olszewska (Budapest: L'Harmattan, 2013), 438–60.

13 Ondřej Sekora, 'Novoroční předsevzetí' (New Year's Resolutions), *Eva*, 1 January 1929, 9.

14 'Paní Hana Benešová v toaletě a crepsatinu barvy slonové kosti' (Mrs Hana Benešová in a toilette of ivory crepe-satin), photographed by František Drtikol, *Eva*, 15 December 1929, 3.

15 In Central Europe, the winter ball season involves hundreds of formal dances, many of them organised by professional groups. Miloš Forman's film *Hoří, má panenko* (*The Fireman's Ball*, 1967) sets its satire of Czechoslovak life under Communism at one of these events.

16 See *Moderní dívka*, October and November 1924.

17 'Taneční umění' (Dance art), *Eva*, 15 January 1930, 18.

18 See, for example, 'O Milče Mayerové' (About Milča Mayerová), *Eva*, 15 December 1928, 24.

19 The department Život a práce žen (Women's Life and Work) normally appeared as the final editorial page, just before the advertisements. Photo essays on work appeared more occasionally.

20 Karel Horký, 'Eva,' *Fronta*, 25 December 1930, 56–8.

21 For example, see 'Cena zdraví' (The Price of Health), *List paní a dívek*, 12 November 1924, 10 and the weekly feature 'Co vařit?' (What to Cook?) beginning with *List paní a dívek*, 12 November 1924, 11. See 'Domácnost' (Household), *Eva*, 15 December 1928, 20, for a page devoted to holiday meals. An article relating to fitness is 'Rytmika a její kulturní význam' (Rhythm and its cultural significance), *Eva*, 1 January 1929, 17.

22 Sokol exercise was promoted by the nationalist Sokol movement, similar to the German *Turnverein*.
23 'Jak se strojí ženy různých národá' (How women of various nations dress), *Eva*, 1 March 1930, 18–19.
24 Landrová, 'Evino roucho od pravěku až na naše časy' (Eva's garments from prehistory to our day), *Eva*, 1 October 1930, 9.
25 An advertisement for folk costume appears in *Lada: Kulturní rodinný čtrnáctideník* (*Lada: Cultural Family Biweekly*), 5 June 1927, 83. The long-haired woman advertisement 'Care for your hair!' appeared on the inside covers of *Lada's Modní svět* (*Fashion World*), 5 January and 20 January 1927, and frequently in *Lada: Kulturní rodinný čtrnáctideník* of the same year. A different company advertised in Pražanka with a similar image, beginning with volume 1, number 21, 1925, 11.
26 Todd Huebner, 'The multinational "nation-state": The origins and the paradox of Czechoslovakia, 1914–1920' (PhD diss., Columbia University, 1993).

5 Make Any Occasion a Special Event
Hospitality, Domesticity and Female Cordial Consumption in Magazine Advertising, 1950–1969

Rochelle Pereira-Alvares

> Women readers are of great interest to us in our Cordial advertising [. . .] use of women in liquor advertisements can be fraught with danger. If the advertising is not prepared with skill and taste it could turn women (and men) away from the product. We think if one word had to be chosen to express our feeling about the use of women in advertising, it would be subtlety.[1]

In 1958, the Distilled Spirits Institute (DSI), a self-governing organisation of the distilled spirits industry, lifted a twenty-year ban that had prohibited the portrayal of women in hard liquor advertising. The above words were spoken in 1959 by Donal O'Brien, the Vice President and Director of Advertising at the Hiram Walker distillery, in response to the DSI's decision. With market expansion as a goal, the Hiram Walker distillery wanted to target female consumers, but O'Brien was apprehensive about readers' and critics' reactions. While by the late 1920s it had become more acceptable for middle-class American women to drink alcohol, the act of women drinking remained a stigmatised activity even in the 1950s. Hiram Walker hoped its brightly coloured, fun and fashionable liqueurs (termed cordials in the American context in this period) would appeal to women drinkers and dispel negative connotations about their drinking behaviour.

This chapter explores Hiram Walker's cordial print advertising directed at middle- and upper-class white female consumers in North America in the 1950s and 1960s. It is based on a survey of *Gourmet*, *Sports Illustrated*, *Ebony* and *Life* magazines from 1950 until 1969. A sample of ninety-two Hiram Walker cordial advertisements were examined.[2] Eighty-four per cent of the advertisements appeared in *Gourmet*, and the remaining were found in *Sports Illustrated* and *Life*. However, none ran in *Ebony*, a lifestyle magazine aimed at African Americans, first published in 1945. Contrary to O'Brien's claim that Hiram Walker used subtle appeals to target women, this chapter argues that the distillery explicitly targeted middle- and upper-class white women. Hiram Walker's advertisements addressed women in their capacity as housewives rather than as drinkers of hard liquor in order to imbue alcohol use with respectability. In a period when many women's magazines refused advertisements from liquor manufacturers, I had to turn to some general interest and specialised publications that might have been trying to cultivate a female readership. The use of magazine advertising provides an understanding of some of the normative gender roles in the period, along with how the distilled spirits industry shaped drinking culture in this era. The study offers insight into the distilled spirits industry's advertising messages to normalise women's alcohol consumption by tying it to domesticity and fashion.

Earle MacAusland launched *Gourmet* in 1941 for 'well-to-do' audiences interested in gourmet dining, luxury goods and food travel. Food historian David Strauss states that *Gourmet* was built on the success of male-oriented, urban, gourmet dining societies in the 1920s and 1930s. At its debut, it was intended for an upper-middle-class audience and catered to the male cook even though women made up much of the readership during the war.[3] Manufacturers of higher end products like fine china dinner settings, silver cutlery, gourmet foods, foreign wines, liqueurs and domestic spirits advertised in *Gourmet*. The editorial content and consumer goods advertising indicate that this was not an egalitarian publication. *Gourmet* was aspirational, geared towards readers who wanted to impress others with their sophisticated knowledge of food, rather than a practical guide for those who had to cook on a daily basis. It had a relatively low circulation rate of 100,000 in 1950, which reached nearly 450,000 by 1969.

In 1936, Henry Luce created *Life*, a lifestyle magazine, and founded other popular magazines like *Time*, *Fortune* and *Sports Illustrated*. *Life* documented with large glossy photographs general interest stories about current political events, entertainment, culture and sports. It was hugely successful, with a circulation rate of about 5.5 million in 1950, reaching up to approximately 7.5 million by 1969.[4] *Life* had several imitators, including *Look* and *Ebony*. Luce was a staunch Republican and defender of big business, and his political values shaped the content and tone of the magazine.[5]

American sports fans could pick up their first copy of *Sports Illustrated* in 1954. It began as a magazine dedicated to elitist sports and pastimes like yachting, tennis, equestrian competitions, golf and croquet. It was poorly received by audiences, and therefore Luce decided to cover spectator sports such as boxing, baseball and basketball instead, much to the delight of American readers. The majority of the writers were male and wrote with a male readership in mind, but it did try to appeal to female readers with selected articles. *Sports Illustrated* was the leading sports magazine of its day, and in the years covered in this article, circulation hovered between 1 and 1.5 million.[6]

WOMEN AND DRINK IN A HISTORICAL CONTEXT

In the latter half of the nineteenth and the early twentieth centuries, many middle- and upper-class North American women served and consumed alcoholic beverages at home.[7] Throughout the 1920s, although Prohibition was in effect, middle-class women began to participate in a culture of heterosocial leisure by drinking in certain public spaces, such as cocktail parties, restaurants, social clubs and dance halls.[8] The alcoholic beverage industry contributed to this trend by doggedly trying to normalise drinking after the repeal of Prohibition in 1933.[9]

Even so, female public drinking was not the norm, as society considered drinking spaces such as saloons, taverns and bars to be rough, unsavoury and dangerous places for respectable women. Society regarded such venues as male drinking establishments, associated with masculine virility and sociability, and places where men could relax, have a drink, gamble or search for employment.[10] Anxiety surrounding female alcohol consumption was related to female sexuality and moral preservation. Medical professionals and social observers viewed women's tendency to visit male drinking spaces as a transgression of gender norms and a reflection of women's growing masculinity.[11] Stories about bar-room girls, women who colluded with barkeepers to increase male patron's spending, coloured the front pages of California's major newspapers in the early 1950s.[12] When women did frequent taverns or saloons, they were usually working class, utilised side entrances and drank in seclusion to avoid the gaze of unknown and potentially dangerous men.[13]

Although heterosocial drinking was prevalent in the 1930s and 1940s, it had not supplanted the notion that drinking was a gendered activity, one performed by males.[14] In his analysis of the American brewing industry's advertising practices, historian Nathan Corzine asserts that society regarded alcohol consumption as a masculine leisure activity and argues that brewers had to embrace a domesticated image of alcohol use in order to counter criticism and acquire credibility.[15] From the 1950s, the Hiram Walker distillery likewise adopted a domesticated image of female alcoholic beverage use in an effort to appeal to women and appease critics—but a change in DSI policy had to come first.

Shortly after the repeal of Prohibition in 1933, the DSI established a code of conduct regarding advertising practices to which members were bound. The DSI was a coalition of North American distillers, including Seagram, Hiram Walker and Heublein, that endeavoured to appropriate a standard of respectability for the industry as well as to promote and defend its members' business initiatives. From 1937 to 1958, it banned images of women from alcohol advertising copy and tableaux in the United States. The ban was partially lifted in 1958, but the portrayal of women holding or consuming distilled spirits in print advertisements continued to be prohibited until 1963.[16] Although television became a pervasive form of entertainment in North American homes in the 1950s, in 1948 the DSI chose not to advertise distilled spirits on television.[17] As a result, print publications remained integral to the promotion and success of a distillery's brand image and product awareness.

At the same, the periodicals market was flourishing; between 1945 and 1962, the total number of magazine titles in the US increased from 472 to 706.[18] Editorial staff of general interest magazines imagined a mass, homogeneous audience with shared consumer tastes and economic status, although 'mass' appeal was actually associated with a white middle-class audience and thus excluded other significant groups of people, including African Americans.[19] Even when magazines focused on a special interest, as in the case of *Gourmet* and *Sports Illustrated*, white middle- or upper-class readers were the target audience. Furthermore, journalism scholar David Abrahamson notes that general interest magazines reinforced mainstream values along with a message of conformity in post-war America.[20] However, journalism and media studies scholar Carolyn Kitch argues that magazines were not a reflection of dominant societal values or reality. Instead, she argues, they perpetuated certain versions of womanhood because of their simplicity and recognisability instead of disseminating complex imagery that mirrored the realities of women's lives.[21] The magazines often established and upheld unrealistic expectations or worlds of fantasy that many women chose to ignore. At the same time, they provide insight into understandings of what was deemed the 'good life' in this period—thus when Hiram Walker explicitly targeted female consumers in the 1950s and 1960s, it generally identified them as perfect hostesses and housewives.

THE CORDIAL HOSTESS AND HOUSEWIFE

In the 1950s, distillers like Hiram Walker began advertising their products to women yet a decade later still characterised them as an 'untapped market'. In a *Printers' Ink* article from 1967, Jack S. Birnbaum, a distributor of distilled spirits, advised the industry to simplify bottle labels because 'The woman should be able to examine a bottle of wine or spirits in a liquor store as easily as she picks up a can of beans in a supermarket.'[22] An article from the May 1967 issue of *Liquor Store* magazine, a trade publication, noted female consumers were uninformed about liquor categories and most relied on their husbands' opinions or that of experienced sales staff to make purchasing decisions.[23] In December of the same year, the magazine released an article by George Mosley, the Seagram distillery's advertising manager, instructing retailers to maintain clean stores with tidy displays and shelves, pay close attention to the requests of female customers and remember that the store keeper was 'helping to educate a buyer who wants to be as knowledgeable as her husband'.[24] Yet despite this, the retail industry still often regarded women consumers as unknowledgeable, recalcitrant and whimsical.[25] In *Retail Nation: Department Stores and the Making of Modern Canada*, historian Donica Belisle has demonstrated that retail and department store managers treated female shoppers with condescension and drew distinctions between the 'normal' customer as passive compared to the demanding, unsatisfied, 'deviant' woman.[26]

An article in the July/August 1960 issue of *Round Table*, Hiram Walker's employee magazine, stated that the number of women who purchased liquor and wine for the household had doubled since 1950.[27] The same issue contained an article by Illinois liquor retailer Ben Schwartz, explaining the need for suburban liquor retailers to cater to female consumers. He believed women shoppers were price-conscious compared to male customers, yet also more impulsive, making it easier to up-sell them with attractive displays.[28] According to Schwartz, women preferred sales staff adept at providing food and drink pairings and appreciated the cooking-with-cordials demonstrations held at his store. Demonstrations were one of several techniques that Hiram Walker used to reach out to women; conscious of industry critics and keen to achieve a degree of respectability, the company conformed to perceived prevailing gender norms and industry trends by marketing its line of cordials as beverages suited to respectable, white middle-class women for the duration of the 1950s and 1960s, as the rest of this chapter demonstrates.

In the mid-1950s, the distillery held live cooking demonstrations, beverage tastings and movie screenings. It collaborated with television chefs who cooked with Hiram Walker's products on their programmes. In advertising inserts, the distillery promoted its generic line of cordials as quintessential dessert substitutes and as integral ingredients in dessert recipes in *Life*, *Gourmet* and *Sports Illustrated*. Between 1956 and 1964, Hiram Walker ran an advertising campaign entitled, 'Hiram Walker's cordials: a rainbow of distinctive flavors'. Dining and hospitality were central themes. The campaign stressed heterosocial hospitality with hostesses offering guests brightly coloured cocktails and desserts made with Hiram Walker cordials, clear indications that the distillery was trying to appeal to the female consumer. *Gourmet*'s kitchens tested cocktail and dessert recipes made with Hiram Walker cordials, a fact Hiram Walker boasted about in some of its cordial advertisements. One such advertisement encouraged readers to dine at home rather than go out to a restaurant for dinner. It contained cocktail and dessert recipes women could replicate for their husbands or guests, thereby demonstrating their expertise in the kitchen (see Figure 5.1).

Hiram Walker claimed their cordials had the potential to enliven casserole suppers, add luxury to buffet dinners and contribute a festive glow to informal meals. Advertisements tried to persuade the reader that Hiram Walker cordials could transform casual, mundane domestic dining and entertaining into elegant, luxurious and exceptional affairs. In the October 1956 and March 1957 issues of *Gourmet*, Hiram Walker ran advertisements trying to convince women that cordials were convenient and inexpensive beverages that would thrill and impress guests.[29] Serving cordials could improve a woman's reputation and reinforce her role as the perfect wife or hostess. Many of the cocktail recipes found in the advertisements required women to have several varieties of cordials on hand. They had multiple steps, which

Figure 5.1 'How about stepping in this evening?' Hiram Walker advertisement, *Gourmet*, March 1956, 69.

made the process complicated and potentially costly rather than quick, easy and affordable. The advertisements never recognised or represented women as drinkers of Hiram Walker cordials even though more middle-class American women started to drink in the 1950s.

CORDIAL FASHION AND STYLE

After the DSI revoked its decision to ban women from advertisements in 1958, Hiram Walker started to include images of women in its cordial advertisements. In one example, a woman with short dark hair stood in a pink floral dress, her hand lifted to her face.[30] She may have held a cocktail glass to her lips or in her other hand, but since her image was out of focus, and Hiram Walker was still bound by industry code not to show women consuming alcoholic beverages, the gesture was cryptic. In the foreground and in focus was a white table-top covered with five filled cordial glasses, a white casserole dish and loaf of bread. A bottle of blackberry brandy and crème de menthe also sat on the table. The caption below the image stated, 'Give your casserole suppers a candlelight charm with cordials by Hiram Walker'. The cordials were 'fun to serve . . . and inexpensive, too, whether you buy the standard sized bottle or the smaller flask-shaped size'. A woman's cooking and entertaining skills defined gracious hospitality, which were further enhanced when she used Hiram Walker's cordials at her kitchen and dining table. By evoking the theme of gracious living, the cordials had the ability to transform a simple meal like a casserole dinner into an elegant, special event.

Scenes of chafing dishes, candle-lit table settings or one-dish skillet meals emphasised the traditional gender roles expected of women in these decades. However, the advertisements undermined women's hard work and glamourised domestic chores like cooking and serving by aligning them with sophistication, luxury and elegance. As middle-class incomes grew, magazines like *Life* encouraged readers to surround themselves with tasteful commodities.[31] Food manufacturers were just as enthusiastic to nurture a culture of gracious living and advertised packaged foods as symbols of affluence and creativity with the goal of convincing female consumers to find satisfaction in routine domestic labour.[32] Hiram Walker propagated cultural norms by presenting middle-class women with an avenue for expressing their creativity and impressing guests with innovative, sophisticated recipes made with its cordials. While Hiram Walker's advertisements encouraged women to dress up their ordinary dining and entertaining routines, they also pressured women to impress their husbands and guests in their roles as perfect hostesses. Contrary to O'Brien's admissions, Hiram Walker's cordial advertisements did target female consumers as model wives and hostesses even if not as drinkers of the liquor.

Many of Hiram Walker's other cordial advertising campaigns promoted flower arranging and home décor. In 1968, retail outlets featured display stands with cordial recipe booklets and flower arrangements and the distillery released accompanying magazine advertisements.[33] The following year, Hiram Walker partnered with candle manufacturer Paragon to present a line of slim taper candles coordinated to reflect the colours of the crème de menthe, blackberry brandy, cherry brandy, crème de cacao and anisette cordials. The purpose of the advertising campaign was to create a 'high-style adjunct to gracious living and entertaining'.[34] The advertisements reinforced themes of domesticity and hospitality. They encouraged conspicuous consumption by suggesting women needed to enhance their lives with 'pretty things' like candles and flowers.

Hiram Walker also employed some innovative strategies to gain the attention of potential and pre-existing female consumers. In the 1960s, the company released a few cordial advertisements based on the stereotype of women being interested in fashion. Advertisements endorsed McMullen's Cordial Casuals, a collection of women's travel wear comprising Bermuda shorts, shirts, sheath dresses, skirts and tote bags inspired by Hiram Walker's line of cordials (see Figure 5.2). The outfits' colours corresponded with Hiram Walker cordial names like cacao bean, crème de menthe, black raspberry and apricot. Mint leaves, cacao beans and fruit adorned white-collared blouses which women could pair with solid-coloured linen skirts.[35] Women could find the line at the nearest clothing store and then decide on a 'few bottles of Hiram Walker's Cordials . . . 21 flavors to choose from . . . all of them a snap to serve and delightfully *un*extravagant in cost!'[36] Rather than a subtle reference to female consumers, this was a blatant promotion geared at the stylish woman for whom travel, leisure and relaxation were viable options.

Figure 5.2 McMullen's Cordial Casuals/Hiram Walker advertisement, *Sports Illustrated*, 4 April 1960, 11.

In one advertisement from an April 1960 issue of *Sports Illustrated*, a woman reclined along the trunk of a tree with one leg swung out in front and the other to her side, with her face upturned towards the sky and her arms askew at her sides. Modeling the McMullen Cacao Bean collection, she exhibited a form of ritualised subordination known as body clowning where she posed in playful, child-like enthusiasm with pliant arms and legs.[37] Her body language was open and fluid, leaving her vulnerable to the gaze of the man in the advertisement. In an inset to the left of the primary image, a woman lounged in a boat with arm extended and fingertips pointed at the water, her legs outstretched and crossed at the ankles. In contrast, her male partner and their male Jamaican guide sat upright. Much like the woman expressing body clowning, her body, though clothed, was exposed and lay prone. Compared to the men in the scenes who were composed, the women seemed frivolous and relaxed, possibly communicating the pleasure one derived after drinking the liquor, but the message was understated. Linking female alcohol consumption with fashion and leisure, Hiram Walker built on the idea that female alcohol consumption was not only an act that could be respectable but also one that was lighthearted, pleasurable and fun. The advertisement was only one of a select few to situate women enjoying themselves outside a domestic setting, distanced from the role of the ideal hostess.

CONCLUSION

Beginning in 1958, Hiram Walker personnel stated that the company would employ subtlety when including women in its advertising, but it is evident that this was a tactic to mute criticism. Prohibition ended in 1933, but the alcoholic beverage industry was still wary of offending vocal dry proponents who repeatedly lobbied the US Congress to ban alcohol's sale and advertising. Hiram Walker was comfortable reinforcing many of the traditional roles ascribed to women by the food industry in the 1950s and 1960s, a fact that did not change until the mid-1970s. While some publishers were willing to accept liquor advertisements, many women's publications refused to do so. When magazines did accept such advertisements in these years, they avoided risqué scenes and innuendo in an effort not to alienate their reading audience. Many women in this period chose not to or did not fit the moulds perpetuated by mass media, but others likely aspired to such ideals, because magazines like *Life* sold millions of copies a year.

Hiram Walker had been targeting female consumers for several years prior to 1958, even before female models or characters appeared in cordial advertisements. Once women were permitted in alcohol advertisements, the distillery's cordial advertisements reinforced normative gender roles with themes of hospitality, gracious living and domesticity to garner wider interest among female consumers and develop this new market. Even though the distillery made coy attempts to blur women's faces and was careful not to portray women actually drinking, their cordial advertisements and marketing strategies clearly indicated that the company wanted to develop a female consumer base. The advertisements instructed women to cook certain foods, decorate their tables in a specific way and host friends for supper while making Hiram Walker's products central to their entertaining repertoire. They showed women and potential critics that women and alcohol were compatible without causing offence, provided it was done in carefully controlled ways and environments. Hiram Walker's cordial advertising in the 1950s and 1960s was an effort to gain credibility and normalise heterosocial alcoholic beverage consumption.[38] The distillery's cordial advertising championed domesticity, gracious living and hospitality to endow the Hiram Walker brand name and women's use of alcoholic beverages with respectability.

NOTES

1 'How Hiram Walker feels about women in liquor ads,' *Round Table*, March/April 1959, 2.
2 The survey accounted for twelve issues per year of each publication, even though *Life* and *Sports Illustrated* were weekly magazines, to ensure that an equal number of issues were examined for each title.
3 David Strauss, *Setting the Table for Julia Child: Gourmet Dining in America, 1934–1961* (Baltimore: Johns Hopkins University Press, 2011), 136, 190.
4 'Circulation chart,' *Round Table*, March/April 1959, 14.
5 'The aim of life,' *Life*, 2 June 1962, 1.
6 'Circulation chart,' *Round Table*, March/April 1959, 14.
7 See Catherine Murdock, *Domesticating Drink: Women, Men and Alcohol, 1870–1940* (Baltimore: Johns Hopkins University Press), 56; Craig Heron, *Booze: A Distilled History* (Toronto: Between the Lines, 2003), 207.
8 See Lori Rotskoff, *Love on the Rocks: Men, Women and Alcohol in Post-World War II America* (Chapel Hill: University of North Carolina Press, 2002), 38–9; Mary Murphy, 'Bootlegging mothers and drinking daughters: Gender and prohibition in Butte, Montana,' *American Quarterly* 46 (1994): 174–94; Timothy Olewniczak, 'Giggle water on the mighty Niagara: Rum-runners, homebrewers, redistillers and the changing social fabric of drinking culture during alcohol prohibition in Buffalo, NY, 1920–1933,' *Pennsylvania History* 78 (2011): 33–61; Mary Jane Lupton, 'Ladies' entrance: Women and bars,' *Feminist Studies* 5 (1979): 571–88.
9 John Burnham, *Bad Habits: Drinking, Smoking, Taking Drugs, Gambling, Sexual Misbehaviour, and Swearing in American History* (New York: New York University Press, 1993), 474–5.
10 Cheryl Krasnick Warsh, 'Smoke and mirrors: Gender representation in North American tobacco and alcohol advertisements,' *Histoire Sociale* 62 (1998): 183–222; Murphy, 'Bootlegging mothers,' 178; Lupton, 'Ladies' entrance,' 583.
11 Michelle McClellan, '"Lady Tipplers": Gendering the modern alcoholism paradigm, 1933–1960,' in *Altering the American Consciousness: The History of Alcohol and Drug Use in the United States, 1800–2000*, ed. Sarah W. Tracy and Caroline Jean Acker (Amherst: University of Massachusetts Press, 2004), 267–97.
12 Amanda Littauer, 'The B-Girl evil: Bureaucracy, sexuality and the measure of barroom vice in postwar California,' *Journal of the History of Sexuality* 12 (2003): 171–204.

13 Madelon Powers, 'Women and public drinking, 1890–1920,' *History Today* 45 (1995): 46–52.
14 Rotskoff, *Love on the Rocks*, 59.
15 Nathan Corzine, 'Right at home: Freedom and domesticity in the language and imagery of beer advertising, 1933–1960,' *Journal of Social History* 43 (2010): 843–66.
16 Pamela Pennock, *Advertising Sin and Sickness: The Politics of Alcohol and Tobacco Marketing, 1950–1990* (DeKalb: Northern Illinois University Press, 2007), 45.
17 Pamela Pennock, 'The evolution of US temperance movements since Repeal: A comparison of two campaigns to control alcoholic beverage marketing, 1950s and 1980s,' *The Social History of Drugs and Alcohol* 20 (2005): 14–65.
18 Theodore Peterson, *Magazines in the Twentieth Century* (Urbana: University of Illinois, 1964), 59.
19 Jennifer Scanlon, *Inarticulate Longings: The Ladies' Home Journal, Gender and the Promises of Consumer Culture* (New York: Routledge, 1995), 5.
20 David Abrahamson, 'Reflecting and shaping American culture: Magazines since World War II,' accessed 15 August 2015, http://www.davidabrahamson.com.
21 Carolyn Kitch, *The Girl on the Magazine Cover: The Origins of Visual Stereotypes in American Mass Media* (Chapel Hill: University of North Carolina Press, 2001), 3–5.
22 Ted Sanchagrin, 'The new mix: Whisky and women,' *Printers' Ink*, March 1967, 10.
23 'How retailers see the woman customer,' *Liquor Store,* May 1967, 32.
24 George Mosley, 'Are you sharpening up for today's women's market,' *Liquor Store*, December 1967, 20–1.
25 Susan Benson Porter, *Counter Cultures: Saleswomen, Managers and Customers in American Department Stores, 1890–1940* (Champaign: University of Illinois Press, 1986), 80–94.
26 Donica Belisle, *Retail Nation: Department Stores and the Making of Modern Canada* (Vancouver: UBC Press, 2011), chapter three.
27 'And what'll the *lady* have?' *Round Table*, July/August 1960, 3.
28 Ben Schwartz, 'Why we designed our store for women shoppers,' *Round Table*, July/August 1960, 4–6.
29 'Dinner becomes an event,' Hiram Walker advertisement, *Gourmet*, October 1956, 81.
30 'Casserole suppers, candlelight charm,' Hiram Walker advertisement, *Gourmet*, January 1960, 57.
31 Laura Shapiro, *Something from the Oven: Reinventing Dinner in 1950s America* (New York: Viking, 2004), 27.
32 Shapiro, *Something from the Oven*, 64–5.
33 'Campaign mixes flower, liqueurs,' *New York Times*, 14 March 1962, 60.
34 'The why of a cordials and candlelight program . . .,' *Round Table*, 16 April 1963, 3.
35 'It's new to us—spring in bloom,' *Town Topics* (1960), 7.
36 'It's new to us—spring in bloom,' 7.
37 Erving Goffman, *Gender Advertisements* (New York: Harper Torchbooks, 1987), 50.
38 Rotskoff, *Love on the Rocks*, 202–4.

6 Righting Women in the 1960s
Gender, Power and Conservatism in the Pages of *The New Guard*

Sinead McEneaney

This chapter considers the role of the magazine *The New Guard* in discourse around gender in the new conservative movement in the United States as it redefined itself in the 1960s against the prevailing political climate of liberalism and the countercultural tide of the New Left. Circulation of the magazine was largely among the membership of the Young Americans for Freedom, who published it on a bi-monthly and then monthly basis from March 1961.[1] By looking at the issues of the magazine published between March 1961 and the end of 1968, I want to make two arguments: firstly, that the magazine provided a way for women to develop a public profile within an organisation dominated by men; and secondly, that the portrayal of women in the pages of the magazine (as subjects and authors) reflected a commitment to the politicisation of women in a way that the contemporary New Left still struggled to convey.

In 1962, Murray Kempton proclaimed in the pages of the *New York Post* that 'the conservative revival was *the* youth movement of the 1960s'.[2] He had good reason to believe this: with Richard Nixon's narrow defeat in the 1960 presidential election, many within the Republican Party sought new responses to a resurgent liberalism. By the early 1960s, this response was coming from a generation of younger conservatives who were enthralled by the philosophies of Ayn Rand and Russell Kirk and who made Barry Goldwater their political hero.[3] Only months before the election, in September 1960, then thirty-four-year-old William F. Buckley, Jr hosted a meeting of nearly one hundred young conservatives at his estate in Sharon, Connecticut. Buckley was the founding editor of the *National Review*, which began as a fringe magazine in 1955 aimed at rejuvenating conversations about the American right. By the early 1960s the *Review* had become mainstream and would continue to play a central role in redefining the boundaries of American conservatism.

The meeting of young conservative activists at Sharon produced a statement of purpose which formed the ideological basis for a new group, the Young Americans for Freedom, Inc. (YAF).[4] This was to become the most influential youth organisation on the right during the 1960s, with a national leadership in Washington, D.C. and local chapters at many of the nation's universities. While membership numbers are difficult to verify, the foundation of YAF repositioned the conversation about the future of conservatism further and further to the right. Looking at the career trajectories of leading YAF organisers, James C. Roberts concluded in 1980 that the founding of YAF was 'probably the most important organisational initiative undertaken by conservatives in the last thirty years'.[5]

WOMEN AND THE EDITORIAL DIRECTION OF *THE NEW GUARD*

Part of YAF's early success lay in the publication of its monthly magazine, *The New Guard*. The first issue was published in March 1961, under the stewardship of its first editor, Lee Edwards, and its first Managing Editor, Carol Dawson.[6] It reflected the values of YAF, and the members of its editorial team were all closely connected to YAF's national Board of Directors. From the start, the production quality was much better than newsletters produced by the Left, and in a short time, it evolved into a high quality, glossy magazine. A cross between a college alumni magazine, social diary, corporate newsletter and political magazine, the growth of the organisation meant that it soon became a monthly volume.[7] Covering stories about individual YAF chapters and the national movement, offering advice to young conservatives and running advertisements for other conservative magazines, the content of *The New Guard* was wide-ranging and varied from issue to issue. The magazine was well funded, in contrast with many of its counterparts in the underground press of the countercultural Left. Its purpose was as much to recruit new members as it was to communicate with the existing membership.

As its first Managing Editor, Carol Dawson (later Bauman, when she married fellow YAF-er and future Congressman Robert Bauman) was instrumental in establishing the direction the magazine took. Dawson was born in 1937 and grew up in Indianapolis, Indiana, and later in Washington, D.C. Her parents were both Republican supporters. In the capital, she studied liberal arts at Dunbarton College, a small Catholic college for women, and became heavily involved in political activism through her membership of both the Young Republicans Federation and the Youth for Nixon campaign of 1960. She was a prolific writer for a number of conservative publications, including Buckley's *National Review*.[8] She was a founding member of YAF and served on its Board of Directors from 1960 to 1962, but it was her involvement as Managing Editor of *The New Guard* that maintained her national profile well beyond her stint on the national board. Here she became a poster-girl for conservative women and helped to shape the organisation's message and exert some control on the means of expression.

Dawson was not the only woman on the editorial team of *The New Guard*.[9] In October 1961 she was joined by Mary Weatherly, a graduate of Skidmore College, who was working in the office of Sen. John Marshall Butler (Maryland). Throughout the decade, however, there were relatively few women on the editorial board and few female contributing writers. Nevertheless, *The New Guard* aimed to be a kind of *National Review* for a youth organisation intent on growth and waging war on the New Left and the counterculture. Women's voices were an organic part of that campaign. 'Many kids are revolting against the ruling "establishment" by following the New Left,' said Charisse Taylor in the April 1968 edition of *The New Guard*. 'This is unfortunate,' she continued, 'because the only logical alternative to the existing liberal "establishment" is YAF, not SDS.'[10] Taylor was one of the many women featured in the monthly 'Miss YAF' column, a feature of the magazine from late 1967 onwards that arguably cast politically active women in the role of glossy pin-up girls. Did this portrayal of women necessarily strip them of their political agency, or was it one of a variety of ways that the magazine created space for women's interaction with YAF, alongside their involvement as editors, as contributors, as subjects and as consumers? The rest of this chapter focuses on the ways in which women in the Young Americans for Freedom were involved with and portrayed in the pages of the group's magazine, *The New Guard*.

THE NEW GUARD AS AN 'ANTI-UNDERGROUND' PRESS

Much has been written about the centrality of the underground press to the cultural significance of the American New Left.[11] The do-it-yourself spirit of the *New Left Notes*, the *Berkeley Barb*, the *New York Rat* and the San Francisco *Oracle* (to name but a few) reflected underlying concepts of participatory democracy and anti-establishment values. Only the glossy *Ramparts* stood out as a more polished magazine with higher production values, but it was not without its problems regarding women.[12] Despite claiming to challenge the system, both high quality and underground magazines on the Left often portrayed women in a sexualised manner, encouraging men on the Left to see relationships with women outside of an inevitable nuclear family.[13] Much less attention has been given to the importance of media expression among youth groups on the Right in the 1960s, with most scholarship focusing on the development of alternative media outlets in the 1970s to counteract the perceived liberal bias of the previous decade.[14] Almost no attention has been given to the way that gender was framed in the magazines of the Right during that period.[15] While scholars attach cultural significance to magazines on the Left, those produced by right-wing organisations tend to be discussed only within the larger context of such groups and the movement in general.[16]

There is, however, a growing body of scholarship on women of the Right and New Right. Rebecca Klatch has written extensively about the experiences of conservative women, advancing compelling arguments that women were essential to the grassroots development of the New Right from the 1960s onwards.[17] In her excellent book *A Generation Divided: the New Left, the New Right and the 1960s* (1999), Klatch argues briefly that women in YAF publications were objectified and sexualised much more overtly than they were in comparable left-wing publications, especially those of YAF's counterpart on the Left, the Students for a Democratic Society. Klatch concludes that the 'Miss YAF' section of *The New Guard* was a 'pin-up' section aimed at objectifying women and portraying them in trivial, fluffy terms.[18] She is, of course, correct in her assertion of sexism in YAF: there was chauvinism in most political movements of the left and right in the 1960s. Even so, her claims leave the door open to further investigation into the ways that women used *The New Guard* to establish themselves as prominent members of the organisation, especially within a rigid structure that often militated against their ability to gain influence through formal leadership. Through the pages of the monthly magazine, we get a glimpse of the kinds of contradictions conservative women faced within an organisation that did not claim to be progressive in terms of gender equality and yet actively sought to recruit a female membership. We also get a clearer sense of how some women negotiated power within structures that did not lend themselves easily to this.

One might be forgiven for assuming that the conservatism of YAF would leave women outside the main structures of power and reduce them to the status of what prominent YAF member, Philip Abbot Luce, dubbed the 'house-female'.[19] While gender roles in YAF mirrored those of wider American society, and many of the tea-makers and secretaries were female, there were notable exceptions to the rule. By defining influence in terms of formal leadership—especially chairmanships of local and state chapters—it is easy to forget that there were other less formal avenues to developing power and influence within the organisation. The national magazine offered significant flexibility in that regard. Carol Dawson and Marilyn Manion were among the few women who ever achieved positions of formal leadership at the national level, and they each did so through their contributions to *The New Guard*, which provided a route towards leadership that was separate from, but parallel to, the local chapter system.

RECRUITMENT, POLITICS AND MORALITY

Looking at the articles and advertising on the pages of *The New Guard*, there can be no doubt that YAF was eager to specifically target young women as new recruits. So eager was YAF to appeal to female conservatives that it featured a 'For girls only' column that ran periodically in *The New Guard* as early as 1963 and essentially fused the traditions of the political journal and the women's magazine. There is no sense that this was in any way linked with what we identify as an emerging feminist consciousness on the Left, but by making a distinctive appeal for female readers, *The New Guard* provided traditionalist conservative women with an 'acceptable' way of becoming activists.

This is perhaps not surprising; scholars of women's magazines and romance fiction have written extensively about the conservatism of the genre and the difficulty of separating out a liberating message of inclusivity from a reinforcement of patriarchal expectations and female subjectivity.[20] Although the style of expression in 'For girls only' remained close to that of a glossy women's magazine, contributors to the column never lost sight of the political importance of their message and couched it within language designed to fit with traditional expectations of femininity. In an article entitled 'What the well-dressed girl should think', Elizabeth Foster intertwined a light-hearted discussion on women's fashion with a pointed critique of the liberal agenda and a staunch defence of the YAF leadership.[21] The juxtaposition of content and form gave the article a peculiar tone, but is one example of how women within the organisation used the magazine to forge their own style of participation without really appearing to challenge contemporary gender norms.

This contradiction was a feature of almost all female contributions to the magazine. In the May 1964 issue of *The New Guard*, Marilyn Manion's article 'Politics and the single girl' raised the question of whether women belonged in politics at all. Manion, who described herself on one occasion as a 'born conservative', was a prominent member of YAF who served on the national board of directors and also as national secretary. The daughter of Dean Clarence Manion, a former head of Notre Dame's law school, Manion worked for her father's conservative think tank the Manion Forum.[22] Her perspective on political engagement reflected that of many women in youth movements of the 1960s, including the Civil Rights movement: she chose not to run for formal political office herself (either in the YAF, or in local or national politics). Instead, she concentrated on behind the scenes activity, helping 'to spur conservative activity and thought [. . .] [persuading] someone to run. I guess,' she said, 'I'd go as far out on a limb as I could get—for somebody *else*' [emphasis in the original].[23]

Playing off the title of Helen Gurley Brown's bestselling *Sex and the Single Girl* (published two years earlier), Manion's article replicated the form of a traditional advice column with the edge of political satire.[24] The word play was not accidental; the magazine had published a review of Gurley Brown's book in the December-January 1963 issue, provoking quite some reaction in the letters pages. The review was scathing, criticising the book for urging women to use their looks rather than intelligence to get ahead and casting it as 'little more than shallow sophisticated smut'.[25] Becky Keller, from St Petersburg in Florida, was one of the many who registered their disdain in the letters pages, not only with the book itself, but with the decision to review it in the first place, especially as many high school readers already got 'enough filth and lewdness from television and magazines of questionable character'.²⁶ *The New Guard*, Keller suggested, should be a 'beacon of moral strength as well as political enlightenment'. The review of the book, and the reaction to it, revealed the broad church of YAF. This was an organisation that sought to embrace traditional conservatives, social conservatives and libertarians of various views. Defining the political agenda of the group, and the position of women within it, was an ongoing debate.

Speaking directly to these tensions, Manion set out to establish the uniqueness of the YAF woman and her suitability for politics. Despite her own reluctance to run as a candidate, Manion used the article to encourage young women to join organisations like YAF and to engage in politics more broadly. Her approach was half dating advice, half politicking: young women should not heed political stereotypes. The YAF 'bachelor girl' is neither the 'old stereotype of the plump lady in the wrinkled suit and flowered hat, who sponsors creamed-chicken-on-toast luncheons at which other ladies looking remarkably like her all sit around and plan how to plan the *next* luncheon'; nor is she the 'young mother who puts in a good ten hours a week of typing, telephoning and precinct-polling in between her washing, ironing, and baby-sitting chores'; and she is certainly not the woman who, 'armed with a formidable, fierce expression and a low, raspy, unfeminine voice, was convinced that she should be running things'. Manion points out, a little tongue-in-cheek, that 'if you are smart, you can go right ahead and run things as long as you let the men think *they* are running them [. . .]'.²⁷

The main point of Manion's article was to highlight the position and the importance of single, college-age girls, or 'bachelor girls', within the YAF, and to send the message that there was room in politics for a new style of female conservative. YAF women were not, for example, the 'little old ladies in tennis shoes' of the increasingly fringe John Birch Society.²⁸ But underscoring the whole article is the message that men would not discriminate against women within YAF because they would 'actually welcome *anybody* to the cause because there are precious few volunteers as it is'.²⁹ Couched within a language of women's magazine-meets-recruitment drive, Manion's message was twofold: in the first instance, women should not become political activists in order to meet men, even though YAF *was* a social environment as well as a political one. Secondly, Manion was keen to underscore that YAF men would not see political engagement as a negative quality; YAF women were not undateable. Despite claims of sexism within the organisation, articles like Manion's demonstrated the efforts of YAF women to develop authentic political voices within this non-threatening 'advice column' genre.

MISS YAF: A CONSERVATIVE PIN-UP?

In October 1967, a new regular column appeared in *The New Guard*, which set out to showcase female YAF-ers' political and personal qualities. Called 'Miss YAF', the column was a monthly one-page spread featuring several photos of the chosen woman alongside a fairly lengthy interview-biography. Much like the 'Miss America' contest, Miss YAF was chosen not only for her physical attributes, but also for her exemplary commitment to the politics of YAF. The 'Miss YAF' column essentially served as a showcase for ambitious young women within the organisation and afforded them an opportunity to be known and applauded by the national membership. Through this column, a profile emerges of young women who were not only politically active and politically ambitious, but also displayed the qualities lauded by Marilyn Manion in her 1964 article on politics and the single girl.

In some issues of *New Guard*, 'Miss YAF' replaced the more sober 'Focus on State Chairmen' column, which offered details on the biography and political achievements of the mostly male state chairmen.[30] The contrast between the two columns is stark. 'Miss YAF' was a more personable column, featuring large pictures and pithy quotes from its subjects. By contrast, the more sombre 'Focus on State Chairmen' carried photos of serious-looking men and detailed their outstanding achievements in conservative politics. The distinction is important: even though the biographical text of each Miss YAF highlighted political activity, the images themselves are quite passive, likely constructed for the male gaze and aimed at reinforcing the message that conservative women would not lose their feminine appeal by involvement in politics. The images were carefully framed to depict the traditional 'girl next door'. In much the same way as Manion's recruitment message used the non-threatening language of an advice column, so too was the political activism of these women couched in the non-threatening image of wholesome American womanhood. Through the 'Miss YAF' column, women became both consumers of a political platform and objects of consumption.

All of the women featured as Miss YAF shared certain characteristics. They were all white, and presented as heterosexual. They were all students: this is particularly interesting given YAF's insistence that they were a 'youth' movement rather than a 'student' movement. The choice to showcase these college-going women was clearly aimed at competing with student movements on the Left, but also reflected the desire to present YAF as a movement of intellectuals, educated men and women, who were to be the leaders of the future. Nevertheless, the columns tended to open with a detailed description of the age profile and physical attributes of the subject, including hair colour and height. This was not 'Miss America', but the descriptions and accompanying photos situated these women within the beauty queen genre. Belying the beauty queen trope, all of the women were serious activists who shared several social, political and aspirational traits, as well as a clear commitment to conservative politics. The women featured in the 1967 and 1968 issues all held some position of formal leadership at chapter or at state level, or both. They were often involved not only in YAF but in related conservative groups, notably Young Republicans. Generally, they became involved in YAF through 'mainstream' conservative activities, especially political campaigning for a Republican candidate during an election. Some traced their early political awareness to the 'Goldwater for President' campaign of 1964. All of them agreed that the politics of their families, and particularly their fathers, influenced their propensity towards conservative politics. The breadth of their political engagement was impressive. In October 1967, Miss YAF was a nineteen-year-old from California, Elizabeth Lee. She had been introduced to politics during the Goldwater campaign and became chairman of the Pacific Palisades YAF. By 1966, she was organising the 'Youth for Reagan' drive to support Ronald Reagan's campaign for the governorship of California. She was chosen as a 'Reagan girl' and was subsequently promoted as coordinator for all sixty YAF 'Reagan girls' in western Los Angeles county. By 1967 she was active in support of US involvement in the Vietnam War, serving as a 'VIVA girl' (Victory in Vietnam Association).[31]

Similarly, Karen Jo Setterfield, Miss YAF for November 1967, was both a 'Goldwater girl' (1964) and a 'Reagan girl' (1966). Like Lee, she also worked at the California state YAF office, and was a seasoned organiser. Louisa Porter, a twenty-one-year-old junior at Indiana University, Bloomington and Miss YAF for May 1968, was an activist and 'victory girl' for the Student Committee for Victory in Vietnam. The column highlights that the real value of Porter's role lay in her external engagement, and stresses that 'YAF and SCVV received much publicity as a result [of Porter's activism].'[32] Acting as a public, softer face of conservatism, these women spoke to a new audience, and YAF rewarded its female activists with media coverage on a national scale and with promotional possibilities within the organisation at the local and national level.[33]

The images of these women, intended to reinforce expectations of traditional femininity, are disrupted somewhat by the description of their political activities. To paraphrase Marilyn Manion, Miss YAF belied the old stereotypes of the female politician. The 'Miss YAF' column also raises serious questions about the accuracy of Phillip Abbott Luce's assessment of women within the organisation. Coming from a background as an activist leader in both SDS and YAF, Luce appears to have viewed success and leadership in terms of national leadership and perhaps undervalued these other roles fulfilled by women, which were central to the development of the organisation. These women were not the 'house-females' to whom he referred, the secretaries who were unable to wield any real political power.[34]

While the ranks of national leadership tended to be male-dominated, clearly women advanced within YAF through distinctive routes and participation styles at local levels and through engagement with the magazine. Many Miss YAF women *did* hold positions of formal power in local chapters. Elizabeth Lee served as chairman of the Pacific Palisades YAF. Karen Jo Setterfield was chairman of South Peninsula YAF in 1965–66. Jorene Jameson was chapter historian to the Philadelphia YAF chapter. Jo Ramsden was chairman of the University of New Mexico YAF chapter. Kathy

Forte founded Dunbarton YAF and served as its vice-chairman and also as the treasurer of District of Columbia (State) YAF.[35] All these women were both powerful and well respected within the organisation. They capitalised on all of the avenues open to them within YAF, both formal and informal. Not only were they 'Goldwater girls' or 'Reagan girls', they were committed activists on a number of fronts, from picketing companies to campaigning for Republican candidates, and importantly, supporting the drive for victory in Vietnam.

CONCLUSION

It is perhaps too easy to simply dismiss the 'Miss YAF' column as a manifestation of sexism. There was undoubtedly considerable chauvinism within the organisation, as there was in similar groups on the Left. Conservative women, not unlike their left-wing counterparts, struggled to find their political voice within a group that was ideologically traditionalist. *The New Guard* provided one outlet for this exploration. While the media darling of the SDS—the progressive magazine *Ramparts*—ran into trouble with feminists over its treatment of women's liberation issues, *The New Guard* provided an avenue for discussion of women's political activity. Mirroring the non-threatening imagery and language of women's magazines, the advice offered by Manion and others did nothing much to challenge dominant ideas about women's roles in wider society. But this emphasis on juggling politics and social expectations of marriage and family was largely consistent with the value systems of the group, as it struggled to reach out to women and men of different political backgrounds.[36] Contrary to what one might expect in a conservative group, YAF women wielded power in the production and content of *The New Guard*. In the editorial room and the writers' room and in the content of the stories, the magazine offered unique opportunities for women who often found themselves searching for political space in the wider organisation and beyond.

NOTES

1 Membership figures in 1961 were officially gauged at 25,000, but these figures are most likely highly inflated. Not all members paid the two additional dollars on top of the membership fee, and exact circulation figures are hard to determine. Nevertheless, Gregory L. Schneider points out that the official membership was not a clear indicator of influence, but that in reality the influence of Young Americans for Freedom was much wider than its official membership might suggest. For more detail, see Gregory L. Schneider, *Cadres for Conservatism: Young Americans for Freedom and the Rise of the Contemporary Right* (New York: New York University Press, 1998), 40–2.
2 Murray Kempton, *New York Post*, 5 March 1961, 2; John A. Andrew III, *The Other Side of the Sixties: Young Americans for Freedom and the Rise of Conservative Politics* (New Brunswick, NJ: Rutgers University Press, 1997), 83;

Paul Lyons, *New Left, New Right and the Legacy of the Sixties* (Philadelphia: Temple University Press, 1996), 53. Although Kempton's comment was tongue in cheek, M. Stanton Evans made similar comments in the second issue of *The New Guard* in April 1961, 8, in which he claimed that the conservative movement represented 'the future of the country'.

3 Lee Edwards, 'The other sixties: A flag waver's memoir,' *Policy Review* 46 (1988): 58.

4 'The Sharon Statement,' reprinted in Andrew, *The Other Side of the Sixties*, 221–2 and in Rebecca E. Klatch, *A Generation Divided: The New Left, the New Right and the 1960s* (Berkeley: University of California Press, 1999), 341–2.

5 James C. Roberts, *The Conservative Decade: Emerging Leaders of the 1980s* (Westport, CT: Arlington House, 1980), 25; Andrew, *The Other Side of the Sixties*, 216.

6 Wayne Thorburn, *A Generation Awakes: Young Americans for Freedom and the Creation of the Conservative Movement* (Ottawa, IL: Jameson Books, 2010), 51; Andrew, *The Other Side of the Sixties*, 69.

7 Jonathan M. Schoenwald, *A Time for Choosing: The Rise of Modern American Conservatism* (New York: Oxford University Press, 2011), 246.

8 'Girl on the go,' *The New Guard*, 3 June 1963, 15; Andrew, *The Other Side of the Sixties*, 69.

9 Biographical information for Carol D. Bauman from *New Guard*, 3 June 1963, 15 and *New Guard*, 8 April 1968, 23; Margaret M. Braungart and Richard G. Braungart, 'The life-course development of left- and right-wing youth activist leaders from the 1960s,' *Political Psychology* 11 (1990): 257–65.

10 Charisse Taylor, quoted in 'Miss YAF' column, *New Guard*, 8 April 1968, 21. SDS refers to the Students for a Democratic Society, one of the largest student groups on the Left in the US during the 1960s.

11 Abe Peck, *The Life and Times of the Underground Press* (New York: Pantheon Books, 1985); John McMillian, *Smoking Typewriters: The Sixties Underground Press and the Rise of Alternative Media in America* (New York: Oxford University Press, 2011).

12 *Ramparts* was founded in 1962 as a new outlet for progressive Catholics who wanted to provide a forum for debate on contemporary social and moral issues. By 1964 it had been taken over by a chaotic mix of left wing activists, writers and journalists, who turned the publication into the national voice of the counterculture. The editor, Warren Hinkle III, ran afoul of women's liberationists when he sanctioned the publication of a headless woman on the cover of the February 1968 issue, prompting complaints that *Ramparts* represented women as having 'two tits, no head'. For more on *Ramparts*, see Peter Richardson, *A Bomb in Every Issue* (New York: The New Press, 2009).

13 See Barbara Ehrenreich's discussion of this phenomenon with relation to mass-market magazines, in *The Hearts of Men: American Dreams and the Flight from Commitment* (New York: Anchor Press, 1983).

14 For example, prominent former YAF activists Richard A. Viguerie and David Franke discuss this in *America's Right Turn: How Conservatives Used New and Alternative Media to Take Power* (Los Angeles: Bonus Books, 2004). For a more academic discussion, see James Brian McPherson, *The Conservative Resurgence and the Press: The Media's Role in the Rise of the Right* (Evanston, IL: Northwestern University Press, 2008).

15 In *A Generation Divided: The New Left, the New Right and the 1960s* (Berkeley: University of California Press, 1999), Rebecca Klatch briefly discusses

sexism in *The New Guard* (166, 175). In her book *Wives, Mothers and the Red Menace: Conservative Women and the Crusade Against Communism* (Boulder: University of Colorado Press, 2008), 42–3, Mary C. Brennan outlines women-sponsored and women-run newsletters produced by grassroots conservative groups in the 1950s and 1960s.

16 Over the past twenty years or so, historians have paid more attention to the story of 1960s conservatism, recognising that there has been an imbalance in the historiography of the decade. Building on George Nash's early work in *The Conservative Intellectual Movement in America since 1945* (New York: Basic Books, 1976), John A. Andrew's *The Other Side of the Sixties*, Gregory Schneider's *Cadres for Conservatism* and Lisa McGirr's *Suburban Warriors* (Princeton: Princeton University Press, 2001), they go some way to counteract a sixties historiography that privileges the experiences of the New Left and the counterculture.

17 Rebecca E. Klatch, *Women of the New Right* (Philadelphia: Temple University Press, 1987) and Klatch, *A Generation Divided*. For more recent work on women in grassroots activism since the 1980s, see Ronnee Schreiber, *Righting Feminism: Conservative Women and American Politics* (New York: Oxford University Press, 2008); Michelle Nickerson, *Mothers of Conservatism: Women and the Postwar Right* (Princeton: Princeton University Press, 2012); Donald T. Critchlow, *Phyllis Schlafly and Grassroots Activism: A Woman's Crusade* (Princeton: Princeton University Press, 2005).

18 Klatch, *A Generation Divided*, 166.

19 Phillip Abbott Luce, 'Against the wall,' *The New Guard*, October 1968, 4–5.

20 For example, Janice Radway, *Reading the Romance* (London: Verso, 1984); Ien Ang and Joke Hermes, 'Gender and/in media consumption,' in *Mass Media and Society*, ed. James Curran and Michael Gurevitch (London: Edward Arnold, 1991), 307–28.

21 Elizabeth Foster, 'What the well-dressed girl should think,' *The New Guard*, March 1963, 42–3.

22 Biographical information for Marilyn Manion can be found in *The New Guard*, February 1963, 17; Braungart and Braungart, 'The life-course development,' 257–65.

23 Interview with Marilyn Manion, *The New Guard*, February 1963, 17.

24 Marilyn Manion, 'Politics and the single girl,' *The New Guard*, May 1964, 8–9.

25 J. A., 'How to stay single,' *The New Guard*, December–January 1963, 19.

26 Becky Keller, 'Letter to the editor,' *The New Guard*, May 1963, 2.

27 Manion, 'Politics and the single girl,' 8–9.

28 Stanley Mosk and Howard Jewel, 'The Birch phenomenon analyzed,' *New York Times Magazine*, 20 August 1961, 12; Nickerson, *Mothers of Conservatism*, xviii.

29 Manion, 'Politics and the single girl,' 9.

30 The first female state chairman was Judy Whorton, a senior at Howard College in Birmingham. She was elected in 1963 as chairman of Alabama YAF (*The New Guard*, November 1965, 22). Only a very small number of women were elected as state chairmen during the 1960s, but the number increased by the end of the decade. In 1968 Zan Clark was South Carolina chairman, Candace Sorenson was chairman of Wisconsin YAF and Eva Bushman served as chairman of Oregon YAF (*The New Guard,* March 1969, 10).

31 Elizabeth Lee, 'Miss YAF,' *The New Guard*, October 1967, 25.

32 *The New Guard*, May 1968, 21.

33 Karen Jo Setterfield, 'Miss YAF,' *The New Guard*, November 1967, 23; Louisa Porter, *The New Guard*, May 1968, 21.
34 Luce, 'Against the wall,' 4–5. This concept of the 'house-female' plays on the concept of the division between 'house-slave' and 'field-slave', and suggests that prominent men like Luce may have seen YAF women as doing domestic work in a privileged position.
35 All conclusions and biographical details based on the 'Miss YAF' column. Elizabeth Lee, *The New Guard*, October 1967, 25; Karen Jo Setterfield, *The New Guard*, November 1967, 23; Jorene Jameson, *The New Guard*, December 1967; Jo Ramsden, *The New Guard*, February 1968, 23; Charisse Taylor, *The New Guard*, April 1968, 21; Louisa Porter, *The New Guard*, May 1968, 21; Kathy Forte, *The New Guard*, Summer 1968, 25.
36 Klatch details the tensions between traditionalists and libertarians in chapter six of *A Generation Divided*.

Part III
Women, Magazines and Employment

7 Getting a Living, Getting a Life
Leonora Eyles, Employment and Agony, 1925–1930

Fiona Hackney

Nowadays, far from being a disgrace to work, it is a disgrace not to.[1]

[V]ery few human beings can stand leisure; something atrophies, and they become degenerate. It is the busy woman who makes time to read, to think, in a word to Live who is best fitted to be a wife, a mother, and a friend.[2]

Leonora Eyles (1889–1960), the author of both epigraphs above, remains a relatively unknown figure today, yet her work as a British journalist, novelist and author of sociological texts was both prolific and impressive.[3] Her eclectic journalistic output includes articles for literary periodicals such as *Time and Tide*, newspapers—she contributed to *The Daily Herald* and *The Times*, for instance—and correspondence columns for magazines. In the rapidly expanding market for women's magazines in the 1920s and 1930s she carved out a niche for herself as one of the country's most respected 'agony aunts', reaching out to 'thousands of women—as sisters and daughters, mothers and lovers, as workers in both the home and the public workplace, who read her columns avidly'.[4]

A lifelong socialist, Eyles rejected an economic and social order based on competition and insisted that relationships of subordination between men and women were equally damaging. These ideas inform and structure her writing. It was, however, her ability to communicate them through her lived experience of insecurity—the legacy of a traumatic childhood, marked by her alcoholic father's bizarre and unpredictable behaviour and the premature death of her mother—that makes her work so distinctive and affecting. Eyles' story of struggle and survival, from riches to rags and back to riches again, is the stuff of magazine fiction. In her memoir she explains how a talent for writing and a strong sense of religious and political ethics as a Christian Socialist sustained her through hardships in early adult life (not least when she had to raise her young children alone), instilling a deeply felt need to address poverty, hardship, inequality and injustice through her writing, something that emerges strongly in her work as an agony aunt.[5]

Part of Eyles' originality was her belief in popular media as a conduit for social change. This was particularly true of the correspondence page, which she regarded as a space for readers to share what could often be highly challenging problems, including poverty and ill health, even abuse, as well as romantic dilemmas. For Eyles, the magazine problem page was a serious concern and, at a time when often there were few other places to turn, she worked to forge a supportive community that was both 'imagined' and, on occasion, met in real life.[6] This chapter explores that process and considers how Eyles created a particular ethos and sense of community for readerships in different magazines. It focuses on the period from 1925–1929, when she edited columns for *Modern Woman*, a consumer monthly targeted at middle-class housewives and professional women, and the left wing *Lansbury's Labour Weekly*, an independent labour publication whose declared aim, in its editor's words, was to appeal to and convert 'men in the workshop and women at the washtub who are not yet class-conscious'.[7]

Careful comparison of these pages (the topics selected, the tone and nature of advice and the approaches she adopted) suggests a mode of progressive cross-pollination, as Eyles adapted strategies from the socialist press to give agency to *Modern Woman* readers, while shaping a feminist sensibility for the *Labour Weekly's* readership. Such hybridising tendencies additionally inform her fiction and non-fiction writing as well as her journalism; all were connected in Eyles' political-literary imaginary. It is no coincidence, for instance, that the destitute heroine of her first novel, the best-selling *Margaret Protests* (1919), saved her family by selling abortifacients through magazine small ads, while polemical texts such as *Women's Problems of To-day* (1926), *Careers for Women* (1930) and *Common Sense About Sex* (1933) were drawn from her experience as an agony aunt. Reading across the various genres that Eyles wrote suggests how powerfully she developed, and communicated, her ideas in the spaces between fiction and 'real life'. The problem page, a semi-public/semi-private construct which dealt in raw emotion, albeit often in coded form, provided an ideal vehicle for this.

The 1920s was a decade of progress and upheaval when women gained the vote, entered Parliament and local government, and worked in factories, offices and shops alongside men in increasing numbers.[8] The 1921 census showed over half a million women in the labour force—a figure that omitted the large numbers of uninsured workers, for instance, in domestic service— and numbers of insured female workers grew more rapidly than men.[9] To employ Sally Alexander's vivid metaphor, 'Office cleaners, packers, shop assistants, typists became the unlikely and suddenly visible shock troops of industrial restructuring.'[10] In magazines and other media, the working woman was principally characterised as young and single. The bob-haired bachelor or business girl who worked in an office earning a little extra cash to spend on cigarettes, lipstick, the pictures or new dress styles to a large extent reflected real change. Between 1901 and 1931, more than two-thirds of working women were under thirty and more than three-quarters of them

Figure 7.1 (Margaret) Leonora Eyles (née Pitcairn) (Mrs D.L. Murray), photograph by Howard Coster, 1934 © National Portrait Gallery, London.

were single, while the most dramatic shift was in the occupational distribution of women away from domestic service and the textile industries to 'white-blouse' office and secretarial work.[11] A large number of women in the over-thirty-five age group, however, also worked, and trends began to reverse after 1931 when single women comprised 51 per cent of the female workforce aged over thirty-five.[12] Above all, there was a marked tendency for single women of all ages and classes to work, resulting in a degree of disposable income that made them an important target audience for consumer magazines wishing to attract advertising.

Published in 1925, *Modern Woman*, as its title suggests, was consciously modernising. The strapline, 'The journal with the new spirit of the age', further underlined the magazine's progressive intent.[13] The first editorial in June addressed 'the woman of to-day' and promised a 'new era both in journalism and in the lives of women'.[14] The young, fashionably dressed business girl and the successful career woman became symbols of the freedoms, real or imagined, that modern life offered. The expanding field of employment in, for instance, modern hotels or on ocean liners was explored in 1927: 'The sea as a career for women' explored Miss Victoria Drummond's employment as a marine engineer, as well as openings for stenographers, hairdressers and shop assistants.[15] A 1929 series about successful career women, such as advertising executive Florence Sangster, beautician Helena Rubinstein and the educationalist Margaret MacMillan, was designed to appeal to the publication's target audience of professionally minded women.[16] Yet with a formal marriage bar in place in teaching and the civil service, and an informal bar operating in occupations such as journalism, the prevailing idea that a 'woman's place' was in the home persisted.

One of a group of consumer monthlies which magazine historian Cynthia White describes as offering women readers an 'intimate personal service, with a secondary emphasis on entertainment', *Modern Woman* promoted the value and quality of advice delivered by named experts such as Eyles.[17] This marked a turning point in women's publishing, which was reorientated away from the servant-keeping leisure classes towards the middle ranks. Styling itself 'the magazine that HELPS and ENTERTAINS' [emphasis in the original], *Modern Woman* was organised into nine Service Departments across five areas of interest: housewifery and child craft, fashion and appearance, home decoration, 'personal' (which included the correspondence page) and children. With a cover price of six pence for around eighty pages of fiction, features and additional colour inserts, these middle-market consumer monthlies depended heavily on income from selling space to advertisers. While editors fiercely defended the independence of editorials, visually appealing advertisements were increasingly grouped persuasively alongside appropriate content and scattered throughout the magazine.[18]

Eyles, perhaps surprisingly, was enthusiastic about the educational benefits and liberating power of advertising. In *The Woman in the Little House* (1922), her crusading book based on first-hand experience of bringing up her family in ill-adapted housing in Peckham, she applauded the 'columns of advice about dress, health and toilet matters' in magazines, which could stir women from 'lethargy, complacency or hopelessness' by making 'Mrs Britain and her sisters dissatisfied with themselves and their surroundings'.[19] She was not alone in holding such views. Jennifer Scanlon, in her analysis of the American *Ladies' Home Journal*, highlights the 'social service goals' of advertising in the period when progressive women with backgrounds in suffrage or social work moved into advertising in the belief that they could better improve women's lives.[20] In England, Ethel M. Wood, a Director of the Samson Clark agency and a prominent advocate of women in advertising, shared this concept of a 'service' ethos in advertising, which in Britain aligned with the public service ethos of such organisations as the BBC.[21] Additionally advertising, as Eyles later noted, was the only field in which women were appointed to posts with salaries anything like those of men and with 'a chance of work of real scope and responsibility'.[22]

In 1909 the author and playwright Cicely Hamilton had called for a new sense of fellowship among women, a 'feminine class-consciousness' that could be fostered through awareness of disadvantages held in common.[23] In the early decades of the twentieth century the correspondence or agony column, which by this stage was firmly established as women's domain, offered a space in which concerns could be shared and a common sense of female identity forged beyond class, at least to some degree.[24] As a socialist and a feminist, Eyles grasped the potential of the problem page to connect with women, inspire them and galvanise them to action. The next section will explore some of the strategies she developed to 'raise consciousness' in the socialist press.

'PROBLEMS OF REAL LIFE': *LANSBURY'S LABOUR WEEKLY*

George Lansbury, socialist leader of Poplar council and later leader of the Labour Party, launched *Lansbury's Labour Weekly* in February 1925 as the only independent Labour paper.[25] Contributors included such notable figures as the Labour MP Ellen Wilkinson and the socialist and journalist Raymond Postgate. Eyles wrote a weekly column, 'The woman's part', which outlined a progressive agenda for women. Her first rousing editorial introduced the central theme of 'wakening' those who were 'passively enduring' lives with 'half a dozen children and thirty shillings a week to feed and clothe them', or living in 'two rooms in Bethnal Green and Deptford trying to keep decency about them'.[26] Passionate about the power of female agency, Eyles argued that the 'nation is in the little homes'. She believed that if she could inspire women with a vision, a 'picture of the world as they could make it', they would be stirred to direct action to bring about change.

Competition from the *Sunday Worker* soon halved the *Labour Weekly's* circulations. Lansbury fought back with a new format that adapted strategies from the capitalist press for socialist ends. Innovations included 'popularly written, entertaining and useful articles and stories' and 'bright' visuals that, interestingly, he claimed would make the paper 'truly representative of the lives and feelings of the people'.[27] In effect this meant stronger visual content: a striking pictorial cover (red, of course), sketches and cartoons, sheet music ('great Labour battle songs'), a 'tit-bits' style 'two-minute Socialist sermon', human interest stories in the form of moving dramas from the police courts, a sports column and, despite the paper's opposition to capitalism, increased advertising.[28] Eyles contributed investigative journalism and fiction about the dramas of everyday life. She even ran a short story competition for readers—billed as 'the *human* story, a tale of real people up against real life'—but it was on her 'Problems of real life' correspondence page where readers' stories were most often to be found.[29]

'Problems of real life' was penned by Eyles under the name Martha. The pseudonym referenced the biblical figure whose association with domestic management and active service in the community symbolised Eyles' commitment to direct action through domestic agency. The column covered an amazingly diverse range of topics, from housing, health and fears about mental illness to sexual urges, requests for work, marriage tangles, pension difficulties and dreadful cases of poverty, abuse, drunkenness and debt.[30] Two inter-related themes dominate: unemployment, which Eyles described as '[t]he only problem that beats me', and the terrible personal consequences of poverty and financial instability.[31] 'All the time I am getting letters from people asking me to relieve them of their kiddies', Eyles wrote, referring to the pitiful parents and desperate single mothers with illegitimate babies searching for someone to 'take on the job of caring' until they 'get on their feet'.[32] The flipside of unemployment was the fantasy of a career, and letters from young people dreaming of the glamorous fields of writing, modelling and fashion regularly appeared in the column.[33]

Eyles' replies were supportive yet realistic; 'Nothing in art or, indeed in any walk of life is won without effort', she advised a young flour mill worker who wanted to draw for the illustrated weeklies.[34] Ever the pragmatist, she warned an aspiring young journalist that 'Writing too much for Labour papers will make you get a propagandist style.'[35] A woman whose husband was unemployed and 'must make money to feed the children' asked about the viability of homeworking with knitting machines. '[N]ot a money-making proposition', Eyles cautioned, suggesting that it would 'be safer to hire a sewing machine and do mending and making'.[36] A sharp rejoinder to a letter complaining about spendthrift workers when the middle-classes struggle on reduced capital reminds us that the right to work was a foundation of her socialism: 'we don't believe that people should live on dividends. Everyone should work [. . .]. You who do not work are really bankrupt, because you cannot redeem your money by your labour', she tartly replied.[37]

Most striking, perhaps, is the manner in which the column shaped a community identity and operated as a shared resource. Eyles' rhetorical yet highly personal style was instrumental in this. Readers were addressed as 'friend' and 'comrade', while offers and requests for rooms, jobs and material support were printed alongside advice in the form of a friendship club or mutual support agency. A young amputee, for instance, secured work on a farm but was unable to do his job because his crutches were worn and inadequate. Eyles appealed for contributions to purchase an artificial limb.[38] Particular ventures built momentum over the weeks, notably a scheme titled 'Martha's children' that collected and redistributed clothing for families in distress.[39] On occasion Eyles offered personal help to intervene with the Welfare Committee or to lend her flat as a venue for Russian classes, for instance.[40] Eager to instill Christian values of charity she, nevertheless, refused to shy away from revolution and urged her readers to view their daily struggles as 'epics' that would inspire others to rise up and 'smash the system that causes them'.[41]

'FROM ONE WOMAN TO ANOTHER': WORKING FOR THE CAPITALIST PRESS

The publisher George Newnes, who backed the left wing *Daily Herald,* also published *Modern Woman,* where Eyles' correspondence page, 'From one woman to another', ran for five years until October 1929. In contrast to *Lansbury's Labour Weekly, Modern Woman's* target audience comprised career women, suburban housewives and the daughters of the expanding middle-classes.[42] Many had gained the vote in 1918, and their numbers would expand in 1928 with the granting of full enfranchisement to women. For Eyles, writing for a commercial publication that professed progressive intentions must have represented an important opportunity to reach and inspire this potentially powerful new audience of professional women and housewife citizens.[43] Like *Good Housekeeping, Modern Woman* presented itself as a 'forum for rational debate'.[44] Its model of modern, home-based femininity, which accommodated and even enhanced participation in public life, had obvious appeal for Eyles. Her column, moreover, represented a chance to carve out a space in the mainstream women's press; a counter-public sphere in which the notions of community and (working) class consciousness forged in *Lansbury's Labour Weekly* could be inflected for a female readership.[45] 'Women talk to each other in a way that men don't share', Eyles observed in *The Woman in the Little House,* and her belief in the power of female reciprocity and community informed her column's title and its editorial ethos.[46]

It is difficult to describe 'From one woman to another' as an agony column, partly because it was as likely to deal with questions about training and employment as romantic dilemmas.[47] Eyles adopted an 'intimate and subjective voice to get alongside her readers'.[48] 'Voice' was, and remains, a vital means of communicating a magazine's 'personality'; it helped guarantee a publication's reliability and build rapport with its readership. Nowhere was this more important than on the correspondence page, which addressed readers' public, private and intimate lives. Among a sample of fifty women consulted about their memories of reading magazines, many described how, on opening their publication, they routinely turned to the problem page first, along with a serial if they were following one.⁴⁹ Yet in contrast to the sentimental, moralising tone and conventional guidance about 'boy trouble' or etiquette dispensed by more orthodox aunts, such as the generic Mrs Marryat at *Woman's Weekly* or even *Woman's* Evelyn Home (both journalistic pseudonyms), Eyles' advice could be challenging, was often surprising and she used her real name.

Her first editorial made a virtue of the fact that her instruction was grounded in hard-won experience, long before she read 'Havelock Ellis, Bloch or Freud'.⁵⁰ The synthesis of the drama of lived experience with contemporary scientific thinking on sexology and psychiatry was characteristic of Eyles, who described herself as 'one who had been through the vales of affliction and come out smiling, smashed, ideals dragged in the mud, everything lost'.⁵¹ Uncompromisingly frank, she was not afraid to unsettle established feminine norms. Older women, in particular, were encouraged to assert their needs above those of others; Eyles had no truck with self-sacrifice. When, for instance, thirty year old 'Alice'—who had been left to 'scrape along' on £100 a year after devoting her life to nursing an invalid aunt—received a marriage proposal from a man who drank, Eyles did not equivocate: 'men drink to escape and marriage to him would be an unending burden to carry'. 'Learn a profession' and be 'self-reliant', she instructed, adding '[s]ome women rejoice in sacrifice, and find greater pleasure in it than in a life of comfort. And then, too, some women would rather have torture than loneliness. But don't say I didn't warn you.'⁵² Ever attuned to the heroism of everyday lives, Eyles remarked on the 'epic' quality of the letters she received, both at *Lansbury's Labour Weekly* and *Modern Woman*.⁵³ '[A]lmost all the people who write to me seem to be doing heroic things and doing them with every possible obstacle against them', she remarked in *Modern Woman*, before going on to reflect on the correlation between 'fiction and real life'.⁵⁴ Dramatising her own life, Eyles also dramatised the lives of her readers in order that they might see themselves in sharper focus; a form of emotional, social and political consciousness-raising that was grounded in her experience of 'direct action' socialism.

'How shall I get my living?' was the question around half her correspondents asked, Eyles later recalled in *Careers for Women* (1930). A central aim was to expand the parameters of respectable female employment; 'No longer now is every girl forced to live dependent on her parents or a husband, or become a teacher, dressmaker, nurse, shop-assistant, or domestic worker', she declared.⁵⁵ In her *Modern Woman* page she dealt with questions about office work, hairdressing, beauty culture, childcare, midwifery, librarianship, dressmaking, teaching, film, fashion illustration, writing and journalism, music (in orchestras, cinemas and cafes), handicrafts, small business, religious and voluntary work, as well as domestic service, cookery and related occupations.⁵⁶ An emphasis on professional occupations reflected the magazine's middle-class readership, but Eyles was careful to include low-cost alternatives. While other magazine columnists engaged in reimagining employment from a female perspective, none responded so directly to readers' circumstances as Eyles, nor were their responses grounded in her politics and activism.[57]

Numerous requests for information about how to earn a living from feminine endeavors suggest the plight of middle-class households facing financial constraints; '[h]undreds of girls' wanted to 'commercialize' their accomplishments, Eyles maintained.[58] 'Maidie', who had two musical children but could not support them through a long training, enquired which instrument was best from the 'money-earning point of view', while 'Kit' in Devon asked how to turn 'a good art training into money'.[59] The aspirations of the magazine's youthful readers were markedly similar to those of *Lansbury's Labour Weekly's* young socialists, with many dreaming of work in the glamorous fields of journalism, fashion and film.[60] Eyles' advice, however, differed. Whereas *Modern Woman* readers were encouraged to be ambitious and improve their prospects—Violet, for instance, was told that she was 'obviously superior' to basic office work and should attend evening classes, learn languages and shorthand—job security was foregrounded as a principle concern for the *Weekly's* readership.[61]

The 'vexed question of equal pay for equal work' was never discussed; it may have been considered inappropriate in a commercial magazine whose business was the culture of feminine self-improvement.[62] Believing passionately that matching a girl's training to her aptitude would go at least some way towards redressing inequalities in the workplace, Eyles urged *Modern Woman* readers to plan for a career and seek out job satisfaction, advice rarely given in *Lansbury's Labour Weekly*. Details about training, pay and conditions in the recently professionalised field of midwifery, in Froebel and Montessori methods of teaching, beauty culture and hairdressing were offered to help women get 'out of the rut' and avoid frustrated ambitions. Eyles herself had wanted to be a gardener or a doctor but was forced to train as a teacher, an occupation she loathed.[63] Those without funds were directed to apprenticeships or opportunities to train on the job.[64]

Proponents of Domestic Economics in America strove to elevate home industry into a 'household science', a theoretical and practical reassessment of women's activity that reached out into wider society.[65] The Labour Party's Women's Labour League saw home as potentially a base for the empowerment of women and put forward demands for material change in living conditions as well as in the routines of housework.[66] Eyles was similarly optimistic about the future for professionalised domestic work within the context of an active female citizenship and an expanded state that had the radical potential to redefine the public sphere as a 'domesticated' public life.[67] In 1929 in *Modern Woman*, she predicted that domestic service 'bids fair to be the sort of job a High School or Secondary School girl will like to take up'.[68] 'Mothering careers' occupied a separate category in *Careers for Women* (it consisted of 'hand work', 'creative work' and 'routine work'). Housewifery, which included domestic science, cookery and domestic service, was ascribed a 'very high place', the equivalent of such 'almost godlike tasks as medicine and teaching' for, as Eyles explained:

> There is no work of higher importance to the nation than the running of a home and all that it implies; for lives are still largely lived in our homes, and unless they are made comfortable by efficient housekeeping, and unless the health of the people is maintained by good and intelligent cooking, all the work of teaching, doctors, statesmen, artists, and poets is undone.[69]

Concerned to raise the status of domestic work, she was critical of the limited specialism that resulted from division of labour in factories, preferring to celebrate the 'quick-witted, nimble fingered' domestic servant who is 'full of resource'. Few letters from domestics appeared on Eyles' page, however, and features about domestic service in magazines were generally addressed to mistresses rather than maids, even in tuppenny weeklies.[70] This, no doubt, was due to the aspirational nature of popular magazines, which promoted the pleasures of marriage and a 'home of one's own' above more radical ideals of the professionalised well-trained, well-paid domestic worker and housewife citizen.

While some in the socialist movement imagined a future in which technology would abolish housework, for Eyles the knowledge and skills associated with domestic work and home crafts would make an important contribution to the brave new world of women's employment.[71] The 1920s and 1930s witnessed a craft revival with courses, specialist publications and information about how to make things for the home springing up everywhere, including in women's magazines.[72] Eyles envisaged a raft of small businesses developed from domestic skills in needlework, embroidery, cookery and other crafts, which could be run from home, providing independence and, in many cases, essential income. 'There is a great demand, nowadays, for hand-made things of all sorts, from underwear to lampshades and bags; hand-made wooden goods are also popular', she told *Modern Woman* readers in 1927.[73]

The question of how to make money at home reappeared a few months later when a 'crop of letters' requested advice. Make 'distinctive things that will sell at fairly low prices to middle-class people', such as children's clothes for mothers who 'don't like factory made ones yet cannot afford West-End prices', Eyles advised, revealing a keen sensitivity to the dilemma of holding cultural aspirations on restricted means.[74] The difficulty of monetising accomplishments that were regarded as leisure activities, or were central to what the historian Claire Langhamer terms the 'definitional ambiguity' of housework, is documented by Steven Gelber in his fascinating study of the American hobby crafts movement.[75] Gelber argues that, while handicraft hobbies 'passively condemn the work environment by offering contrast to meaningless jobs', they are inherently conservative because they reinforce a conventional work ethic by integrating 'the isolated home with the ideology of the workplace'.[76] Whereas Gelber's analysis only makes sense when, as he puts it, 'remunerative employment' exists elsewhere, Eyles' focus on the liberating potential of home crafts as a means for women to lay claim to and reimagine work speaks to a period when women experienced very real difficulties finding secure, well-paid work of an equal status with men.[77]

The spectre of the 'untrained woman' haunted Eyles' page.[78] She developed a chapter in *Careers for Women* from the numerous 'pathetic letters' from middle-class married or elderly women (most likely *Modern Woman* readers) 'begging' for information about how to make money from home work 'without the neighbors knowing'. 'The next generation will not suffer as they have done', she vowed.[79] Her response was to transform dependence into independence through action, advising women to 'strike out' and find work based on their caring and domestic skills, or identify 'some need of the community, and set to work to fill it'.[80] Suggestions ranged from running a boarding house to a business serving the needs of struggling working women; 'a fair number of young mothers of illegitimate children are trying pluckily to maintain their standard of living and bring up the child unaided', she remarked, drawing no doubt on her experience at *Lansbury's Labour Weekly*.[81] Young women who contravened established codes of respectability were also at risk. 'Elsie', who was forced to leave home after falling in love with her mother's lodger, asked how to secure a post as a 'companion'; try 'mother's help [. . .] earning a living and doing a great human service', Eyles replied.[82] Inspired by her Christian ethics and her knowledge of the networks of reciprocity that operated in working-class neighborhoods, Eyles imagined a system where an expanding female workforce would outsource domestic needs (food, mending, childcare) to well-paid professionals or small businesses run by untrained yet entrepreneurial women.[83]

'[A] lifetime of complete independence and of supporting my family alone' shaped Eyles' deeply held views on the controversial topic of the working wife.[84] Like Olive Schreiner and Vera Brittain, she was highly critical of parasitic middle- and upper-class women who married to be 'kept', but unlike them she identified the working-class wife who is 'never anything but a financial asset to her husband' as a model for rethinking 'modes of living'.[85] Rather than undermining marriage and motherhood, Eyles extended and revalued it, arguing that the working wife who contributed her share of the household expenses was the equal of, and a valid alternative to, the stay-at-home wife. Her advice, nevertheless, varied according to a woman's circumstances; for Eyles, motherhood remained perhaps the most important job. 'Eileen', who hated housework and wanted to return to dressmaking against her husband's wishes (he wanted to support her himself), was told to dismiss this 'old-fashioned idea [. . .]. You would be much happier with a job you can do well than one you do badly'.[86] In contrast, 'Mrs A', who worked, employed a maid, was 'bored stiff' and contemplating an affair, was sternly reproached for taking marriage 'on the surface'. 'Leave your work, stay at home and run your house and have a baby as soon as possible. Then you will see what marriage means', Eyles rebuked.[87] Her ideal was for women to be 'useful to the community, financially self-supporting, and spiritually at home in their working environment', inside and outside the home.[88]

'A Home or Business of Their Own': The Self-Reliant Woman

> It isn't that women are not good employees; they are, but their conditions of employment are often very hard, and offer little outlet for their immense creative ability. There is not wealth to be made in these small, personal undertakings, but there is a living and a Life, which to most thinking people matters most.[89]

For many single and some married women, finding a job became an accepted part of growing up and becoming a woman in these years.[90] Selina Todd reports that 'self-sufficiency gained through secure employment' was a central theme in her interviews with working-class women, while all but a few of the women readers I contacted had worked, at least before marriage; the working girl heroines of fiction were recalled with particular affection.[91] Oral testimonies show that paid work, the conviviality and little extra spending money it implied, was central to a shared imaginary of modern womanhood.[92] Magazines, with their experimental career columns, features about successful women and articles exploring office girl gripes, offered readers a space to reflect critique and dream about what the world of work might be and might mean.

Eyles' column, which was shaped by her personal experience, feminist, political and religious convictions, as well as her belief that revolution starts in the home, made an important contribution to the discourse of modern work identities, including that of the housewife and mother. Just as George Lansbury adopted targeting strategies from the capitalist press to extend the reach of socialism, Eyles adapted a working-class ethos of communality and socialist strategies of direct action to the mainstream women's press to raise consciousness and increase agency.

This revolution of domestic and private life, nevertheless, was not without its critics. While favourably reviewing *The Woman in the Little House* in 1922, Stella Browne, the forthright advocate of birth control, remained unconvinced by Eyles' belief that a socialist state would emerge without extensive structural change.[93] More recently, Maroula Joannou has argued that Eyles' fiction represents an 'escape from, rather than an assault on, patriarchal values'.[94] However, Browne referred to a polemical piece and Joannou to the novels; neither writer considers the rich network of connections between Eyles' journalism, her fiction and non-fiction writing. It is when we attend to this, to how certain themes develop and emerge through and across genres, that the truly pioneering and radical nature of her work begins to emerge.

Sensitive to different readerships and their constituencies, Eyles was also alert to problems, aspirations and experiences that might be shared across genres and across classes, particularly when the audience was women.

CONCLUSION

Whether aimed at socialists, working wives, middle-class professional women, housewives, a broad popular readership (*Margaret Protests* was a best seller), or any combination of these, Eyles' writing shares a socially concerned ethos expressed through a democratic cross-fertilisation of difficulties, hopes and dreams. The problem page, which encouraged readers to voice their stories, connected and informed the other writing in a network of inter-textual storytelling and mutual knowledge exchange. Themes such as 'improved conditions for workers' weave in and out of texts, and are honed, deepened and given impact through personal testimony.[95] The urgent need for support services for working mothers was discussed in *Lansbury's Labour Weekly* in 1925, the Labour publication *Women's Problems of To-day* (1926) and informed Eyles' advocacy of domestic and caring careers in *Modern Woman* (1929).[96] These ideas were drawn together in *Careers for Women* (1930), where Eyles visualised a 'more rational communal life' with communal kitchens and nurseries staffed by well-trained, well-paid professionals: an interconnected system in which women of all ages, abilities and social classes could work together according to their interests and abilities, whether those be running a 'small-holding', 'shop-keeping', 'professional mothering' or 'various art and craft works'.[97]

Eyles understood the struggles, contradictions and frustrations of self-reliant womanhood and encouraged her readers to withstand them. When 'Joyce', a Sydenham schoolmistress who longed to marry, complained that her independent status discouraged men, Eyles reproved, 'It is only convention that men don't like self-reliant women.'[98] Only a year before in *Good Housekeeping,* however, she had revealed how becoming a divorcee had led her to question deeply held assumptions about independence, blaming her 'pride' at being self-reliant for the breakdown of her marriage.[99] A decade later she candidly confessed the strain incurred by trying to be a mother, wife, businesswoman (she ran a small poultry farm), writer and political activist. Struggling to be so many things, she feared that she succeeded at none, resulting in a 'feeling of inadequacy' that made her ill for a time.[100] This was written at the end of the 1930s when, married to D. L. Murray (editor of the *Times Literary Supplement*) and penning an agony column for the high-selling *Woman's Own,* Eyles had re-entered the middle-class mainstream, both in her professional and private life. She remained politically informed and empathetic, however, and her ability to speak frankly and bravely about the complex social, economic, emotional and psychological effects of being a woman was perhaps her greatest achievement as an agony aunt. Eyles took the problem page seriously. She understood how it could disseminate and validate female experience, taking it into the mainstream while encouraging women to demand more; not only a 'living', that is, but also a 'life' that was rewarding *and* fulfilling.

NOTES

1 Leonora Eyles, 'From one woman to another,' *Modern Woman*, October 1925, 72.
2 Leonora Eyles, *Careers for Women* (London: Elkin Mathews & Marrot, 1930), 11.
3 Maroula Joannou, *'Ladies, Please Don't Smash These Windows'*: *Women's Writing, Feminist Consciousness and Social Change 1918–38* (Oxford: Berg, 1995), 54–76. Also see Juliet Gardiner, *The Thirties: An Intimate History* (London: Harper Press: 2010), 55, and Sheila Rowbotham, *Dreamers of a New Day: Women Who Invented the Twentieth Century* (London: Verso, 2010), 54, 77–9, 100, 119, 226. Over twenty titles are listed under Eyles' name in the British Library catalogue.
4 Joannou, *Ladies*, 64. This chapter is developed from research undertaken for my doctoral thesis: Fiona Hackney, ' "They opened up a whole new world": Feminine modernity and the feminine imagination in women's magazines, 1919–1939' (PhD diss., Goldsmith's College University of London, 2013), which forms the basis of the monograph *Women's Magazines and the Feminine Imagination: Opening Up a New World for Women in Interwar Britain* (London: I. B. Tauris, in press).
5 Leonora Eyles, *The Ram Escapes* (London: Nevill, 1953).
6 Benedict Anderson, *Imagined Communities: Reflections on the Origin and Spread of Nationalism* (London: Verso, 1983).
7 George Lansbury, 'Our Next Issue,' *Lansbury's Labour Weekly*, 13 June 1925, 7. Both titles were published by George Newnes. From 1932 Newnes published the popular weekly, *Woman's Own*, with Eyles as correspondence page editor and agony aunt.
8 Gerry Holloway, *Women and Work in Britain Since 1840* (London: Routledge, 2005).
9 The 1921 census shows 5,036,727 working women out of a total female population of 14,959,282 and 5,606,143 women workers in 1931 out of a total female population of 16, 410,894. Jane Lewis, *Women in England, 1870–1950: Sexual Division and Social Change* (London: Harvester Wheatsheaf, 1984), 146–9.
10 Sally Alexander, *Becoming a Woman, And Other Essays in 19th and 20th Century Feminist History* (London: Virago, 1994), 206.
11 Highest participation (79 per cent) was amongst eighteen to twenty-year-olds, the rate falling dramatically after the age of twenty-four. Miriam Glucksmann, *Women Assemble: Women Workers and the New Industries in Inter-War Britain* (London: Routledge, 1990), 41. Clerical jobs for women increased during and after the First World War, and by 1931 women accounted for 42 per cent of the clerical workforce. Selina Todd, 'Poverty and aspiration: Young women's entry to employment in inter-war England,' *Twentieth Century British History* 15 (2004): 122.
12 Holloway, *Women and Work*, 150. If older, these single women were unlikely to marry and therefore more likely to work until retirement. Lewis, *Women in England*, 149; Katherine Holden, *The Shadow of Marriage: Single Women in England 1914–60* (Manchester: Manchester University Press, 2007).

13 The subtitle may refer to the prominent modernist architect Le Corbusier's journal, *L'Esprit Nouveau*, which was published in Paris at this time. Audited circulation figures for *Modern Woman* were 95,000 a month in 1938; actual readership is likely to have been three times this figure. Cynthia White, *Women's Magazines 1693–1968* (London: Michael Joseph, 1970), Appendix V.
14 *Modern Woman*, June 1925, 7.
15 For more on Victoria Drummond, see Virginia Nicholson, *Singled Out: How Two Million Women Survived Without Men After the First World War* (London: Penguin, 2007), 107–9, 242, 258.
16 E. M. B., 'The sea as a career for women,' *Modern Woman*, August 1927, 71; 'This wonderful world: the women who succeed: Advertising executive Florence Sangster,' *Modern Woman*, September 1929, 40. The 1919 Sex Disqualification (Removal) Act removed barriers to women's entry into the professions. The total number of women registered as professionals, however, only rose from 350,000 in 1921 to 390,000 in 1931. Holloway, *Women and Work*, 149.
17 White, *Women's Magazines*, 96. Other consumer titles include: *Good Housekeeping* (1922), *Woman and Home* (1926), *Wife and Home* (1929), *Mother* (1936), *Woman's Journal* (1927).
18 Author's interview with Mary Dilnot, who worked as a 'sub' at *Woman's Weekly* in the 1930s and later became editor. 2 February, 1995.
19 Leonora Eyles, *The Woman in the Little House* (London: Grant Richards, 1922), 101–2. Annie Britain, the symbolic heroine, was intended to represent an ordinary English working-class woman, wife and mother.
20 Jennifer Scanlon, *Inarticulate Longings: The Ladies' Home Journal, Gender, and the Promises of Consumer Culture* (London: Routledge, 1995), 183–5.
21 Ethel M. Wood, 'Advertising as a career for women,' *Modern Advertising*, Vol. 1 (London: New Era Publishing, 1925), 180.
22 Eyles ruefully contrasted advertising with her experience of journalism, where women, no matter how highly qualified, were generally relegated to 'women's page stuff'; even then male editors complained that they could not find women with 'enough brains and education' to supply the copy required. Eyles, *Careers*, 19.
23 Cicely Hamilton, *Marriage as a Trade* (London: The Women's Press, 1909), 129.
24 Robin Kent, *Aunt Agony Advises: Problem Pages Through the Ages* (London: W.H. Allen, 1979).
25 John Shepherd, *George Lansbury: At the Heart of Old Labour* (Oxford: Oxford University Press: 2004).
26 Leonora Eyles, 'The woman's part,' *Lansbury's Labour Weekly*, 28 February 1925, 4.
27 George Lansbury, 'Our next issue,' *Lansbury's Labour Weekly*, 13 June 1925, 7.
28 Advertisements, which occasionally ran on the problem page, included those for publications advising on birth control, such as Marie Stopes' 'A letter to working mothers' and Margaret Sanger's 'Family limitation,' *Lansbury's Labour Weekly*, 7 November 1925, 15. Eyles and Stopes corresponded between 1926 and 1927; while Eyles could not deal with birth control in her column because it caused trouble in the Labour Party, she offered readers information privately. Joannou, *Ladies*, 66–7, and *Lansbury's Labour Weekly*, 5 September 1925, 2.
29 Leonora Eyles, 'Can you write a short story?,' *Lansbury's Labour Weekly*, 5 December 1925, 2.
30 I read every column during the first year of publication (twenty-five issues). Themes covered are quite diverse and difficult to classify. Aside from

work-related problems and unemployment, topics that appeared repeatedly include: illegitimate children, debt, pension problems, marital problems, loneliness, health (from morning sickness to consumption), homelessness, finance (bogus insurance), accidents, drink, crime, sex outside marriage and dress etiquette, as well as love problems, blushing and stammering.

31 Martha, 'Problems,' *Lansbury's Labour Weekly*, 3 October 1925, 2.
32 Martha, 'Problems,' 20 June 1925, 2.
33 For instance: Martha, 'Problems,' 5 September 1925, 2; 5 December 1925, 15.
34 Martha, 'Problems,' 5 September 1925, 2.
35 Martha, 'Problems', 5 September 1925, 2.
36 Martha, Problems', 5 September 1925, 2.
37 Martha, 'Problems,' 29 August 1925, 2.
38 Martha, 'Problems,' 5 December 1925, 15.
39 See for instance, Martha, 'Problems,' 15 August 1925, 2.
40 Martha, 'Problems,' 31 October 1925, 2.
41 Martha, 'Problems,' 20 June 1925, 2.
42 *Modern Woman's* monthly sales were about half those for *Good Housekeeping*; it targeted middling households with incomes of £500 p.a. White, *Women's Magazines*, 95 and Appendix V. During my research with readers, I only came across one woman who read the magazine regularly, Marjorie Denut, who was a teacher.
43 Caitriona Beaumont, *Housewives and Citizens: Domesticity and the Women's Movement in England, 1928–1964* (Manchester: Manchester University Press, 2013).
44 Judy Giles, *Women, Identity and Private Life in Britain, 1900–50* (London: Macmillan Press, 2004), 123; *Modern Woman,* June 1925, 7.
45 For a discussion of counter-public sphere and print culture, see Mark S. Morrison, *The Public Face of Modernism: Little Magazines, Audiences, and Reception 1905–1920* (Madison: University of Wisconsin Press, 2001); Ann Ardis and Patrick Collier, eds., *Transatlantic Print Culture, 1880–1940: Emerging Media, Emerging Modernisms* (Basingstoke: Palgrave Macmillan, 2008).
46 Eyles, *The Little House*, 132–3.
47 I looked at twenty-one issues of the problem page from 1925–1929. Out of a total of 107 letters, thirty-five dealt with employment; forty-one with personal issues and relationships; twelve with finance and the home; eleven with single and married women's or couples' problems; eight discussed sexual relationships and birth control.
48 Sheila Rowbotham, *Dreamers*, 79.
49 For a discussion of methodology and details about the readers and journalists interviewed, see Hackney, 'They opened up a whole new world'.
50 Leonora Eyles, 'From one woman to another,' *Modern Woman*, June 1925, 72.
51 Eyles, 'From one woman'.
52 Eyles, 'From one woman,' September 1925, 72.
53 Martha, 'Problems,' 20 June 1925, 2.
54 Leonora Eyles, 'From one woman,' October 1925, 72.
55 Eyles, *Careers*, 9. Careers discussed include: the medical profession, engineering, veterinary surgery, welfare and social service, dairy farming, aviation, photography, education, crafts and woodwork, gardening, secretarial and office work, shop assistant, dress design and fashion drawing, beauty culture, domestic work and homemaking. The emphasis on forging a path in

the professions and business was echoed in Julia Cairns, ed., *Careers for Girls* (London: Hutchinson, undated but in the 1930s), which included chapters on medicine by Winifred C. Cullis, advertising by Ethel M. Wood, business and commerce by Lady Rhondda, as well as accountancy, dentistry, journalism, engineering, architecture and the bar, alongside a chapter on marriage and home-making by Lady Asquith.
56 Eyles, 'From one woman,' October 1925, 72; November 1925, 68; December 1925, 76; March 1927, 84; July 1927, 88; August 1927, 80; September 1927, 88; November 1927, 180; December 1927, 10; January 1929, 96; February 1929, 92; March 1929, 96; April 1929, 100; May 1929, 96; June 1929, 100; July 1929, 96; August 1929, 96; October 1929, 61.
57 For instance, the journalist Elidor Briggs covered teaching, nursing, 'outdoor careers' and 'careers of service' in her career column in *Modern Woman* in the 1930s. She identified radiography, journalism, commercial traveller, window dresser, clerical and secretarial work and advertising as promising careers, arguing that the latter was 'one of the most interesting and suitable kinds of work for women'. *Modern Woman*, August 1932, 30.
58 Eyles, 'From one woman,' November 1925, 68.
59 Eyles, 'From one woman,' August 1927, 80; February 1929, 92.
60 For instance, Eyles, 'From one woman,' April 1929, 100; August 1925, 72.
61 Eyles, 'From one woman,' June 1929, 100.
62 She did, however, discuss the question of equal pay in her book. Eyles, *Careers*, 22.
63 Eyles, 'From one woman,' October 1925, 72. Eyles, *The Ram*, 91
64 Eyles, 'From one woman,' July 1927, 88; November 1925, 68; March 1929, 96.
65 Charlotte Perkins Gilman and Ellen Swallow Richards were examples of such proponents. Rowbotham, *Dreamers*, 125.
66 Rowbotham, *Dreamers*, 130.
67 Lucy Delap, *The Feminist Avant-Garde: Transatlantic Encounters of the Early Twentieth Century* (Cambridge: Cambridge University Press, 2007), 145–53.
68 Eyles, 'From one woman,' May 1929, 96.
69 Eyles, *Careers*, 36.
70 'Engaging a domestic worker,' *Modern Woman*, December 1926, 68; 'Teach your maid,' *Home Chat*, 11 August 1934, 271.
71 Rowbotham, *Dreamers*, 138.
72 Fiona Hackney, 'Use your hands for happiness: Home craft and make-do-and-mend in British women's magazines in the1920s and 1930s,' *Journal of Design History* 19 (2006): 24–38; Pat Kirkham, 'Women and the inter-war handicrafts revival,' in *A View from The Interior, Women and Design*, ed. Judy Attfield and Pat Kirkham (London: The Women's Press, 1989), 174–83.
73 Eyles 'From one woman,' September 1927, 88.
74 Eyles, 'From one woman,' December 1927, 100; Eyles, *Careers*, 21.
75 Claire Langhamer, *Women's Leisure in England 1920–60* (Manchester: Manchester University Press, 2000), 36.
76 Steven Gelber, *Hobbies: Leisure and the Culture of Work* (New York: Columbia University Press, 1999), 19–20.
77 Gelber, *Hobbies*, 3. Jane Lewis, ed., *Labour and Love: Women's Experience of Home and Family, 1850–1940* (Oxford: Blackwell, 1986). Current interest in an alternative crafts economy has resulted in a revival of these debates today. See Fiona Hackney, 'Quiet activism and the new amateur: The power of home and hobby crafts,' *Design and Culture* 5 (2013): 169–94.

78 The term also appeared in *Woman's Weekly*'s career column in 1919, where it was described as a 'terrible mishap' and referred to those who, without benefit of skills or experience, had to support themselves and often dependents: largely war widows at this time. 'Chats,' *Woman's Weekly*, 18 October 1919, 316.
79 Eyles, *Careers*, 5–6, 50–65.
80 Eyles, *Careers*, 61, 65. In this she built on the ideals of the arts and crafts movement, but extended these into the home and beyond the realm of trained professionals. Jude Burkhauser, ed., *Glasgow Girls: Women in Art and Design 1880–1920* (Edinburgh: Canongate, 1990).
81 Eyles, *Careers*, 64.
82 Eyles, 'From one woman,' August 1925, 64.
83 She was not alone in this, as feminists such as Olive Schreiner also 'reworked work'. See Rowbotham, *Dreamers*, 193–209.
84 Eyles, *Careers*, 22.
85 Vera Brittain, *Women's Work in Modern England* (London: Noel Douglas, 1928); Olive Schreiner, *Women and Labour* (London: T. Fisher Unwin, 1911). Eyles went so far as to blame the 'vexed question of equal pay for equal work' on parasitic wives who 'blackleg' those, such as herself, who 'refuse to be kept'. Eyles, *Careers*, 22–3.
86 Eyles, 'From one woman,' July 1927, 88.
87 Eyles, 'From one woman,' June 1929, 100.
88 Eyles, *Careers*, 32.
89 Eyles, *Careers*, 8–9.
90 Alexander, *Becoming*, 207.
91 Todd, 'Poverty and aspiration,' 140; Hackney, 'They opened up a whole new world,' 286.
92 Penny Tinkler, 'Women and popular literature' in *Women's History: Britain, 1850–1950*, ed. June Purvis (London: UCL Press, 1995b), 132–56; Langhamer, *Women's Leisure*.
93 Lesley A. Hall, *The Life and Times of Stella Browne: Feminist and Free Spirit* (London: I. B. Tauris, 2011), 102.
94 Joannou, *Ladies*, 76.
95 Her novel *Hidden Lives* (London: Heinemann, 1922) follows the desperate struggle of the young doctor, Helen Clevion, to help women in the Staffordshire potteries establish a community centre and nursery. Poisonous working conditions in the potteries was the subject of a series of investigative pieces she wrote for *Lansbury's Labour Weekly* in 1925: 'Death in the teacup,' 19 September 1925, 7; 'Chained to the slums,' 26 September 1925, 13.
96 Eyles, 'The woman's part: Amusements,' *Lansbury's Labour Weekly*, 28 March 1925, 14; Leonora Eyles, *Women's Problems of To-day* (London: The Labour Publishing Co., 1926); Eyles, 'From one woman,' May 1929, 96; March 1929, 96.
97 Eyles, *Careers*, 8, 27.
98 Eyles, 'From one woman,' January 1929, 96.
99 Leonora Eyles, 'The unattached woman,' *Good Housekeeping*, 1928, in *Things My Mother Should Have Told Me: The Best of Good Housekeeping 1922–1940*, ed. Brian Briathwaite and Noëlle Walsh (London: Ebury Press, 1991), 74–5.
100 Leonora Eyles, 'Have you failed?,' *Good Housekeeping*, 1930s, in *Things My Mother*, 164–5.

8 'Corresponding with Men'
Exploring the Significance of Constance Maynard's Magazine Writing, 1913–1920

Gretchen Galbraith

For Constance Maynard (1849–1935), founding Mistress of Westfield College (later incorporated into the University of London), the process of writing for magazines after retirement enabled her to engage publicly with major debates of the day and, in her view, achieve new social and mental freedom. This chapter focuses on one article, 'Love which is not the fulfilling of the law', which appeared in *The Hibbert Journal* in 1917. *The Hibbert*, published in London and Boston from 1902 to 1968, was one of several well-regarded British periodicals of the era devoted to intellectual discussions of philosophy and religion. Publication in *The Hibbert* gave Maynard a broader audience and positioned her as a peer of its predominantly male contributors. Her topic, the ethics of warfare, represented her effort to integrate her intellectual and spiritual beliefs while engaging a wider world, both of which had been unavailable to her as Westfield's Mistress. Maynard saw her efforts at publication as contributions to key discussions of the day; opportunities to promote causes and ideas dear to her as well as a series of conversations that widened her circle of friends and intellectual peers, her writing enabled her to set aside past restrictions that had, in her view, limited her (mental) freedom. She believed that in writing for these new audiences she had 'become one of the thinkers of the world.'[1]

Raised in an evangelical Anglican family that derived its wealth from South African investments, Maynard made a series of choices that set her apart from her sisters and from most of her peers, beginning with attendance at Girton, one of England's first residential colleges for women and later part of the University of Cambridge.[2] Maynard intended Westfield, the women's college she created in 1882, to be a religiously based alternative to her experience as a member of that first generation of women students at Girton.[3] Later, membership of this close-knit community of educated professional women became a crucial aspect of Maynard's daily and emotional life.[4] At the same time, she chafed at the circumscribed familial and social roles available to professional women. When she adopted six-year-old Effie, while unmarried and serving as Westfield's Mistress, she deliberately rejected the divide between profession and motherhood taken for granted in her generation and class while acknowledging that that same profession had precluded (heterosexual) marriage.[5] Yet, while refusing these divisions, she never satisfactorily resolved for herself the tensions created by her efforts to integrate work and family or to unite scholarship 'with living faith'.[6]

Maynard was what Joan Hind Stewart has called a 'cusp' figure: her life straddled two centuries and she seized upon but could not fully engage with new possibilities for women in higher education; hence she was not quite in step with her younger or more secular peers, nor fully able to speak the language of the next generation.[7] In 1916, she wrote of the importance of speaking the 'language of one's age' and played with the idea that she was divided in two—her self and her race experience.[8] At least one publisher, however, frankly suggested that her tone was 'too "instructive" to meet the taste of the day [. . .]'.[9] Maria Tamboukou also speaks to the transitional nature of this generation of educated professional women's lives: they lived with a reality still constructed by convention and yet dreamed of and experienced new freedoms that 'education, economic independence and "a room of their own" could offer them'. Tamboukou argues that the techniques women used 'to map their existence would be in a form of continuous resistance' even when they could not see clearly where they were going.[10] Maynard's efforts at writing for publication became a means of rebellion against the limitations of familial and professional obligation for which she lacked a map.

Maynard's sex-segregated upbringing and professional duties had imposed limits on her public actions.[11] Like her fellow education pioneers, she had steered away from controversies that would harm her institution and the cause of women's education. Yet in private, her desires, beliefs and interests had extended beyond the limits imposed by professional obligations. In 1888, while struggling over whether to adopt Effie, she wrote,

> When I accepted the College, I *knew* I was giving up marriage; *that* was settled, + I looked in the face, but I did *not* know I was forever giving up this. The day I was elected Mistress of Westfield, I cried the whole morning [. . .] I seemed flooded by a sense of sorrow utterly beyond control as I heard the harsh grating of the convent gate closing behind me.

She consoled herself that 'Duty, interest, love, all lie there. Make the most of them, count each grain, for it is your whole stock.'[12] She had also experienced disappointment in her efforts to maintain a spiritually centered social life at Westfield, and her beloved Divinity Program was short-lived largely because Westfield's board of directors and its younger staff did not share Maynard's enthusiasm.[13] By the time of her retirement in 1913, she was exhausted by what had come to feel like a losing battle to maintain spirituality at Westfield's heart. She had also dissolved her adoption, though not the relationship, having concluded under pressure from colleagues and family that Effie was morally and spiritually unsuited to be her daughter.

RETIREMENT AT SUNDIAL: 'I WILL BE MYSELF'

Early in retirement, settled into her newly purchased Sundial Cottage, Maynard looked back on those years at Westfield with mixed feelings: when 'the whole Family', including her closest colleagues, had arrived, 'It was taken out of my hands, criticized and changed. It was all right, + a very good thing, for in my hands it would not have been a College at all; perhaps a Protestant sort of Convent, like Port Royal, but not a College.' Despite her conclusion that it was 'a very good thing', she viewed the price paid as 'the suppression of myself.' Not once since the start of the second year, thirty years before, had she been herself, and the 'distinctive things' she had to give, affection, the 'union of Faith and Reason', were wasted. But at her retirement cottage, she wrote, 'I will be myself all though [sic], a disciplined wiser self [. . .].'[14] A year later, as World War I began, she was determined to get some war poems published. After an initial rejection, she 'rebelled' and sent them off to another publisher. 'Never have I been permitted to go outside Westfield, + attain success, never [. . .].' When the poems were accepted, she determined to publish them anonymously 'because I dread Westfield criticism.'[15]

These poems were not Maynard's first venture into writing for publication. In the years just before and during her retirement, Maynard wrote for a public audience. She published a number of books and wrote essays and tracts for various religious societies.[16] She also had articles accepted in *Contemporary Review*, *Nineteenth Century* and *The Hibbert*, all three of which had reputations for serious intellectual discussion and a liberal outlook. In all of her writing for publication, Maynard seems to have avoided any connection to the 'feminised space' of the women's popular periodicals that proliferated in her lifetime, most likely preferring the intellectual focus, formality and seriousness of the *The Hibbert* and *Contemporary Review* to the informal chattiness of women's magazines.[17]

However, as the comments from her journal suggest, there was a marked difference between her writings before and after retirement. The former, limited in scope and bearing titles such as *Between College Terms* and 'A Farming Holiday', focused on nature study, fruitfully spent holidays, curricula appropriate for women's colleges and educationally focused religious and philosophical essays.[18] In contrast, in retirement she challenged pacifist spiritual opposition to warfare, asserted women's crucial role as the 'makers, teachers, and guardians of the next generation' and attempted to intervene in debates over evolution and humanism.[19] Writing for magazines at Sundial, feeling freed from past restrictions, Maynard could re-work issues that had preoccupied her throughout adulthood and selectively engage with a wider world than had ever before been available to her. Yet she initially saw her retirement as a continuation of her professional life's restricted focus on the wellbeing of Westfield and its students.

On the first page of the diary devoted to recording life at Sundial, Maynard's reflection on how fully work had consumed her for over twenty-five years lacks the regretful tone of other entries: 'The break with Westfield, my one thought, my one duty, my interest, my joy, is of a difficulty all but incredible + all life appears blank + empty, as though the breaking of the tie would break my heart too.' She goes on, 'Yet I come of a long-lived race' and so must prepare for at least another fifteen years. She planned to fill it with work on behalf of 'Old Students. It is rather like a family.' Current students, like children in the nursery, could be 'delegated to other hands,' but those taking their places in the world 'are like the half-grown lads + girls with whom the Mother, + no one else, can deal.'[20] Echoing earlier moments in which she had likened her professional role to motherhood,[21] a theme she would pick up again in 'We Women' (1919), she calculated that by the time she retired 550 or 660 'Old Students' would be 'out + at work in the world [. . .]. This surely is responsibility enough for any one.'[22]

'SOMETHING REAL TO SAY': SEEKING A WIDER AUDIENCE

Perhaps, though, this goal was not enough. Even in 1909, as she planned for retirement, she was already writing in hope of publication. During a moment when not only had her offer on a parcel of land been refused, but four publishers had turned down a manuscript, she wrote, '[t]hese blows are rather staggering, + seem to give me a check in life [. . .]'.[23] By 1915, two years into retirement, she was more optimistically engaged in several writing projects that represented the expanding scope of her ambition and sense of purpose: she would continue to devote energy to her 'Old Students' through visits and a circular letter, but she would seek a wider audience too.

Through 1915 and 1916, the war's impact grew around her in the form of 'swarms of khaki' at Waterloo station, German Zeppelins in the skies above her village and a young relative's visit just before heading to the front.[24] Now preoccupied with the ethical and religious implications of 'the rights of the war', Maynard developed her thinking on the subject by preparing lectures and sending off manuscripts in multiple directions.[25] She appears to have been motivated to intervene in the growing debate about how best members of the Religious Society of Friends (Quakers) could live out their pacifist ideals.[26] Her excitement increased as she found time to write and to place early drafts of her argument for publication. Having seen an old student off, one of many visitors to Sundial through the years, she had 'four beautiful, windless, golden autumn days alone, + was seized with a feverish anxiety to get my thoughts on non-resistance still more clear [. . .]. I felt as though I were lifting an almost crushing weight, but it was got through at last.' Hoping to give a lecture on the subject in her community and 'still more to get an article into some really good review', she sent it to the *Nineteenth Century*, figuring that there was 'hardly one chance in 100' that it would be accepted.[27]

Two months later, she was working steadily and with purpose: '[t]he early morning writing goes on energetically, + all now has to do with the War of course. I wonder if it is any use. I feel as though I had something real to say.'[28] She had success publishing in 'a good + obscure little Paper' for teachers and in 'a solid work of the Society of Friends'. However, her efforts to reach a wider audience were frustrated: she had submitted a 'longer + more complex' version to *Nineteenth Century* but '[t]hey *don't* print it, + *won't* return it, + I have no second copy.' Meanwhile, she sent another article 'at once better written + more daring + more religious' to the editor of the *Oxford Papers for War Time*. '[H]e replied very kindly' but had just closed the series, '[S]o now it has gone to the *Hibbert Journal*, there is as yet no reply.'[29] For Maynard, this process was both frustrating because of delays, misunderstandings and her ambition to reach a broader audience and yet also exhilarating because she had 'something real to say'.[30]

She developed a strategy of working on multiple projects simultaneously—often ten at a time—and of developing an argument across various media, sometimes presenting talks as a way to refine her writing, sometimes trying to publish an essay as prelude to a lecture series. Practicing a speech before local League of Honour people she had to tea, '7 each time,' she noted 'how keenly they enjoyed having a few leading statistics [. . .] drummed into them'.[31] For a paper on women during the war, 'Order Within + Defense Without', she 'took more trouble over this than on any,' wading through Government Blue-book statistics 'to find out which classes of crime were preventable by women and early training'. 'It has in it a great many valuable things, I really think, + yet when yesterday I read it aloud' to neighbours, 'I could feel it aimed at too much, was crowded + jostled with thoughts,' having 'in an exaggerated degree the faults my writings always shew [sic]. It must be chopped into fragments' and sent off. 'It is disappointing, but I will not give up.'[32] When she was not doing a series of speaking engagements or travelling, she devoted mornings to writing and reading (on average, 100 books a year) and afternoons to visits or leading 'Ladies Classes' and Mothers' Meetings.[33]

These passages about how she developed and disseminated her arguments also illustrate how, for Maynard, publication and speech-giving served to connect her to organisations and individuals now that she had left behind Westfield's institutional ties and structures. While finishing up several war-related essays in late 1915, she was planning other projects: 'I want, ambitiously enough, to help the whole Evangelical Church by writing an article on "Christian Unity"', which she hoped would have the 'practical outcome' of reviving two Evangelical organisations. 'All this is in view of a long series of visits I am arranging [. . .] to speak wherever I can on these subjects, but I should like an article or two written, printed, + re-printed, before I start. The prospect is immense [. . .].'[34]

A month later she had cut the article down for one organisation, '+ they were pleased. Going to print it for immediate use.' The deleted portion, 'which is the more interesting part, I shall read to Sir W. Mackworth Young', a new correspondent who had retired from the Indian Civil Service: 'he will advise me whether it will serve as an explanatory letter'.[35] She then noted, perhaps wistfully, 'It is odd, but having lived the whole of my life among women, I now take pleasure in corresponding with men', and followed with a list of her male correspondents, their varying responses to her writing, reflections on their characters and the nature of these friendships. One Quaker correspondent whose advice she had sought on a paper appealing to Friends to take up Red Cross and minesweeping work she 'already counted a friend, drawing nearer'. When he responded critically to her draft article on pacifism, she concluded that he 'entirely misunderstands it' but sympathetically recorded his frustration at the 'deplorable' utterances of 'our leaders in the public papers'.[36] In private she described the war as 'now wildly exciting, as inch by inch on the detailed map we make headway' and deplored the 'most miserable Pacifism' in an essay she had read.[37] That sense of carrying on a conversation with friends she admired, but could not entirely agree with, carried over into her published writing.

WRITING, 'THE REAL BUSINESS OF LIFE'

In 'Love which is not the fulfilling of the law', the article finally published in *The Hibbert* in 1917, Maynard addressed the question whether pacifism was the correct moral response to warfare or whether instead the 'national decision' to enter war stands Christianity's 'stringent test'.[38] *The Hibbert: A Quarterly Review of Religion, Theology and Philosophy* seems to have been a good fit for Maynard, as its authors, many of them clergy or university faculty, wrote about the relationship between science and faith and social and educational reform. *The Hibbert's* first editors, Lawrence Pearsall Jacks and G. Dawes Hicks, were a professor of philosophy and theology at Oxford and a professor of British philosophy at University College, London, respectively. Among the few other women contributors to this volume of *The Hibbert* were the reformers Helen Bosanquet and the colourful Duchess of Warwick. Male contributors included modern historian John Arthur Ransome Marriott, philosopher John Beattie Crozier and physicist Sir Oliver Lodge. The inclusion of Maynard's article in the same volume as these better known and respected intellectual voices was deeply significant to her.

Establishing her authority to speak by giving evidence from science, society and scripture, Maynard drew first upon science to challenge the pacifist premise that all life must be valued equally: 'Turn for a moment to biology and read half a page about parasites, and judge if their life is a good thing.' In the case of the sunfish, he carries so many uninvited passengers—barnacles, isopods and trematodes—that 'he seems to be crammed with foreign living matter more than with his own organs [. . .]. If all lives are of equal value, the fish decidedly ought to be eaten through and through by his half-million guests, and only patiently live as long as he can that he may unselfishly support them.' Similarly, 'brave, learned, gentle Germany, is being devoured, mind, heart, and soul, by enemies that have arisen from within [. . .]'. She asks, 'are we to be "one" with the military despotism [. . .], the most cruel tyranny, the most unbridled lust? Are we to take the part of the malignant arm of Germany against the main body of her good and home loving people?'[39]

Passing from the natural to the social realm, Maynard suggests that relationships founded on love alone 'account for scores of divorces, hundreds of broken hearts, and thousands of disappointed lives,' hinting darkly that the suicides of young girls in the Thames were due to their mistaken belief in 'Love' as 'the supreme authority of life'. She asks, is this mistake to be 'magnified from the individual to the nation, and so bring ruin, not on the single home, but on the whole world'?[40] From this dramatic warning, she leads readers to biblical evidence that while Christians must embrace forgiveness on an individual level, that rule cannot apply to other aspects of life. Outside religion, 'there is a wider ring where "Moral Law" is recognized as right and good'. In this wider ring of 'all but universal agreement [called] The State, or the Collective Conscience', we confront the necessity of using force to create order: 'Behind the order must lie the ultimate power to punish disobedience, or the order is fragile and fictitious. That which would be wrong in the region of personal religion becomes right and necessary in the region of communal ethics.' Similarly, forgiveness appropriate for the individual is a luxury that a nation can ill afford and would itself be 'a crime, a transgression of the highest right'.[41]

Maynard cites scriptural authority for her argument about the proper use of force: 'not in parable or metaphor but in direct and open terms, our Lord shows that the exertion of physical force is right in defence of the State, and wrong in defence of the Church'.[42] She exhorts readers to recognise Britain's duty as 'a kingdom that above all others stands for the three great foundation-stones of the State, Justice, Liberty, and Beneficence. In defence of such a kingdom the opposition of arms to the very death is to be expected; is necessary, is right, is to be approved and honoured.'[43] Having differentiated individual religious obligations from communal ethics, Maynard circles back to connect individual sin with national action: '[a]re we as a nation worthy to be the champions of this spotless cause? The godless vanity of many of the rich, the besotting drink of many of the poor, seem to shout aloud, No, no, not worthy.' Invoking the authority of direct experience, she quotes a letter to *The Times* by an officer at the Eastern Front: '"the real war is against social evils, and the real battleground in the hearts of men. Not until there is some marked improvement in the atmosphere at home dare we hope or even wish for victory."' She concludes, 'while peace is used for the degrading evils of self-indulgence, the energy and sacrifice of war only shine the brighter. But this is another subject.'[44] In essence, communal ethics dictated war, the success of which in turn required combatting individual sin.

In this single article written in retirement, Maynard brought together beliefs about the relationship of religion to both science and society that she had held in tension throughout her professional life. Intrinsically linked to her correspondences and public speaking, writing 'seems to be the real business of life,' she reflected in her journal entry summing up 1917, the year 'Love' appeared.[45] In 1923, she described writing as 'the real centre of life'.[46] Again in 1927, 'I *do* so want to do a little good through my writing before I go hence.'[47] Writing for magazines gave Constance Maynard a way to address, if not to reconcile, conflicting ideals and, with the authority of the title 'First Mistress of Westfield' after her name, she could in retirement step into a world wider than the one available to her while she served as her college's leader.

Like any *The Hibbert* contributor, Maynard was now open to the routinely robust critiques of the journal's readers; responding to an article published in the same issue that hers appeared in, a correspondent described its 'gratuitous' assumptions and 'extraordinary' views.[48] Shortly after returning from a cycling tour, Maynard makes note of her first response in the form of a letter, 'I think I have not yet remarked that I got my article on Pacifism into the *Hibbert Journal* [. . .] it is a real joy to me to be in the *Hibbert* at last. I tried in vain once before. This has brought a comment or two, notably one from Sir Lawrence Jones, Bart,' questioning her suicide statistics. This query prompted a letter to her source at the Mission of Hope who confirmed Maynard's figures. Soon afterwards, her correspondent appeared in person: 'On this day, Sat., Sir L. Jones was suddenly announced, a delightful figure, tall, battered-looking, grey-haired, gentle of voice,' who had ' "just run down [to call on an old friend] + hearing you were so *very* near, I thought I might venture", +c, +c. He was charming, + we talked in confidence over the subject in hand.'[49]

More formal responses followed in the pages of *The Hibbert*. The first, by J. W. Campbell, opens by assuming general agreement with Maynard's 'cogent argument' that it is the duty of nations to fight for civil and ethical reasons but considers Maynard to be on 'more debatable ground' in drawing the line at resistance to ethical wrongs: 'I am not forgetting the lofty standpoint of the writer, but we must take human nature as it is plus spirituality.' The rest of the essay focuses on the point that Maynard had ignored many historical examples of nations and groups rising up to resist 'religious tyranny'.[50] The Editor's note that followed picked up on Jones's point about the suicide figures she had quoted: they were 'very different from those furnished by the Commissioner of Police for the Metropolis'. Maynard's account of 365 bodies in the Thames and seventy in the Serpentine was in stark contrast to the Commissioner's figures of fifteen and two.[51]

Maynard did not respond directly to these critiques, which were perhaps less overtly condescending than critics of older women writers a century earlier.⁵² However, in an August 1917 journal entry, in the context of sorrowfully reflecting on the published lists of war dead, she urges that we 'must look to the cause, the total, the aim, to cheer ourselves on at all. I have written my article against Pacifism in the *Hibbert Journal*, + now it is so much liked by "the good" it is being reprinted.'⁵³ In December 1917, she notes that *The Hibbert* article was 'a real success; reprinted + sold + given away'.⁵⁴ For her, publication was also about starting conversations that she continued through lectures and redistribution of her essays; she plowed the seven pounds she earned for this article back into paying to have copies of her *A True Mother* book shipped to worthy recipients.⁵⁵

Maynard continued to publish in *The Hibbert*. By late 1918, she had had 'We Women' accepted and was at work on eleven more articles and several book manuscripts: 'This is, at any rate a record of industry, + some of it is of value. I see that by the effect on others.'⁵⁶ The following year also brought changes in her circumstances: after the death of her brother Harry, she moved for a time to Wimbledon to share her sister-in-law's home. The move seems to have been prompted less by finances (she had come into two inheritances since retirement and before that drew on £800 a year in savings and investments) than by a growing sense of loneliness and the stresses of keeping up her retirement cottage. On her last night at Sundial, she wrote, 'It is quite wonderful what these long solitary years have done for me. When I left Westfield, I could barely "write," and now I feel judgment, + conviction + even "style" have come to me, + I enter the arena as one of the thinkers of the world.'⁵⁷

In December, she noted that her reply to an article on Humanism for *The Hibbert* 'has been the saving of me, as forcing me to consider + state clearly the grounds of my hope'.⁵⁸ In her first entry for January 1920, 'this curious "Houseless but not Homeless Year," ' she lists ten goals. The ninth was 'To get into correspondence with Men through the *Hibbert*.'⁵⁹ She did just that. Her article on humanism, 'Is Christ Alive To-day? Two or Three Witnesses', published in 1920, garnered two responses to which she gave her own response and then she kept the conversation going by reprinting and distributing her article.⁶⁰ That December she tallied up her 'accounts' and found herself 'rich': in addition to sufficient funds to spend on scholarships, donations and subscriptions, she had 'complete social freedom, + go where I choose; + mental freedom, + read + write as I will, without supervision or submission to my surroundings'.⁶¹ In the seven years after retiring, Maynard believed that she had found a path from rebellion against past restrictions to a role as one of the 'thinkers of the world', which for her was crucially linked to both mental and social freedom. Having left behind the 'family' of Westfield College, she had worked hard to create a 'style' of her own that enabled her to find her way into conversations with fellow (male) *Hibbert* contributors and readers and to engage in a wider world as she integrated her intellectual and spiritual beliefs.

NOTES

1. Constance Maynard, 'Green Book' (1919), 266–7, 275–6, in 'The diaries of Constance Maynard, Founding Principal of Westfield College', University of London, Microfilm, 14 reels (Harvester Microform Publishers, 1987).This chapter relies on three of her five journals: *Effie Diaries*, *Green Book* and *Sundial Diaries*. Maynard's papers can be tricky to date precisely because she sometimes transcribed and revised earlier entries.
2. Regarding Maynard's Evangelical upbringing, see Catherine Beatrice Firth, *Constance Maynard: Mistress of Westfield College* (London: George Allen & Unwin, 1949), 13–15; Pauline Phipps, 'Faith, desire and sexual identity: Constance Maynard's atonement for passion,' *Journal of the History of Sexuality* 18 (2009): 265–86.
3. For Maynard's central role in founding Westfield College, see Firth, *Maynard*, 133; see also Joyce Senders Pederson, 'The reform of women's secondary and higher education: Institutional change and social values in mid and late Victorian England,' *History of Education Quarterly* 19 (1979): 61–91.
4. Martha Vicinus, *Independent Women: Work and Community for Single Women, 1850–1920* (Chicago: University of Chicago Press, 1985).
5. She later privately celebrated the 'marriage' of two female friends; *Sundial*, 1917, 254; *Effie Diaries*, 1888, 48–51.
6. Regarding Maynard's efforts to reconcile faith and science at both Girton and Westfield, see Firth, *Maynard*, 125–7, 264–8, and *Green Book*, 1917, 75. She recorded her struggle to integrate profession and family in the *Effie Diaries*, 1888, 42–50.
7. Joan Hinde Stewart, *The Enlightenment of Age* (Oxford: Voltaire Foundation, 2010), 18.
8. *Green Book*, 1916, 354; 1916 (new volume), 13. See Katharina Rowald on the contemporary ascent of scientific language and emphasis on mothers and race in *The Educated Woman: Minds, Bodies and Women's Higher Education in Britain, Germany and Spain, 1865–1914* (New York: Routledge, 2010), 49.
9. *Green Book*, 1919, 213.
10. Maria Tamboukou, 'Of other spaces: Women's colleges at the turn of the nineteenth century in the UK,' *Gender, Place and Culture* 7 (2000): 247–63.
11. Maynard only won her parents' permission to attend Girton with the promise that she would return home after one year. See Firth, *Maynard*, 103.
12. *Effie Diaries*, 1888, 48, 50.
13. Firth, *Maynard*, 283–8.
14. *Green Book*, 1913, 141–2.
15. *Green Book*, 1914, 252–3. She noted that she spent more on the publishing than she made on sales: *Sundial Diaries*, 1915, 77, 90.
16. She wrote for the National Sunday School Union, the Society for Promoting Christian Knowledge and the British and Foreign Bible Society.
17. See Margaret Beetham's excellent analysis of the 'feminised space' of women's magazines in *A Magazine of Her Own? Domesticity and Desire in the Woman's Magazine, 1800–1914* (London: Routledge, 1996).
18. Maynard's publications shortly before retirement, in chronological order: 'A farming holiday,' *Contemporary Review* 88 (1905): 90–103; 'Maligned November,' *Contemporary Review* 88 (1905): 843–8; *The Value of Holy Scripture: A Paper for Students in Women's Colleges* (London: British and Foreign Bible Society, 1907); *Between College Terms* (London: James Nisbet, 1910); *An Alpine Meadow* (Edinburgh: Oliphant, Anderson and Ferrier, 1912).

19 Quote is from 'We women,' *The Hibbert* 17 (1919): 463–72. A sample of her writings, 1914–1920: 'From early Victorian schoolroom to university: Some personal experiences,' *Nineteenth Century* 76 (1914): 1060–73; 'Love which is not the fulfilling of the law,' *The Hibbert* 15 (1917): 479–92; 'We women,' *The Hibbert* 17 (1919): 463–72; 'Is Christ alive to-day? Two or three witnesses,' *The Hibbert* 18 (1920): 361–77.
20 *Sundial*, 1911, 2.
21 *Effie Diaries*, 1888, 48–51.
22 She maintained contact with former students through visits and a circular letter. *Sundial*, 1911, 1–2. This entry about 1906 is dated 1911.
23 She concluded that she would have to pay to publish the book herself. See *Sundial*, 1909, 67.
24 *Sundial*, 1915, 153, 157; 1916, 185.
25 *Sundial*, 1915, 153.
26 She never directly connects this debate to passage of the Compulsory Service Acts in 1916. See Thomas Kennedy, 'Many Friends do not know "where they are". Some divisions in London Yearly Meeting during the First World War,' *Quaker Theology: A Progressive Journal and Forum for Discussion and Study* 11 (2005): no page, accessed 25 June 2015, http://quakertheology.org/issue-11-contents.htm.
27 *Sundial*, 1915, 156.
28 *Sundial*, 1915, 171–2.
29 Regarding writing projects underway in December 1915, see *Sundial*, 1915, 171–2.
30 *Sundial*, 1915, 171.
31 *Sundial*, 1915, 172. Leagues of Honour were established to encourage members to uphold moral standards that might be endangered in a time of war.
32 She had carried through on this plan by January 1916: *Sundial*, 1916, 185.
33 While she does not detail her role in these local women's groups, these entries would suggest that, here too, she sought to bring a religious perspective to social ills.
34 *Sundial*, 1915, 173.
35 *Sundial*, 1916, 185.
36 *Sundial*, 1916, 186.
37 *Sundial*, 1916, 205, 225.
38 Maynard, 'Love which is not the fulfilling of the law,' *The Hibbert* 15 (1917): 479–92.
39 Maynard bolstered her scientific analogy by citing Patrick Geddes and John Arthur Thomson, *Evolution* (London: Williams and Norgate, 1911). On the influence of scientific discourse at this time, see Rowald, *The Educated Woman*, 10, 11.
40 Maynard, 'Love,' 483.
41 Maynard, 'Love,' 486.
42 The passage she refers to is 'If my kingdom were of this world, then would my servants fight' from John 18: 36.
43 Maynard, 'Love,' 492.
44 Maynard, 'Love,' 492.
45 *Green Book*, 1917, 108–9.
46 Firth, *Maynard*, 300.
47 Firth, *Maynard*, 300.
48 'Discussions,' *The Hibbert* 15 (1917): 673–4.
49 *Sundial*, 1917, 248–9.

50 'Discussions,' *The Hibbert* 15 (1917): 674–6.
51 'Discussions,' *The Hibbert* 15 (1917): 674–6.
52 See Devoney Looser, *Women Writers and Old Age in Great Britain, 1750–1850* (Baltimore, MD: Johns Hopkins University Press, 2008).
53 *Green Book*, 1917, 64–5.
54 *Green Book*, 1917, 294–6.
55 *Sundial*, 1917, 249.
56 *Sundial*, 1918, 80.
57 *Green Book*, 1919, 266–7.
58 *Green Book*, 1919, 275–6. She wrote in response to an article on humanism by Sir Roland Wilson.
59 *Sundial*, 1920, 161.
60 Maynard, 'Is Christ alive to-day? Two or three witnesses,' *The Hibbert* 18 (1920): 361–77; related correspondence appeared on pages 591–2 and 803.
61 *Sundial*, 1920, 201.

9 The Married Woman Worker in *Chatelaine* Magazine, 1948–1964

Helen Glew

The increased participation of married women in the paid labour force was one of the significant demographic shifts in Canada after the Second World War. The suitability and ramifications of this were widely debated in the press, amongst employers and in other public arenas. *Chatelaine*—the only magazine for women produced (as opposed to circulated) in Canada by the late 1950s[1]—discussed this new phenomenon widely, with it featuring as a recurring topic in editorials and articles throughout the 1950s and into the 1960s. This chapter examines in depth the contributions of *Chatelaine* to the debate about working wives, analysing both the direct and deliberate commentary on the issue and, importantly, the more implicit ways the married woman worker was represented in the magazine.

Given *Chatelaine*'s position in Canadian culture, considerable academic attention has been paid to it. The most significant study is Valerie J. Korinek's *Roughing it in the Suburbs*, which examines the production of *Chatelaine* and, in particular, reminds us of the multiple layers and competing discourses in each issue of the magazine, and thus the complexities that must be considered when reading it.[2] Kaitlynn Mendes also offers important discussion of mid-1950s *Chatelaine* and the columns by Dr Marion Hilliard.[3] There has been less specific discussion of magazines and their coverage of the issue of married women and paid work in the mid-twentieth century, although Jane Marcellus makes an important contribution for the inter-war US.[4] The work of Joanne Meyerowitz in reassessing US women's magazines in the post-war period provides an informative and overdue corrective to Betty Friedan's assertions about women's magazines in this period, which, as Meyerowitz notes, historians have tended to adopt uncritically.[5] Friedan argued that magazines in the post-war US were key components in creating 'the feminine mystique', depicting womanhood as glorified through domesticity and motherhood. Meyerowitz, in revisiting these publications, shows how magazines were much more wide-ranging, ambivalent and contradictory in their coverage, ultimately upholding the ideal of marriage for women but far less so the ideal of domesticity.[6] The findings presented in this chapter largely correlate with Meyerowitz's on the US context.

Chatelaine was published monthly and, as was typical for magazines of this type, featured articles and editorials on a wide range of topics assumed to be of interest to women, advice columns (increasingly written by the Chatelaine Institute), as well as fiction and a significant amount of advertising. *Chatelaine* routinely published a readers' correspondence page, meaning that there was a culture of reader critique of the publication. This was particularly significant, as it gave readers additional perspectives and could present a challenge to, or agreement with, the various discourses being offered by the magazine.[7] The analysis for this chapter has been conducted by looking at each issue of the magazine for 'even' years in the period 1948–64. This allows an appreciation of the time period as a whole whilst also providing an opportunity to look at seasonal coverage, serialisation of materials which often spanned several issues and to trace reader interaction with the magazine. *Chatelaine* imagined and spoke to a white readership, with immigrants and 'new Canadians' discussed as though they were all of European heritage.[8] Like other women's magazines of this time, it assumed heterosexuality and that married women would bear children. In this sense there was a specific, embedded idea of what being a married woman meant. The magazine saw the comfortable middle-class wife as its ideal reader, though as Korinek has pointed out, there is evidence to suggest that *Chatelaine* was read by significant numbers of women from lower-middle and working-class backgrounds who did not always fit the profile the advertising department had in mind.[9]

Both within issues of *Chatelaine* and elsewhere, the post-war debate about wives and paid work was framed principally around middle-class women, as it was assumed that these women had a choice about whether they worked, while working-class women were considered more likely to have to work out of financial necessity.[10] With the disruptions to employment practices caused by the Second World War and the dismantling of some of the marriage bars in women's employment in the post-war period, it was clear that married women's participation in the labour force was changing, although public and policy-making discourse on the issue remained contentious and vociferous.[11] Statistics illustrate the increased participation of married women in the labour force. In 1951, 30 per cent of the female workforce in Canada was married, but a decade later, half of the female workforce was married.[12] However, this was not merely a result of changing perceptions of married women's roles: it also reflected the fact that women on average were marrying at an earlier age than previously.[13] That said, in 1961, four out of five wives were still not in the workforce, despite the marked increase in married women's labour force participation as a whole.[14] When considered alongside each other, these statistics provide a clue as to why there were continuing debates and anxieties about wives working: despite visible change in this period, for many women marriage still meant leaving the waged economy.

CHATELAINE'S DISCOURSES ON MARRIED WOMEN AND EMPLOYMENT

Throughout the period considered here, articles in *Chatelaine* that were specifically about the issue of married women and paid work tended to advocate it—cautiously at first, and then more confidently. This compares favourably to the British edition of *Good Housekeeping,* an equivalent publication in style and intended readership, whose discussion of these issues disappeared in the early 1950s.[15] *Chatelaine*'s advocacy always brought with it an element of debate or disagreement from readers, and the creation of discussion might well be seen at least in part as a means to increase reader numbers as well as providing a space to air the issues.

The reasons why married women's employment was generally supported by successive *Chatelaine* editors and writers are significant in themselves, but are also important for what they signify about the magazine's conceptions of womanhood and gender roles in this period. There was often an elision (in the magazine and elsewhere) between wives and mothers because it was expected that women would have both identities. This was, of course, rooted in long-standing and conventional conceptions of marriage and womanhood. Therefore there was relatively little space for the idea of a 'career woman' simply marrying and continuing her career indefinitely: it was assumed that children would follow sooner or later but that the wife might continue in paid employment until the birth of the first child. It was then assumed that women might, if they chose, resume work when all children were in school. This really meant part-time work in practice, given that there was no suggestion of men adopting childcare responsibilities. At the same time, it was conceded that relatively few households would be able to afford paid help with housekeeping and childcare to enable either an earlier return to work or a mother to work full-time hours.[16]

In the late 1940s, *Chatelaine* included less coverage of the married woman in paid work than there would be in future years. Significantly, a married reader with children, who needed to work for financial reasons, raised the issue of paid work via a letter to the editor.[17] One article featured a woman who began paid work on a part-time basis, as it was better for her state of mind. Tellingly, this was a piece in a section called 'Women in Revolt'.[18] In March 1950, there was a deeply provocative piece that attributed a whole range of negative characteristics to housewives who did not work outside the home, including resentment towards their husbands, laziness and an interest in little besides domesticity. Around 500 letters were received from readers in response, a considerable number of which were in opposition to her views.[19] In April, an article on the year's typical bride and groom made it clear that the bride planned to continue working until she had children.[20] In July, Byrne Hope Sanders' editorial directly tackled the increase of wives in paid work, which contrasted with another two years previously in which she conceptualised the majority of married women as housewives only. Sanders attributed married women working to post-war consumerism, arguing that '[o]ur modern way of life demands so high a standard in the homes we live in, the cars we drive, the education we want for our children that it is more and more difficult for one wage-earner to support it.'[21] She invited readers to discuss what they thought of the increase in working wives, suggesting that two incomes for a family might come at the expense of a wife's happiness. She seemed to see satisfaction in working as well as homemaking for professional women only, rather than for potentially all women, which was perhaps an interesting comment on the paid work typically available to women. Sanders was clearly not convinced that the employment of married women outside the home was necessarily a positive development, though she did recognise it had to be a woman's choice.[22] Thus the issue was directly raised by the editorial, but the near-equivalency given to both sides of the debate perhaps revealed her lack of surety, a fear of causing offence or a sense of apprehensiveness about the debate she was helping to open up.

By the early to mid-1950s, *Chatelaine* portrayed self-fulfilment as the chief reason for a married woman to choose to work outside the home. The writing of experts—sociologists and doctors in particular—was fundamental in establishing and bolstering this perspective. *Chatelaine* devoted space in two issues in 1952 to extracts from Sidonie M. Gruenberg and Hilda Sidney Krech's book, *The Many Lives of Modern Woman* (1952), which addressed the choices faced by middle-class women after they had married, borne children and then considered whether or not to return to the workplace. The extracts were notable for foregrounding the notion of choice and the idea that women were not to be condemned for choosing either housewifery or a paid career outside the home, or some combination of the two. They advocated part-time work as a means of securing fulfilment without the heightened stress of having to balance two full-time roles.[23] The extracts were apparently well received by readers.[24]

The expert most regularly called upon in the mid-1950s was Dr Marion Hilliard, a Toronto-based doctor specialising in women's health. Although *Chatelaine* is widely acknowledged as being at its most feminist during Doris Anderson's tenure as editor between 1957 and 1977, it is important—as Mendes has also argued—to acknowledge the contributions of Hilliard to the magazine in the mid-1950s. As Mendes observes, Hilliard offered numerous strands of feminist thought in her columns, even if some aspects of her message remained conservative.[25] She was a strong advocate of married women's paid work as a means of personal fulfilment, along the same lines as Gruenberg and Sidney Krech.[26] Like those contributions, Hilliard's advice also elicited reader comment. One reader reported enjoying the 'pandemonium' of being a housewife, and two other readers argued that they had enough to do in the home but also that housewifery equipped them with many skills that could be used in the workplace.[27]

In addition to expert columns, *Chatelaine* regularly featured profiles of women who combined work and marriage (often as well as raising a family). However, these could be difficult for average readers to identify with. The women were often writers—frequently the magazine's own contributors—or trained in another profession which allowed a high degree of flexibility.[28] There was thus often a limit to how far these women could act as role models for those married women who sought to emulate others who had re-entered the workplace. The 'Women of . . . ' feature visited cities and towns across Canada and profiled women who were active or prominent in local communities, some of whom were also wives in the workforce.[29] In this way, *Chatelaine* offered coverage of successful women alongside profiles of individual women who might be deemed to be aspirational, but there was rarely discussion in these or the 'expert' columns of the specific factors which allowed women to combine paid work and the other commitments of marriage.

This was amended somewhat in June 1958, when *Chatelaine* published a supplement of several pages somewhat romantically titled 'The Wife with a Job . . . Her Risks . . . Her Gains . . . Her Chances of Happiness . . . '. The supplement acted as its most solid affirmation yet that married women working outside the home were a permanent feature of contemporary life, presenting the issue in mostly positive terms. It featured contributions from the anthropologist Margaret Mead, Marion Royce (the Director of the Women's Bureau of the Federal Department of Labour) and practical tips from the Chatelaine Institute on household management whilst in employment. This was the first detailed discussion of strategic household management for the working wife or mother in the issues sampled for this chapter. In her contribution, Mead argued that one of the chief obstacles was the husband or child who expected a mother to 'fulfill their every need' and was ahead of her time in arguing that wives' and husbands' jobs had to be taken equally seriously when planning for the future, with homemaking to be shared or delegated to paid help.[30] Interestingly, there was no comment on the supplement from readers in subsequent issues where pieces of this nature usually excited comment. It is possible, though, that the decision to include it in a special supplement, which had the effect of semi-detaching it from the rest of the magazine, meant readers took it less seriously or saw it as different from other magazine content.

In 1960, an article confidently asserted that 'there is no longer any stigma attached to the working married woman'.[31] By 1964, *Chatelaine* was detectably more comfortable with the idea of married women's choice to work and also less shy about the problems that still beset women in this regard. In a foreshadowing of sentiments expressing in coming decades, Doris Anderson's January 1964 editorial argued:

> We are beginning to realise that the roles we assume aren't neatly labelled 'wrong' or 'right', and the choices don't automatically cancel

one another out. [. . .] it is possible to be a mother and not be a self-sacrificing 'mom' [. . .]. We've always been told, we women, that we 'can't have our cake at eat it, too'. But today we almost can—and without robbing a husband or children of their full share of attention and love, or ourselves of our right to be women.[32]

In June, Anderson took critics of working mothers to task for blaming women for 'problem children' with no evidence, whilst challenging legislators to create laws and practices which would support the working mother.[33] There was, therefore, a discernible new confidence about asserting the rights, needs and problems of the working mother.

OTHER PERSPECTIVES ON THE WORKING WIFE

Alongside the narrative of personal choice and fulfilment to be gained from paid work, *Chatelaine* also addressed other aspects of the debate. This both acknowledged that some readers might have a different perspective and allowed room for doubt and contestation to emerge, as well as arguments against, or problems with, married women's paid work. The levels of debate and coverage thus revealed the ongoing need to discuss the issue. As Veronica Strong-Boag has remarked of the Canadian popular press, the very fact that the issue was discussed so often suggests unease about married women's paid work and signals the extent of contestations over the practice.[34]

The debate emerged in a variety of different ways on *Chatelaine*'s pages. For example, around the same time as Hilliard's advice about wives working, other articles expressed bitterness or negativity about the confines of housewifery—rather than the positives of paid work—which then generated reader correspondence in support or critique.[35] Dr Reva Gerstein's articles were predicated on married women not being able to work and having to accept their traditional position, telling wives to 'learn to live with yourself' and not to focus on the career or lifestyle they might have had if they had not married, reminding them that once the children were in school they would be able to resume work outside the home.[36] At the same time, the magazine also ran a 'Makeover for a Working Wife' contest, the winner of which was a woman who was working out of necessity owing to her husband's illness rather than by choice.[37] In featuring the winner, the magazine both presented the stark realities some working wives faced and brought a less-prominent factor in the debate to the fore.

Furthermore, in November 1958, an article by Eileen Morris—who had also contributed to the June 1958 supplement—reflected on recent wider criticisms of working mothers and asked whether married women were working in greater numbers because there was no longer a place in society for stay-at-home mothers.[38] One reader threatened to cancel her subscription in response to this 'trash'.[39] In January 1960, the magazine published

Anita Birt's 'Married Women, You're Fools to Take a Job', which attracted both strong agreement and disagreement from readers, signalling the still very divided views on married women's employment.[40] By 1962, Christina McCall Newman was able to write a piece pointing to the huge demographic shift in the workplace brought about by married women's participation and argued in another article for the need to see housewives as people.[41] Thus her writing captured a nuance only possible at this stage of the debate and demographic change: the need to value housewifery for its own sake.[42] This was markedly different from the praise of housewives and mothers in previous periods because housewifery was now discussed in terms of choice and not as the default. At the same time, some contributors to *Chatelaine* began to situate the working wife as more of a standard position, even if the commentary they offered detracted from this or outwardly criticised married women and paid employment.

Significantly, though, other articles not directly about married women and paid work offered piercing criticisms of the wife in the labour force and pointed to underlying cultural unease. An article titled 'How to Fight the Other Woman' presented a cautionary tale in which it was argued that a wife who earned an income (and perhaps a larger one than her husband) had to respect her husband as breadwinner and chief provider for the household and not flaunt her wealth, otherwise the husband may be tempted to cheat—in this particular example with the stenographer in his office.[43] This was a stark warning to uphold traditional gender roles. More worryingly, a June 1960 article on 'The Problem of the Terrible-Tempered Husband' by Violet Munns, of the Neighbourhood Workers' Association in Toronto, effectively named the wife's work as one of the central causes of the husband's domestic violence, which in turn had caused the wife to start seeing another man at work. The article suggested that '[t]he Hahns were a classic, if somewhat violent, example of the kind of strain a working wife can place on a marriage'. It did also state that Mr Hahn had had a difficult upbringing but, notably, made it clear that Sally Hahn giving up her job and 're-committing' to the marriage was key to the resolution of the problem: '[n]ow the household revolves, as it must to survive, around Karl Hahn. At last report, he's keeping his temper and his wife.' The fact that the household revolves around Karl does not appear very reassuring and the wider warning was clear throughout: married women working could be a catalyst for marital violence, and a key way to stop the violence was for the woman to return to the home.[44] Even though the article was not overtly about the working wife, the unease with her as a figure was clear.

THE MISSING WORKING WIVES: FICTION AND ADVERTISING

Throughout this period, although *Chatelaine's* articles and editorials directly on the subject of the working wife were broadly positive, it was clear that tensions, reservations and occasionally undercurrents of fear remained. Nowhere were the latter elements clearer than in *Chatelaine*'s fiction, where continuing discomfort with the re-casting of women's roles was readily apparent. Advertising, on the other hand, came across as largely blind to women's changing roles.

As Michelle Smith has argued for the period before 1945, *Chatelaine*'s fiction was designed to portray situations and contexts with which women in Canada could identify.[45] The emotional conundrums surrounding paid work for wives and particularly mothers featured increasingly in fiction in the 1950s. By foregrounding the issue of a career outside the home, these short stories served variously as cautionary tales, attempts to envision solutions or as ways of displaying self-sacrifice surrounding this central dilemma facing women. The vast majority had a conservative message, which encouraged re-embracing the home and often featured an epiphany by the central female character about her 'true role'.[46] The two stories in this sample where the working wife continued her job involved in one case a near-affair by the husband as a warning to the wife of the need to rebalance her focus. In the other, set far away from Canada in a Guatemalan village, a wife manipulated her husband by appearing to change her mind in order to persuade him that their joint participation as a husband-and-wife team in work outside the home was a good thing.[47]

Advertising complicated messages about changing roles for women. Although editors had little control over the content of advertising, companies trying to reach a consumer market through female homemakers (whether part- or full-time) ended up—deliberately or otherwise—supporting traditional ideologies about domesticity, femininity and the male breadwinner. Advertising was, of course, necessary for magazines' survival. As Doris Anderson explained in her autobiography, '[y]ears after the women's movement was well-established, I would be challenged regularly for running [. . .] sexist ads in *Chatelaine*. I always explained that magazines depended on ads for their revenue.'[48]

As a result, *Chatelaine* was full of advertising that largely targeted the married homemaker, but there were one or two conspicuous advertisements designed to address the married woman worker. Twice in 1954, a full-page advertisement was carried for Weston's baked goods which appeared to salute the married woman in paid employment. The image depicted a woman in work clothes punching a time clock in a factory, carrying her coat and bag. The text was ambiguous enough to apply to both married women with children and those who did not (yet) have children. It also firmly situated the working wife's contributions as patriotic and as 'helping to build two big projects . . . the Canadian Future and the Canadian Home' [ellipses in original]. The wife was 'the not-so-silent partner help[ing] her husband hold the line on both fronts. This is the way a family grows . . . and with such families Canada reaches new horizons of happiness and achievement' [ellipses in original].[49]

A similar version of this advertisement depicted a family of farmers on the prairies, with the copywriters also managing to sneak in a joke about 'chick chores'.[50] Arguably this depiction of married women working posed less of a challenge to traditional conceptions of womanhood because women's labour on family farms had long been accepted. However, what is more significant in both cases—particularly in the 'time clock' version of the advertisement—is not that women's domesticity was highlighted alongside her place in the paid work economy but that there was such an overt image of a woman working outside the home in the early 1950s.[51] These advertisements are important examples because they explicitly showed married women in the workforce, whilst the bulk of the advertising in the magazine largely drove home notions of domesticated womanhood and coexisted somewhat uneasily with some of the messages elsewhere in the magazine.

Throughout this period, *Chatelaine* was unafraid to insert itself into the debate about wives working outside the home and, on balance, to advocate it. However, the reservations about the working wife described in letters, intimated by asides in various articles that were ostensibly about other issues and in *Chatelaine*'s fiction—along with the complexities of advertising—represented numerous subtle or less-than-subtle ways in which positive messages about working wives were challenged or undermined. Collectively, the different aspects of the magazine highlight the ambiguities about the issue, the complexities of the debate and in some cases the underlying fears about what were perceived as rapidly changing gender roles for women.

NOTES

I would like to thank the Department of Social & Historical Studies at the University of Westminster, who funded this research, and the staff at Library & Archives Canada, Ottawa, and the Thomas Fisher Rare Book Library at the University of Toronto, where I undertook this research. I am very grateful for the helpful comments from conference delegates at the Women in Magazines conference, Kingston University London (2012), and from the editors and peer reviewers of this volume. Thanks also to Corinna Peniston-Bird, Simon Avery, Hannah Elias and Patrick Stribley for their advice and comments.

1 Valerie J. Korinek, *Roughing It in the Suburbs: Reading* Chatelaine *Magazine in the Fifties and Sixties* (Toronto: University of Toronto Press, 2000), 35. The French language version, *Châtelaine*, did not begin publication until 1960.
2 Korinek, *Roughing It*, 15 and *passim*.
3 Kaitlynn Mendes, 'Reading *Chatelaine:* Dr Marion Hilliard and 1950s women's health advice,' *Canadian Journal of Communication* 35 (2010): 515–31.
4 Jane Marcellus, *Business Girls and Two-Job Wives: Emerging Media Stereotypes of Employed Women* (Cresskill, NJ: The Hampton Press, 2011).
5 Joanne Meyerowitz, 'Beyond the feminine mystique: A reassessment of postwar mass culture, 1946–1958,' *Journal of American History* 79 (1993): 1455–82; Betty Friedan, *The Feminine Mystique* (New York: Norton, 1963).
6 Meyerowitz, 'Beyond the feminine mystique,' 1457–8, 1470.

7 For a discussion of reader critique of *Chatelaine* in this period, see Korinek, *Roughing It*, 79–97.
8 For a discussion of citizenship issues in *Chatelaine* in the inter-war period, see Michelle Smith, 'Fiction and the nation: The construction of Canadian identity in *Chatelaine* and *Canadian Home Journal* during the 1930s and 1940s,' *British Journal of Canadian Studies* 27 (2014): 37–53.
9 Korinek, *Roughing It*, 100, 176.
10 See, for example, Jennifer A. Stephen, *Pick One Intelligent Girl: Employability, Domesticity and the Gendering of Canada's Welfare State, 1939–1947* (Toronto: Toronto University Press, 2007), 109, 163–4; Veronica Strong-Boag, 'Canada's wage-earning wives and the construction of the middle-class, 1945–1960,' *Journal of Canadian Studies* 29 (1994): 5–25; Joan Sangster, 'Doing two jobs: The wage-earning mother, 1945–1970,' in *A Diversity of Women: Ontario, 1945–1980*, ed. Joy Parr (Toronto: University of Toronto Press, 1995), 100.
11 See, for example, Ruth Roach Pierson, *'They're Still Women after All': The Second World War and Canadian Womanhood* (Toronto: McClelland & Stewart, 1986); Joan Sangster, *Transforming Labour: Women and Work in Post-war Canada* (Toronto: University of Toronto Press, 2010); Stephen, *Pick One Intelligent Girl*; Strong-Boag, 'Canada's wage-earning wives'. See also Library & Archives Canada, RG 30 13105 4805-X2 'Employment of married women,' which covers the late 1940s and the 1950s.
12 Alison Prentice et al., *Canadian Women: A History* Second Edition (Toronto: Harcourt Brace, 1996), 351, 355.
13 Sangster, 'Doing two jobs,' 100.
14 Alison Prentice et al., *Canadian Women*, 351, 355.
15 See issues of *Good Housekeeping* (UK edition) for the period 1948–1964 and Cynthia White, *Women's Magazines, 1693–1968* (London: Unwin, 1970), 141–2, 185.
16 See, amongst a large range of articles Dr Reva Gerstein, 'Learn to live with yourself: How to be yourself,' *Chatelaine*, August 1956, 6–8; Dr Marion Hilliard, 'Stop being just a housewife,' *Chatelaine*, September 1956, 11, 90; 'The wife with a job,' *Chatelaine*, June 1958, 61–6.
17 Reader's letter, *Chatelaine*, February 1948, 3
18 'Women in revolt,' *Chatelaine*, May 1948, 34
19 Beverly Gray, 'Housewives are a sorry lot,' *Chatelaine*, March 1950, 26; 'Housewives blast business girl,' *Chatelaine*, June 1950, 14–15.
20 Wilma Tate, 'Bride with a future,' *Chatelaine*, April 1950, 31.
21 Byrne Hope Sanders, editorial, *Chatelaine*, April 1948, 3; Byrne Hope Sanders, 'Working wives outside the home,' *Chatelaine*, July 1950, 3.
22 Sanders, 'Working wives,' 3. See also Korinek, *Roughing It*, 260–2 for a discussion of this piece.
23 Extracts from Sidonie M. Gruenberg and Hilda Sidney Krech's book *The Many Lives of Modern Woman*, in *Chatelaine*, August 1952, 16–17, 48, 52–4; September 1952, 13, 52–4.
24 'Reader takes over,' *Chatelaine*, October 1952, 2.
25 Mendes, 'Reading *Chatelaine*,' 517–18; *passim*.
26 Hilliard, 'Stop being just a housewife,' 11, 90; Marion Hilliard, 'There was never a better time to be a woman. . . . ,' *Chatelaine*, April 1958, 12. Hilliard's book was also posthumously serialised in *Chatelaine*. See, for example, 'The challenges of modern life,' *Chatelaine*, April 1960, 18.
27 'Reader takes over,' *Chatelaine*, November 1956, 2–3.
28 See, for example, Claire Wallace, 'I got here the hard way,' *Chatelaine*, February 1952, 11–12, 43; Chatelaine Centre profile on Mada Gage Boulton, *Chatelaine*, August 1952, 56. One exception to the freelancing rule was

Frank Lowe, 'She helps you put your best foot forward,' *Chatelaine*, November 1952, 18, which was about Canada's top shoe salesperson.
29 For example, 'The women of Winnipeg,' *Chatelaine*, February 1954, 11; 'The women of London [Ontario],' *Chatelaine*, April 1954, 11.
30 'The wife with a job,' *Chatelaine*, June 1958, 61–6.
31 'A special *Chatelaine* guide for the woman who is going back to work,' *Chatelaine*, September 1960, 37.
32 Doris Anderson, editorial, *Chatelaine*, January 1964, 1.
33 Doris Anderson, editorial, *Chatelaine*, January 1964, 1.
34 Strong-Boag, 'Canada's wage-earning wives'; see also Korinek, *Roughing It*, 6–7.
35 Phyllis Lee Peterson, 'Don't educate your daughter,' *Chatelaine*, September 1954, 18–19, 67–8; 'A single girl tells why I hate wives,' *Chatelaine*, March 1956, 11; 'Reader takes over,' 2.
36 Dr Reva Gerstein, 'Learn to live with yourself,' *Chatelaine*, February 1956, 9; Dr Reva Gerstein, 'Learn to live with yourself: How to be yourself',' *Chatelaine*, May 1956, 6–8.
37 'Makeover for a working wife,' *Chatelaine*, April 1956, 28.
38 Eileen Morris, 'Are mothers obsolete?,' *Chatelaine*, November 1958, 37.
39 'The last word is yours,' *Chatelaine*, December 1958, 76.
40 Anita Birt, 'Married women, you're fools to take a job!,' *Chatelaine*, January 1960, 12–13, 41; 'The last word is yours,' *Chatelaine*, March 1960, 148; 'The last word is yours,' *Chatelaine*, April 1960, 164.
41 Christina McCall Newman, 'All Canadians are equal except women,' *Chatelaine*, February 1962, 34–5, 89; Christina McCall Newman, 'Why can't we treat married women like people?,' *Chatelaine*, April 1962, 25.
42 As told to Christina McCall Newman by Martha Wasserman, 'Why mothers mix up their daughters for love and marriage,' *Chatelaine*, October 1962, 31.
43 Dorothea Goetz, 'How to fight the other woman,' *Chatelaine*, May 1952, 7.
44 Violet Munns, 'The problem of the terrible-tempered husband,' *Chatelaine*, June 1960, 42.
45 Smith, 'Fiction and the nation,' 37–8, 44, 52.
46 See, for example, Ethel Gordon Wilson, 'The wrong kind of mother,' *Chatelaine*, May 1956, 14; Jean C. Clark, 'Little boy bluebird,' *Chatelaine*, March 1962, 31, 127.
47 Sheila MacKay Russell, 'The sisters,' *Chatelaine*, November 1960, 41; Mary Jane Rolfs, 'A woman's dreams,' *Chatelaine*, November 1962, 41. For a discussion of some of the *Chatelaine* fiction which dealt with married women's employment in the later 1960s, see Korinek, *Roughing It*, 234–6.
48 Doris Anderson, *Rebel Daughter: An Autobiography* (Toronto: Key Porter Books, 1996), 173.
49 Weston's advertisement, *Chatelaine*, June 1954, 75. My reading of this is a little different from Korinek's, though this serves to underline her point that advertisements could offer multiple readings. Korinek, *Roughing It*, 129–31. For comparison, see also the less-striking Weston's advertisements in August 1954, back cover, which featured a married female nurse.
50 Weston's advertisement, *Chatelaine*, October 1954, 38.
51 One other example of an advertisement which acknowledged that women worked outside the home was for *Encyclopaedia Americana* in *Chatelaine*, April 1964, 86.

10 Nanny Knows Best?
Tensions in Nanny Employment in Early and Mid-Twentieth-Century British Childcare Magazines

Katherine Holden

> With a baby, an experienced Nurse, once she is used to that baby, knows exactly what to do for him and why he is crying. Were it her own baby her task would be lessened, but so often Mother worries when baby cries and thinks there is something wrong with him. If a mother has a really good competent nurse would it not be better if she left the baby entirely to nurse.[1]

The extract above, taken from a letter to *Nursery World* in the mid-1920s, illustrates tensions often found in households that employed nannies, or nurses as they were often called before the Second World War. This chapter examines letters of this kind in British childcare magazines from the 1900s to the 1950s. It suggests why these publications were a valuable public space for nannies and mothers to air views and concerns which could not easily be expressed face to face or in private letters; it shows how some of their disputes and disagreements can be connected to the class and marital status of the mother and the nanny; most importantly it explores interdependency and ambivalence in relationships between mothers and nannies revealed in the letters they sent.

Before examining these letters, some background on nanny employment practices in this period is necessary. The first point to note is that the job of a nanny was generally carried out by single and usually childless women. For unmarried women in this period, work with children offered them both a professional status and personal satisfaction. But this was also a gendered expectation which did not always sit comfortably with their marital status, particularly when they were employed as childcare experts to look after children in the parental home.[2] Recruiting live-in help with childcare was much more common among upper- and middle-class families before the Second World War than it is today. Domestic service was by far the biggest employer of women, although census categories which include nannies and nursemaids under domestic servants make it difficult to tell exact numbers of childcare specialists.[3] In the wealthiest homes at the start of the century, nannies were generally from working-class backgrounds and trained on the job.

It was usual for the nanny to take sole charge with the mother's role in childcare often limited to spending an hour with her offspring in the evening in what was known as 'the children's hour'.[4] However, by the inter-war years, a greater emphasis on motherhood and the social and economic value of the child to the nation raised maternal expectations of their helpers; some mothers now looked for professionally trained nannies. A falling birth rate led to smaller families, and as the mother's involvement in her children's upbringing increased in importance, so also did the amount of time she spent with them. Sharing care with nannies became more common and by mid-century an expanding female employment market and dwindling supply of servants meant that many nannies were expected to do housework as well as childcare.[5]

With mothers and nannies thus no longer occupying such separate spheres there were more opportunities for conflict between them. In order to comprehend the intensity of exchanges between correspondents, we need to consider the roots of feelings generated more widely within nanny employment, a subject explored in greater depth in my book *Nanny Knows Best: the History of the British Nanny*. Because nannies were allocated much of the physical and emotional work of mothering, they often became deeply attached to their charges. But they also had to reconcile their feelings with knowledge that the child did not belong to them. In the context of today's migrant nannies, sociologist Arlie Hochschild described the love and care they give their charges as having been extracted from them by the global capitalist order in the same way as gold and other raw materials were extracted from colonial nations.[6] This is an important insight which exposes exploitation, yet it gives little sense of agency on the part of the nanny and does not take account of their gains rather than simply their losses: the satisfaction nannies take in giving and receiving love and in doing their job well.

Cameron Macdonald in her book *Shadow Mothers* explores the relationships between mothers and nannies in contemporary America. She argues that the doctrine of 'intensive motherhood' leads nannies to devalue their own relationship with the child in order to ensure that the child's love and attention is focused on the mother; this creates the illusion that the mother is the primary carer.[7] Evidence that some nannies focused children's attention on their parents can also be found in private correspondence in the first half of the century. For example Elfie, a nanny to the upper-class Beamish family in East Sussex in the 1920s, wrote to her employers:

> I have wished so often that you could peep at us especially when I draw!!! A boat sailing to Mum—all sorts of nice things are in the hold for you and Dad only I haven't time to enumerate them [. . .] but it has just helped them think of and *for* you and to *do* something for you.[8]

Elfie and other nannies employed by this family also sent letters and drawings composed by their charges to their mother and father (often annotated by the nanny) which helped to keep the relationship alive at a distance. However, unlike twenty-first-century American nannies, British nannies' letters in this period suggest the high value they assigned to their work, particularly when they were left in sole charge, evidenced by how well the children were being looked after. As we shall see, these views are expressed more directly and powerfully in nannies' letters to magazines where they did not have to consider their employers' interests and could assert that they, not the mother, knew best.

Nannies' gains when they were in sole charge could, however, represent loss for the mother, particularly in her lack of direct contact with her children. Mothers who can afford nannies are now often in high-powered jobs,[9] but upper- and upper-middle class women in the early and mid-twentieth century who did no paid employment might be equally fully occupied. This could simply be the demands of a complicated social calendar, but might equally involve extensive unpaid philanthropic work or supporting a husband in his career at home or abroad. The mother could have work, a husband and a life which did not depend on being with her offspring. But to achieve this she was dependent on a nanny whose total attention was given to her children. The fact that a trained nanny might come from a similar class to the family she worked for made things even more complicated and mothers struggled with boundaries, not always knowing how far to treat nannies as employees or as one of the family.

Thus it is clear that that the dynamics of power and interdependency in nanny employment ran two ways. The nanny wielded power because the mother was dependent on her for childcare, and she often had greater expertise than the mother. Nannies also left mothers helpless if they chose to leave the family unexpectedly, though their departures also often caused much heartache both for the nanny and child in her care. The mother had power over the nanny in that she could hire or fire her, determine the conditions in which she worked and undervalue the nanny's relationship with the children in comparison with her own. While many nannies and mothers created satisfying and happy relationships based upon their mutual dependencies and needs, tensions could arise even in the happiest situations.

CORRESPONDENCE IN *NURSERY WORLD* AND *NORLAND QUARTERLY*

We can see some of these tensions played out in the magazine *Nursery World*, which first appeared in 1925 and quickly became an important source of information on childcare.[10] With a mainly middle-class readership, it was targeted not just at mothers but also at nannies, who if they were trained, often came from middle-class backgrounds. One of the magazine's aims was to help nannies keep in touch with one another, both through its correspondence pages and through 'The Nursery World Friendship League'. This was a column where nannies advertised for others to keep them company, to go for walks together in the afternoons or socialise with in their time off. The fact that this was recognised as a problem is indicative of the isolation many nannies experienced and the limitations of their time off, which made it harder to meet people than if they had been in jobs with regular hours.

The *Nursery World* correspondence pages were entitled 'Over the Teacups', a name associated with femininity previously used in the Victorian magazine *Woman at Home*.[11] In the 1920s the page was illustrated by a drawing of letters on a tea table and in the 1930s of women meeting together for a cosy chat.[12] Yet, while the column's purpose was to foster a sense of community among its readers, many letters were far from cosy in tone.[13] As well as affirmations of the value of the work nannies did and the support they gave mothers, it became a forum for heated debates about the frustrations mothers and nannies felt in their relationships with one another and their feelings about the children.

These letters are important to examine because, as Cynthia White found in her classic study of women's magazines, the letter page became one of

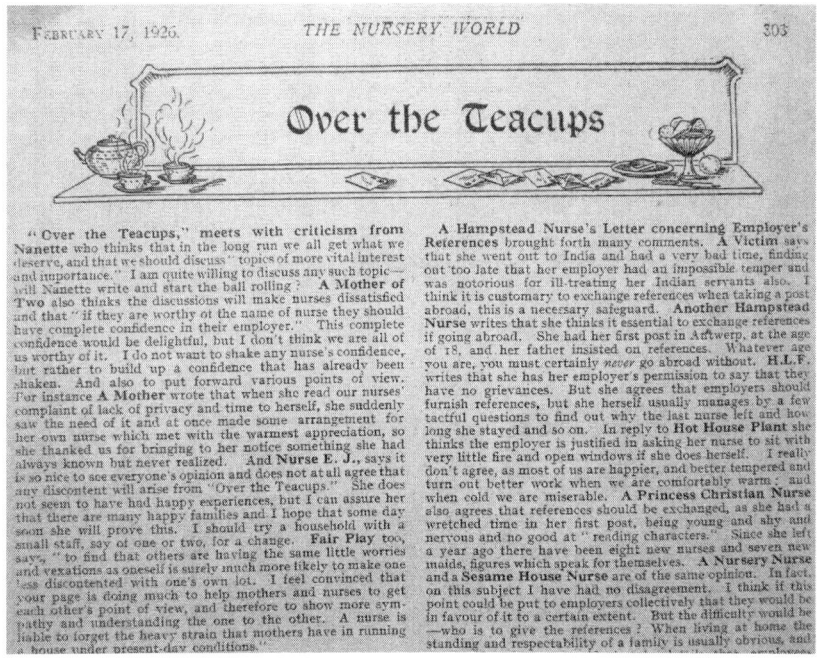

Figure 10.1 'Over the Teacups', reproduced courtesy of *Nursery World*.

the most popular features of women's magazines during the twentieth century, with the average reader turning to it before reading anything else.[14] Doubts have been cast on correspondence pages' authenticity, with letters selected for entertainment value rather than being in any way representative, and sometimes having been made up by editors. Yet, as Margaret Beetham asserts, 'The letters page [. . .] offers readers a place and some power to participate in negotiating the meaning of their social identity in public print.' The letter embodied 'a set of narrative and social conventions' that readers recognised. 'It offered versions of women's life stories for readers to match or contest, whatever the level of their sophistication as readers.'[15] This was particularly important for nannies, who usually gave their versions of life stories anonymously and expressed feelings which, if openly voiced to an employer, might have cost them their jobs. The difference is striking between nannies' often quite dull and formulaic letters in private collections which tell their employers how good and happy the children are and the much more vibrant ones they wrote to *Nursery World* complaining about difficulties in their jobs. Mothers were equally frank. While they might have been afraid to express their annoyance directly to a nanny who could easily leave them without notice, they spoke their mind in no uncertain terms in letters to *Nursery World*. Debates were often long-running, with readers answering one another's letters and taking issue with childcare experts' views as well as those of other mothers and nannies.[16]

Similar letters can also be found in college magazines, such as the *Norland Quarterly*, newsletter of the Norland Institute, Britain's most prestigious nanny training college. This magazine was sent to subscribers, mostly either former students wishing to keep in touch with the College and their classmates, or employers interested in the latest ideas about childcare. Here a different kind of editorial bias was in operation. Nannies could not write anonymously, as the magazine editor was usually the college principal or a member of staff. While they may have chosen the most entertaining letters to publish, editors were anxious not to alienate employers by allowing their students to say anything too critical.[17]

CHILDCARE REGIMES: THE INTERFERING MOTHER AND THE EXPERIENCED NURSE

The content of letters and advice columns reflects changes in childcare theories over the period. Until the Second World War, training manuals were dominated by the ideas of the New Zealand born writer Truby King and the American behaviourist psychologist John Watson, who advocated strict routines, fresh air and keeping a physical and emotional distance between mother or nanny and child.[18] Children's nurses were taught to let children cry, with one text in the 1920s going as far as to advocate complete separation of a newborn baby for twenty-four hours from its mother, leaving it alone in a quiet room and in the worst cases sedating it in order to solve feeding problems.[19] These views suited many nannies. Like the nanny who wrote the letter at the start of the chapter, they found it easier to keep discipline if children did not have too much maternal contact and often labelled mothers as interfering.

Other nannies wrote to *Nursery World* in the mid-1920s complaining that it hurt them to see children being spoiled by their mothers, which made the nanny's task so much harder.[20] They were also actively debating the roots of this problem and ways it could be prevented. A nanny who trained at the Princess Christian College (the main rival of Norland) took issue with the view put forward in an article on 'interfering mothers' that psychology (a subject in vogue in the magazine[21]) was 'only common sense'. She pointed out that it was psychology that had taught her to anticipate conflicts and "be before" to prevent the screams, the difficulties and troubles of ordinary nursery life'.[22]

Similar letters reflecting on difficulties in mother/nanny relationships also appeared in the *Norland Quarterly* throughout the century. For example, in 1909, Nurse Cicely Colls, who was feeling lonely and desperate to 'let off steam', wrote a long letter offering advice to younger nurses about how to deal with the demands of different employers. She was exasperated at being told both that 'she was too "intelligent to be a children's nurse"' and being denied the right to rely on her own judgment and to manage her own nursery. She had to be careful how to express these feelings and her advice to younger nurses was to cultivate a sense of humour 'as one of the best gifts in this very contradictory world'. Yet the seriousness of her message, that Norland nurses really did know best, is apparent in her advice: 'So now I try to be adaptable and give in on unimportant "points". But do not change your opinion regarding things that *do* matter, because your employer has different ideas'. Cicely was not, however, allowed to get away entirely with giving advice which might have alienated mothers, and her letter prompted the editor and founder of the college, Emily Ward, to remind her Norland Nurse readers to 'never make game of your employers'.[23]

Mothers who objected to being described as difficult and interfering were equally forthright in expressing their concerns about being excluded from the nursery and having their authority threatened. One 'harassed mother' writing to *Nursery World* believed her nurse was not inculcating the right values in her children, which she saw as 'courage, honesty and self-control':

> Every mother worth her salt has ideas on the upbringing of her children; when every suggestion is presumed to be an aspersion on the nurse's efficiency, how is she to put these ideas into force [. . .]. I am faced with the choice of letting things slide or losing my nurse.[24]

Keeping hold of nannies could be difficult in such circumstances, particularly in a period when the old hierarchies of domestic service relationships no longer seemed so stable. Yet their interdependent positions also gave mothers and nannies a strong investment in coming to terms with differences. Another nanny explained:

> When taking a new post, I make it clear that I want the Mother to share in the nursery life and uphold my authority as I uphold hers. I can go for a holiday, knowing that the nursery routine will go smoothly, and that the children will be happy, as the mother knows their whims as well as Nanny does.[25]

This letter suggests middle-class mothers' increasing involvement in their children's care in the inter-war years. However it was not always easy for mothers to achieve the balance they desired. The Honourable Mrs de Gray highlighted the difficulty she had to find an experienced nurse who did not want to be in sole charge. Filled with misgivings by the 'careless, noisy, and rough specimens' of nurses she met in other people's houses, her request to an agency for a nurse who 'could work under the mother's supervision and yet not be under twenty-five' yielded 'nobody suitable [. . .] not a soul with any experience materialised'.[26] Only by a stroke of luck did she eventually find a woman between thirty and forty, with previous experience as a nurse or help, willing to work under her.

One mother who found the views of nurses trained under Truby King style regimes particularly irksome was Ursula Bowlby, wife of the psychiatrist John Bowlby, who pioneered the theory of 'maternal deprivation' (now known as attachment theory). Ursula Bowlby was both influenced by and offered evidence for her husband's views on the importance of mothers looking after their own children. Her private diaries and unpublished writings in the 1940s show her hostility to the unmarried baby expert who had never had a child of her own, particularly nurses who were employed to look after babies during the first month of their lives. Bowlby believed these nurses infantilised mothers, pressuring them into believing that nanny must know best, and she stated her determination to be her 'own head nurse'.[27] In April 1941 she wrote to *Nursery World* to complain about nurses' objections to dummies:

> In reply to 'Poor but Contented's' letter I should like to say that my baby age 15 months has always had a dummy and I imagine she will give it up naturally at the age of two. My husband, a doctor, thinks a dummy is a brainwave, so long as you sterilise it and only give it when the baby is getting off to sleep. I quite expect that this statement will rouse a passion of indignation in the breast of many a trained nurse but the normal mother does not like to hear her baby scream itself to sleep and you can't sterilise a thumb![28]

MULTIPLE CARERS AND NANNY LOSS: PSYCHOANALYTIC PERSPECTIVES

While Truby King continued to hold sway in many nurseries until the Second World War, Ursula Bowlby's writings show that by the late 1930s and 40s his theories were beginning to be challenged by psychoanalysts who regarded a close bond between mother and child as important for child and adult health and wellbeing. Another childcare expert who took this position was Susan Isaacs, analyst and author of a number of books on child development, who had observed young children closely in a nursery setting. Isaacs encouraged mothers to relate closely to their children and engage with their feelings.[29] Writing in *Nursery World* during the 1930s under the pseudonym Ursula Wise, she was also one of the first advice columnists to identify difficulties for children in having multiple carers.

Wise was concerned with the effects of nanny loss. Writing to a woman whose daughter, after initially accepting a new nanny, began to cling to her mother, she explained that this behaviour was rooted in a lie told to the child that her old nanny was going on holiday. Wise insisted that the child must have seen through the lie and that the mother needed to acknowledge her loss. Similar problems, including tantrums, were also reported by a nurse who had recently left a post. She had been accused by her former employer of having spoiled her charge, a little girl to whom the nurse had been devoted. Wise suggested that the loss of her nurse and disturbance of her accustomed routine had aroused 'a general resentment in the child's mind' and was causing her headstrong behaviour. She advised mothers not to change nurses too often and to 'balance against the present ills, those arising from the mere facts of the change'.[30]

Experts in *Nursery World* also began to acknowledge how difficult leaving a child was for a nanny. As 1950s psychologist Phyllis Hostler pointed out, 'It is always difficult to believe when we have served well and faithfully, that any other will do or be as much loved. One of the hardest things a nurse can be called upon to face, is to hand over her charge to another, wholly and undivided.'[31] Whatever the reasons for a nanny's departure, partings could be traumatic. One nanny who shared with *Nursery World* readers in 1946 her agony at leaving a much loved charge was amazed to receive so many letters in response expressing sympathy. Her last charge was the nearest to her heart and, although she could now think of him without the terrible heartache she used to have, the letters and gifts she sent were not acknowledged and she had heard nothing more of the child.[32] There was no explanation for this particular family's silence but, while many mothers did stay in touch with former nannies, those who cut contact were often motivated by jealousy, finding it hard to acknowledge the importance of the nanny's relationship with the child.

Mother has the product

"The child has become to one a doll, to sit sweet and clean on one's knee for half-an-hour when visitors come, to enchant briefly with pretty ways or astoundingly clever remarks."

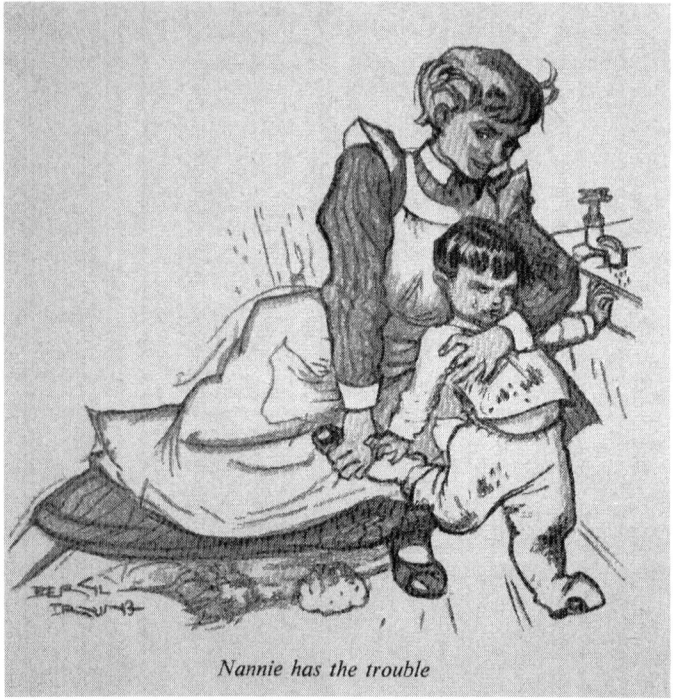

Nannie has the trouble

Figures 10.2 and 10.3 Illustrations for the article 'Mother and/or Nanny' in *Nursery World* by Phyllis Hostler, December 1956. Reproduced courtesy of *Nursery World*.

CLASS CONFLICTS: THE OLD FASHIONED NANNY AND THE LADY NURSE

As mothers became more involved in their children's care, the issue of a nanny's class background became more difficult to manage. From the late nineteenth century some mothers had become so concerned that their children might adopt the behaviour and manners of the lower classes that they began to recruit women from a 'respectable' background to do childcare, usually known as 'lady nurses'. This was not, however, always viewed as a better option and other mothers preferred having a nanny who could be treated more like a servant. In *Nursery World* in the 1920s, mothers debated lady nurses' unreasonable needs to be waited on and whether or not they should be treated as family. Mothers also discussed the difference between lady nurses and the old-fashioned nannies they recalled nostalgically from their own childhoods and whose superior qualities they praised. By contrast one 'harassed mother' bemoaned the petty bourgeois ideas of her college-trained nurse, which she believed were making her children appallingly priggish.[33]

Another correspondent was anxious to dispel the idea that there should be any difference between nannies and lady nurses and thought that they should be treated the same socially since they did the same work.[34] In response to this the editor pointed out the class differences between the two positions, assuming that a nanny would make her own friends and socialise with servants, while a lady nurse would be utterly lonely without the companionship of her employer and should not be forced into too much contact with servants. One lady nurse pointed out the difficulties of her position when visiting a hotel and being forced to have meals with waiters, and insisted on eating meals only with people of her own social position. The editor's reply shows the uncertain position lady nurses occupied in a society where class barriers were beginning to break down:

> I take it that you were engaged as a lady nurse; that is to say that you were not engaged as a nurse, and incidentally happened to be a lady. If being a lady is part of your job, that position should certainly be upheld by your employer [. . .]. This is not snobbery: it is due to yourself and others to uphold the status of the lady nurse. But I shall be very glad of other opinions.[35]

Yet for employers, socialising with lady nurses was not as easy as this advice suggests. The article entitled 'Those Interfering Mothers' by Joan Bateson pointed out how important it was that readers recognised they lived in a changed world. She posed the problem in relation to her own self-sacrificing old-fashioned nanny who had dedicated her life to children and 'never took one minute off day or night'. This was the regime under which she believed most employers had been brought up. There were now opportunities for them to develop friendships with the new younger lady nurses that would never have happened in the past. However she also recognised the difficulties of negotiating a relationship in which class divisions were much less clear. Was she or was she not one of them and what relationship did she bear to old-fashioned nannies?

> What should we call her [. . .] ? Where ought she to feed? Will she hate your friends, or will she want to know them? If you are smoking, do you offer her a cigarette? Is she in fact like ourselves inside, or has she some relationship to the starched miracle of our own childhood?[36]

The problem all these examples illustrate is the clash between professional and personal relationships, as boundaries became blurred between a nanny's position as servant, professional worker, family member and family friend.

Loneliness was a common complaint from lady nurses who felt socially isolated. But one nurse had a sympathetic understanding of the difficulties her presence in the household caused and prioritised the needs of the married couple over her own. She also offered a clear analysis of the advantages and disadvantages of the different households. In her former position where she was 'one of the family', she never had a minute to herself and was heartbroken when she had to leave. But however lonely she felt in her new post, where she was alone in her room after 7pm, she was determined to stay and work with the mother, acknowledging the mother's right to have ideas about her own children.[37] The shift in her position from a family member to a professional relationship is made very clear.

It was not, however, only the lady nurses who gave their opinions. An 'old-fashioned nurse' argued that 'there can be and often is a very true friendship between mother and nurse even if she is of the "old-fashioned Nanny" type'.[38] Perhaps some mothers found it easier to depend on and be friends with an old-fashioned nanny who knew her place than they did with a single woman of their own class who did not. Like the nineteenth-century governess, lady nurses were in a more ambivalent position, a threat as much to a mother's relationship with her husband and her sexual identity as a wife.

POST-WAR NANNIES: THE DEMISE OF THE LADY NURSE

Lady nurses finally disappeared following the collapse of live-in domestic service after the Second World War and specialist nannies in sole charge were only now required in the wealthiest homes. Mothers writing to *Nursery World* at the height of post-war austerity during the cold, wet summer of 1946 despaired of getting any live-in childcare at a price they could afford, often having to manage with only a daily help:

> Nannie is unnecessary; home help doesn't sound very attractive; mother's help doesn't convey my meaning. I need someone equivalent to the

army aide de camp who can be relied on to pull their weight under any and every circumstance; but I feel only the celestial regions will ever fulfil my requirements.[39]

Another mother said she would gladly have had an ex-nanny as a general help whom she could trust with the children overnight, while a nanny insisted that although she would be willing to lend a hand with housework on occasion, her work should really be in the nursery. Nannies and mothers endlessly debated how much time off they should have, whether or not housework should be included in addition to childcare and what the job should be called. Trying to cope with 'rations, coupons, housekeeping, sickness etc.', a mother longed for a 'really jolly, understanding, honest-to-goodness soul who is not too superior' and asked readers to invent a title for the type of helper she required. Another responded that nurses who 'assisted with extraneous tasks were now valued much more highly than departmental nurses' and argued that their status should be raised; 'assistant housewife would more fittingly describe the finest preparation for wife and motherhood'.[40] Furthermore, some women, who had to manage without help during the war, were critical of mothers who demanded nannies. Post-war propaganda on the undesirability of mothers leaving their children added fuel to these debates, and by the mid-1950s one woman went so far as to condemn a mother who wanted her child to be trained by an expert, pointing out that he was not a 'circus animal'.[41]

CONCLUSION

The shifting relationships of power, authority and interdependence between mothers and nannies revealed in childcare magazines are important to explore because, as Alison Light showed in her study of Virginia Woolf's relationship with her servants, we cannot understand middle-class married women's social relationships and productivity outside the home without also investigating the care relations within it.[42] Moreover, where childcare is concerned, the lives and voices of the women who gave care have largely remained invisible. The difficulty for upper- and middle-class women to admit their dependence on nannies was connected to their own conflicted and gendered position in relation to the outside world. The evidence given in this chapter of emotional tensions within the home, whether related to class, professional knowledge or marital status, is part of a wider history of service relations in twentieth-century Britain. But they also speak to us today. For as Light has pointed out, how we tolerate our inevitable dependence on those who do our dirty work, those who care for us and care for our children, 'is not a private or domestic question but one which goes to the heart of social structures and their inequalities'.[43]

NOTES

1. Letter from Miss Ritchie, *Nursery World*, 23 December 1925, 112.
2. Katherine Holden, *The Shadow of Marriage: Singleness in England 1914–1960* (Manchester: Manchester University Press, 2007), chapter eight.
3. It has been estimated that the number of nannies in any given year between 1850 and 1939 lay somewhere between a quarter and half a million. See Jonathan Gathorne-Hardy, *The Rise and Fall of the British Nanny* (London: Weidenfield and Nicholas, 1993), 181.
4. See Jane Hamlett, *Material Relations: Domestic Interiors and Middle-Class Families 1850–1910* (Manchester: Manchester University Press, 2010), chapter three.
5. Katherine Holden, *Nanny Knows Best: The History of the British Nanny* (Stroud: The History Press, 2013).
6. Arlie R. Hochschild, 'Love and gold,' in *Global Woman: Nannies, Maids and Sex Workers in the New Economy*, ed. Barbara Ehrenreich and Arlie R. Hochschild (London: Granta Books, 2002), 26.
7. Cameron L. Macdonald, *Shadow Mothers, Nannies, Au Pairs, and the Micropolitics of Mothering* (Berkeley, CA: University of California Press, 2011), 126–7.
8. Letters from nannies to Mrs Beamish with news of Tufton and John. CLW/1/6/2 n.d. (c. 1920s), Baron Chelwood Papers, East Sussex Record Office.
9. See Barbara Kline, *White House Nannies: True Tales from the Other Department of Homeland Security* (New York: Tarcher/Penguin Group, 2006).
10. Jenna Bailey, *Can any Mother Help Me? Fifty Years of Women's Friendship Through a Secret Magazine* (London: Faber and Faber, 2007), 3.
11. Margaret Beetham, 'The reinvention of the English domestic woman: Class and "race" in the 1890s' woman's magazine,' *Women's Studies International Forum* 21 (1998): 226.
12. Bailey, *Can any Mother Help Me?*, 10.
13. Bailey, *Can any Mother Help Me?*, 3.
14. Cynthia White, *Women's Magazines 1693–1968* (London: Michael Joseph, 1970), 128.
15. Beetham, 'The reinvention of the English domestic woman,' 225–6.
16. Editions of *Nursery World* over one year were surveyed every ten years in 1926, 1936, 1946 and 1956. Some additional correspondence from intervening years in *Nursery World* taken from other sources is also included in the analysis. The content of letters has been analysed in relation to the advice of childcare experts in the magazine.
17. Editions of the *Norland Quarterly* over a six-month period were surveyed every five years using the same methodology as with *Nursery World*.
18. Christina Hardyment, *Dream Babies: Childcare from John Locke to Gina Ford* (London: Francis Lincoln Ltd, 2007), chapter four. See, for example, M. Truby King, *Mothercraft* (London: Simkin, Marshall Ltd. 1934), 4–5; 'Modern woman, 1929,' in Tanith Carey, *Never Kiss a Man in a Canoe: Words of Wisdom from the Golden Age of Agony Aunts* (London: Boxtree, 2009), 103.
19. D. A. Kennedy, *The Care and Nursing of the Infant for Infant Welfare Workers and Nursery Nurses* (London: William Heinemann, 1930), 49.
20. 'Over the teacups,' *Nursery World*, 24 February 1926, 328, and 28 April 1926, 544.
21. See, for example, Eustace Chesser, 'Simple psychology for women,' *Nursery World*, 20 January, 1926.

22 'A Princess Christian nurse,' *Nursery World*, 24 February 1926, 328.
23 Letter from Cicely Colls and editorial by Emily Ward, *Norland Quarterly*, December 1909.
24 'A harassed mother,' *Nursery World*, 24 February 1926, 327.
25 'Miss Reynolds,' *Nursery World*, 13 January 1926, 184.
26 The Hon. Mrs De Gray, 'Finding a nurse,' *Nursery World*, 26 May 1926.
27 Ursula Bowlby, 'Experiences of motherhood. 1939–54,' and 'Happy infancy'. PP/Bow/P.3, Wellcome Library, Archives and Manuscripts.
28 'A doctor's wife,' *Nursery World*, 16 April 1941.
29 Philip Graham, *Susan Isaacs: A Life Freeing the Minds of Children* (London: Karnac Books, 2009) 208–15.
30 These letters to *Nursery World* in the 1930s were republished in Susan Isaacs, *Children and Parents: Their Problems and Difficulties* (London: Routledge and Kegan Paul, 1968), 3–4, 48–50.
31 Phyllis Hostler, 'Mother or nurse,' *Nursery World*, 20 December 1956.
32 Letter to *Nursery World*, 22 August 1946.
33 'A harassed mother,' *Nursery World*, 24 February 1926, 327.
34 'An interested mother,' *Nursery World*, 27 January 1926, 232.
35 'Molehill,' *Nursery World*, 30 December 1925, 136.
36 Joan Bateson, 'A mother's advice to nurses: An answer in effect to "those interfering mothers,"' *Nursery World*, 10 February 1926.
37 'Surrey nurse's advice to lonely nurses,' *Nursery World*, 3 March 1926, 351.
38 'An old fashioned nurse,' *Nursery World*, 24 February 1926, 327.
39 Letter to *Nursery World*, 15 August 1946.
40 Letters in *Nursery World*, 18 April 1946; 27 June 1946; 11 July 1946; 15 August 1946; 5 September 1946; 19 September 1946; 10 October 1946.
41 Letter to *Nursery World*, 25 October 1956.
42 Alison Light, *Mrs Woolf and Her Servants* (London: Penguin, 2007).
43 Light, *Mrs Woolf*, 314.

Part IV
Young Women in Magazines

11 The American Girl
Ideas of Nationalism and Sexuality as Promoted in the *Ladies' Home Journal* during the Early Twentieth Century

Cheyanne Cortez

Emblazoned on the February 1903 cover of the *Ladies' Home Journal* is the profile of 'Mr Gibson's American Girl' (Figure 11.1). In this drawing, Gibson encapsulated his idea of the American Girl. The tagline, 'THE MAGAZINE WITH A MILLION', atop the page declares the status of the *Ladies' Home Journal* as the first magazine to have one million subscribers. This cover thus announced two facts: the widespread presence of the *Ladies' Home Journal* in the American home and equally widespread fascination with 'the American Girl'. Depicted as beautiful and charming, the Girl was an archetype for the American middle class. Typified as an unmarried young white woman between the ages of eighteen and twenty-five, she navigated her life with charm, joy and beguiling naïveté. She was selfishly altruistic, candidly artificial and incorrigibly attractive. She was America's sweetheart, adored by the nation and emulated by young women across the country.[1] Her dynamic characteristics allowed for both personal connection and greater national approval. This chapter is an examination of the American Girl as an icon of United States idealism in accordance with mass cultural constructs of race and female sexuality, using how she was represented in the *Ladies' Home Journal* in the early twentieth century as its focus. My survey of the *Journal* follows the tenure of its most influential editor, Edward W. Bok, whose editorship from October 1889 to December 1919 corresponded to the time when it was one of the most widely read and successful magazines in the country.

THE AMERICAN GIRL ARCHETYPE

The public celebrated the American Girl in magazines, newspapers, songs, plays and mass-produced products. Her cultivation and veneration provided the changing country with an evident and glorified identity. In her book, *Imaging American Women: Idea and Ideals in Cultural History* (1987), Martha Banta argued that the public's adoration of the American Girl was symptomatic of a greater national identity crisis, and the saturation of Girl imagery functioned as a publicly sanctioned ideal of race and social status for men to worship and for women to emulate.[2] The country was fascinated and attracted to the Girl as a representation of desirable 'American' qualities.

It is important to recognise the American Girl as a personification of the United States, unlike Columbia, the allegory of the North and South Americas. This clarification of these commonly misapplied terms and female figures enhances our understanding of the American Girl as a manifestation of United States character and national pride that was embodied by young women. Columbia is associated with the 'New World' and the discovery of the Americas by Christopher Columbus. Columbia wears clothes of Greco-Roman antiquity and adapts monumental postures embodying peace, bounty and liberty. The American Girl, on the other hand, wears the latest fashions and performs popular everyday activities. Columbia exists equally in the past, present and future, unlike the American Girl, who is rooted in the present and therefore must conform to contemporary American culture. No one is expected to become Columbia, but one may emulate the American Girl.

THE *LADIES' HOME JOURNAL* AND ITS EDITOR, EDWARD BOK

As the personification of the United States at the turn of the last century, the American Girl was utilised in magazines as part of the pedagogy of a national identity, functioning as a visual definition and form of instruction in what it is to be 'American'. During this golden age of magazines, publications were the taste-creators of American culture and one of the most influential magazines was the *Ladies' Home Journal*.[3] Established in 1883 by Cyrus H. K. Curtis and originally edited by his wife, Louise Knapp Curtis, the *Ladies' Home Journal* began as an eight-page middle-class woman's monthly magazine. Within six years, it had expanded to thirty-two pages and had over 440,000 subscribers, more than double any other women's and general interest magazine at this time.[4] In 1889, Curtis hired a new editor, Edward K. Bok, a Dutch immigrant and successful twenty-six year-old advertising director at Charles Scribner's Sons publishing house and editor of the national news syndicate, Bok's Syndicate Press.[5] The fact that Bok, a man, was the editor of the most popular US woman's magazine was not seen as unusual: the publishing world was very much a male domain in the late nineteenth century. However, in his autobiography, Bok acknowledged the criticisms of his career in understanding feminine intuition and the fact that the public was often surprised by his masculine nature. The key to Bok's success with the *Journal* was that he was a highly perceptive and intuitive businessman with a firm understanding of the American psyche. He emigrated from the Netherlands with his family as a boy and described his childhood as an 'experiment in Americanization', a process of social interactions and cultural adaptations.[6] Bok observed during his 'Americanization' that the American public was always ready to recognise and follow a leader; he provided that leadership through his strong editorial voice in the *Journal*.

While the *Ladies' Home Journal*'s direct competitors, such as *McCall's* and *Good Housekeeping*, offered similar content of household management advice and sewing and fashion patterns, Bok's magazine was a 'problem solver' that was informative, intimate, entertaining and efficient, offering a variety of news, politics, fiction and fashion with service departments for housekeeping, health and personal advice. The *Journal* proved to be the most influential, with over one million subscribers by 1903, while *McCall's* did not reach that benchmark until 1908 and *Good Housekeeping* had achieved a mere 300,000 subscribers in 1911 when it was purchased by William Randolph Hearst.[7] The *Ladies' Home Journal* was often referred to as the 'monthly Bible of the American home', and under the ministry of its influential editor, it dictated proper and appropriate ideas, values and goals to the American woman and her family.[8]

One of the *Ladies' Home Journal*'s largest audiences and the focus of Bok's greatest editorial concern was the young woman (or girl, as she was referred to) between the ages of eighteen and twenty-five. The *Journal* dedicated several advice columns over the years to her, including 'Side Talk with Girls' by Ruth Ashmore, 'Girls' Problems', 'Good Health for Girls', Margaret Sangster's 'Heart to Heart talks with Girls' and 'Pretty Girl Questions'. The magazine also published the book, *Side Talk with Girls* (1896), as a continued discussion from the department of the same name. Ashmore's dedication read:

> To the American Girl. Wherever she may be I dedicate this book. I respect her independence, I honor her goodness, and I love her sweetness. She makes the most charming of friends, the best of wives, and the trusted of mothers. These three positions in life will, I hope, represent her future.[9]

'From schoolroom to altar', the *Journal* advised young women on issues of health, romance, fashion, friendship, social etiquette and culture.[10]

Additionally, the *Ladies' Home Journal* printed special Girl, Romance and Bridal issues that were dedicated to young women, with such features as 'The American Girl Two-step', 'What 100 Girls would like to Be' and 'My Greatest Experiences as a Girl and How I Met It'.[11] Stunning images of American Girls by famous illustrators, including Charles Dana Gibson, Harrison Fisher and Howard Chandler Christy, regularly appeared on *Journal* covers. Poster-size prints of these featured covers were available for purchase by mail, and over 100,000 copies sold in one year.[12] The American Girl was the *Journal*'s most popular and profitable cover girl.

Although the *Ladies' Home Journal* was not a political magazine, its editorials and illustrative covers offered insight into the racially charged political and social agendas of mass culture in the United States in the early twentieth century. While this chapter focuses on the American Girl archetype as the ideal young woman, as depicted in the magazine, there was actually little, if any, opposing imagery presented in the *Ladies' Home Journal*. Bok had very specific and strong ideas about modern American womanhood. While his editorials recognised the progressive societal changes of the time, he wished to counter conflicting female figures, such as the politically radical New Woman and the sexually promiscuous Evil Girl, with images and articles expounding the virtues of the more conservative woman, wife and mother.[13] Bok understood the American Girl to be a politically moderate and socially conventional young woman, as illustrated in a five-part series *American Girl* by the illustrator Howard Chandler Christy, published in 1900. In this series of images, she was depicted in various scenarios, including 'at church' and 'at sport', presenting a visual diagram of the appropriate social activities for young women.[14] For Bok, the New Woman and the Evil Girl did not represent his readers and therefore were not illustrated and only peripherally acknowledged in his magazine.

The February 1903 cover, 'Mr Gibson's American Girl', exemplified the racial and eugenic agendas of the early twentieth century. Her distinctly Anglo-Saxon profile is set adrift in a crimson sea. The crown of silky locks atop her head softens the line of her elegant brow. Her small straight nose is

Figure 11.1 Charles Dana Gibson, 'Mr Gibson's American Girl', *Ladies' Home Journal*, February 1903.

delicate and sweet. The graceful line of her profile indicates the statuesque body not represented on the page. The American Girl appears on the *Journal* cover like an effervescent cloud that accumulated on its surface. Gibson always maintained that his famous Gibson girls were not representations of any particular woman but a collection of American types. In 'The Origin of a Type of the American Girl', author Richard Davis proclaimed the influential power of Gibson's illustrations: 'It is as though Gibson had set up a standard of feminine beauty and sent it broadcast through the land by means of the magazine and periodicals, to show his countrywomen of what they were capable and of what was expected of them in consequence.'[15] The American Girl was a manifestation of human potential in a democratic environment, and the power of her image was meant to inspire the nation.

A magazine cover should be considered a form of cultural propaganda. Every magazine carries both explicit and implied messages to a targeted audience and promotes these messages on its covers.[16] In his analysis of early twentieth-century advertising, cultural historian Roland Marchand explains the 'hypodermic needle' theory to describe the power of media images to inject certain attitudes and ideas into the minds of the audience; this repeated imagery constructs frames of reference.[17] While Marchand acknowledges that the theory is flawed (it does not allow for people's choice to not believe the ideas being forced upon them), he stresses that the repeated imagery carries specific messages that the public may accept as truths. In this context, the America Girl cover of the February 1903 issue of the *Journal* should be analysed as both a message and a messenger of American identity.

THE AMERICAN RACE

The American Girl was not a political figure and not representative of the body politic, but this does not negate her use as an anchor for a distinct political and social agenda. Examining the significance of a person's political identity as manifested in their physical appearance, Elaine Scarry in *The Body of Pain: the Making and Unmaking of the World* (1985) stipulates that a person's national identity is usually learned, unconsciously and effortlessly, at a very early age.[18] She cites French sociologist Pierre Bourdieu on the physical embodiment of identity: 'The principles em-bodied [sic] in this way are placed beyond the grasp of consciousness [. . .] nothing seems more ineffable, more incommunicable, more inimitable, and therefore, more precious, than the values given body, *made* body by the transubstantiation achieved by the hidden pedagogy [. . .]'.[19] The principles embodied are unconsciously done; therefore they cover indefinite boundaries and cannot be adequately expressed. The allusive and abstract nature of a national identity is thus more sacred than the material reality. The American Girl was not representative of the body politic, but her body was made public and therefore was political. The *Ladies' Home Journal* was a conduit for transmission of these multifaceted messages that she embodied.

Many social changes were in process in the United States at this time: there was a steady influx of immigrants, while urban overcrowding was associated with growing levels of pollution and poor living conditions. Fears of racial degeneration by perceived inferior 'white' peoples increased racial tensions.[20] In addition, during the second half of the nineteenth century, there developed a pseudo-scientific dialogue to refine and redefine the concept of the 'white' race. The arrival of large numbers of non-Anglo-Saxon European immigrants into the US generated fear among the local population, who labelled the immigrants as degenerate 'white' breeds who threatened to corrupt and cripple the purity of the American (Anglo-Saxon) people and the greater republic. Blending science and cultural observations, native (Anglo-Saxon) born Americans debated the viability and political fitness of non-Anglo-Saxon white peoples based on observational measurements of physical, social and economic differences, with little consideration of pre-existing cultural and environmental conditions. The American Girl was a declaration of United States standards meant to assuage these fears. In his book *The American Girl* (1906), a sentimental proclamation of the type, the author and illustrator Howard Chandler Christy defined her as an exemplary testament of racial superiority and evolutionary advancement:

> Never before has the world offered full opportunity for the perfecting of the highest type of womanhood; never before have the selected individuals from all the races of the world been brought together under such conditions as to come to the best of which they are capable. And apart from sentiment, uninfluenced by any narrow patriotism, trying simply to see clearly the causes at work and their necessary results, we may confidently declare that the American Girl in the future will become a veritable queen of the kingliest of races.[21]

Representing the best of the white races, Christy proclaimed her to reign supreme over all other nations. The American Girl was a physical and psychological ideal, and the move to establish and cultivate her in turn provided the country with the security of an Anglo-Saxon national identity.

The concept of an American race as portrayed by the *Ladies' Home Journal*'s American Girl cover allows us to consider how she represented a homogeneous culture for an increasingly racially diverse nation. In his influential work, *Whiteness of a Different Color: European Immigrants and the Alchemy of Race* (1998), historian Matthew Frye Jacobson described the construct of race as a construct of power: who belongs, who is deserving and who is capable.[22] 'Race' was a form of control and 'white' was synonymous with superiority. The concept of a white race was central to the foundation of the United States; its significance is expressed in the first naturalisation law of 1790 that limited citizenship to 'free white persons'. To better understand the American Girl's racial significance, it should be acknowledged that a distinction between ethnicity and race did not exist in nineteenth-century America, rather there was a fluidity and hierarchy of whiteness. Immigration policies, such as the 1887 Dawes Act (which granted Native Americans citizenship based on their individual renouncement of tribal practices) and the Chinese Exclusion Act of 1882 and the Geary Act of 1892 (which barred Chinese immigration and refused to grant citizenship to Chinese resident aliens), were enacted based on the belief that a culturally, if not racially, homogenous population was a requirement for American citizenship.

The rising immigration of peoples from Europe caused many native-born Americans of northern European ancestry to doubt the equality of whiteness and others' 'fitness for self-government'.[23] Between 1865 and 1914, over 25 million immigrants entered the United States. Prior to 1890, most were from northern Europe, predominantly fair-skinned and Protestant, but after 1890 the majority were olive-skinned and Catholic or Jewish, from eastern and southern Europe. Many United States-born people of Protestant Anglo-Saxon origins considered these 'new immigrants' to be racially inferior, culturally backwards and economically threatening. Symptomatic of the burgeoning immigrant population in America at this time was a growing idea of nativism, an anti-immigrant sentiment that developed early in the founding of the country with roots in the 1798 Alien Act, which limited the rights of unnaturalised immigrants. The nativist sentiment came to the forefront of American culture and politics with the founding of the Immigrant Restriction League in 1893. Members of this national society expounded the theory of eugenics against non-northern European immigrants. Nativists disregarded environmental and economic conditions and blamed these peoples for the epidemics, overcrowding and crime plaguing US cities. Nativists were extremely xenophobic and viewed each new wave of immigrants as societal pollutants who encroached upon their own independence and democratic rights.[24]

The nativist Charles Davenport, in *Heredity in Relation to Eugenics* (1911), warned the American public that 'the population of the United States will, on account of the great influx of blood from South-eastern Europe, rapidly become darker in pigmentation, smaller in stature, more mercurial [. . .] more given to crimes of larceny, kidnapping, assault, murder, rape, and sex-immorality [. . .]'.[25] Combining heritable traits with environmental factors, Davenport condemned entire peoples as unfit and caustic to society. Similarly, in 1914, sociologist Edward Ross expressed his anxiety over the increased immigrant population, believing that America would soon be 'swamped and submerged by an overwhelming tide of latecomers from the old-world hive'.[26] Likening them to a deadly swarm, Ross viewed the sheer number of these peoples as a form of terrorism. In reaction to this perceived problem, nativists used eugenic principles and ethno-racial categories of whiteness to distance themselves, biologically and politically, from the recent immigrants.

Fueled by anthropological theory, the United States government employed eugenic principles of race to define and legitimise citizenship. Eugenicists sought to delineate the physical traits of an exclusively 'American' race that would properly express the ideals and strengths of the country. Anthroposophical studies flooded mass culture with pseudo-scientific diagrams charting humans on racially biased hierarchical scales of intelligence and integrity.[27] Favouring the northern European Anglo-Saxon race, eugenicists cited the physiognomic regularity of Anglo-Saxon features, in comparison to non-Anglo-Saxon features, as evidence of greater intelligence and moral superiority. These ideas may seem disturbing today, but such views provide a clearer understanding of how eugenic beliefs were enacted in politics and depicted in mass culture. In this context, the American Girl's whiteness and the extreme regularity of her features were the embodiment of her nation's superior race, intelligence and ethical code.

THE ANGLO-AMERICAN GIRL

Returning to the February 1903 *Ladies' Home Journal* cover, the American Girl is set against an opaque background in a fashion similar to the physiognomic illustrative figures in which racial portraits are depicted against empty backgrounds. Her pale skin and Anglo-Saxon features enhance her 'beauty'. Her skin is soft and fair, the fullness of her cheek revealing her health and vigour. Her voluminous and glossy hair is piled atop her head to expose a firm jawline and long neck, while the shape of her nose and defined chin imply the refinement and strength of her spirit. The subtle pout of her lips and soft gaze of her eyes indicate her intelligence and charm. Her gaze is bold and clear; her features are feminine and white. She is beautiful, she is confident, she is healthy; she is a testament of superior Anglo-Saxon Protestant American stock.

One of the American Girl's greatest mass cultural advantages was her standardised 'white' appearance that allowed for an almost infinite number of versions of herself without deviating from her racial origins. As a national identity, her symbolic function stabilised and substantiated American culture. The physical exhibition of the American Girl on the February 1903 cover of the *Ladies' Home Journal* demonstrated clearly to the reader who could (and also who could not) embody the American race. Those who did not resemble her appearance were seen as less American, marginalised citizens. Women of colour were never considered to be the *Journal*'s audience and therefore were rarely depicted in it. In terms of mass culture, visual representations of racial minorities as individuals, rather than as denigrated stereotypes, would disrupt the homo-racial hegemony of America. To be 'American' was to be white. There were obvious advantages for citizens who were white or could pass for white. To be white carried real and attributed privileges of social opportunity, legal representation and financial freedom. By simple extension, therefore, the American Girl symbolised not merely the liberty of being a US citizen but also the privilege of being white.[28]

Young women around the country were praised for embodying the American spirit. The April 1902 *Ladies' Home Journal* article 'The President's Daughter' introduced President Theodore Roosevelt's teenage daughter Alice as a real-life American Girl: 'Alice Roosevelt is the typical American girl in the best sense of the word; modest, self-reliant, democratic [. . .]'.[29] Her personality and physical attributes embodied national values and behaviours; she represented the country's promise and potential and presented a model for *Ladies' Home Journal* readers to live up to. The American Girl thus served as a prototype and, on a higher level, as part of a strategy for hegemonic discourse between the dominant and subordinate racial classes in the United States.

PREVENTING RACIAL SUICIDE

Concurrent with the definition and celebration of a national race was the country's fear of its degeneration and possible extinction. Declining birth rates among white-middle class families was a major concern in the western world. Commonly referred to as 'race suicide', the declining birth rate was feared across Europe and the United States owing to a widespread fall in population growth that generated anxieties of racial annihilation. Over the course of the nineteenth century, the American family size decreased by half. In 1800, the average family had seven children; by 1900 the average was 3.54 children.[30] In contrast, birth rates in 1900 among recent immigrant families were much higher: in Buffalo, New York, for example, Polish families averaged eight children and Italians had an average of eleven children per household.[31] These disproportionately large families gave rise to widespread concerns that the majority of Americans were no longer of Anglo-Saxon origin. It was feared that these new Americans would overrun the country, ultimately leading to the nation's downfall.

Many theorists explained the declining birth rates among native-born white couples as a result of a deterioration in women's physical and mental constitutions, caused by over-exertion in their pursuit of advanced degrees, employment outside the home and suffrage. As a result, young women's physical and reproductive fitness became of national interest. Gynaecologist William H. Walling, in his book *Sexology* (1904), which linked sex and morality, stressed that good breeding was entirely dependent on the physical improvement of the Girl as the future mother of the American race.[32] W. I. Thomas, an American sociologist and social psychologist, wrote *Sex and Society* in 1907 as a guide to avoiding the destruction of maidenly innocence in the modern world.[33] Physicians, psychologists and sociologists concentrated their efforts on understanding the role of female health in the maintenance and improvement of the white race in the face of challenges to traditional western culture.[34]

The American obstetrician and gynaecologist, George J. Engelmann, who was also the author of *The American Girl of To-Day: Modern Education and Functional Health* (1901), outlined his concerns and medical recommendations for promoting women's physical health in an address to the Southern Surgical and Gynaecological Association in November 1890. Engelmann argued, 'The importance of female hygiene and the social dangers which threaten the health of the America Girl, bearing closely upon our common welfare; it concerns layman and physician; it concerns not alone the individual, but the State, in its broadest sense.'[35] His address positions the Girl as a manifestation of the American race, a breed to be cultivated and the nation's greatest investment. He continued, '[although] woman is the exponent of a nation, indicative of its development, of its growth or depreciation, the American woman is more closely linked with the state and fate of her nation than is the woman of other countries'.[36] Therefore, more than her European counterparts, the American Girl was essential to the success of the nation as a result of her more direct (democratic) involvement in the greater society.

Many medical professionals, Engelmann among them, recommended moderate exercise to combat women's biological failings and strengthen their mental and physical health. In the June 1900 *Journal,* Bok published Dr S. Weir Mitchell's editorial 'When the College is Hurtful to a Girl,' voicing concerns over college girls' unhealthy emphasis on intellectual pursuits which supposedly could lead to physical and mental health complications. He reported that the lack of physical exercise during exam time caused, in some cases, girls to experience 'emotional neurasthenics' and 'hysterical breakdowns'.[37] Popular activities including tennis, golf, basketball and cycling were recommended as sources of physical exercise and social entertainment for young women. The *Journal* article, 'Are Athletics Making Girls Masculine?: A Practical Answer to a Question Every Girl Asks', by Dr Dudley A. Sargent, Director of the Harvard Gymnasium, reassured readers that rather than leading to a masculinisation of the female sex, exercise belonged to 'the progressive stages of the evolution of mankind'.[38] Moderate physical and intellectual exercises created a well-rounded young woman, the best kind of woman to be a future wife and mother.

Many *Ladies' Home Journal* covers featured the American Girl enjoying athletic activities, including canoe races, golf, tennis and ocean bathing. Politically, racially and economically, the Girl's active lifestyle was explicitly American. The *Ladies' Home Journal* encouraged athleticism, as in the article, 'Why and How Girls should Swim' (August 1910), and offered recommendations for physical exercise with the reassurance that it would benefit the American Girl and consequently improve the race.[39] Beginning in the early 1900s, the *Journal*'s monthly column, 'Good Health for Girls', by Emma E. Walker, MD, offered young women medical advice, beauty tips and recommended physical exercises. In another article, 'Why Golf is Good for Girls', Walker pointed out that golf uses nearly all the muscles of the body, sharpens the mind and improves the appetite and the circulation.[40] This column often included a five-minute exercise routine accompanied by a demonstrational photo of a young woman performing the movements. The reader was left in no doubt that the health benefits derived from such exercise were, in essence, part of the American Girl's patriotic duty.[41]

A young woman's primary duty was to marry. Physicians and scholars at the turn of the last century warned against the rogue woman who deliberately shirked her biological duties and societal conventions to be a wife, bear children and manage the home. The independent unmarried woman was seen as a menace to society, indirectly encouraging immorality, contributing to the degradation of the race and ultimately the fall of civilisation. There was a general consensus among the medical and pseudo-medical fields that woman's involvement in the public sphere acted against her biological nature and was reproductively damaging.[42] Popular theorists' publications, including the evolutionist Herbert Spencer's *Principles of Ethics* (1887) and the sociologists Patrick Geddes and J. Arthur Thomson's *Evolution of Sex* (1889), asserted that the biological differences between males and females were evidence of their differing abilities.[43] Women were deemed physically and mentally inferior to men and therefore were unfit for public sphere activities.[44] With declining birth rates as apparent confirmation, it was claimed that the public activities of New Women, female social reformers and suffragists had an adverse effect on the human race.[45] In 1912, former President Theodore Roosevelt publically expressed his fears of race suicide in the *Outlook* magazine article, 'Women's Rights: The Duties of Both Men and Women', claiming the danger of women's emancipation was not in the vote but their delay of marriage caused by their active public roles.[46] Roosevelt asserted that marital duty was more important than individual men and women's rights, 'for unless the average man and the average woman live lives of duty, not only our democracy but civilization itself will perish'.[47] Quoting British physician and eugenicist Dr C. W. Saleeby, he claimed the delay of marriage was not only detrimental to the nation but also harmful to a woman's health. Both Saleeby and Roosevelt warned that delaying marriage (read as socially approved sexual intercourse) stunted a woman's physical development, 'indirectly encouraging male immorality and female prostitution'.[48] Making the assumption that women did not have sex or children out of wedlock, Roosevelt believed women who resisted marriage shattered the biological harmony between the sexes and would be responsible for the United States' social downfall. Therefore, in order for the American race to survive, it was a young woman's patriotic duty to marry and procreate. Bok, as editor of the most successful magazine aimed at young white American women, was perfectly poised to deliver that message.

Bok's May 1908 *Journal* article, 'The American Girl: An Editorial', directly criticised the American Girl's neglectful mother and her New Woman (read as 'masculine') demands for suffrage and a more active political and professional role in society. The New Woman mother, he claimed, was absent from the home, neglectful of her duties and failed to deliver maternal guidance. Despite these detrimental circumstances though, Bok believed the American Girl would persevere. For him, it was the Girl's responsibility to continue the noble cause of motherhood: 'Upon her rests the future of an American motherhood that will give to her children what has so largely been withheld from her.'[49] With pure heart and feminine intuition, according to Bok, the American Girl would save the nation.

Before the Nineteenth Amendment granted American women the right to vote in 1920 (although in practice few women of colour were able to exercise the franchise), women were socially and politically defined by the men in their lives. In addition to her doting father, the American Girl's heart belonged to her sweetheart. She was unmarried but, according to the *Ladies' Home Journal*, her goal in life was to be a wife and mother. The biological and social harmony created by her romantic interests and eventual marriage served as a form of charity and self-sacrifice towards the greater good of the nation. The *Journal's* book *Side Talk with Girls*, by Ashmore, advised young women to be socially (and racially) mindful in their search for love. 'Be pleasant and agreeable to all who may be in your own social world, but give no one man the right to especially claim you until the veritable Prince Charming appears.'[50] In matters of love, the Girl's modern world was transformed into a chivalric narrative; she became a princess waiting for her prince. However, more than romantic, Ashmore reminded her readers to be selective, and to ensure she fell in love with a man of her own social (racial) status.

The American princess was also present in Christy's description of the Girl's first love. He encouraged her chaperone to allow her to experience the thrill of courtship. He wrote 'How else shall the little Princess learn to know her own kind from the baser-born?'[51] Such exposure would enable her to discern and distinguish herself from (racially) inferior men. The American Girl was treated like a purebred in matters of love and marriage. The *Ladies' Home Journal* also recommended the use of a chaperone in courtship.[52] In an editorial warning against risqué behaviour, Bok tells the Girl, 'Young men soon lose their respect for such a girl exactly in proportion as she allows them any familiarity.'[53] He calls to his readership to 'make clearer in the minds of our young women that proper deportment in a girl is her great and only safeguard, and the one which will win for her the esteem of her own sex, and the respect of the best and truest men'.[54] Bok continues by reminding young women of the direct link between a respectable woman and the greater good of society through her husband. Avoiding the risk of a misstep or indiscretion not only helped young women to protect their reputations; it also served to preserve and improve the United States of America.

Mass culture teaches young women whom to love and more importantly how to be loveable.[55] Early-twentieth-century mass culture promoted the concept of marital bliss as an unequivocal attraction between a man and a woman. Sexologists, psychologists and biologists alike encouraged expression rather than repression of sex within the sanctity of marriage; the couple's sexual intimacy ensured social harmony. Therefore passion became fundamental to the American Girl's viability. In the *Ladies' Home Journal*, the American Girl's sexuality was addressed monthly in the advice columns and special Romance issues and novelettes, while the magazine's covers celebrated the innocence of young love. The *Journal* advice columns were littered with lovers' quarrels and pining poetry. Its novelettes and serialised romances, such as 'Love Stories of some American Girls' and 'A Live Ember', emphasised the man's domination and the submission of the American Girl, further reaffirming their gendered societal roles.[56] Barbara Welter, in *Dimity Convictions* (1976), has argued that romance novels are tools for sexual instruction, teaching how a woman loves a man and her social and emotional expectations.[57] Thus the American Girl's virginal sensuality was treated as a fact of human nature and was cultivated through romantic imagery and fiction to maintain her sexual vitality for her eventual application in matrimony. Filling young women's heads and hearts with passionate love stories was healthy and beneficial to good breeding.

Like a blossom at the peak of its perfumed perfection, the American Girl was ripe with heated passion. In a society still influenced by nineteenth-century ideas about women's inability to control their passions, the American Girl was also at high risk of throwing herself at the first man she met, thereby posing a real danger to the values of American society. She had to be reined in by social conventions.[58] In his editorial, 'Breaking down Fences', Bok threatened those girls who pushed social boundaries of appropriate sexual behaviour too far:

> It is a very fine line which divides unconventionality in a girl's deportment from a certain license and freedom of action, which is so fraught with danger—a very, very fine line. And yet on one side of the line lies a girl's highest possession: her self-respect and on the other side her loss of it.[59]

He identified the loss of a girl's virtue as the loss of her value to the greater good of humanity. Warning the girl of the cavalier charmer, the *Journal*'s 'Side Talk with Girls' advised, 'Listen to no word of love that is not followed by the suggestion of an early marriage.'[60] This delicate manipulation of innocent frivolity was difficult to manage; however, as long as the game ended in marriage to a proper suitor, the American Girl's romantic dalliances were partially forgiven.

The *Journal* published numerous Bridal Numbers, giving thousands of hopeful romantics and fortunate fiancées a chance to see the latest in bridal fashion and decor. To be the American Girl Bride was the apex of her existence and highly coveted. As such, she was the embodiment of patriotic and patrimonial perfection. Many *Journal* covers featured the blushing bride demurely bowed in prayer, proud of her accomplishments and honoured to serve her duty as wife and future role as mother. In 'The Greatest Period in a Girl's Life', a 1911 *Journal* illustration series by Harrison Fisher, the Girl's life began with 'The Proposal' and concluded with her and her husband doting over 'Their New Love', a sweet infant. Together with her handsome groom they were united in purpose: to love one another as companions and to provide the country with their perfect progeny, serving the county by ensuring the next generation of the superior American race.

CONCLUSION

The American Girl was symptomatic of early-twentieth-century social and racial unrest in the United States. Her Anglo-Saxon appearance and primed sexual health served to placate a racially and culturally fractured people. She was a manifestation of American potential, meant to inspire and assuage the nation's majority against the rising minority whom many saw as a threat to the pure democracy of their forefathers and their future nation itself. And while her 'life' ended with marriage and motherhood, references to the America Girl stop with the United States' involvement in World War I. The American Girl's 'child', the 1920s flapper, may have been a celebration of modern youth but carried with her the tarnish of innocence lost.

With regards to the *Ladies' Home Journal*, the magazine served as a catalyst in the development of a modern American culture and national identity. An evaluation of the American Girl as typified in the *Journal* reveals her to be an icon of optimism and conservator of femininity at the beginning of the new century. As Ashmore's *Side Talk with Girls* dedication proclaimed, her future was to be a charming friend, wife and mother. The *Journal*'s advice columns and editorials assisted in delineating the American Girl's expectations and duties to herself, her family and her country. Bok's outsider mentality allowed him to be more aware and observational about Americans, tapping into the people's pride, desires and insecurities. The *Journal*'s Girl was a mass cultural identity meant to reassure, and for some, to convince, that America was a superior and united (white) people.

The power of magazines and their imagery is in their ability to be seen, shared and experienced by a racially diverse and physically dispersed people—perceivably uniting them into a cohesive and harmonious society. Every publication has a personality and there develops a relationship between the physical magazine and the reader, a shared intimacy when it is brought into the home.[61] Bok's *Ladies' Home Journal* offered the latest news, information and entertainment. It developed a friendship with its readership based on trust, understanding and amusement. The *Journal*'s Girl provided a charming friend, sister and daughter for all Americans. We read magazines not to see what we have but what we can attain; the American Girl read to see not herself, but what she could be.

NOTES

1. Charles Gibson's illustration 'The glorification of the "American Girl,"' in which a young woman stands on a pedestal waving the American flag with a raucous crowd reaching up, waving and cheering from below, was originally featured in a double spread Fourth of July Tribute in *Life*, 30 June, 1892.
2. Martha Banta, *Imaging American Women: Idea and Ideals in Cultural History* (New York: Columbia University Press, 1987).
3. John William Tebbel and Mary Ellen Zuckerman, *The Magazine in America: 1741–1990* (New York: Oxford University Press, 1991), 57.
4. Frank Luther Mott, *A History of American Magazines: 1885–1915*, vol. 4 (Cambridge, MA: Harvard University Press, 1957), 537–9.
5. Edward K. Bok, *The Americanization of Edward Bok* (New York: Charles Scribner's Sons, 1921).
6. Bok, *Americanization of Edward Bok*, 18–29.
7. Mott, *History of American Magazines*.
8. Jennifer Scanlon, *Inarticulate Longings: The Ladies' Home Journal, Gender, and the Promise of Consumer Culture* (New York: Routledge, 1995), 4.
9. Ruth Ashmore (Isabel Allderdice Sloan Mallon), *Side Talks with Girls* (New York: Charles Scribner's Sons, 1896), iv.
10. The term 'school room to altar' was used by Ella Wheeler Wilcox in 'Between school-room and altar,' *The Ladies' Home Journal*, December 1890, 2.
11. Ada Gertrude Wood, 'The American Girl two-step,' *The Ladies' Home Journal*, June 1903, 13; Helen Hamilton, 'What 100 girls would like to be,' *The Ladies' Home Journal*, January 1903, 3. The series 'My greatest experience as a girl and how I met it' was published in installments in the *Ladies' Home Journal* beginning in July 1912. This series of articles were written by *Journal* readers and gathered through a prize contest.
12. Bok, *Americanization of Edward Bok*, 245.
13. Bok, 'At home with the Editor,' *The Ladies' Home Journal*, October 1894, 14. In his editorial, Bok argues against the New Woman because she appears to belittle the influence of the woman in her home. For more New Woman scholarship, see: Martha H. Patterson, ed., *The American New Woman Revisited: A Reader, 1894–1930* (New Brunswick, NJ: Rutgers University Press, 2008) and Laura L. Behling, *The Masculine Woman in America, 1890–1935* (Chicago: University of Chicago Press, 2001). The term Evil Girl is coined by Carolyn Kitch in *The Girl on the Magazine Cover: The Origins of Visual Stereotypes in American Mass Media* (Chapel Hill: University of North Caroline Press, 2001). I prefer the term Naughty Girl to imply her mischievous and yet naïve frivolity.
14. The *Ladies' Home Journal* illustrations consisted of 'The American Girl at church,' March 1900; 'The American Girl as a bride,' April 1900; 'The American Girl on the Farm,' May 1900; 'The American Girl at college,' June 1900; 'The American Girl at her sports,' July 1900. Carolyn Kitch makes a similar point regarding a six-series illustration titled 'The American woman' which was aimed at the *Journal*'s mature audience and produced by Alice Barber Stevens in 1897. Kitch, *The Girl on the Magazine Cover*, 17–36.
15. Richard Harding Davis, 'The origin of a type of the American Girl,' *The Quarterly Illustrator* 9 (1895): 6.

16 Bok, aware of the American Girl's visual power, chose to print 'Mr Gibson's American Girl' on the February, 1903 cover, the same month it was announced that Gibson had signed an exclusivity contract with the *Journal*'s competitor *Collier's*. The public was confused and curious about for whom Gibson was working. In March, *Collier's* published a formal letter to clarify the situation and the *Journal* received some free publicity.
17 Roland Marchand, *Advertising the American Dream: Making Way for Modernity, 1920–1940* (Berkeley: University of California Press, 1985), xx.
18 Elaine Scarry, *The Body of Pain: The Making and Unmaking of the World* (New York: Oxford University Press, 1985), 109.
19 Pierre Bourdieu, *Sketch for a Self-Analysis* quoted in Scarry, *The Body of Pain*, 110–11.
20 For more information about white racial tensions in America during the late nineteenth and early twentieth centuries, see: Edward J. Blum, *Reforging the White Republic: Race, Religion, and American Nationalism, 1865–1898* (Baton Rouge: Louisiana State University Press, 2005) and David A. Gerber and Alan M. Kraut, eds., *American Immigration and Ethnicity: A Reader* (Palgrave Macmillan: New York, 2005).
21 Howard Chandler Christy, *The American Girl: As Seen and Portrayed by Howard Chandler Christy* (New York: Moffat, Yard and Company, 1906), 11–12.
22 Matthew Frye Jacobson, *Whiteness of a Different Color: European Immigrants and the Alchemy of Race* (Cambridge, MA: Harvard University Press, 1998), 6.
23 Jacobson, *Whiteness of a Different Color*, 13.
24 For more information about American Nativism, see: John Higham, *Strangers in the Land: Patterns of American Nativism, 1860–1925* (New Brunswick, NJ: Rutgers University Press, 2002); and Brian N. Fry, *Nativism and Immigration: Regulating the American Dream* (Berkeley: University of California Press, 2011).
25 Charles Davenport, *Heredity in Relation* (1911) cited in Lori Jirousek, 'Mary Antin's progressive science: Eugenics, evolution, and the environment,' *An Interdisciplinary Journal of Jewish Studies* 27 (2008): 66–7.
26 Edward Ross, *The Old World in the New: The Significance of Past and Present Immigration to the American People* (1914) cited in Jirousek, 'Mary Antin's Progressive Science,' 61.
27 Banta, *Imaging American Women*, 117–24.
28 For more information about race and immigration in the United States at the turn of the last century, see: Jacobson, *Whiteness of a Different Color*; Ewa T. Morawska, *A Sociology of Immigration: (Re)Making Multifaceted America* (Basingstoke: Palgrave Macmillan, 2009); David M. Reimers, *Other Immigrants: The Global Origins of the American People* (New York: New York University Press, 2005).
29 Clifford Howard, 'The President's daughter,' *The Ladies' Home Journal*, April 1902, 5–6.
30 John D'Emilio and Estelle B. Freedman, *Intimate Matters: A History of Sexuality in America* Second Edition (Chicago: University of Chicago Press, 1997), 58, 174.
31 D'Emilio and Freedman, *Intimate Matters*, 185. It is important to consider higher birthrates among the immigrant population in the context of early marriage, rural traditions and lack of information about birth control.
32 William H. Walling, *Sexology* (Philadelphia: Puritan Publishing Company, 1904)—reprinted as part of the series *Sex, Marriage, and Society* by Arno Press Inc., 1974.

33 William Isaac Thomas, *Sex and Society: Studies in the Social Psychology of Sex* (Chicago: University of Chicago Press, 1907).
34 Behling in *The Masculine Woman in America* argues that the study of modern sexuality and psychology during the turn of the last century established a gender-biased foundation of 'natural' and 'healthy' human behaviour in western culture that carried through and evolved in the twentieth century.
35 George J. Engelmann, *The Health of the American Girl as Imperiled by the Social Conditions of the Day* (Philadelphia: W. M. J. Dornan Publishing, 1891), 3.
36 Engelmann, *The Health of the American Girl*, 5.
37 Dr S. Weir Mitchell, 'When the COLLEGE IS HURTFUL TO A GIRL,' *The Ladies' Home Journal*, June 1900, 14.
38 Dudley A. Sargent, 'Are athletics making girls masculine?,' *The Ladies' Home Journal*, March 1912, 11.
39 Annette Kellermann, 'Why and how girls should swim,' *The Ladies' Home Journal*, August 1910, 11.
40 Emma E. Walker, 'Why golf is good for girls,' *The Ladies' Home Journal*, May 1902, 24. The *San Francisco Chronicle*'s 'Sports that are beauty builders for the school and college girl,' 21 September 1913, includes a portion of Dr Walker's *Journal* article verbatim.
41 Barbara Welter, *Dimity Convictions: The American Woman in the Nineteenth Century* (Athens: Ohio University Press, 1976), 16–17.
42 Some of the literature, primarily from feminist historians, argues that this was one approach used by men to reinforce patriarchal systems. For more, see Carroll Smith-Rosenburg's *Disorderly Conduct: Visions of Gender in Victorian America* (Oxford: Oxford University Press, 1985). Lois Banner discusses the dynamic interplay of education, sexuality and physical activity in shaping the cultural image of femininity in the twentieth century. Lois Banner, *Women in Modern America* (New York: Harcourt Brace Jovanovich, 1974).
43 Lorna Duffin, 'Prisoners of progress: Women and evolution,' in *The Nineteenth-Century Woman: Her Cultural and Physical World*, ed. Sara Delamont and Lorna Duffin (London: Croom Helm, 1978).
44 Behling's *The Masculine Woman in America* is an examination of how the US suffrage movement was translated into a fear of female sexual inverts and over-sexualised women. The extremes of femininity were believed to disturb the balance of society and lead to the country's downfall.
45 The first published use of the term 'New Woman' was by Sarah Grand, a British woman's rights activist and novelist, in the distinguished *North American Review*. Sarah Grand, 'The New Aspect of the Woman Question,' in *The American New Woman Revisited: A Reader, 1894–1930*, ed. Martha H. Patterson (New Brunswick, NJ: Rutgers University Press, 2008), 29–34.
46 Theodore Roosevelt, 'Women's rights: The duties of both men and women,' in *The American New Woman Revisited*, ed. Patterson, 108–13.
47 Roosevelt, 'Women's rights,' 108.
48 Roosevelt, 'Women's rights,' 109. In *Parenthood and Race Culture: An Outline of Eugenics* (New York: Moffat, Yard and Co., 1909), C. W. Saleeby claimed that delay of marriage would lead to the fall of civilisation.
49 Edward Bok, 'American Girl: An editorial,' *The Ladies' Home Journal*, May 1908, 1.
50 Ashmore, *Side Talks*, 15.
51 Christy, *The American Girl*, 43–4.
52 As early as November 1884, the *Journal* article 'When girls deceive their parents' warned that liberties permitted the American Girl were something of

which to be proud, as long as they were not abused. 'How girls deceive their parents,' *The Ladies' Home Journal*, November 1884, 1.

53 Edward Bok, 'At home with the Editor,' *The Ladies' Home Journal*, April 1892, 12. In the article, Bok defines risqué behavior as when a girl is not wicked nor improper but 'They are just a little careless—especially careless in their attitude toward men.'

54 Bok, 'At Home with the Editor,' 12.

55 For more information about women's sexuality in the early twentieth century, see: Elizabeth K. Menon, *Evil by Design: The Creation and Marketing of the Femme Fatale* (Chicago: University of Illinois Press, 2006); Welter, *Dimity Convictions* ; June Sochen, *Enduring Values: Women in Popular Culture* (New York: Praeger, 1987).

56 Anne Virginia Culbertson, 'Love stories of some American Girls,' *The Ladies' Home Journal*, July 1902, 7. Julia Magruder's short story 'A live ember' was featured as a two part series in the *Journal*'s August and September 1892 issues and previewed in the December 1891 issue as 'when the strife of affection in two hearts silently burns'. *The Ladies' Home Journal*, December 1891, 4.

57 Welter, *Dimity Convictions*, 18.

58 Henry James' *Daisy Miller* (1879) and Theodore Drieser's *Sister Carrie* (1900) are cautionary tales for the American Girl to stay within the boundaries of social convention. Barbara Welter comments in *Dimity Convictions* that 'Daisy Miller is at least absolved by her death.' Welter, *Dimity Convictions*, 10–11. Many historians have discussed late nineteenth- and early twentieth-century ideas about women's sexuality: See for instance Behling, *The Masculine Woman in America,* which identifies the over-sexed *femme fatale* as a counter to the masculine woman, and the danger she presents to the values of American society. In addition, John D'Emilio and Estelle B. Freedman claim that a new sexual order in America sprang from the suffrage movement, which included the overly passionate female: D'Emilio and Freedman, *Intimate Matters*. Maria Elena Buszek's *Pin-Up Grrrls: Feminism, Sexuality, Popular Culture* (Durham, NC: Duke University Press, 2006) argues that the Pin-Up Girl developed as a culturally approved, non-threatening sexualised female.

59 Bok, 'Breaking down fences,' *The Ladies' Home Journal*, August 1897, 14.

60 Ruth Ashmore, 'The voice of the charmer,' *The Ladies' Home Journal*, January 1891, 17.

61 For more about the taste-creator relationship between magazines and their readerships, see Ellen Gruber Garvey's *The Adman in the Parlor: Magazines and the Gendering of Consumer Culture, 1880s to 1910s* (Oxford: Oxford University Press, 1996). Garvey discusses the complexity of the magazine as a sterile public world of goods that exists in a private world of the home.

12 A Taste of *Honey*
Get-Ahead Femininity in 1960s Britain

Fan Carter

In April 1960, UK publisher Fleetway launched *Honey* magazine for 'teens and twenties'.[1] It was the first of a number of titles that started in the 1960s which targeted the teenage reader or 'single girl', as the market was often referred to. It soon became synonymous with a new, fashionable and 'get-ahead' femininity, but unlike the younger weekly title *Jackie* (D. C. Thompson, 1964–93), the more radical, celebrated and short lived, *Nova* (Newnes, 1965–75) or the internationally successful *Cosmopolitan* (National Magazines, launched in the UK in 1972), to date *Honey* has received less attention within histories of publishing and feminist media criticism.[2]

This chapter seeks to offer a re-evaluation of *Honey* focusing on its launch and development in the 1960s. During this time, the magazine evolved a distinct editorial style and innovative approach to branding which helped to establish the new genre of young women's fashion magazines as a major force within the British magazine market. The chapter argues that rather than viewing *Honey* as simply a functional vehicle for growing consumer advertising and a consequence of the shifting balance of power between editorial and advertising content, it is precisely its focus on fashion that enabled *Honey* to carve out a distinctly new image of youthful femininity that resonated with readers.[3] This youthful femininity was articulated in terms of 'get-ahead' aspirations, mobility and consumer style.

The chapter addresses three specific concerns relating to the making of this new youthful magazine. First it locates the emergence of *Honey* within the contemporary discourses of marketing and consumer capitalism as characterised by Mark Abrams' *The Teenage Consumer* (1959) and contemporary trade accounts.[4] Here the teenage magazine emerges as the rational solution to advertisers' needs, matching the consumer with niche advertising copy in a sympathetic context. Second, the chapter considers how the editorial approach and marketing initiatives of the magazine developed a distinct brand identity for the title in a decade marked by growing consumer culture and rapid social change. Third, it explores the specific ways in which the teenage girl was imagined and addressed within the pages of the magazine itself. In so doing, the chapter argues that *Honey* constitutes an important figure in the wider historical and critical landscape of women's magazines scholarship, marking out the beginning of a new and distinctive format for young women's titles and commercially mediated constructions of young fashionable femininity.

The analysis that follows is based on a ten-year sample of *Honey*, from its launch in 1960 through to the end of 1969. Four issues from each year were examined and a full record of contents was made to establish editorial themes and formats and to identify advertising patterns. This was supplemented with research from contemporaneous journalism drawing on the trade and consumer press as well as market research reports and industry figures, where available.

THE MAGAZINE MARKET AND THE SINGLE GIRL

In 1959 the market researcher Mark Abrams published his analysis of the newly identified British teenage consumer market for the London Press Exchange, one of Britain's largest advertising agencies at the time.[5] While the report details the intricacies of spending on particular consumer goods, there are a number of broader headline themes that emerged which are worth noting here. In general, the teenage consumer's leisure world was predominantly a social one, lived outside of the home; there was significant spending on clothing and other non-durable items, while print media, newspapers and importantly for this chapter, magazines, were particularly popular with this market. Abrams rounded off his report noting that print media would be a potentially lucrative area to develop and expand given teenagers' appetite for expendable reading matter.[6] His conclusions amounted to a rallying cry to publishers and marketers alike to develop the right products to capture this teenage market. Commentators in the trade press noted that within the world of marketing at least, attitudes to young people were changing rapidly from ones of concern, to those of commercial interest: 'the old cry of "what are the youngsters coming to" has given way to "What are the teenagers coming to buy?"', proclaimed *World Press News and Advertisers Review* in their own special report on the teenage market published the following year.[7] The right media selection was crucial to providing a sympathetic and trusted context for products, they advised, noting that 'many media planners rate the magazines which cater for the well-known tastes of the teenage reader as the best advertising media of all'.[8]

While Abrams' report acknowledged that popular consumer culture aimed at this new market was largely formed in response to the taste preferences and cultural practices of working-class males who enjoyed higher spending power than their middle-class and female counterparts,[9] he paid particular attention to significant changes to the social and employment opportunities for girls. Focusing on the new openings in manufacturing and clerical work, Abrams noted that this afforded working-class girls in their teens and twenties greater opportunities than ever before, particularly in terms of independence, leisure time and most importantly, consumer spending power. In so doing, Abrams identified some of the defining characteristics of the young female consumer as she would be imagined more broadly, and across class distinctions, within commercial discourses of the 1960s; that is her relationship to the world of work, which was increasingly articulated in terms of a 'job with prospects' or even a 'career'. These were girls who were out and about, making their way in modern Britain; travelling to work on public transport, negotiating the subtleties of office etiquette, meeting up with friends after the office or shop floor closed and, importantly, spending much of their leisure time shopping for 'the look'. Elsewhere referred to as the 'independent typist', single girls belonging to this demographic were exactly the readers that magazine publishers set out to attract.[10]

The late 1950s had seen the launch of a number of magazine titles that anticipated the new teenage consumer described by Abrams. However, these were generally cheap weekly magazines that concentrated on romantic fiction and comic strip stories, such as *Valentine* (Fleetway, 1957–74), *Roxy* (Amalgamated Press, 1957–63), *Marilyn* (Amalgamated Press, 1957–65) and *Mirabelle* (IPC, 1956–77). The monthly *Vanity Fair* (National Magazines, 1949–72) was aimed at the affluent 'teen and twenty market' and focused on a decidedly middle-class 'social scene'.[11] In addition, teenage girls reported reading the best-selling mass weeklies *Woman* and *Woman's Own* in significant numbers.[12] Magazine journalists and historians Joan Barrell and Brian Braithwaite describe the magazine market of the late 1950s and early 1960s as volatile, characterised by frequent new launches, closures and mergers of titles along with an increasing concentration of ownership among publishing companies, leading in 1968 to the formation of the International Publishing Corporation Limited, more commonly known as IPC.[13] The search for a successful magazine for the young woman, both the 'independent typist' and 'young married',[14] made a significant contribution to these changes in the magazine market as publishers sought the ideal balance between editorial, advertising and circulation required to sustain a thriving title.[15] In pursuit of this new market, two new monthlies were launched in 1960: Fleetway's *Honey* and the perfect bound *Flair*, from Newnes, along with a weekly magazine, *Date*, from Odhams.[16] A further nine titles, from assorted publishers, opened throughout the decade, each seeking to capitalise on the new, young female market.[17]

'WE'RE HERE TO SERVE YOU, AND HAPPY TO DO SO': ESTABLISHING THE *HONEY* BRAND[18]

Honey was launched amid a fanfare of publicity and a party at the Mayfair Hotel, London. The pop star Cliff Richard sang a theme song for the magazine, while professional dancer and television personality, Lionel Blair, together with his wife Joyce, choreographed a dance in celebration.

According to news reports, the party was attended by 'debutantes and glamorous girls from stage and screen, the Army, Navy and Air Force, international airlines, departments stores, ballet, nursing, GPO [the General Post Office] and the photographic and modelling worlds'.[19] The guest list gave some indication both of the imagined readership and the wide advertising spread contained in the first editions. *Honey* set out to cater for a distinctly middle-class market, but one that was increasingly identified in terms of consumption rather than the traditional markers of income and profession.[20] In anticipation of the launch, Fleetway had courted advertisers with the promise that '[T]hese girls spend money on products they'll see in *Honey*'. They confidently declared: '[t]here's no other medium like *Honey*. There's no waste in *Honey*. It goes straight to the heart of a profitable, brand-free market. It's the only full-sized monthly glamour magazine for these girls—and remember, *they* are the mothers and housewives of tomorrow.'[21]

Fleetway's pitch articulated the double positioning of the new young female consumer: individual and independent today and a housewife and mother in the future. *Honey's* advertising was organised as a 'group buy' with other titles in the Fleetway stable, a common practice in the market at the time. In the early issues, small advertisements for rufflette tape, Anadin and even traditional British lace jostled alongside full-page colour features for *Max Factor* cosmetics and *Maiden Form* brassieres. The 'group buy' policy would later contribute to the decline and closure of the magazine,[22] but in its early days it guaranteed a steady stream of advertising copy, enabling *Honey* to boast frequently that it carried the greatest number of advertisements across the company.[23]

As *Honey's* position as an authoritative guide to the new fashion market grew more assured, it garnered increasingly desirable advertising, especially in the form of glossy, colour campaigns for the new synthetic fibre brands, such as Orlon and Bri-Nylon. These lucrative accounts were seen as an index of a magazine's status as a fashion leader and were highly prized.[24] The fact that *Honey* was able to attract such advertising, more commonly seen in the up-market fashion titles of *Vogue* and *Queen*, is indicative of its success in the period.

This good relationship with advertising was not just a commercial consideration for the title but specifically part of its brand image and editorial positioning. *Honey* clearly delivered potential consumers to expectant advertisers but also saw its role as serving its readers, ensuring they had the best advice on which to base their consumer purchases. *Honey* prided itself on delivering accurate consumer information to its readers, supplementing the advertising with lists of stockists and up-to-date coverage on fashion and beauty in its editorial pages. *Honey* quickly launched a readers' enquiry service, enabling readers to request accurate stockist information on any products featured in the magazine. It frequently carried reader offers for cosmetics and gave away free gifts in cover mounts.[25] Later, *Honey* ran competitions for larger consumer items, including a record-player in 1961 and, more dramatically, the chance to win a Mini in 1964.²⁶ In the early years, *Honey* forged connections across the wider world of teenage consumer culture. It ran a disc club, offering members specially selected compilations of current hits, and for a short time hosted a weekly radio show, 'the *Honey* Hit Parade', on Radio Luxemburg.²⁷

Honey's position as a trusted intermediary between the market and the consumer was further endorsed through its early efforts at brand extension in the form of *Honey* boutiques and hair salons. First launched in February 1965, these were located within department stores and sometimes in independent shops. They were lauded as places where local '*Honeys*' could not only purchase the clothes advertised in the pages of the magazine but also receive advice and guidance from trusted professionals. The announcement supporting the launch of the first ever *Honey* Boutique in Schofields, Leeds, took up a whole page in the February 1965 issue. Presented as a notice, it was placed in the middle of an otherwise blank page and starts:

> Where can you find the *Honey* look? How frustrating is it to see mouth-watering clothes and accessories in *Honey* [. . .] and then find the bubble bursts when you tackle the local shops? . . . Oh yes—we've heard you wail—and we're doing something about it!²⁸

Within the year there were a further twenty-six *Honey* Boutiques stretching from Hull to Plymouth and a number of *Honey* Hair Salons in provincial department stores, such as Lewis', where customers were promised a professional and modern service.²⁹ The salons and boutiques were hung with *Honey* signage and often featured in the magazines alongside profiles of the shop assistants or owners who ran them, who became known as the '*Honey* girls'.³⁰

The magazine was produced with a full-colour cover and saddle stitch binding.³¹ Smaller than the mass weeklies *Woman* and *Woman's Own*, and with cheaper production values than the elite titles of *Vogue* and *Queen*, at the same time it was equally distinct from the 'love comics' previously read by adolescents and remarked upon by Abrams.³² *Honey* covers were always bright, clean and visually arresting. The use of the bold lowercase typeface in the masthead contributed to its modern and youthful appearance. Early covers featured photographs of couples in traditional, romantic poses, but these soon gave way to more adventurous and creative designs. Cover lines addressed the reader from the start, often employing the imperative as illustrated in the cover below, where readers were invited to 'Take off [. . .] Put on [. . .] Cut out [. . .]'. This example (see Figure 12.1) plays with the conventional aesthetics of the magazine cover, the choice of a full length body shot over the more common close-up together with the unusual body pose and obscuring eyewear construct an image which is arresting and distinctly modern.

While the idea of service was established as the framing editorial device from the early editions, under Jean McInlay's editorship the magazine had

Figure 12.1 *Honey*, June 1965, with kind permission of © Time Inc., UK Ltd and The British Library.

a somewhat staid tone, resembling that of a sensible older sister rather than friend and equal. Her first editor's letter began in a rather timid manner, asking:

> Ever felt a bit **shy** meeting new folks? Yes? Then you'll know exactly how we're feeling now, meeting you for the first time.
>
> We hope you like us, and that *Honey* will be one of your closest friends, as months pass and we get to know each other.
>
> What **fun** lies ahead of us? Discs and dancing. Old friends and new. Adventure. In fact all manner of exciting interesting, **simply shattering** things. [emphasis in the original][33]

Readers failed to be drawn to the stuffy approach, and as a consequence the magazine was slow to build its circulation.[34] Notwithstanding this mismatch of verbal tone and target market, *Honey* made an instant impact on the industry with its use of rising talents within the world of publishing and photography. The first issue alone carried work by Terrance Donovan and Michael Ward, and the November 1960 issue featured profiles on Don McCullin and David Bailey, who advised readers 'if you're to be a good fashion photographer, the first essential is to develop a good fashion sense'.[35]

While the early tone of the magazine may well have been miscalculated, it soon developed a distinctive editorial address towards its readers, positioning them as confident, independent and demanding young women. Audrey Slaughter, who was to become a dynamic and dominant figure in new women's publishing ventures for several decades, replaced McInlay in 1961 and took charge of the then ailing publication, developing a clear editorial address to accompany a distinctive and innovative brand.[36] Her letters were both familiar and flattering towards her readership.[37] She was wary of making assumptions about her readers and their preferences, and described them here, in an editorial letter, as savvy, fun and ambitious young women far beyond the easy grasp of some market researcher's slick profile:

> *Honey* readers aren't interested only in fashion, beauty and beat. You talk about holidays, careers, boyfriends, cooking, cars. About 50% of you go abroad [. . .] and we find that contrary to the opinion of those know-it-all statistics men, your careers mean more to you than a stop-gap before marriage. You talk several languages learned at night-school. You learn to cook the *cordon-bleu* way; you plan to revolutionise design and industry [. . .] [you are] everything that is young, gay and going far.[38]

Slaughter was certainly the driving force in making *Honey* such a success in the 1960s. Under her editorship, circulation grew to a respectable 185,000 by 1965, overtaking *Vanity* Fair (140,000) and *Flair* (144,800). It went on to exceed 200,000 the following year.[39] Slaughter is credited with having generated a particularly creative and dynamic culture within the editorial team. A *Times* profile of Slaughter from 1972, by which time she had gone on to launch *Petticoat* for Fleetway and then set up *Over 21* as an independent venture, made much of her personal approach, driven by 'feeling' and 'hunches' rather than marketing formulae.[40] Slaughter's editorial style was often considered risky by Fleetway's management. In 1963, she famously sent the photographer Michael Ward to Liverpool to cover The Beatles in concert at the Cavern. She was determined to put them on the cover in 'op art' fashions, despite complaints of the management who could not understand why a group of long-haired nobodies, who would never amount to anything, should make the cover of their magazine. Slaughter remarked later of the cover, 'it was a mess, but we were speaking the right language'.[41]

Under Slaughter's editorship, *Honey* pushed the boundaries of accepted publishing models. Not only was she responsible for the launch of the *Honey* Boutiques, she also organised the purchase of a second-hand bus, which was painted with the *Honey* masthead, and used it to tour the country with her editorial team.[42] Her beauty team ran seminars in provincial department stores and offered readers the chance to go on *Honey* beauty weekends. At various points the *Honey* team went on location and published special regional editions from 'the north' and 'south-west' with readers offering tips on local nightlife, modelling clothes and undergoing make-overs.[43] '" Catch us wearing those?" giggle Diana and Fiona of Leeds, pointing to our skin tight-sweater. "Why not try them on", challenges Gillian. So they do . . . and they're sold. Help . . . how do we get them to take them off again?'[44]

The magazine's tone also displayed a sophisticated degree of self-referentiality for the period. The July issue of 1965 carried the cover-line, 'This is I hate *Honey* month: lots of reader critics tell us why', which became the theme for the entire issue. The editorial responded to readers' queries and complaints across the breadth of the contents. Readers asked, 'Where are the photos of pin-ups', the hair styles for girls without a 'Maison Albert' on the corner and affordable fashions for students, school girls and first jobbers?—and *Honey* responded.

FASHIONING A NEW FEMININITY: THE GET-AHEAD *HONEY* GIRL

The world of *Honey* magazine was a wide and relatively open one. The magazine did not limit its readers' horizons to shopping and settling down, and instead took an instructive and educative approach in its features. It was known for its varied content, eschewing the common reliance on a high number of regular features and opting instead for theme-based special issues.[45] *Honey* ran general interest features on architecture and planning, reviewed the Paris collections through the eyes of Royal College of Art students, Ossie Clark and Brian Harris (October 1965), commented on political elections (October 1963) and asked searching questions about girls' experience of loneliness (February 1968). It also offered decorating tips for first flats and gave advice on moving to the 'big city' and choosing new flat mates. Considerable attention was paid to careers, with profiles of a wide variety jobs regularly appearing in the magazine. While more traditionally feminine jobs, such as modelling, acting and secretarial work featured highly, the magazine also covered less obvious careers, including a profile of a woman driver and increasingly regular articles on going to university and volunteering.[46]

The magazine's attitude towards sex and relationships reflected the rapidly changing social context of the period. At the start of the decade, the magazine confidently instructed readers to avoid the perils of a necking session: 'Quicker than a penguin sliding down an icicle, that's how quickly a necking session can turn into a jam session. And **you're** the one in a jam', it advised in the August 1960 issue [emphasis in the original].[47] However, by

1965, in articles such as 'Dating before Mating', the magazine was implicitly acknowledging that its readers had sexual relationships. By 1966, Audrey Slaughter had written the booklet *Birth Control and the Single Girl*, which readers could send for.[48] At the time this was considered a bold move by a magazine, and Slaughter was interviewed by the BBC about her permissive stance.[49] By the end of the decade, *Honey* editorials were asking whether marriage was still necessary, publishing articles on unmarried mothers and regularly running advertisements for Durex contraceptives.[50] While this was in keeping with other young women's magazines of the period, Slaughter's early championing of information on contraception should not be discounted.[51]

Central to the *Honey* brand was its coverage of fashion, with each edition giving a significant number of pages to thematic fashion spreads. *Honey*'s fashion journalism carved out a distinct niche between the high-end glossies, such as *Vogue* and *Queen* with their focus on the exclusive world of couture and the Paris shows, and the popular mass weeklies, such as *Woman* and *Woman's Own* with their more pragmatic and limited approach. *Honey* was well placed to capitalise on the rapid expansion of the fashion markets in this period and the emergence of designers such as Mary Quant and brands such as Biba, which came to epitomise the 'swinging sixties'. The magazine's fashion journalism in the 1960s can be characterised by a number of features. There was a commitment to a service ethos, delivering information and choice to readers, along with a distinct visual style often characterised by vibrant poses, witty layouts and use of graphics integrated into thematic fashion spreads. There was also a rhetorical code in which fashion—being knowledgeable of, keeping up with and making selections within—was constructed as both fun and central to the making of a particular feminine self.[52]

This feminine self is one which might well be characterised as 'get-ahead': ambitious, optimistic and enterprising. Histories of the 1960s and also of post-war youth culture draw attention to youth as a signifier of social change and a conduit for both the anxieties and optimism these changes stimulated.[53] The 'get-ahead' femininity of the *Honey* girl articulated these in particular ways. While she delighted in fashion and took pleasure in constructing her 'look', she was more than a clotheshorse. Citing an editorial from 1967, Janice Winship notes that fashion in the magazine 'symbolised an individuality young women were searching for beyond the confines of their looks'.[54] The emphasis on fashion, then, was not simply a mode of individualisation, but carried with it a broader set of discursive configurations relating to the optimism and ambitions of youthful femininity.

This individuality was one that was often articulated through the pose of the model's body, which emphasised animation and movement over the static poses of traditional fashion photographs. In many of the fashion pages, the *Honey* girl is quite literally on the move—striding out, striking a pose and going far. This rhetorical code is explored by Hilary Radner in her discussion of fashion photography and the single girl in the 1960s.[55] She argues that movement constitutes a significant theme in 1960s' photography. Models are captured moving across the frame, or shot outside amid cityscapes or in a documentary style; this new visual code, she continues, is representative of a 'culture in transition', a visual connotation of modernity and one which was epitomised in the figure of the single girl. The new consumer who moves through the city and through the photographic frame is an active feminine subject, and, argues Radner, quoting Helen Gurley Brown, 'the single girl is known for what she does rather than who she belongs to'.[56]

While pitching to a mid-market readership and with considerably less budget for art direction than was available to up-market magazines, the photographic style of *Honey* fashion spreads in the 1960s share something of these 'movement images' from the higher end of the market. If anything, this visual trope is even more evident in *Honey*, where pages feature multiple images, photo montage and bold graphics. The creativity of *Honey* fashion shoots of the time is recalled by beauty editor, Pat Baike, who notes that, 'We would evolve a new look on a photo session and there wasn't even a hairdresser or a make-up artist, just me, the photographer and the model [who] would turn up with an impeccable kit of makeup and hair accessories.'[57]

Honey fashion spreads introduced new and upcoming models, and from the outset modelling was featured as an aspirational career.[58] Twiggy was the cover model in October 1966, while Cathee Dahmen, the dual-heritage American and Chippewa model whose tight-permed hair became a much copied, if short lived, trend, was profiled in November 1967.[59] From the late 1960s *Honey* also employed black models on a regular basis in fashion and beauty features, although not going so far as to use them as cover models.[60] While black musicians had featured regularly since its launch, reflecting the popularity of Motown and the acceptance of black performers within music genres more generally, questions of race and representation remained absent from the magazine for much of the decade. Towards the end of the 1960s though, *Honey* began to challenge the invisibility of black identities within the magazine, both through the use of black models in fashion spreads and in features that specifically addressed issues of discrimination.[61] *Honey* also used 'real' women in their fashion and beauty features, both readers and, on occasion, members of the editorial staff who were given the *Honey* look.[62] Like Helen Gurley Brown's single girl, the *Honey* girl was a worker.[63] She might be an office girl, a student or shop assistant, but she was active, aspiring and going places.

CONCLUSION

This chapter has offered a reappraisal of the birth and development of one particular magazine which addressed the increasingly commercially and socially significant market of the 'teen and twenties' in the 1960s and has explored the way in which the 'single girl' was imagined within discourses of marketing and magazine journalism. *Honey* broke with existing models of publishing for teenagers, presenting a world of consumption based on fashion and leisure rather than romance and comic strips. It harnessed the ambitions of advertisers and retailers to build brand loyalty among this new and aspiring market with ambitious and innovating marketing strategies, such as the *Honey* Boutiques, and in so doing anticipated approaches that would become more commonplace in the following decades.

Honey articulated a particular image of youthful femininity that was mobile, ambitious, fashionable and self-fashioning. As noted by Winship and Radner, this spoke to wider ambitions and aspirations for individuality and emphasised agency over conformity and tradition. However, this get-ahead femininity was also one that became problematised in social critiques and popular commentary as the decade went on. Mainstream commentators callously dismissed the 'dolly bird' and 'swinging London' in a critique which had gender as well as class inflections, while the growing women's liberation movement, which was to preoccupy the next decade, also found fault with it.[64] However, although noting the ways in which these freedoms were tightly contained within a consumerist logic, it is important to acknowledge the contribution *Honey* magazine made both to the magazine market and also to opening up narratives and images of opportunity and agency for young women in the period. It generated both 'copycat' publications, such as *19* (launched in 1968), and was the precursor to titles aimed at a younger market, such as the weekly *Petticoat* (launched in 1966). *Honey* successfully established a new format of magazine for the mid-market that was fashion forward and had a distinct editorial style that addressed its readers as exacting equals with high expectations. The particular construction of femininity assembled across its pages resonated with young women whose dreams and aspirations extended beyond the confines of the fashionable consumer subjects pictured there.[65]

NOTES

1 This was the first strapline for the magazine and first appeared in July 1960. This later changed to 'Young, gay and get ahead' in June 1961, under the editorial leadership of Audrey Slaughter.
2 See Angela McRobbie's work on *Jackie* magazine in *Feminism and Youth Culture: From Jackie to Just Seventeen* (London: Routledge, 1991) and Alice Beard 'Put in just for pictures: Fashion editorial and the composite image in *Nova* 1965–1975,' *Fashion Theory: Journal of Dress, Body and Culture* 1 (2002): 247–60 for detailed accounts of both magazines. See also Laurie Ouellette's analysis of the development of *Cosmopolitan* under Helen Gurley Brown, 'Inventing the Cosmo Girl: Class identity and girl style American dreams,' *Media, Culture & Society* 21 (1999): 359–83 and Jennifer Scanlon's biography of Helen Gurley Brown, *Bad Girls Go Everywhere* (New York:

Oxford University Press, 2009). For a discussion of *Honey* magazine in this period, see the seminal studies by Cynthia White, *Women's Magazines 1693–1968* (London: Michael Joseph, 1971) and Janice Winship, *Inside Women's Magazines* (London: Pandora, 1987).

3 See Cynthia White's account of the shifting balance of power between advertising and editorial in the 1950s in White, *Women's Magazines*, 156.
4 Mark Abrams, *The Teenage Consumer* (London: London Press Exchange, 1959).
5 See 'Visit of the Institute to the London Press Exchange Limited,' *Journal of the Royal Statistical Society,* Series D (The Statistician) 13 (1963): 47–53 for an overview of the agency in the period.
6 Abrams, *The Teenage Consumer*, 17.
7 Brian Braithwaite and Joan Barrell reproduce the article in its entirety in *The Business of Women's Magazines* second edition (London: Kogan Page, 1988), 42–4.
8 'Teenage market feature,' *World Press News and Advertisers Review*, 4 March 1960, 26.
9 On this point, see also Selina Todd and Hilary Young, 'Baby-boomers to 'beanstalks': Making the modern teenager in post-war Britain,' *Cultural and Social History* 9 (2012): 451–67 for a discussion of the working class specificities of teenage affluence in the post-war period.
10 This term is used by Linda Christmas to describe the young women's magazine market as defined by Abrams and the publishing industry in the early 1960s. Linda Christmas, 'If Over 21, state Over 21 . . . After *Vanity Fair* Audrey Slaughter has a new baby,' *The Guardian,* 25 February 1972, 11.
11 The first four titles are cited by Abrams as constituting a small but significant percentage of teenage consumer spending in his report, *Teenage Consumer*, 8. White attributes the successful launch of *Vanity Fair* to its wider social appeal in contrast to the ill-fated *Mayfair*, launched three years earlier and with a much narrower, elite market appeal. White, *Women's Magazines,* 139.
12 Abrams, *Teenage Consumer,* 10. It is likely that girls were reading their mothers' or older sisters' magazines, which, while not targeting teenage readers directly made some efforts to address them in particular features.
13 Braithwaite and Barrell summarise these, noting the successive buyouts of Newnes, Odhams and Fleetway to produce IPC Media in 1968. This effectively concentrated much of the young women's market into one large publishing conglomerate. Braithwaite and Barrell, *The Business of Women's Magazines*, 169.
14 In his analysis of advertising to 'ordinary women' in the 1950s and 1960s, Sean Nixon notes that while Abrams' study focused on the rise of the teenage consumer, other market research of the period concentrated on different sectors within the youth market, such as 'young married' and 'young home makers'. Sean Nixon, 'Understanding ordinary women: Advertising, consumer research and mass consumption in Britain, 1948–1967,' CRESI Working Paper number: 2009–03 (2009), 8 note 9.
15 This combination is sometimes referred to as the 'three-legged-stool' of publishing theory. See Jason Whittaker, *Magazine Production* (Abingdon: Routledge, 2008), 1–29.
16 This term refers to the binding of the magazine, where pages are glued to a central spine. It commonly distinguishes quality 'glossies' from cheaper productions that are stapled.
17 The list of monthly and weekly publications in chronological order as catalogued by Braithwaite and Barrell included: 1963 *Jackie,* D.C. Thompson

Ltd (weekly); 1964 *Diana*, D.C. Thompson Ltd (weekly), *Fabulous*, Fleetway (weekly); 1965 *Nova*, IPC (monthly); 1966 *Annabel*, D.C. Thompson Ltd (monthly), *Hers*, Pearsons (monthly), *Petticoat*, Fleetway (weekly), *Trend*, City Magazines Ltd (weekly); 1968 *19*, IPC (monthly).

18 Jean McInlay, 'Editor's letter,' *Honey*, April 1960, 2.
19 'Fleetway stage a song-and-dance send off for *Honey* at May Fair,' *World Press News and Advertisers Review*, 18 March 1960, 1. The General Post Office (GPO) was responsible for postal telecommunication services and would have attended as a potential employer of young women.
20 The relationship between class and magazine readership is not necessarily straightforward, as the National Readership Survey (NRS) discriminates readerships in terms of social grade. In the 1960s, this would have been based on the occupation of the 'head of household' rather than the respondent. Girls and young women would normally have been classified in terms of their fathers' occupation rather than their own. See Winship, *Inside Women's Magazines*, 164, for further discussion of the NRS categories.
21 Full-page advertisement for *Honey* magazine, *World Press News and Advertisers Review*, 29 January 1960, 2.
22 See Anna Gough-Yates' discussion of the closure of *Honey* in 1986, where she argues that the 'group buy' policy at IPC contributed to the magazine's abrupt closure. Gough-Yates notes that much of the advertising, which appealed to a traditional feminine consumer, was out of step with the editorial rebrand of the magazine in the 1980s. Anna Gough-Yates, *Understanding Women's Magazines, Publishing Markets and Readerships* (London: Routledge, 2003), 82.
23 The editor's letter of issue 85 began with the exclamation, 'If you're staggering under the weight of this issue, let me tell you it's a record. This is the largest issue of *Honey* we have ever produced, and it carries more advertising than any Fleetway woman's magazine has ever done.' *Honey*, April 1967, 3.
24 Braithwaite and Barrell, *Women's Magazines*, 38.
25 '"Fabulous Gala Lipstick offer" 7 lipsticks for 3s 6d,' *Honey*, August 1961, 13; '*Honey* hair clip,' *Honey*, October 1965, cover. The gift was accompanied by a feature on how to style hair using the featured hair clip, 'Ten headliners to start you off,' 78–9.
26 *Honey* celebrated its first anniversary with a competition to win a Decca record player, inviting readers to organise a playlist of ten singles. *Honey*, April 1961, 124. 'Win a Mini, or £500 cash,' *Honey*, July 1964, cover.
27 The radio show, *Honey Hit Parade*, began in April 1961 with the D. J. Kent Walton on Radio Luxemburg. *Honey*, April 1961, 75.
28 Advertisement for Leeds *Honey* Boutique, *Honey*, February 1965, 38.
29 These were launched within Lewis' department stores in Leicester, Manchester, Birmingham, Hanley and Blackpool in 1965 and were tied to existing salons. *Honey*, November 1965, 78–9.
30 See, for example, the main launch feature for the boutiques, 'Be a black and white girl,' which ran to twelve pages and comprised composite pages of black and white fashion spreads accompanied by small inset photographs and pen portraits of the *Honey* girls at each of the featured boutiques. *Honey*, April 1965, 56–69.
31 This refers to the use of central staples to bind the pages.
32 Abrams, *The Teenage Consumer*, 10.
33 Jean McInlay, 'Editor's letter,' *Honey*, April 1960, 2. This first letter was simply signed 'The Editor' rather than naming McInlay. Indeed, despite being the magazine's first editor, little mention is made of her within it, in contrast to

her successor Audrey Slaughter, who is often mistakenly credited as responsible for launching *Honey.*

34 White, *Women's Magazines*, 172, notes that the early 'big sister' tone adopted by the magazine was unpopular with readers.
35 'We'd like you to meet . . . ,' *Honey*, November 1960, 111.
36 There is no evidence to suggest that McInlay was sacked, although this may have been the case. It may also have been common practice to launch new titles with an established staff editor before investing in new talent.
37 Audrey Slaughter was the youngest editor of a woman's magazine in the Fleetway group. Having entered journalism at the age of eighteen as a typist on *Woman* (Odhams 1937–), she went on to join Fleetway two years later in the paper pattern department. Slaughter was fashion editor for *Woman's Illustrated* (Fleetway, 1936–61) when she was asked to take over the then failing *Honey*. She became Editor in Chief of *Honey* and her sister magazine, *Petticoat*, in 1966, but left the publishing house (by then IPC) for a short stint on the *Evening News*. Slaughter returned to publishing in 1970 as editor of *Vanity Fair* (National Magazine, 1949–72), but left when it was sold to IPC in 1972 to make way for the launch of the British version of *Cosmopolitan*, having turned down the editorship. Working with a group of journalists from *Vanity Fair*, Slaughter launched *Over 21* in 1972 as an independent venture with Ms Publishing. For profiles on Slaughter and her publishing career see Linda Christmas's, 'If Over 21 . . . ' in *The Guardian,* 25 February 1972, 11, or Prudence Glynn, 'Audrey Slaughter: Back in circulation,' *The Times,* 24 April 1972, 7.
38 White, *Women's Magazines,* 172, attributes this to the February 1965 issue, however it seems more likely that this extract is taken from the issue of November 1966, which featured an extensive report of the results of the magazine's Readers' Survey.
39 Figures taken from White, *Women's Magazines*, appendix V.
40 Glynn, 'Audrey Slaughter: Back in circulation,' *The Times,* 24 April 1972, 7.
41 Christmas, 'If Over 21 . . . ,' 11. See also *Honey,* June 1963, cover.
42 The bus appears in the contents page of the issue entitled 'To the North,' *Honey,* February 1965, 3. It is photographed from the side, with Audrey Slaughter behind the wheel and various members of the editorial team seen through the windows and climbing onto the open doors at the rear. This episode is recalled in an editorial article written to commemorate the final issue of the magazine, 'And now the end is near. . . . Goodbye forever,' *Honey,* September 1986, 46.
43 'No quiet on the northern front,' *Honey,* February 1965, 24–5.
44 *Honey*, February 1965, 10.
45 White, *Women's Magazines*, 173.
46 'Elizabeth Jones, 28, professional driver,' *Honey,* August 1961, 38–9.
47 Abigail Van Buren, 'To neck or not to neck,' *Honey,* August 1960, 14–16.
48 Keith Cameron, 'Dating before mating,' *Honey,* November 1965, 16–17; Audrey Slaughter, *Birth Control and the Single Girl*, *Honey,* October 1966, 130.
49 Reported in the editorial section of Melbourne daily newspaper *The Age,* 28 September 1966, 2.
50 'Free, young and female: But God help you if you have a baby and no husband,' *Honey,* April 1968, 114–15.
51 Helena Mills discussed the changing coverage of sexuality in young women's magazines in the period. Helena Mills, 'Young women in love: Media, gender and the heterosexual career in 1960s Britain' (paper presented at the

'Consuming/Culture: Women and girls in print and pixels' conference held, Oxford Brookes University, UK, 5–6 June, 2015). See also Hera Cook, 'Nova 1965–1970: Love, masculinity and feminism, but not as we know it,' in *Love and Romance in Britain, 1918–1970*, ed. Alaina Harris and Timothy Willem Jones (Basingstoke: Palgrave Macmillan, 2015), 225–44.
52 See Roland Barthes, *The Fashion System* (London: Vintage, 2010), on the structure of fashion pages, and Joanne Entwistle, *The Fashioned Body* (Oxford: Polity, 2000), on the discursive practices of fashion and identity.
53 See Dominic Sandbrook, *White Heat: A History of Britain in the Swinging Sixties* (London: Abacus, 2009) and William Osgerby, *Youth in Britain since 1945* (Oxford: Wiley-Blackwell, 1997) on youth culture in the 1960. For a general discussion of fashion and youth culture in the 1960s, see Christopher Breward, *Fashioning London: Clothing and the Modern Metropolis* (Oxford: Berg, 2004).
54 Winship, *Inside Women's Magazines*, 62.
55 Hilary Radner, 'On the move: Fashion, photography and the single girl in 1960s,' in *Fashion Cultures: Theory, Exploration and Analysis*, ed. Stella Bruzzi (London: Routledge, 2000), 128–42.
56 Helen Gurley Brown cited in Radner, 'On the move,' 135.
57 'Take a good look: 26 years of *Honey* beauty,' *Honey*, September 1986, 46.
58 'So you want to be a top model?,' *Honey*, April 1960, 91.
59 'Meet Cathee, will she change the way you look?,' *Honey*, November 1967, 76–7. The article reports that Dahmen cut and curled her hair on the advice of a photographer, giving her a distinctive look.
60 'Ain't got no English Rose, big blue eyes, usual looks, peaches and cream,' *Honey*, April 1969, 70–1; 'Calico alla campagna,' *Honey*, April 1970, 78–9.
61 See, for example, 'Too bad she's black as well,' *Honey*, August 1968, 60–1, which addresses racial discrimination within the education system, and 'Can't she get anyone better?,' *Honey*, April 1969, 84–5, on mixed race relationships.
62 See, for example, a fashion spread featuring students from Cambridge and the country girls from Wisbech, *Honey*, February 1968, 30–41.
63 See Ouellette, 'Inventing the Cosmo girl', for a discussion of *Cosmopolitan* magazines and Helen Gurley Brown's particular construction of the single girl.
64 See, for example, Christopher Breward, David Gilbert and Jenny Lister, *Swinging Sixties* (London: V&A Publications, 2006) for a discussion of the mythologising of the term 'swinging London'. See Anna Gough-Yates, '"A shock to the system": Feminist interventions in youth subculture—the adventures of *Shocking Pink*,' *Contemporary British History* 26 (2012): 375–403 for a useful overview of second wave feminist critiques of mainstream women's magazines.
65 See, for example, the life stories collected in Sara Maitland, ed., *Very Heaven: Looking Back at the 1960s* (London: Virago, 1988).

Part V
Women's Bodies from Second Wave Feminism to the Twenty-First Century

13 Popular Feminism and the Second Wave

Women's Liberation, Sexual Liberation and *Cleo* Magazine

Megan Le Masurier

Cleo magazine was launched in Australia in November 1972. It was a mainstream magazine, much like American and British *Cosmopolitan*, and vied for a similar demographic of younger women open to new ideas about gender equality and sexual freedom. *Cleo*, however, was more overtly committed to engaging with ideas of women's liberation than *Cosmopolitan* and was produced for a specifically Australian readership. Within the mainstream of the Australian magazine landscape at the time, *Cleo* was extraordinary in its departure from the general focus of women's magazines on homes, husbands, children, recipes, royalty and the accoutrements of a traditional femininity.[1] The scant academic work that has been done on Australian magazines of the period of the second wave (late 1960s to early 1980s) gives no indication of *Cleo*'s feminist enthusiasm. Australian feminists in the 1970s took their cue from Betty Friedan's excoriating analysis of women's magazines as the primary force that kept women trapped inside the home.[2] Like their contemporaries in Britain and America, feminists and scholars either ignored or disparaged women's magazines of this period. The mainly British tradition of work that does refer back to 1970s magazines, such as the incipiently global title *Cosmopolitan*, recycled the conclusions of earlier feminists about their tokenistic, 'fake' feminism.[3] Angela McRobbie, for example, confidently generalised that women's magazines in the 1970s were full of 'deep conservatism' in terms of feminism.[4] But deep conservatism was not in evidence in *Cleo*. As Jennifer Scanlon also concluded in her recent study of Helen Gurley Brown, the editor of US *Cosmopolitan*, there was indeed an engagement with the idea of women's liberation (and sexual liberation) in this influential magazine in the 1970s.[5]

The politics of women's liberation was steeped in everyday life, a space that women's magazines had colonised for their journalism many decades before. It therefore makes intuitive sense that women's magazines would provide evidence of *some* kind of engagement with the new ideas about equality for women that were erupting in the West from the late 1960s. Indeed, a small clutch of mainstream publications were launched in the early years of women's liberation in Australia, designed for the 'new' young women at this time, which responded positively to feminist ideas.

Magazines such as *Pol* (1968–, inspired by the British *Nova*), *Cleo* (1972–) and the Australian version of the US-based title *Cosmopolitan* (1973–) were published, alongside the expected effervescence of small scale, more radically feminist magazines that were appearing in countries where women's liberation was taking hold.

'We equipped the rebels with knowledge and thus stoked the fires of revolution', wrote *Cleo*'s first editor Ita Buttrose.[6] In the pages of *Cleo*, there was a lively debate and multi-voiced negotiation of much of the social and cultural ground unearthed by second wave feminist activists in feature journalism, interviews, reader letters and the questions and answers appearing in the doctor and advice columns. From 1972 to 1985, when a new editor shifted the magazine's focus away from such overt engagement with feminist ideas, there were stories on the politics of housework and the double shift, on abortion, contraception and sexually transmitted diseases, women's health and childbirth; stories on domestic violence, rape and women's refuges; on sexual harassment and sexism; the pressure to partner and have children and the competing desire to find fulfilling work and a career. There were stories on girls' education, on feminist consciousness-raising and the women's liberation movement around the world.

Although Buttrose may have retrospectively claimed *Cleo* as a revolutionary force, *Cleo*'s type of feminism was not radical. There was no analysis of patriarchy or call for the dismantling of the family and the state. The editorial agenda was recognisably that of liberal feminism, with a wash of the less revolutionary ideas of women's liberation. *Cleo* was a mainstream magazine designed to maximise profit for its owner, Kerry Packer, and his large magazine company, Australian Consolidated Press. But commercial success does not necessarily negate the possibility of a magazine engaging in popular feminist politics. Indeed, there was enough rich material in the issues of *Cleo* published in the period of the second wave to provide evidence for a different story to be told about the role of women's magazines in aiding the development of feminist consciousness amongst their 'ordinary' women readers.

Cleo's readers were mainly lower to middle class, based on average income, and the majority were under thirty-five. Almost three-quarters were married. Thirty per cent of Australian women between the ages of thirteen and twenty-four read *Cleo*.[7] At this point in Australia's history, less than 40 per cent of girls completed high school education.[8] In 1971, just 31.5 per cent of the university population was female and only a small minority came from working-class backgrounds.[9] By contrast, women involved with the women's liberation movement were 'almost without exception women who had had some university education'.[10] The readers of *Cleo* were women who had neither the education nor the freedoms of youthful middle-class privilege, neither the support networks nor the articulate anger of the more radical feminists. These women were developing their own more pragmatic and personal interpretations of feminism, tempered by the many competing demands of their particular life situations. They may not all have identified as 'Women's Libbers' or 'feminists', but they absorbed many of the ideas about equality and independence and attempted to put them into practice.

One definition of popular feminism is that women may be influenced by feminist ideas but not necessarily identify with the feminist label. Joanne Hollows and Rachel Moseley in their work on feminism and popular culture push this further, arguing that second wave feminism 'was partly constituted through the popular'.[11] Susan Sheridan, Susan Margarey and Sandra Lilburn, in their study of representations of feminism in Australian newspapers, go further still: 'It is impossible to draw a firm line between feminism "in actuality" and feminism in the media-sphere.'[12] This chapter adds another layer of meaning by focusing on how sexual liberation was integrated into popular feminism. For *Cleo* and its readers, sex was a constant point of discussion, often framed in terms of equal rights and gender inequality.

WOMEN'S LIBERATION/SEXUAL LIBERATION

Women's liberation and sexual liberation were entwined in the optimistic early years of second wave feminism. As Jane Gerhard writes, 'Feminists in the late 1960s joined sexual liberation to women's liberation, claiming that one without the other would keep women second-class citizens.'[13] Lynne Segal notes that for all the confusion and uncertainty, 'liberated' heterosexual experiences could be 'a delight in the affirmation of self':

> The fight against sexual hypocrisy and for sexual openness and pleasure provided much of its [women's liberation's] early inspiration, as women decided that pleasure was as much a social and political as a personal matter. These issues were not only central to the genesis of feminism, they remain central to the majority of women's lives today.[14]

The ideas of sexual liberation continued into the early years of the second wave. The Australian feminist historian Jill Julius Matthews reflected that 'For a while in the early seventies, feminism was able to hold on to both positions: the end to be achieved by overcoming women's oppression was a human liberation in which true equality and freedom in sexuality as in all else would be enjoyed by all.'[15]

This connection began to unravel as the 1970s unfolded and second wave feminists contested the meaning of sexual liberation for women—a period known as the 'sex wars'.[16] Some judged heterosexuality harshly, publicly denouncing it as anything from sleeping with the enemy to legalised prostitution, masochism or patriarchal brainwashing.[17] Feminists such as Carol Smart have described the intensity of this debate, saying, 'It was as if there were really only two available positions; one which seemed to gloat over the mistakes of heterosexual women and one which seemed to apologise for being heterosexual.'[18]

Amber Hollibaugh captured the shift that had occurred in just over ten years of the second wave: 'Part of my attraction to feminism involved the right to be a sexual person. I'm not sure where that history got lost.'[19] However, one of the places that connection continued to be asserted was in the popular feminism of a magazine like *Cleo*. Women's right to the freedom and erotic enjoyment they perceived men to be having, the dismantling of the double standard and disconnecting sex from shame was part of *Cleo's* basic editorial philosophy and part of its popular interpretation of feminism.

Anne Woodham, one of *Cleo's* feature journalists, recalled that the all-day editorial meetings involved the entire staff and came to resemble monthly consciousness-raising sessions: 'Those story conferences were practically therapy sessions, the pride we took in lowering our inhibitions. Orgasms? We described them in poetic detail. We laid them as on an examining table and picked them over. Frigidity, impotency, homosexuality, lesbian mothers, menstruation. Nothing, but nothing, was taboo.'[20] Of the new women's magazines in the 1990s, McRobbie writes:

> The idea that sexual pleasure is learnt, not automatically discovered with the right partner, the importance of being able to identify and articulate what you want sexually and what you do not want; the importance of learning about the body and being able to make the right decisions about abortion and contraception, the different ways of getting pleasure [. . .] each one of these figured high in the early feminist agenda.[21]

She could have been describing *Cleo's* editorial philosophy. For all the talk of liberation and the social changes taking place, for all the talk about sex, we should not forget that many people in Australia in the 1970s were sexually conservative and the level of ignorance about bodies and sexual practices was high. Sex before marriage, 'living in sin', unmarried motherhood, illegitimate children given up for adoption, illegal abortion, even getting a prescription for the Pill, were still sites of shame, anxiety and social controversy. These issues were under challenge in the 1970s, but for many young women it was a confusing time. In 1971, the average age of marriage was twenty-one and the teenage birth rate was the highest in Australia's history, at 55.5 per thousand of population. In 2001, by comparison, it was 17.6 per thousand.[22] The 1971 figure is extraordinary and suggests young women in confusion and dramatic transition about sexual behavior, ignorant or unable to access contraception in a society where abortion was still illegal but enticed by the rapidly changing cultural and social environment to experiment with sex.

A *Cleo* feature story about the importance of sex education for girls was filled with anecdotes from ordinary women who spoke of the guilt-ridden messages about sex received from their mothers:

> I remember her saying when I was about 16: 'If you ever feel tempted, just see my face before you'. [. . .] And the very first time I did go to bed with someone I really did see her face, this sad face being terribly disappointed in me. I suffered giant guilt and I was convinced that the next morning I would be dappled with this scarlet rash, invisible to everyone else but her, which would let her know immediately that I was no longer a virgin.[23]

The journalist who wrote the story, Patricia Johnson, also interviewed Robyn Clark, a health worker from the overtly feminist Leichhardt Women's Health Centre in Sydney. Clark spoke of the levels of sexual ignorance, especially amongst migrant women and those with strong religious backgrounds:

> There is still that vicious circle of morality versus pleasure, thinking only of the man's pleasure, never of her own. When a woman can't have an orgasm, the first step is to encourage her to masturbate. But it has never occurred to the majority that they could. They find it so distasteful after all that earlier conditioning that they simply can't.[24]

At a time when sex education was barely provided by schools, parents and doctors, *Cleo* became one of the most important regular forums for explicit and non-judgmental sexual information for young women (and men, who comprised one third of *Cleo*'s readers if not buyers) in Australia. The young women who read *Cleo* had been raised on respectability, restraint and sexual ignorance but they were being hailed by the popularised discourses of sexual liberation to take on the new ethos of 'sophistication' and 'sexiness'. The clash produced much anxiety, evident in the doctor and adviser pages. 'The number of letters which arrive for the *Cleo* Doctor each month is staggering', stated a special *Dear Cleo Doctor* booklet; 'It concerns us that women know very little about their bodies, that they are too embarrassed to seek medical advice—and that even after they consult a doctor they are quite ignorant of their condition and the treatment they are receiving.'[25] The booklet provided a list of questions to ask doctors and encouraged women to be more assertive and demanding. The *Cleo Adviser Booklet*, based on the 'hundreds of letters' that were sent to the magazine's advice column every week, was even more explicit. With a barely contained anger it stated, 'doctors, lawyers, even parents may be wrong. They are limited by their own view of the world, their own conditioning, their own fears and prejudices.'[26]

It is easy to disparage advice columns as a lesser kind of journalism. Michael Schudson, for example, defines journalism as dealing only with serious matters of the public sphere: 'Journalism is the business or practice of producing and disseminating information about contemporary affairs of general public interest or importance.' Advice columns, by his definition, would be 'hard to dignify [. . .] as publically important'.[27] As a genre that evolved in women's magazines over many decades, however, advice columns have provided a space for women to share personal problems, to find solace and support. Furthermore, as Meryl Altman writes, 'So often an anxiety about sex, women and gender, turns into an anxiety about genre.' This trashing of trash can be 'an unsuccessful way of stopping women's mouths'.[28] The advice column is a genre of journalism where the boundaries between private and public, of what knowledges should and should not be spoken in public, are challenged. In the *Cleo* advice column, especially towards the end of the 1970s, we hear not moralism or prescription but support and a pluralistic acceptance of different sexual practices. The kind of advice offered by Wendy McCarthy, a second wave feminist activist and the *Cleo* adviser from 1978–84, provided an avowedly feminist source of support for readers.

THE SEXUALLY ACTIVE WOMAN

With its high level of reader interactivity, *Cleo* also provided a sense of community in which shame could be aired and possibly alleviated. As Michael Warner argues, 'Isolation and silence are among the common conditions for the politics of sexual shame. Autonomy requires more than civil liberty; it requires the circulation and accessibility of sexual knowledge.'[29] There was a lot of sex work to do here for and by 'ordinary' women in the 1970s, and especially those women who were isolated from social formations where sexual liberation or feminist discussion groups were active.

Cleo attempted to break down one of the traditional and oppressive polarities of heterosexuality and gender—of masculinity as active and femininity as passive. This was quite a radical position at the time and was surprisingly evident in *Cleo*'s feature journalism and in the readers' letters. Sex was not represented as something to be exchanged or endured for a meal ticket or social mobility, nor was it represented as something extracted from women as unwilling victims of phallic domination. Women were being provided with the techniques and attitudes to *do* sex—not have it *done to* them. This did not necessarily mean having sex with more men; it meant women learning about their bodies, taking control of their own pleasure, with men or without them. It was a huge shift in sexual practice for women and it was clearly a challenge for many women to engage in active sexual practices, such as masturbation, using vibrators, sexual fantasy or oral sex, and to take an active 'woman on top' role in penetrative sex with men: 'I wanted to be more of an equal, to initiate some of the ideas. But he didn't like that. Some kind of power struggle began to upset the works,' wrote W. H. Manville in a January 1973 article.[30] The theme was echoed several years later in a piece by journalist Lonnie Barbach, stating, 'One erroneous expectation is that the man should be the authority on sex—that the man is responsible for the woman's orgasm. But men do not have any magical answers and they are not capable of reading a woman's mind.'[31]

Exhorting women to disrupt the traditional expectation of sexual passivity was not only continuous throughout the 1970s; *Cleo* presented it as a feminist position. Anne Woodham observed that the feminist questioning of 'stereotyped sex roles' was allowing women to 'take a more active part in suggesting love-play', but most women were still conditioned to take their cues from male partners and remained unsatisfied.[32] By 1982, however, the phenomenon of the sexually assertive woman was commonplace in the pages of *Cleo*. In a satire on the traditional advice column, 'Dear Aunti Susan' responded to spoof reader questions:

Dear Aunti Susan,
A male friend of mine says he is fed up with women who put the hard word on him—he can't stand it. What do you think?

Dear Reader,
The poor dear. He probably feels like a sex object! Aunti Susan's heart bleeds for him. Many men have failed to understand that the woman's movement has changed the way many women feel about this attitude among men. And while it is never proper etiquette for anyone to put the hard word on anyone else, women have certainly emerged from the 70s feeling freer to make their sexual wishes clear. Instead of waiting to be asked, and pretending to be coy, women are trying to get what they want. Men have always done so. Aunti Susan suggests you present your friend with a copy of *The Female Eunuch*, the seminal sex book of the 70s.[33]

An article in *Cleo* by Betty Dodson, US feminist and doyenne of masturbation, pointed to the importance of self-exploration for women to understand their own sexual responses and to find pleasure, with or without men: 'Sexual skill and the ability to respond are not natural. It has to be learned and practiced.'[34] These were themes *Cleo* repeated constantly throughout the years 1972–85. Dodson argued strongly against the sexual double standard in which society approved of men who were 'aggressive (independent) and sexually polygamous' but women were expected to be 'non-aggressive (dependent) and sexually monogamous'.[35]

There was a huge gap, however, between advising women to masturbate and readers' actual sexual practices. 'Beth' of NSW (New South Wales) sent *Cleo* a letter that reminds us just how difficult and shameful masturbation was for many women:

When I was 10 I used to masturbate. I was caught masturbating by my parents and ever since then I have felt guilty even though I know it's perfectly normal. My mother does not come straight out and say anything about my masturbating, she makes snide, nasty remarks, which upset me. My husband has not caught on to her remarks yet and I feel

I should tell him but I am ashamed. [. . .] My problem is wrecking my sex life. I feel ashamed of my body because of what I have done. Please help before it is too late.[36]

Embarrassment, shame, anxiety and the difficulty for some in engaging in the expanding repertoire of sexual practice are constants in the readers' letters. An exchange on the letters pages over oral sex adds another element as well: the way more adventurous sexual practices had become a marker of a woman's 'liberation' and her modernity and how this 'erotic capital'—or refusal of it—could be used to judge others. J. H. of NSW had found a feature discussing oral sex 'disgusting, unclean and revolting [. . .] I nearly threw up [. . .] I couldn't believe what I read. How any woman can put her mouth near a penis or a man put his mouth near a vagina is beyond me.'[37] The response to this letter from other readers was almost violent: 'If you could liberalise your views on oral sex as well as sex as a whole your husband might just regain his potency'; 'Oral sex is a clean wholesome way to satisfaction'; 'Wake up to yourself JH.'[38]

The vibrator was another new challenge for women—and for some men too. In 1972, the quality broadsheet *The Australian* had described sex shops as 'a pimple on the face of tolerance', and the courts were convicting the purveyors of such obscenity. Sex shops, their catalogues and vibrators were controversial. *Cleo*, however, championed the sex aid as 'fashioned solely to increase the pleasure of women [. . .]. Of the myriad devices concocted to please us—usually clitoral or vaginal stimulators—only three are designed to titillate heterosexual males.'[39] In fact, it was suggested that vibrators were so good at providing better, more reliable orgasms that women might be tempted to dispense with partners altogether: 'Many women express fears of becoming dependent on them for sexual release once they start [. . .]. Liberated women demand to know exactly what is wrong with being dependent on a vibrator?'[40]

THE POPULAR ORGASM

It sounds like a tautology. Is there an unpopular orgasm? The pages of *Cleo* demonstrate a constant engagement with women's right to orgasm and a recognition that this was indeed a feminist issue. The orgasm in the 1970s became a site of deep feminist debate. Amongst many feminist theorists, if you were not pursuing clitorally focused sexual pleasure, then the orgasms you were having were deeply unpopular. Anne Koedt insisted on the primacy of the clitoris for the 'feminist' orgasm, that the vaginal orgasm was a myth and that men and penetrative sex were unnecessary for female orgasmic pleasure.[41] Orgasm became the symbol of women's sexual liberation in *Cleo*, as it had in some of the early writings and discussions of second wave feminists. But although *Cleo* certainly ran stories about the role of the clitoris for orgasm, within the multi-voiced pages of women's popular journalism, many different sexual experiences were explored and accepted. For *Cleo*, the issue was not *how* women found their pleasure but *that* they found it. Sexual pleasure was framed as a woman's right, and involving men in the discussion and experience was important. 'For centuries pleasure in sex was regarded as reserved for men only', wrote Anne Woodham in one of her features; 'Now women see their own needs and want men to know.'[42]

Although *Cleo*—like *Cosmopolitan*—was aimed at heterosexual women, it did acknowledge that not all women's sexuality was inclined towards men. There were occasional articles about lesbian sex and positive reader responses. In 1974, for example, a first person feature entitled 'I am a lesbian. The frank story of a woman who came to terms with herself', was quickly followed by 'The shy homosexual woman'. Journalist Kirsten Blanch visited a regular social night for homosexual women in a suburban Melbourne home and talked with the women there, aiming to represent the 'frightening other' as ordinary: 'There is not a single, radical, liberated, aggressive butch among them. They are the proverbial silent majority of lesbianism, ordinary women with almost nothing in common except their preference for relationships—sexual and otherwise—with people of their own sex.'[43]

Lesbian readers started to write to *Cleo* in response. Reader, NSW, wrote of the pretence still involved with socialising as a lesbian in public and the abuse she received:

> I buy *Cleo* regularly and read 'The Shy Homosexual Woman'. This article and previous articles have done a great deal to destroy the nasty bitch 'offering boiled sweets to young girls' image that lesbians—I still hate the word—have unfortunately acquired. I am 23 and camp and have lived for the past three and a half years with a girl I love [. . .] I have been through the trauma of not believing myself to be camp and finding excuses but now I would never change.[44]

Cleo presented the often conflicting knowledge of experts (sexologists, psychologists, doctors, sex counsellors, feminists) and the similarly varied knowledge (and questions) of its readers in a mixed language of sexual science, how-to practical tips and descriptions of erotic pleasure. The result was a productive demotic babble. Letters kept pouring in to the *Cleo* Doctor and the *Cleo* Adviser. 'What is an orgasm?' 'How does it happen?' 'Why won't it happen?' 'Am I normal?' Readers were admirably unable to determine whether their problems with orgasm were medical or social/cultural ones. In this democratisation of 'sexpertise', any clear meaning of 'normal' female orgasmic sexuality almost dissolved, as the following excerpts, a handful from hundreds, begin to show.

Writing to the *Cleo* Doctor, a reader from NSW was disturbed by her inability to have an orgasm through penetration: 'I have reached orgasm many times by manual stimulation of my clitoris by my boyfriend. However, attempts at reaching orgasm through intercourse have failed miserably. I am quite unmoved [. . .] feel nothing, left out and inadequate.'[45] She added that because she could just as easily experience clitoral orgasm 'without him,' the sexual experience 'feels false'. This reader was having a 'feminist orgasm' and it was not what she wanted. By contrast, in response to an article asserting 'out with Sigmund Freud's vaginal orgasm, in with the clitoral orgasm', 'Freud Forever', as the reader described herself, wanted to take issue with the feminist 'experts' and demanded public recognition of the existence of the vaginal orgasm:

> [T]here has been mention in previous issues of 'the myth of the vaginal orgasm'. I feel I must let the women readers of *Cleo* know that I can have both clitoral orgasm and vaginal orgasm. Clitoral through masturbation and vaginal through intercourse. Both sensations are different, so much so that I dislike having my clitoris stimulated before intercourse as it tends to diminish vaginal orgasm sensation. Please acknowledge that at least some women do experience two types of orgasm.[46]

Clearly there were women whose bodies could not agree with the new feminist orthodoxy of clitoral supremacy and felt symbolically annihilated by the dismissal of their orgasms.

For Dawn from Victoria, *Cleo*'s 'The little man in the boat' article about the clitoris and how women should not fake orgasms gave her 'the words to say it':

> For the past three years I have tried to explain what I wanted to my husband but couldn't seem to get through to him. I read the article then gave it to my husband to read that night in bed. I won't say it was a complete success but at least he knows what I want now, and for the first time I am really enjoying sex.[47]

Similarly, after a story on the G spot in 1981, 'Reader' from Victoria could barely contain her relief at the validation this article provided:

> At last someone else realises there is another spot for orgasm. I had many long-standing relationships in which I had never experienced an orgasm other than clitoral despite a variety of positions. Then, with a very special guy it happened [. . .] I was away. This was to happen many times [. . .]. My friends have doubted that it was an orgasm, saying they only experienced the clitoral variety [. . .]. It was so good to read your article as I have always been sure that it was a true orgasm and not a figment of my imagination.[48]

Cleo was unquestionably focused on orgasm as the symbolic site of women's right to a gender equality of sexual pleasure. But how orgasm should occur was far from normative. One of the unsung strengths of the intimate style of sex journalism in women's magazines is that its reliance on the voice of the 'sexpert' *as well as* the anecdotal voice of the amateur inevitably results in a picture of the pluralities of female sexuality. There is just too much to be said and too many voices. This democratic generosity of popular journalism can open up the possibilities of female sexuality, not shut them down. It is a feminist desire, articulated without direct mention of feminism itself, and one of the meanings of popular feminism.

CONCLUSION

This chapter has focused on the sexual liberation content of *Cleo*'s popular feminism rather than its coverage of other issues important to the Women's Liberation Movement.[49] Why does this topic matter? Why does the story of ordinary women's engagement with the ideas of sexual and women's liberation need to be told? The answer, partly, is that the role of ordinary women in the history of second wave feminism has been silenced by the histories that focus on the radicals and activists. Their work, of course, was vital to the emergence of a movement for gender equality. However, ordinary women too struggled for equality within the limitations imposed by class, race and limited education. Their stories matter and they have left their traces in the pages of this women's magazine.

The ideals behind the second wave were based on the 'personal is political'. The changes women fought for needed to occur in the public sphere, but also in private. Gender equality needs to be felt and embodied. In the vision of the early women's liberationists, female sexual pleasure was a right to be fought for. As they became embroiled in sometimes bitter internal debates as the 1970s progressed, this vision disappeared, but it was carried forward in popular feminism. The ordinary women who left the imprints of this struggle in *Cleo*, and the magazine that emerged to give them a voice, deserve a place in a more inclusive history of the second wave.

NOTES

1 Susan Sheridan, Lyndall Ryan, Barbara Baird and Kate Borrett, *Who Was That Woman? The Australian Women's Weekly in the Postwar Years* (Sydney: University of New South Wales Press, 2002), 5.
2 Betty Friedan, *The Feminine Mystique* (Ringwood, Victoria: Penguin, 1963), 68.
3 Marjorie Ferguson, *Forever Feminine: Women's Magazines and the Cult of Femininity* (Aldershot: Gower, 1983); Janice Winship, *Inside Women's Magazines* (London: Pandora, 1987b); Ros Ballaster et al., *Women's Worlds: Ideology, Femininity and the Woman's Magazine* (London: Macmillan, 1991);

Ellen McCracken, *Decoding Women's Magazines: From Mademoiselle to Ms* (London: Macmillan, 1993).
4. Angela McRobbie, *In the Culture Society: Art, Fashion, and Popular Music* (New York: Routledge, 1999), 46.
5. Jennifer Scanlon, *Bad Girls Go Everywhere: The Life of Helen Gurley Brown* (Oxford: Oxford University Press, 2009).
6. Ita Buttrose, *Early Edition* (Melbourne: Macmillan, 1985), 151.
7. McNair Anderson Associates P/L, *Print Readership Survey. National Magazine Readership, 1974* (Sydney: McNair Anderson Associates, 1974).
8. Tom Roper, *The Myth of Equality* (Melbourne: North Melbourne Education Department, National Union of Australian University Students, 1970), 51.
9. Sharyn Pearce, *Shameless Scribblers: Australian Women's Journalism 1880–1995* (Rockhampton: Central Queensland University Press 1998), 200.
10. Anne Summers, 'After Germaine . . . what now?,' *Pol*, 29–31 December 1972, 30.
11. Joanne Hollows and Rachel Moseley, 'Introduction,' in *Feminism in Popular Culture*, ed. Joanne Hollows and Rachel Moseley (Oxford: Berg, 2006), 15.
12. Susan Sheridan, Susan Magarey and Sandra Lilburn, 'Feminism in the news,' in *Feminism in Popular Culture*, ed. Hollows and Moseley, 26.
13. Jane Gerhard, 'Revisiting "the myth of the vaginal orgasm": The female orgasm in American sexual thought,' *Feminist Studies* 26 (2000): 465.
14. Lynne Segal, *Straight Sex: The Politics of Pleasure* (London: Virago, 1994), xi–xii.
15. Jill Julius Matthews, *Sex in Public: Australian Sexual Cultures* (St Leonards, NSW: Allen & Unwin, 1997), xii.
16. Carol Siegel, *New Millennial Sexstyles* (Bloomington: Indiana University Press, 2000), 5.
17. Kath Albury, *Yes Means Yes: Getting Explicit About Heterosex* (Crows Nest, NSW: Allen & Unwin, 2002), 33–8.
18. Carol Smart, 'Collusion, collaboration and confession: On moving beyond the heterosexuality debate,' in *Theorising Heterosexuality: Telling it Straight*, ed. Diane Richardson (Maidenhead: Open University Press, 1996), 168.
19. Amber Hollibaugh writing in Deidre English, Amber Hollibaugh and Gayle Rubin, 'Talking sex: A conversation on sexuality and feminism,' *Feminist Review* 11 (1982): 42.
20. Anne Woodham, 'A time of camaraderie & change,' *Cleo*, November 1981, 122.
21. McRobbie, *In the Culture Society*, 57.
22. Anne Summers, *The End of Equality* (Milsons Point, NSW: Random House, 2003), 29.
23. Patricia Johnson, 'Can you ruin your daughter's sex life,' *Cleo*, January 1977, 84.
24. Johnson, 'Can you ruin,' 85.
25. *Dear Cleo Doctor* insert, *Cleo*, July 1976, 60.
26. *Cleo Adviser Booklet* insert, *Cleo*, July 1975, 42.
27. Michael Schudson, *The Sociology of News* (New York: W. W. Norton & Company, 2003), 11.
28. Meryl Altman, 'Beyond trashiness: The sexual language of 1970s feminist fiction,' *Journal of International Women's Studies* 4 (2003): 12.
29. Michael Warner, *The Trouble with Normal: Sex, Politics, and the Ethics of Queer Life* (Cambridge, MA: Harvard University Press, 2000), 171.
30. W. H. Manville, 'I was a sleep around girl,' *Cleo*, January 1973, 65.
31. Lonnie Barbach, 'How to enjoy your sensual self,' *Cleo*, October 1975, 93.

32 Anne Woodham, 'What women wish their men would remember,' *Cleo*, December 1974, 18.
33 Susan Anthony, 'Dear Aunti Susan,' *Cleo*, November 1982, 96.
34 Betty Dodson, 'Getting to know your body,' *Cleo*, December 1974, 207.
35 Dodson, 'Getting to know,' 207.
36 Beth, NSW, '*Cleo* letters,' *Cleo*, June 1982, 34.
37 J. H., NSW, '*Cleo* letters,' *Cleo*, December 1977, 240.
38 '*Cleo* letters,' *Cleo*, March 1978, 144.
39 Nikki Campbell, 'Sex aids: Helpful or harmful?,' *Cleo*, April 1973, 43.
40 George Mazzei, 'The vibrator,' *Cleo*, February 1978, 44.
41 Anne Koedt, 'The myth of the vaginal orgasm,' in *Radical Feminism*, ed. Anne Koedt, Ellen Levine and Anita Rapone (New York: Quadrangle Books, 1973 [1970]), 198–207.
42 Woodham, 'What women wish,' 15.
43 Blanch, Kirsten, 'The shy homosexual woman,' *Cleo*, July 1974, 72.
44 Reader, NSW, '*Cleo* letters,' *Cleo*, October 1974, 178.
45 '*Cleo* Doctor,' *Cleo*, January 1976, 65.
46 'Freud Forever,' no address, '*Cleo* letters,' *Cleo*, September 1974, 178.
47 Dawn, Victoria, '*Cleo* letters,' *Cleo*, June 1981, 184.
48 Reader, Victoria, '*Cleo* letters,' *Cleo*, September 1981, 240.
49 This coverage has been discussed elsewhere by the author. See Megan Le Masurier, 'My other, my self,' *Australian Feminist Studies* 22 (2007): 191–211.

14 How *Ladies' Home Journal* Covered Second Wave Health, 1969–1975

Amanda Hinnant

The women's health movement (1969–75) was one of the most successful accomplishments of second wave feminism in the United States.[1] In addition to the overriding grievance that the male-dominated American medical industry operated under sexist biases, some of the specific health concerns included childbirth, contraception and sterilisation.[2] The common thread running throughout was the desire for women to have agency over their own bodies. Participants in the women's health movement spent a great deal of time distributing informal and formal publications about women's health.

Today, women's health news is a popular subject in gendered and nongendered mainstream publishing. During the late 1960s and early 1970s, as evidenced by the movement's demand for more information, women's health news was not as available or thorough. The impetus for this chapter is to explore what information about women's health readers were getting at this time from mainstream sources and how it was rhetorically shaped. During second wave feminism, did women's publications cover any of the issues brought to the fore by the women's health movement?

To answer this question, I examined health information published in the prominent women's service magazine *Ladies' Home Journal* (*LHJ* or the *Journal*) between 1969 and 1975—key years for the women's health movement. Close textual analysis was needed to establish the ways in which women's health issues were represented in the magazine and the messages that its coverage attempted to convey. As a later section discusses, feminists have condemned women's magazines as patriarchal commercial enterprises focusing on a narrow range of socially prescribed female roles; we might thus expect a prominent example of the genre, such as *Ladies' Home Journal*, to avoid dealing with radical and politicised issues. As a result, I expected the women's health movement topics to be scarce and less revolutionary once filtered through the pages of traditional women's magazine publishing. However, as this chapter shows, this was not always the case. In fact, this chapter offers an important example in an effort to understand how magazine journalism can reflect, reject or enhance ideas put forward by a social movement. Coverage can influence the trajectory of a movement if people feel their voices and demands are being registered or ignored. Before turning to the findings from the magazines later in this chapter, I first review literature on the women's health movement and the significance of the *Ladies' Home Journal* historically and at that time.

THE WOMEN'S HEALTH MOVEMENT

The women's health movement evolved along with the broader Women's Liberation Movement. In second wave feminism consciousness-raising groups in the late 1960s, tales of medical mistreatment were common.[3] The central critiques women had about the system were patient-physician interaction, access to information and the right to decision making in health matters;[4] as feminist scholar and journalist Flora Davis notes, 'From the beginning, feminists took the position that the patient had a right to all the facts.'[5] Thus, the main tactic employed to help women gain control over their health care was education. The Boston Women's Health Collective, which began when a group of women decided to educate themselves about the female body, is credited with starting the movement in 1969.[6] Subsequently publishing *Women and Their Bodies* in 1970, which evolved into the bestselling, internationally published *Our Bodies, Ourselves* in 1973, the Collective's goal was to inform women so that they could take action: 'Rejecting the role of passive patient, women learned to be assertive, to ask tough questions, to do their own research, to insist on certain tests, to refuse others and to demand that doctors take their ailments seriously.'[7] The great success of the movement was the creation of a 'new aggressively informed class of consumer'.[8] Education that would lead to self-determination was a first priority and a common cause within the movement.

Within the larger Women's Liberation Movement, the health movement can be seen as either consistent with feminist principles or at odds with them. Davis points out that health issues are fundamental, but dissimilar to women's rights: 'Often more uncomfortable to deal with than legal or economic rights, body issues are seen to be at the root of the age-old prejudices against women.'[9] Professor of public health Sheryl Ruzek observes the paradox of the women's health movement stemming out of the larger women's movement: 'for feminists have often decried a focus on women's bodies and especially their reproductive organs or functions; usually they minimise the differences between the sexes'.[10] In contrast, the women's health movement focused on these biological differences. Later, science journalist and professor Claudia Dreifus clarified the connection between women's liberation and women's health: 'When women have dominion over their biologic functions, only then, I'm convinced is liberation possible.'[11]

Members of the women's health movement engaged in three forms of activism: changing consciousness, providing health-related services and struggling to change established health institutions.[12] The first step in countering the system became gathering information and reducing the knowledge differential between patient and practitioner: 'To do something about doctors who were condescending, paternalistic, judgmental and non-informative, they [Boston Collective] decided they would have to learn more about their own bodies.'[13] While some health movement organisations existed to change the structure of the health care system or to provide direct medical services, many functioned to provide information, including the Boston Women's Health Book Collective, the Women's Health Forum's *HealthRight*, New Moon Communications, the National Women's Health Network and the San Francisco Women's Health Center.[14]

In the original *Women and Their Bodies,* the writers advise that these papers 'are meant to be used by our sisters to increase consciousness about ourselves as women, to build our movement, to begin to struggle collectively for adequate health care, and in many other ways can be useful to you'.[15] While their emphasis was on educating women about their bodies, consciousness-raising was a fundamental goal as well. The chapter titled 'Women, Medicine and Capitalism' begins with a quote from philosopher Herbert Marcuse: 'Health is a state defined by an elite.'[16] This statement situates the health movement within a class critique, and the same chapter went on to describe how the expertise and power gap between physician and patients is solidified by various elements, including education, dress and language. All of these help to mystify the medical elite, which, they argued, is the main cause of the power allocation.

The activism of teaching women about their bodies both concerned and infuriated physicians. Ruzek writes that in the traditional medical setting, physicians believe information in the hands of patients to be dangerous. A physician interviewed at the time said to Ruzek: 'You just can't give women information without causing a lot of trouble.'[17] Participants at a public forum on health care decision making at the University of California San Francisco pointed out that as women were gaining medical knowledge, they were demanding a greater voice in their care. One surgeon on the panel complained that women were insisting on lumpectomies in the place of radical mastectomies 'on the basis of things they had read in women's magazines'.[18] This points to the fundamental goal of learning about medicine and reducing the knowledge differential: women's self-determination.

In writing about the women's health movement, Ruzek makes a distinction between individual and communal action: 'in this movement, client power is *not* limited to individual efforts to "beat the system." Instead focus is on group action to bring about change on a societal level, and in face-to-face interaction between the patient and the physician.'[19] Thus, the women's health movement advocated for change on both the individual level and the institutional/societal level. Those different levels, however, point to the distinction between liberal feminism and radical feminism within the women's health movement. A liberal feminist critique of the health care system tended to be about sexual equality in education and employment in medicine, the sexist attitudes of male doctors and the 'right to know' nature of women's health information.[20] 'The liberal critique approached the problem of medical care at the point most visible to the middle- or upper-middle-class consumer, the private office of the physician or specialist.'[21] This individual approach could only have a limited effect on the system.

Alternatatively, the radical feminist element within the women's health movement went beyond consumer resistance to emphasise alternate modes of health care. More specifically, a radical feminist critique focused on dismantling the patriarchal structure of medicine (rather than just inserting women into it), creating 'self-help' alternatives for women to take matters into their own hands and equipping women with the information to override physicians' judgments about their own treatment.[22] Like liberal feminists, radical feminists sought to increase knowledge and thus the 'ability of patients to resist their infantilisation at the hands of those who possess that knowledge'.[23] Though the method of education is the same, the ends are somewhat different. Whereas liberal feminism sought to share in the knowledge power of the health care system, radical feminism sought to subvert the system itself. That said, education was a common goal among all involved in the women's health movement.

WHY THE *LADIES' HOME JOURNAL*?

Women's magazines have provided a rich focus for feminist analysis. Betty Friedan indicted mainstream women's magazines for glorifying a domesticated identity of American femininity that was stifling and divergent from reality.[24] With millions of readers, women's magazines have been and continue to be an important cultural medium for female readers, and the *Ladies' Home Journal* was a pioneer in the field.[25] The *Journal* was founded in 1883 as a response to advertisers who wanted to reach a female demographic.[26] It was the first magazine to reach one million readers in 1904.[27] Additionally, the middle-class female readership of the *Journal* represents the demographic that journalists Barbara Ehrenreich and Deirdre English argue make up the consistent 'client caste' to the medical profession.[28]

The *Journal* is ideal for this analysis for a few reasons. It had a history with feminism that predated its second wave. Gender historian Jennifer Scanlon writes about how the magazine reflected the developing consumer culture and resisted feminist principles of the first wave in the late nineteenth and early twentieth centuries. An early editor of the *Journal*, Edward Bok, opposed the push for suffrage: 'Suffrage threatened not only Bok's vision of the woman at home, living the simple life, but also the very purpose of his magazine, which offered women advice and products for their individual and domestic, rather than collective and political, lives.'[29] Bok retired just before the Nineteenth Amendment became law in 1920, and the *Journal* subsequently modernised its political stance. Once the suffrage amendment passed, the magazine advised women to join the already existing political parties and be active in the League of Women Voters, rather than support the more radical National Women's Party. The presence of domestic responsibilities did not decrease in the magazine as civic life increased—the *Journal* promoted both public and private service.

These attempts to reconcile women's private and domestic roles with more public activity were never entirely successful, though. In 1970, the magazine's office was the target of a second wave feminist sit-in, with members of several feminist groups organising a coalition to protest against what they perceived as the magazine's unrealistic representation of women and women's issues.[30] At the end of the day-long sit-in, John Mack Carter, then editor-in-chief and publisher, negotiated to allow members of the coalition to write an eight-page feminist supplement to the August 1970 issue. Additionally, the *Journal*'s managing editor, Lenore Hershey (who replaced Carter as editor-in-chief in 1974) was quoted as saying that the time for reporting on women's liberation activities and organisations had passed: 'We don't feel that we have to say "Look, we're for women's lib, we have an article by Betty Friedan." We can say that month after month we are putting things in our magazine.'[31] Hershey's comments are telling in that she denies the movement credibility while insisting that the *Journal* had incorporated a new message for women. Due to the magazine's chequered engagement with feminism's first and second wave, the *Journal* provides an ideal case study for understanding how women's health movement issues were covered by a mainstream outlet at the time.

LADIES' HOME JOURNAL HEALTH COVERAGE DURING THE WOMEN'S HEALTH MOVEMENT

In order to analyse the *Journal's* health coverage during the time of the women's health movement in the US, I have conducted a qualitative textual analysis, which is a method concerned with revealing a text's latent meaning, rather than eastablishing factual accuracy.[32] First, I determined the core health topics addressed by the movement using five formative texts.[33] This list of topics provides a basis of comparison between what was on the women's health movement agenda and what were deemed to be important issues in the *Journal*. Second, I did a close reading of all 142 articles that were about the ten core topics: sexism in medicine, contraception, abortion, pharmaceuticals, childbirth, surgery, menstruation/menopause, gynaecology, health care access and general women's health issues. Finally, in order to systematically document and understand the issues as they appeared in the *Journal*, I coded the articles for tone and context and worked to determine the latent meaning of the magazine articles in connection with the political and rhetorical missions of the women's health movement. The eight-page feminist supplement that appeared in 1970 as a result of the sit-in provides a succinct contrast to the regular *Journal* coverage. Future research would benefit from exploring how readers interpreted these articles.

All of the articles listed appeared in the regular 'Medicine Today' column, written first by Phyllis Wright, MD, with medical columnist David Zimmerman, and then exclusively by Zimmerman after May 1970, unless denoted as appearing elsewhere in the publication. I review how a number of the core topics were addressed by the *Journal* and compare that coverage to the movement's approach and goals. Overall, the *Journal* attentively presented women's health news as news. Beyond educating the reader as a form of consumer advocacy and awareness, the *Journal* provided little agitation for change and thereby distinguished itself from movement literature. As the following discussion demonstrates, however, three examples from the early 1970s contained a strong liberal feminist agenda. The feminist supplement, the excerpt of *Our Bodies, Ourselves* and the 'Encyclopedia of Women's Bodies' all offered an explicit message that women should be educated about their bodies, so as to play a more active role in their medical treatment.

On the general topic of sexism in medical care and women's right to information, the *Journal* published nine stories. Many of these items described the general state of affairs and did not take an advocacy stance. There was one item, however, that stood out as making a more politically overt argument, an article which included excerpts from a leaflet produced by the federal government and intended to be included in each package of oral contraceptives. After 'organized medicine, population planners and drug makers attacked the leaflet' for being too honest and detailed about the potential side effects of oral contraceptives, a shorter version with less explicit warnings was substituted.[34] The excerpts in the *Journal*, which included refernce to blood clots and other side effects, were from the original explicit draft and did not appear in the government's revised version. Providing readers with the original controversial version of the product warnings was consistent with the ethos and stance taken by the women's health movement that women have a right to *all* information.

On a related topic, articles about women in medicine typically reported on how women face barriers in the field and the paltry percentage of female physicians in practice. An item in February 1971 included quotes from medical school deans who admitted to discriminating against women applicants.[35] An article in the *LHJ*'s 'Working Woman' column by Letty Cottin Pogrebin in April 1974 discussed the sexism directed at women physicians and how the women's movement helped to legitimise their roles.[36] Lastly, in a feature article about medical secrecy in February 1975, the *Journal* quoted medical ethicist Robert A. Veatch as saying, 'We've got to have more equality between patient and physician [. . .]. Every patient must have the right to participate in the medical decisions that affect his or her destiny [. . .]. Truth is your right.'[37] This speaks to the women's health movement's central goal of decreasing the power gap between patient and physician.

While the *Journal's* editorial content was not explicit in supporting that goal, the choice of material and favourable quotations at least suggest some sympathy with the position.

LADIES' HOME JOURNAL AND CONTRACEPTION

Of all of the women's health stories published in the *Journal*, contraception stories were the most frequent. The first article in the *Journal's* January 1969 issue, titled 'What "the Pill" does to husbands', is unlike most of the other contraception articles published in that it included more social commentary and less serviceable information about birth control. Though this article carried no feminist message, it did offer some interesting criticism of husbands who complained about the Pill. It was argued that when women stopped denying men sex, men had to face their own emotional and sexual immaturity that had remained latent when sex was less forthcoming, before the Pill. In the article, Dr Ralph Greenson remarked, 'Woman power is just like black power, and it's going to have a similar impact. Faced by the growing public effectiveness and independence of women, men have traditionally reacted as if their masculinity were under attack.'[38] This noteworthy quote conflates two of the most powerful social movements of the time, and discusses the Pill as a liberating choice for women rather than an apolitical medical choice.

The majority of the *Journal's* contraception coverage concerned the Pill's side effects and other new forms of birth control, such as the morning-after pill,[39] the IUD (intrauterine device that prevents fertilisation and implantation)[40] or Depo-Provera (a hormonal contraceptive delivered as a three-monthly injection).[41] The articles were informative about risks associated with contraceptive devices, as in the earlier example, but unlike in the women's health movement literature, they did not question why these new forms of contraceptive device were not more rigorously tested before being put on the market. That said, an April 1969 feature on the Pill asked why doctors were losing faith in it. The *Journal* quoted Dr Herbert Ratner as saying, 'Safety [. . .] should be established before, not after, a drug is placed on the market. It is truly scandalous to think that 8,000,000 women remain on this vast, uncontrolled experiment we call the birth control pill—especially when alternative safe methods are freely available.'[42] In quoting outraged physicians about the lack of research on the Pill, the *Journal* was, in this instance, reflecting one of the key causes of the women's health movement.

The recurring articles on the Pill (and one on Depo-Provera) foster the idea that women should know more about medical discoveries. The *Journal* did not, however, consistently question the Pill's usage. A feature in August 1971 downplayed the risks associated with the Pill, glossing over them with the argument, 'Pregnancy itself is 15 times riskier than the Pill.'[43] The DES (diethylstilboestrol) cancer debacle, faithfully covered by the women's health movement, was mentioned only twice in the *Journal* between 1969 and 1975.[44] In November 1971, the *Journal* reported on the fatalities of teenage daughters with vaginal cancer caused by their mothers' exposure to DES during pregnancy.[45] The article urged mothers who had been prescribed DES to take their teen daughters to a gynaecologist. This is a classic example of individual-oriented service journalism that does not question the social implications of the lack of research.

Another contraceptive, the IUD, received attention from the *Journal* in a straightforward news format. A 1975 article about the bacteria-prone IUD, the Dalkon Shield, outlined the debate within the US Food and Drug Administration.[46] The piece evaded an explanation of the precise nature of the problems being attributed to the the Dalkon Shield and concluded that most IUDs were effective and safe. Though in May 1975 the deadly consequences of the Dalkon Shield's porous string were not definitive, the article made no refernce to the fact that, in 1974, Planned Parenthood stopped prescribing the Dalkon Shield.[47] Therefore the *Journal's* coverage fell below the educational standards of the women's health movement.

One final form of contraception that the *Journal* covered was sterilisation, which is a form of birth control rarely covered in mainstream magazines today. The women's health movement addressed sterilisation from two perspectives: women should be free from forced sterilisation but should have a right to sterilisation as a form of birth control if desired. The *Journal's* coverage of sterilisation was basically informative about types available and there were no articles about forced sterilisation of poor women or women of colour. There were, however, a couple of articles about the right to sterilisation. In June 1975, for instance, the entire 'Medicine Today' column was devoted to laproscopic sterilisation. While most of the article described the procedure in detail, it concludeds with two paternalistic paragraphs:

> Though every woman has the right to be sterilized—even if she has no children—each doctor also has the right to decide which operations he will perform. For example, Dr Gottlieb will not sterilize a childless woman. And many hospitals demand the husband's approval [. . .]. A woman should be absolutely certain when she chooses this procedure.[48]

This article's conclusion infantalises women, and runs entirely contrary to the women's health movement's goal of women's self-determination.

Like the rest of the contraception stories, which provided information but did not challenge the system, the sterilisation stories in the *Journal* did not push any boundaries. Overall, the *Journal* provided information on contraceptives but failed to address the social implications of the paucity of research or the absence of a regulatory body controlling the marketing of contraceptive devices. Although the *Journal's* effort to keep readers abreast of news about contraception, in order to help them make individual choices, was admirable, its lack of advocacy for reform indicates the *Journal*'s dissonance with the women's health movement.

OTHER WOMEN'S HEALTH MOVEMENT ISSUES: FROM SURGERY TO CHILDBIRTH

Another topic central to the the women's health movement was unnecessary surgery, which movement activists believed was where the power differential between patient and physician was most pronounced. In the *Journal*'s first of seven articles about unnecessary surgery, published in May 1972, the author quotes a doctor who advised anyone contemplating surgery to get a second opinion, implying fallability of the physician.[49] In September of that same year, consumer activist and Green Party politician Ralph Nader wrote in his regular *Journal* column about unnecessary surgery, commenting that some 500 women died every year from unnecessary hysterectomy. Though Nader's column was about surgery in general, and not restricted to hysterectomy and mastectomy, he did take a consumer advocacy position, writing that 'more people are aware of their rights as consumers of health care and more are willing to take action when they believe their rights are abused'.[50]

'Medicine Today' in June 1974 was devoted to the topic of breast surgery and the choice between radical mastectomy and the less radical lumpectomy. David Zimmerman, the *Journal*'s resident medical columnist, outlined the debate: should women have a choice between radical or conservative surgery? He wrote, 'The possibility of conservative surgery has been hailed by some feminists who assail surgeons—most of whom are men—for performing "castrating" operations on women that they would never dare to do on men.'[51] Here Zimmerman explains the women's health movement position on control over surgery but takes the side of conventional medicine that advocated mastectomies. Though the power to decide still lay in the hands of the surgeon, the article addressed the point that women preferred to have a choice, but he stopped short of advocating this choice for women to seize agency. In December 1974, the *Journal* reported that the radical mastectomy had been no better in preventing cancer recurrences than the more conservative lumpectomy.[52] Although the *Journal* raised awareness about the different types of surgery, the message stopped short of telling readers to demand a choice in surgical option.

The *Journal* had several stories on do-it-yourself pap smears between 1969 and 1971 and even a story on menstrual evacuation (a method of do-it-yourself abortion) in May 1973.[53] Both of these gynaecology topics were important to the women's health movement. The *Journal* stressed the fact that the do-it-yourself exams should not be considered adequate replacement for visiting one's physician since the doctor screens for other kinds of cancer. As a result, it did not advocate a direct challenge of the gynaecological establishment.

There were topics where the *Journal* went beyond a liberal feminist approach and advocated systematic reform, notably abortion and childbirth. Twelve of the *Journal*'s fourteen articles on abortion appeared before the Supreme Court decision in 1973 to legalise abortion, and they all contained calls for reform to abortion laws in various states. In July 1970, the *Journal* published a guide to legal abortion in the nation, advising readers of the various regulations in place as well as the pending legislative and judicial actions in progress across the country. The article called the abortion laws unrealistic, given the safety of medical procedures at the time, and expressed hope for medical insurance plans to cover abortion when the laws were liberalised.[54] The article acted as a tool for individual women seeking abortion, but also criticised the system.

Another topic addressed with a surprisingly collective tone was childbirth. The *Journal* did not discuss many alternate forms of (non-hospital based) childbirth, focusing instead on the different new approaches to childbirth being offered by hospitals, rather than questioning the power dynamic between patient and doctor. But in the August 1970 feminist supplement, in an article entitled 'Babies are Born, Not Delivered', the author described her experience of giving birth in a patriarchal hospital situation. She ended her piece, 'Women are, as a group, capable of effecting change that would make the system responsive to us rather than continuing as victims of the system.'[55] While this article would not appear typical of the *Journal*, the following year, in June 1971, there was an item which began, 'Who delivers babies? Obstetricians? Or mothers?' The article was about a feminist sociologist, Dr Alice Rossi, who argued that women are disempowered by the birthing experience. Rossi says 'the whole paraphernalia of medicine [. . .] serve the function of retaining the dominant status of the attending physician, and thus prevent a woman from seeing the reality of the birth situation: that the physician is at her "side" while she gives birth, not her lordly "deliverer"'.[56] This article sent the message that the reader should question the system. It has little to do with individual solutions and deals instead with the structure of medical misogyny. When the *Journal* did discuss childbirth during this period, it was on a systematic level. This differs from the usual tendency within women's magazines towards the individual rather than the collective, a 'therapeutic feminism' style of writing, which utilises a self-help tone and approach as opposed to focusing on broad social issues.[57]

CONCLUSION

In an unusual direct link between the *Journal* and the women's health movement, the *Journal* published part of *Our Bodies* without an editor's note disavowing the content (as with the 1970 feminist supplement). In explaining who wrote the book, the *Journal* states that the authors had become 'convinced that women need to learn about their bodies in order to have control over them—and over their lives'.[58] The inclusion of the *Our Bodies* excerpt in 1973 represents a shift in attitude for the *Journal* from 1969. In 1969, an article about a 'healthier bosom' says that the guide is intended 'to help you know more about your breasts, but not to help you make judgments about your health. Leave that to your doctor.'[59] After 1969, this paternalistic tone was largely absent.

Like the women's health movement, the *Ladies' Home Journal*'s coverage of women's health information between 1969 and 1975 attempted to inform female consumers about their bodies. Along with the examples discussed, it also included articles on menstruation, menopause and pap smear tests for cervical cancer.[60] But unlike the women's health movement, the *Journal*'s coverage during the women's health movement did not always convey a feminist view of health; it rarely editorialised for systematic change and it seldom addressed misogynist social structures as problematic. This analysis of how the core issues of the women's health movement were reflected in the pages of the *Journal* between 1969 and 1975 demonstrates that the *Journal* offered surface patterns that were consistent with the mandate of the movement, but its fundamental approach to women's health issues was discordant with the movement. The *Journal*'s content included educational material about women's health movement issues that would help readers to become better medical consumers. In this sense, there was overlap with the movement's coverage of health issues. However, the information represents a 'therapeutic feminism' style of writing, which resorts to a self-help tone instead of focusing on social issues.[61] Also absent from the *Journal* content was the explicit argument that women should be in control of their bodies. There are exceptions to this argument, of course, but by and large, the *Journal* stuck to factual journalism without advocating for change.

When the *Journal*'s women's health content could be categorised as feminist, it typically falls on the liberal end of the spectrum rather than expressing a radical feminist standpoint. The point that 'power is knowledge' was shared by both the liberal and radical perspectives on women's health. While some of the topics the *Journal* covered, such as abortion, childbirth and health care, could be categorised as making radical statements about women's collective experiences, the tone was typically liberal (working within the system for change). The one characteristic that was both liberal and radical and that was consistently reflected in the *Journal* was that women had a right to know about medical news that affected their bodies and their choices.

In many ways, the *Journal*'s coverage follows the traditional women's magazine paradigm, which usually fails to represent feminism effectively for a few reasons. The self-help, therapeutic approach of mainstream women's magazines centres on individual over collective action. There is a history of feminist issues being co-opted or transformed when they filter into the mainstream media. Mass media cover feminism by anticipating, representing and containing it: 'The political has been collapsed into the personal so that you, the lone individual, are all that matters.'⁶² The women's health movement, however, was distinct from the broader women's liberation movement in a way that allowed some of its messages to avoid being distorted by the transition into the mainstream press. While the women's health movement did try to raise women's consciousness about sexism in medicine and did campaign for broad social change, a big part of its agenda was promoting awareness about women's health issues to individual women so that they might make individual decisions about their care. In fact, the action of educating women about their bodies and raising awareness about dangerous drugs and devices was one of the movement's most powerful lasting legacies. Thus, when the *Journal* included health news to educate its readers about women's health, so that they might be better informed medical consumers, it was helping to accomplish one goal of women's self-determination set by the movement.

Ultimately, in covering issues championed by the women's health movement, the *Journal* was neither always consistent nor always inconsistent with the movement. Although the *Journal*'s rhetorical framework did not permit campaigning for broad social and economic changes or consistent promotion of feminist principles, the magazine's dissemination of women's health information to women's health consumers, even on an individual 'therapeutic feminism' basis, was in line with the women's health movement distribution of health content to individual women.

NOTES

1. Ruth Rosen, *The World Split Open: How the Modern Women's Movement Changed America* (New York: Viking, 2000).
2. Flora Davis, *Moving the Mountain: The Women's Movement in America Since 1960* (New York: Touchstone, 1991), 249.
3. Claudia Dreifus, 'Introduction,' in *Seizing Our Bodies: The Politics of Women's Health*, ed. Claudia Dreifus (New York: Vintage Books, 1977), xxv–xxvi.
4. Sheryl Burt Ruzek, *The Women's Health Movement* (New York: Praeger Publishers, 1978).
5. Davis, *Moving the Mountain*, 228.
6. Rosen, *The World Split Open*, 176.
7. Rosen, *The World Split Open*, 178.
8. Dreifus, 'Introduction,' xxx.
9. Davis, *Moving the Mountain*, 258.
10. Sherly Burt Ruzek, *Women and Health Care: A Bibliography with Selected Annotation* (Evanston, IL: Northwestern University, 1975), 1.
11. Dreifus, 'Introduction,' xx.
12. Rachel Gillett Fruchter et al., 'The women's health movement: Where are we now?,' in *Seizing Our Bodies*, ed. Claudia Dreifus (New York: Vintage Books, 1977), 271–8.
13. Ruzek, *The Women's Health Movement*, 32.
14. Ruzek, *The Women's Health Movement*, 32.
15. The Boston Women's Health Collective, *Women and Their Bodies* (Boston: The Collective, 1970).
16. The Boston Women's Health Collective, *Women and Their Bodies*, 6.

17 Ruzek, *Women and Health Care*, 1.
18 Ruzek, *The Women's Health Movement*, 36.
19 Ruzek, *The Women's Health Movement*, 2.
20 Elizabeth Fee, 'Women and health care: A comparison of theories,' in *Seizing Our Bodies: The Politics of Women's Health*, ed. Claudia Dreifus (New York: Vintage, 1977), 279–97.
21 Fee, 'Women and health care,' 282.
22 Fee, 'Women and health care,' 282–5.
23 Fee, 'Women and health care,' 286.
24 Betty Friedan, *The Feminine Mystique* (New York: Norton, 1963).
25 Jennifer Scanlon, *Inarticulate Longings: The Ladies' Home Journal, Gender, and the Promises of Consumer Culture* (New York: Routledge, 1995), 9–10.
26 Mary Ellen Zuckerman, *A History of Popular Women's Magazines in the United States, 1792–1995* (Westport, CT: Greenwood Publishing Group, 1998), 60–1.
27 Wilma P. Mankiller et al., *The Reader's Companion to US Women's History* (Boston: Houghton Mifflin Harcourt, 1999), 352. *Ladies' Home Journal* is discussed in its early twentieth century incarnation elsewhere in this book: see Cheyanne Cortez, 'The American Girl: Ideas of nationalism and sexuality as promoted in the *Ladies' Home Journal*'.
28 Barbara Ehrenreich and Deirdre English, *Complaints and Disorders: The Sexual Politics of Sickness* (Old Westbury, NY: Feminist Press, 1973), 74.
29 Scanlon, *Inarticulate Longings*, 122
30 Davis, *Moving the Mountain*, 111–13.
31 Sally Wilson Bolstad, 'How magazines reflect social movements: A case study of the Women's Liberation Movement as reflected in three women's magazines' (Master of Arts, University of Missouri-Columbia, 1972), 153.
32 Elfriede Fürsich, 'In defense of textual analysis: Restoring a challenged method for journalism and media studies,' *Journalism Studies* 10 (2009): 238–52.
33 The core women's health movement issues were compiled from: Ruzek, *Women and Health Care*; Ruzek, *The Women's Health Movement*; Davis, *Moving the Mountain*; Rosen, *The World Split Open*; The Boston Women's Health Collective, *Women and Their Bodies*.
34 David R. Zimmerman, 'Medicine today,' *Ladies' Home Journal*, August 1970, 28.
35 Zimmerman, 'Medicine today,' *Ladies' Home Journal*, February 1971, 12–14.
36 Letty Cottin Pogrebin, 'The working woman,' *Ladies' Home Journal*, April 1974, 38–40.
37 Donald Robinson, 'Medical secrecy,' *Ladies' Home Journal*, February 1975, 72.
38 Robert W. Kistner, 'What "the Pill" does to husbands,' *Ladies' Home Journal*, January 1969, 68.
39 Phyllis Wright and Zimmerman, 'Medicine today,' *Ladies' Home Journal*, April 1969, 39
40 Zimmerman, 'Medicine today,' *Ladies' Home Journal*, September 1973, 24.
41 Zimmerman, 'Medicine today,' *Ladies' Home Journal*, February 1974, 26.
42 Barbara Seaman, 'Why doctors are losing faith in the Pill,' *Ladies' Home Journal*, April 1969, 76.
43 Dodi Schultz, 'The family doctors' health guide,' *Ladies' Home Journal*, August 1971, 34.
44 DES had been given to pregnant women to reduce the incidence of miscarriage for decades, until it was discovered to cause cancer in the offspring of women who took the synthetic oestrogen. The US Federal Drug Administration

finally issued a warning to doctors in 1971 advising them to stop prescribing the drug to pregnant women. For a detailed discussion of the DES scandal and its effect on the politics of women's health, see Susan E. Bell, *DES Daughters: Embodied Knowledge and the Transformation of Women's Health Politics* (Philadelphia: Temple University Press, 2009).
45 Zimmerman, 'Medicine today,' *Ladies' Home Journal,* November 1971, 24.
46 Zimmerman, 'Medicine today,' *Ladies' Home Journal,* May 1975, 58.
47 Planned Parenthood is a non-profit organisation which provided (and continues to provide) reproductive health services to American women. For more about the Dalkon Shield scandal, see, for instance: Nicole J. Grant, *The Selling of Contraception: The Dalkon Shield Case, Sexuality, and Women's Autonomy* (Columbus, OH: Ohio State University Press, 1992); Morton Mintz, *At Any Cost: Corporate Greed, Women, and the Dalkon Shield* (New York: Pantheon, 1985).
48 Zimmerman, 'Medicine today,' *Ladies' Home Journal,* June 1975, 111.
49 Zimmerman, 'Medicine today,' *Ladies' Home Journal,* May 1972, 30.
50 Ralph Nader, 'Ralph Nader reports,' *Ladies' Home Journal*, September 1972, 48.
51 Zimmerman, 'Medicine today: Breast cancer,' *Ladies' Home Journal,* June 1974, 22.
52 Zimmerman, 'Medicine today,' *Ladies' Home Journal*, December 1974, 28.
53 Zimmerman, 'Medicine today,' *Ladies' Home Journal,* May 1973, 36.
54 Lawrence Lader, 'A national guide to legal abortion,' *Ladies' Home Journal*, July 1970, 73.
55 Women's Liberation Movement, 'The new feminism,' *Ladies' Home Journal,* August 1970, 67.
56 Zimmerman, 'Medicine today,' *Ladies' Home Journal,* June 1971, 36.
57 Jilliam Sandell, 'Adjusting to oppression: The rise of therapeutic feminism in the United States,' *'Bad Girls'/'Good Girls': Women, Sex, and Power in the Nineties*, ed. Nan Bauer Maglin and Donna Perry (New Brunskwick, NJ: Rutgers University Press, 1996) 21–35; Rosen, *The World Split Open*.
58 Boston Women's Health Collective, 'Defending yourself against rape, our bodies, ourselves,' *Ladies' Home Journal,* July 1973, 62.
59 Judith Ramsey, 'A healthier bosom,' *Ladies' Home Journal,* October 1969, 82.
60 For example, see Phyllis Wright and David R. Zimmerman, 'Medicine today,' *Ladies' Home Journal,* April 1969, 42; Zimmerman, 'Medicine today,' *Ladies' Home Journal,* May 1973, 36.
61 Rosen, *The World Split Open*, 315.
62 Susan J. Douglas, *Where The Girls Are: Growing Up Female with the Mass Media* (New York: Times Books, 1994), 291.

15 *Beauty Trade* and the Rise of American Black Hair Magazines

Carina Spaulding

> They should have a magazine that come out [*sic*] like *Hair Do* for white women. [. . .] They should have a magazine like that for Black women in terms of hair styling [. . .] because *Essence* is the only magazine that I've seen [. . .] that's easily accessible to Black women.[1]

In championing expressions of Black pride, the Black Power movement in America emphasised the importance of recognising and promoting Black beauty within and outside of the African American community. Images of this pride and beauty, however, had yet to reach the pages of most American magazines, and African American women in particular found themselves excluded from the mainstream media. With the launch of *Essence* magazine in 1970, Black women were finally able to find a space dedicated solely to them—a place where varying representations of beauty were prominently displayed.[2] Yet by expressing their displeasure with a continuing lack of visibility in the media, readers such as the focus group respondent quoted above voiced a desire not just for equal representation, but also for access to greater information and choice. As 'mainstream' corporations finally recognised the strength of Black buying power and targeted their advertising, as well as the research and development of new products, towards this newly segmented market, a group of magazines was launched to meet this consumer demand. This chapter addresses a specific subset of magazines that followed *Essence*'s lead in meeting the aspirations and acknowledging the identities of African American women during the 1970s and 1980s: special-interest hair magazines. Through a detailed study of *Beauty Trade* magazine, the leading Black hair trade magazine throughout the latter half of the twentieth century, I explore how the relationship cultivated by publishers and advertisers of Black hair trade magazines created a space for editors to press for continuing racial equality and to promote Black-owned companies, moves that allowed for the entry and rapid growth of consumer magazines into this industry.[3] Yet in doing so, this chapter also considers the industry forces and racial discourses working to hinder the development of these Black-owned specialty magazines.

In her study of the American cosmetics industry, Kathy Peiss argues that it was the turn to national advertising in the 1920s that first forged ties between periodicals, retailers and manufacturers. She notes that these efforts 'spurred consumer demand by coordinating the efforts of manufacturers, advertisers, and retailers—parties who had distinct economic interests but remained mutually dependent'.[4] As mass media grew and then segmented throughout the twentieth century, Black hair magazines particularly reflected these ties and what Rodney Benson calls the media's 'growing dominance of a bottom-line, marketing orientation'.[5] This bottom-line orientation in Black hair magazines eventually developed into greater, 'synergistic' connections between agents in the industry. Nowhere was this 'synergy', defined here as cross-sector mutually reinforcing promotion, more pronounced than in the co-operation between Black hair magazines and Black-owned hair care product manufacturers.

These hair magazines catering to African American women emerged in the 1970s following the launch of mainstream, 'white' hair magazines earlier in the same decade. The success of these mainstream hair magazines—and the growing incomes of African American women—were quickly noted, and a number of publishers soon responded to the demand from Black women for a greater media presence. In his study of *Ebony*, Jason Chambers argues that 'the pursuit of equality in consumption is as much a form of political activism as other, more admired efforts'.[6] Elevating cultural production and the push for consumer citizenship to the level of more traditional understandings of activism, such as marches or sit-ins, is crucial to opening up new understandings of the paths to effecting political change. Consumption, as a part of everyday life, represents a space with heretofore under-recognised potential for considerable power. Following Chambers' argument, this chapter views this first wave of Black hair magazines as an extension of the long fight for racial equality. By using *Beauty Trade* as a case study, I hope to draw out the ways the media function to reproduce and refract (and sometimes run counter to) dominant ideologies. They do so not independently, but in a system where their success is mutually dependent on that of a number of other commercial entities.

CONSTRUCTING A NEW MARKET CATEGORY

To draw out the links between these ideological and economic battles, it is necessary to consider these debates within the wider context of the growing 'glossy' arm of the Black press. As noted by Noliwe Rooks, *Essence* followed a business strategy first pioneered by John H. Johnson when founding *Ebony* in that 'its focus [was] on the particularities of race and gender in such a manner as to create a consumer group'.[7] In a self-perpetuating loop, this ready group of consumers was then advertised to, based on this construction. One further component of *Essence*'s success in creating a ready group of consumers was its encouragement of readers to identify as members of a community—as not just Black, but as Black women. This construction of a consuming community of Black women led to the evolution of the African American segment of the publishing industry from *Essence* to the growth of highly consumer-driven Black hair magazines. By further specialising, moving from a general interest African American women's magazine into a magazine covering exclusively hair and beauty, publishers could attract a significant number of specifically targeted readers and advertisers. The commercial potential of a magazine 'Where black women come first', as *Essence*'s slogan states, was built upon in the following decades; Black hair magazines in particular followed this model, adapting and refashioning methods of reaching consumers as the wider Black hair care industry changed.

This chapter, however, deals with debates that run across both the business and identity dimensions of the industry. Hair magazines act as a prime case study to examine the relationships between magazines, their consumers and advertisers as product information and recommendations, whether in advertising or editorial content, pervade virtually every page of the publication. This may foster the success of the advertiser's company and the economic needs of the magazine, but readers who have turned to the magazine as a source of objective, trustworthy information may ultimately lose out.

This reputation of 'trust' is further complicated by Black hair magazines' position as part of the wider Black press. Peiss argues that Black female readers took pride in Black-owned-and-edited newspapers and magazines and believed them to offer 'factual and trustworthy representations'.[8] Due to advertising concerns, however, representational accuracy was not always at the fore. Bringing Peiss's understanding to the case of Black hair magazines, readers who may have read other magazines' content with a more critical eye might have withheld some scepticism for Black hair magazines. While this might suggest that Black hair magazines could be more effective at manipulating trusting consumers, by providing an outlet for Black-owned companies to advertise, the selling practices in these magazines are more nuanced. Nevertheless, as Ellen McCracken notes, business politics remain key; whether or not the messages espoused by the editorial team mesh with the commercial goals of the publication, advertisers are assured of reaching a group of readers primed to purchase their products.[9]

In studying cosmetics and beauty culture, Peiss further explores the rise of mass production of goods and the ways these commodities moulded definitions of beauty and femininity in the nineteenth and twentieth centuries. Her discussion of African American women is an important resource in understanding the ways Black beauty culture works within and outside of the mainstream beauty industry.[10] She argues that social and economic forces came together to form a national beauty culture, one which excluded Black women. Women's magazines, commercial advertising and the celebrity system all worked to promote the mass consumption of beauty products, yet in many ways African American women continue to be excluded from this so-called 'national' culture.

BEAUTY TRADE: SPEAKING TO RACIALLY CONSCIOUS CONSUMERS

One arena in which Black women's and hair magazines could potentially assert an advantage over mainstream women's or beauty magazines in reaching consumers was through appeals to racial solidarity. Racialised language permeates every issue—if not every page—of these magazines: from editorial decisions as simple as using 'authentic' African American discourses to more complicated moves such as politicising consumption. Black hair trade and consumer magazines follow a tradition also continued by *Ebony*, which politicises the consumption of goods 'for reasons beyond those immediately obvious in the act of consuming',[11] as Chambers explains, or, as Lizabeth Cohen describes it, employs consumption as 'a strategy to achieve economic power'.[12]

In the case of *Beauty Trade*, a popular trade magazine for beauty culturists and salon owners, this economic power was framed as necessary for both consumers and the magazine to achieve. *Beauty Trade*, which had been publishing since 1954 but experienced significant growth in the mid-1970s, became the site of many Black hair care advertisers' first foray into this newly segmented market. Despite a predilection for racialised, separatist language in its editorial content, *Beauty Trade* featured advertising from all of the major brands targeting the ethnic market, though it maintained especially strong ties with Black-owned market leader Johnson Products. In an interview with oral history centre HistoryMakers, George Johnson, founder of the leading Black-owned Black hair care company Johnson Products, noted that despite its pivotal role within the industry, the magazine had long been besieged by financial problems:

> In fact, we carried it, we carried *Beauty Trade* on our back for many, many years. [. . .] I just prepaid the advertising to keep them with, with money to, to stay in business [*sic*]. And that helped me because *Beauty Trade* was the only, it was the only instrument that we could reach hairdressers with, at the time.[13]

This revelation underscores the networks of support between the businesses and magazines involved in the Black hair care industry. Through the promotion of ethnic solidarity, both Black-owned products manufacturers and magazines were able to benefit.

In the January 1976 issue, *Beauty Trade* published a response to a letter they had sent to President Gerald Ford requesting financial support from the government's Minority Business Enterprise programme.[14] The response acknowledged the importance of *Beauty Trade* within the industry and in wider Black culture and promised to work on allocating funds to the magazine. *Beauty Trade* may have been struggling financially by this point, but its editors and publishers were politically active and aware of the affirmative action measures and government benefits available to them. By communicating this political awareness to readers, the magazine highlighted the importance of continuing to push for racial equality. Additionally, by publishing this particular letter, the magazine sent a powerful message to its readers: first, that Black-owned businesses in all primary and ancillary aspects of the Black hair care industry were struggling due to shifting market forces; and second, that government intervention through funding was a potential option open to all Black entrepreneurs. Government programmes existed to help ailing Black businesses, but aid in the form of affirmative action was available only to those who actively sought out these opportunities.

Alongside its explicit discussions of politics, *Beauty Trade* included racialised language throughout its editorial. While this could be considered surprising, as beauty magazines are not generally renowned as sites of political or social action, it becomes less so when considering the source: a beauty magazine targeted at African Americans living during the height the Civil Rights and Black Power movements. Racialised language was typical in advertisements and magazines targeted at African Americans in this period,[15] and the examples found in *Beauty Trade* were not only numerous, but oftentimes also very charged. From celebrating the history of the Black hair care industry to addressing racism within the mainstream beauty industry, racial pride and unity were common topics of the magazine's editorial. *Beauty Trade*'s publisher and editor, Bernice Calvin, publicised improvements to the publication while simultaneously alluding to 'Black Is Beautiful' sentiments: 'We've perfected our color—an expensive process, but it gives you the warm, vibrant color our black skin can exude.'[16] Calvin then parlayed this positive message into an appeal for reader assistance: 'We need your continued support, and good wishes to really keep the only Black Trade Magazine out here. No other Industry can say this.'[17]

Beauty Trade often also gestured to the long tradition of the hair care industry acting as a path to financial independence, for instance by showcasing the success of professionals working in the industry. A regular feature launched in 1976, 'Exciting lifestyle of the professional stylist', upheld the historically perceived traditions of work and status in the Black hair care industry: economic independence, financial success, social mobility and race pride. The inaugural story featured a photo of stylist Joseph Plaskett wearing a fur coat and standing in front of his vintage 1927 Mercedes-Benz, echoing promotional photos of famed Black hair care entrepreneur Madam C. J. Walker, pictured wearing a fur coat and feathered hat while driving her new car.[18]

The magazine was also particularly conscious of keeping its readers aware of racism and prejudice in the wider hair care industry. In reference to a January 1976 national beauty show and hair styling competition, a report in the magazine featured hairstyles modelled on white women, but attributed this incongruity to a failure on the part of the show organisers and participants: 'Once again, no Black model was used in the collection and no style was particularly designed for Black hair, though the inference was that the new styles suited all textures of hair.'[19] The exclusion of Black models and Black hair from hair shows continued to such an extent that, two years later, the magazine featured an entire two-page article and photo spread on the issue. Though noting that Olive Benson, a famous Black stylist of the 1970s and 1980s, had participated in the August 1978 national show, the editors sarcastically maligned the endemic racism of the overall event: 'But then how could we expect back-to-back Black artists, of the four Hair Designers hand-picked, even though, Black women constitute more than 25% of the salon going public? There were no Black Models; it was almost as if no Black models were available.'[20] The article goes on to discuss comments made by Black models and stylists about the poor treatment they had received by the event organisers. The inclusion of these types of articles serves to highlight the frustrations of both the magazine and its readers regarding the continuing marginalisation of African Americans in the mainstream beauty industry, as well as acting as a call to action for its readers.[21]

BEAUTY TRADE: REPRESENTATIONS OF HAIR STRAIGHTENING AND THE 'NATURAL'

The magazine's professed dedication to racial solidarity failed to extend to *Beauty Trade*'s advertising policy, however, as advertisements for a range of companies, both Black- and white-owned, were included throughout each issue. This is unsurprising for a publication beset by financial difficulties; any advertising was good advertising if it could help keep the magazine afloat. Yet racialised language in editorial content sends one message to readers, while the inclusion—and exclusion—of certain images or advertisements sends quite another. McCracken asserts that the readers of special-interest publications 'receive normative messages from the magazines about the roles expected of them as members of these unique groups'.[22] Indeed, for all of these references to racial equality and pride in natural Black beauty, more normative messages, such as the promotion of straightened hair, also pervade the publication. Though hair straightening was criticised by many Black leaders as imitative and assimilative of a white Eurocentric beauty ideal throughout the twentieth century, it was not until the 1960s that unstraightened hair became a widespread socially 'acceptable' option for African American women, in part also due to wider societal connections between long hair and femininity. The Natural, and in particular the Afro, embraced by activists in the late 1960s and 1970s, 'was understood to denote black pride, which became synonymous with activism and political consciousness'.[23]

These normative representations are particularly emblematic in the magazine's photo features. For example, the April 1976 issue, presumably as a nod to that year's bicentennial celebrations, included a hairstyle photo feature titled 'Spirit of '76 for the Black woman!' While the step-by-step instructions note the style can be achieved through a process of relaxing/ perming, blow drying and curling, a large caption on the page opposite proclaims that the customer is 'Free at last!'.[24] The juxtaposition of the text, echoing both spirituals and the words of Martin Luther King, Jr's 1963 speech at the March on Washington, with a photo featuring an expensive and labour-intensive hairstyle, is problematic and inconsistent with the magazine's other political rhetoric, suggesting the ever-present underlying influence of the advertiser.

This seeming promotion of both racial pride and 'assimilative' hairstyling practices in *Beauty Trade* is less surprising in light of the costs associated with creating straightened versus Natural styles; straightened hair required frequent salon trips as well as a number of products and processes in its upkeep, a key concern for the magazine's target market: salon owners, hairdressers and hair care product manufacturers catering to African Americans. McCracken's aforementioned assertion in part maps onto predominant debates amongst feminist theorists, which claim that women's magazines function, in part, to control women's self-image.[25] Yet McCracken also highlights the role of production in this process, and in so doing, moves beyond these potentially limiting arguments positioning the perpetuation of hegemonic beauty ideals as a key driving factor here. She argues that by endorsing and reinforcing normative images, magazines 'create "class" audiences for advertisers by persuading readers to engage in the pseudo-individualized consumption allegedly appropriate to the special roles and obligations of membership in a unique group'.[26] In the case of *Beauty Trade*, this effect is multiplied: readers of special interest magazines are subject to many of the same normative discourses as in general interest women's magazines but have also been explicitly constructed as consumers from the outset, further underscoring the pervasive influences of production.

A message of survival under any circumstances is again communicated in the magazine's advice to stylists. As discussed by Susannah Walker, the Afro and other Natural styles had posed a problem to stylists and product manufacturers, as customers shunned trips to the salon and the use of expensive chemical processes in favour of allowing their hair to grow naturally.[27] The hair care industry's response was to develop products for the new style, effectively commodifying what had begun as a rebellious political statement. However, in the case of *Beauty Trade*, by 1976 the Afro had not only been commodified, but also stripped from its original 'Natural' state. A photo spread featuring a textured hairstyle declared that 'a Relaxer is the basis of these new short 'Fros. The Relaxer is a mild one—"to loosen up the hair"'.[28]

Coupled with this were further declarations by the magazine, in two back-to-back features, proclaiming not only that 'Straight hair is in', but also that 'The Afro is leaving'.²⁹ In the first of the two features, the announcement was predicated on popular Haitian American stylist Mr Frenchie's trip to Paris, where he found that straight hair was more popular among Black women.³⁰ Of Afros, he contended: 'Women are tired of it [. . .]. A fashion fad that has had six big years, it's just running its course. Patrons want hair now—hair that bounces, moves when they move.' His words pose an interesting—and contentious—question: if patrons 'want hair now', what did they consider the Afro or other Natural styles? This distinction highlights the gendered dimensions of the Afro and the ways it was constructed, particularly in the Black community, as a 'masculine' look. As Walker notes, by contrast, 'The more "feminine" Afros sold to women were generally larger and more complex in shape and required more maintenance than those men wore.'³¹ This high maintenance and styling complexity highlight the process of commodification the Afro underwent prior to this period. Indeed, Mr Frenchie's statement, and the magazine's implicit approval of it through the editorial decision to print it, further reduce this previously potent political statement to a mere fashion trend.

Yet despite Mr Frenchie and *Beauty Trade*'s insistence that Natural styles were on the decline, the May 1976 issue of *Beauty Trade* shows that salons were still consistently fielding requests from customers for these looks:

> For those who still want Naturals: No salon should ignore any service! There are some women—though becoming less and less in number—who like the Natural, look good in it and insist on wearing it, even if they change every now and then to a straight style. [. . .] As Hairdressers, you should service them accordingly. For no salon should ignore any service, whether the Stylists like it or not.³²

Language referring to customers 'insisting' on wearing a Natural rhetorically 'others' the look, particularly in conjunction with the lack of models pictured wearing Natural styles throughout the rest of the magazine (although the magazine does concede that some women do 'look good in it'). Additionally, by noting that the number of women requesting the style was 'becoming less and less in number', the magazine subtly reassures stylists that the Natural might soon be a distant memory. The entire discussion of relaxed versus Natural hair and the promotion of straightened styles in this case is, of course, in the interest of increasing sales for the salons, who were the target market of the magazine. Perhaps precisely because of the limitations of this narrow scope of intended readership, in the following two years *Beauty Trade* gradually shifted its focus from writing exclusively to hair care professionals to an eventual official relaunch of the magazine as a consumer title.

As the ethnic hair care market grew to almost half a billion dollars in the 1970s, advertisers and editors both paid increasing attention—and money—to reaching non-hair care professional consumers. Hair magazines, both consumer and trade, have traditionally held popularity with both stylists and salon customers, thereby offering access to a wide group of potential customers. In a focus group led by a minority marketing firm in 1979, a group of African American women were asked to describe where they turn to for information about hair care products or hairstyles. After mentioning that they read 'all types' of beauty magazines for styling ideas, particularly *Essence*, *New Woman* and *Hairdresser's Salon*, one woman offered an explanation of exactly where she read these magazines:

> If you're in a salon that has several beauticians, they have magazines that are sent directly to them, and they have the professional products in there, and they'll do several articles on different products to explain to them what they want and what they want to do for their customers. And I find if you read that, you'll know what they're doing.[33]

Although the focus group was conducted just before the advent of dedicated Black hair magazines, this respondent is not alone; much of the readership of hair magazines comes from salon customers paging through while waiting for an appointment.[34] The response above signals a desire for transparency on the part of consumers. They want to remain informed—not just about new styles or processes, but the best available products needed to create them. Salon owners provided an added service for their customers through their subscription to the magazine. Another respondent noted that she specifically sought out the salon owner's personal magazine for tips: 'One he reads. That tells me a lot because the same products are in there and they explain a lot, you know, just like a book. Tells you everything.'[35] This stresses the importance to both customers and hairdressers of professionalisation, as well as demonstrates the popularity of trade magazines beyond their intended audience. Publishers' growing understanding of this secondary readership likely created an opening for consumer magazines like *Sophisticate's Black Hair Styles and Care Guide*, *Hype Hair*, *Black Hair Care*, and *Try It Yourself Hair!*, among others launched in the 1980s and 1990s.

Following a redesign in 1977 and another in 1978, *Beauty Trade* officially shifted its focus from being a trade publication for beauty professionals to targeting consumers and professionals alike. This relaunch was ultimately unsuccessful, however, as *Beauty Trade* folded shortly thereafter. As Bettiann Gardner, the publisher of Black hair trade magazine *ShopTalk*, commented in her own interview with HistoryMakers:

> When we first started there was a magazine publication called—I think it was *Beauty Trade*. And I would read that. And in the morning when

I'd go to the office and I would read it from cover to cover. And so then that magazine was no longer. So therefore, *ShopTalk* took that place. And we tried to fill that void.[36]

This highlights Black hair magazines' roles in the lives of its readers. In addition, as cultural historian Tom Pendergast argues, product advertisements and the implicit push for consumption were also an important part of cementing this role. Advertisers and editors together created a community and culture for magazine readers.[37] Through tying magazines to readers' lives as a ritual (reading every issue cover-to-cover at work) or even rare pleasure (reading occasional issues at salon visits), readers quickly become attached and loyal to publications such as these.

CONCLUSION

Marjorie Ferguson has argued that 'women's magazines as a social institution and an economic phenomenon have both responded to a pattern of audience demand—and to some extent at least been able to influence it'.[38] Both African American women's magazines and special interest Black hair magazines underscore this observation, as the editorial and advertising content exist to both respond to—and drive the buying habits of—a group of readers. After companies realised the marketing potential of African American women, however, this category quickly grew to both cater to and take advantage of this responsive market segment. The rise of special interest Black hair magazines coincided with greater market diversification, including the entry and expansion of corporations such as L'Oréal, Alberto-Culver, Wella and Procter & Gamble into the realm of Black hair care, in addition to the industry's corporate stalwarts like Revlon and Helene Curtis. Advertisers and publishers alike were eager to reach these new markets, and consumers, in kind, were eager to partake of the increased choice. As Anna Gough-Yates notes, 'In a cultural, economic and political climate oriented around "enterprise" and "the customer", evidence of a special insight into localized and niche markets was fundamental to advertisers' business success.'[39] Hair magazines in particular could provide this 'special insight' and so acted in part as an extension of the beauty features already present in *Essence* and other women's magazines. The arrival of this highly successful category of magazines to the Black hair care professional and consumer markets provided a platform for both beauty culturists and consumers to interact and collaborate with others within the industry. This set a precedent on which Black-owned companies and mainstream corporations were later able to capitalise, facilitating both the rapid growth of consumer magazines targeted to African American women as well as the continued expansion of the Black hair care industry as a whole.

NOTES

1 Respondent, '18–35 hair care focus group, 1979' Tape C, Group 1, 15, ViewPoint, Inc. Archives (Box 14, Folder 1), Vivian G. Harsh Research Collection of Afro-American History and Literature, Chicago Public Library.
2 Noliwe Rooks, *Ladies' Pages: African American Women's Magazines and the Culture That Made Them* (New Brunswick, NJ: Rutgers University Press, 2004).
3 My sampling of *Beauty Trade* for this chapter was selective but covered a representative range of years and issues within these years, including a cover-to-cover analysis of the following issues (all held at the Wisconsin Historical Society, Madison, WI): April 1975, June 1975, January 1976, February 1976, March 1976, April 1976, May 1976, June/July 1977, Fall 1977, October 1978.
4 Kathy Peiss, *Hope in a Jar: The Making of America's Beauty Culture* (New York: Henry Holt, 1998), 125.
5 Rodney D. Benson, 'Tearing down the "wall" in American journalism,' *International Journal of the Humanities* 1 (2001): 107–8.
6 Jason Chambers, 'Equal in every way: African Americans, consumption and materialism from reconstruction to the Civil Rights Movement,' *Advertising & Society Review* 7 (2006): no page numbers, accessed 20 July 2015, http://muse.jhu.edu/journals/advertising_and_society_review/v007/7.1chambers.html.
7 Rooks, *Ladies' Pages*, 148. For more on *Essence* and the role of production on the magazine's relationship to Black feminism during its first decade, see Alexis Pauline Gumbs, 'Black (buying) power: The story of *Essence* magazine,' in *The Business of Black Power: Community Development, Capitalism, and Corporate Responsibility in Postwar America*, ed. Laura Warren Hill and Julia Rabig (Rochester, NY: University of Rochester Press, 2012), 95–115.
8 Peiss, *Hope in a Jar*, 229.
9 Ellen McCracken, *Decoding Women's Magazines: From Mademoiselle to Ms.* (New York: St. Martin's Press, 1993), 283; see also 227.
10 Similarly, Geoffrey Jones places the ethnic beauty industry within an increasingly globalised mainstream industry. His deeply researched work is rich in its discussion of the global mainstream beauty industry. Geoffrey Jones, *Beauty Imagined: A History of the Global Beauty Industry* (New York: Oxford University Press, 2010).
11 Chambers, 'Equal in every way,' no page number.
12 Lizabeth Cohen, *A Consumers' Republic: The Politics of Mass Consumption in Postwar America* (New York: Alfred A. Knopf, 2003), 83.
13 George E. Johnson, Sr (The HistoryMakers A2003.303), Interview by Julieanna Richardson, 18 December 2003, The HistoryMakers Digital Archive, Session 1, Tape 6, Story 7, George Johnson discusses advertising his products, accessed 20 July 2015, http://www.idvl.org/thehistorymakers/iCoreClient.html#/&n=16047.
14 'Help is on the way!,' *Beauty Trade*, January 1976, 30.
15 See Susannah Walker, *Style and Status: Selling Beauty to African American Women, 1920–1975* (Lexington: University Press of Kentucky, 2007), 192–7; Rooks, *Ladies' Pages*, 144–6.
16 Bernice Calvin, 'Changes hurt—but that's progress!,' *Beauty Trade*, January 1976, 13.
17 Calvin, 'Changes hurt,' 13.

Beauty Trade *and the Rise of American Black Hair Magazines* 239

18 'Exciting life of the professional stylist,' *Beauty Trade*, February 1976, 29; Walker, *Style and Status*, 54.
19 'Hair news for spring: The updated wave,' *Beauty Trade*, January 1976, 44.
20 'The big news for '78 fall/winter: No Blacks involved in new fall/winter styles,' *Beauty Trade*, October 1978, 18–19.
21 For more on the mid-century history of Black participation in the fashion industry, see Laila Haidarali, 'Polishing brown diamonds: African American women, popular magazines, and the advent of modeling in early Postwar America,' *Journal of Women's History* 17 (2005): 10–37. It is also important to note that racism in the fashion industry, particularly in the privileging of white or lighter-skinned Black models, is an issue that persists today.
22 McCracken, *Decoding Women's Magazines*, 257.
23 Noliwe Rooks, *Hair Raising: Beauty, Culture, and African American Women* (New Brunswick, NJ: Rutgers University Press, 1996), 6. The term 'Natural', and this capitalised spelling, refers specifically to hair that has not been chemically altered, i.e., straightened through a chemical process. For a deeper discussion of the Afro, see Robin D. G. Kelley, 'Nap time: Historicizing the Afro,' *Fashion Theory* 1 (1997): 339–51; Tracey Owens Patton, 'Hey girl, am I more than my hair?: African American women and their struggles with beauty, body image, and hair,' *National Women's Studies Association Journal* 18 (2006): 40–2; Walker, *Style & Status*, 169–78; Susannah Walker, 'Black is profitable: The commodification of the Afro, 1960–1975,' in *Beauty and Business: Commerce, Gender, and Culture in Modern America*, ed. Philip Scranton (New York: Routledge, 2001), 254–77.
24 James Harris, 'Spirit of '76 for the Black woman!,' *Beauty Trade*, April 1976, 10–11. A photo spread in the magazine features men with Natural hairstyles, however. Hubert Morris, 'Men belong in the hairdresser's hands,' *Beauty Trade*, April 1976, 14–16.
25 See, for example, Susan Bordo, 'Material girl: The effacements of postmodern culture,' in *The Female Body: Figures, Styles, Speculations*, ed. Laurence Goldstein (Ann Arbor: Michigan University Press, 1991); Naomi Wolf, *The Beauty Myth* (London: Vintage, 1990).
26 McCracken, *Decoding Women's Magazines*, 257.
27 Walker, 'Black is profitable,' 254–77.
28 Mr Joseph, 'Short shortie 'Fro,' *Beauty Trade*, February 1976, 32–3.
29 Both articles were based on interviews with Mr Frenchie, a well-known hairdresser in New York City. 'The Afro is leaving,' *Beauty Trade*, March 1976, 8–9; 'Straight hair is in,' *Beauty Trade*, March 1976, 10–1.
30 Walker elaborates on Mr Frenchie and the hairstyling exchange between Europe and America during the 1960s in *Style and Status*, 152–3.
31 Walker, *Style and Status*, 197; see also 194–8 for a discussion of the Afro as both a racialised and gendered style.
32 'For those who still want the Natural,' *Beauty Trade*, May 1976, 24–5.
33 '18–35 hair care focus group,' Tape A, Group 1, 19–20, ViewPoint, Inc. Archives (Box 14, Folder 1), Vivian G. Harsh Research Collection of Afro-American History and Literature, Chicago Public Library.
34 '18–35 hair care focus group,' Tape C, Group 1, 16.
35 '18–35 hair care focus group,' Tape C, Group 1, 16.
36 The magazine continued publication for over ten years under the editorship of Jean Brandon, one of Gardner's self-proclaimed 'best girlfriends'. Bettiann Gardner (The HistoryMakers A2002.168), Interview by Adele Hodge, 26 August 2002, The HistoryMakers Digital Archive, Session 1, Tape 3, Story 6, Bettiann Gardner details her activities as publisher of 'ShopTalk' trade

magazine, accessed 20 July 2015, http://www.idvl.org/thehistorymakers/iCoreClient.html#/&n=6389.
37 Tom Pendergast, *Creating the Modern Man: American Magazines and Consumer Culture, 1900–1950* (Columbia: University of Missouri Press, 2000), 255.
38 Marjorie Ferguson, *Forever Feminine: Women's Magazines and the Cult of Femininity* (London: Heinemann, 1983), 38.
39 Anna Gough-Yates, *Understanding Women's Magazines: Publishing, Markets and Readerships* (London: Routledge, 2003), 60.

Contributors

Fan Carter teaches in the department of Media and Communication at Kingston University, London, UK, where she runs a special study module on gender and lifestyle magazines. She has previously published on teenage magazines and consumer culture, celebrity magazines and cultures of remembrance as well as lifestyle television formats. She is currently writing her first book, a study of *Honey* magazine and consumer culture in the 1960s.

Cheyanne Cortez is an independent scholar whose research interests include nineteenth- and twentieth-century American and European Art and Design with an emphasis on the effects of industrialisation and consumerism in the development of women's identities. Her current scholarship focuses on archetypes of modern femininity depicted in mass media in the United States during the turn-of-the-last-century. She has previously presented at the *Popular Culture Association/American Culture Association National Conference*.

Gretchen Galbraith is Professor of History and Associate Dean for Faculty of the College of Liberal Arts & Sciences at Grand Valley State University in Michigan, US. Author of *Reading Lives: Reconstructing British Childhoods, 1860–1914*, Galbraith's work is principally concerned with Victorian and Edwardian British women's and gender history. She has a long-standing interest in the life and work of Constance Maynard and is currently building a complex project focusing on Maynard's journals that will use digital humanities tools in the service of culture biography. Her work with the Reacting to the Past Consortium, which marries game-based pedagogy with intensive student research, has recently encouraged an interest in the Enlightenment *salon* and the role of women in the production and preservation of knowledge, then and now.

Helen Glew (University of Westminster, London, UK) is a gender and social historian whose research focuses on women and paid work in the late nineteenth and twentieth centuries. She is particularly interested in the ways in which gendered employment policy was formulated and upheld and the lived experience of this policy, as well as in examining public debates about women in the workplace. Her monograph, *Gender, Rhetoric and Regulation: Women's Work in the Civil Service and the London County Council, 1900–1955,* is in production with Manchester University Press and she is the author of several other book chapters.

Fiona Hackney is a design historian and professor in fashion at Wolverhampton University, UK. Her research interests focus on gender, design and print culture in the interwar years, social design and participatory research. Themes include the visual and material culture of women's magazines, crafts, dress and textiles, amateur and participatory practice, creativity and heritage, health and wellbeing. She is currently working on a monograph, *Women's Magazines and the Feminine Imagination: Opening Up a New World for Women in Interwar Britain* (IB Tauris, 2016) and, with colleagues in the UK and US, is co-editing the *Edinburgh Companion to British Women's Print Culture between the Wars* (Edinburgh University Press, 2016). She publishes regularly on print culture, design, craft and participatory practice and has been principal investigator and co-investigator for a number of funded research projects under the Arts and Humanities Research Council's Connected Communities scheme.

Sue Hawkins gained her doctorate in history from Kingston University in 2007, on nursing in Victorian London. In addition to teaching nineteenth-century British social history, she is project manager of the Centre for the Historical Record's (CHR) digitisation projects. These have included projects on nineteenth-century children's hospitals and, in collaboration with Kings College London Archives, a project on the registers of the Royal British Nurses Association. The most recent CHR project is in conjunction with the British Red Cross, and involves the digitisation records relating the Voluntary Aid Detachments during World War I. In 2013, Sue was Principle Investigator (in collaboration with the Royal Society, University of Liverpool and the Rothschild Archive) for an AHRC project, Women in Science Research Network, which has created a network of historians, scientists and social scientists interested in the history of women's involvement in science. A collection of papers from the Network's conference, 'Women in Science', was published as a special edition of the Royal Society's *Notes and Records* in March 2015, edited by Sue along with Claire Jones. Sue's book, *Nursing and Women's Labour in Nineteenth Century: The Quest for Independence*, was published in 2010 by Routledge and came out in paperback in 2012. She has also edited, with Helen Sweet, a collection on colonial nursing: *Colonial Caring: A History of Colonial and Post-colonial Nursing* (Manchester: Manchester University Press: 2015), and has an article currently in press, 'Food, Glorious

Food: The Functions of Food in British Children's Hospitals, 1852–1914' with Andrea Tanner, which will be published in 2016 in *Food and History*.

Amanda Hinnant is an associate professor in the School of Journalism at the University of Missouri, US. Her research interests include health journalism, health disparities, feminist theory, sociology of news and climate change communication. Hinnant has recently focused on how journalists communicate social and environmental determinants of health and how audience members interpret and are influenced by those concepts. Her articles have appeared in *Health Communication, Health Education Research, Journalism & Mass Communication Quarterly, Communication Research, Science Communication, Journalism Studies, Feminist Media Studies* and *Public Relations Review*. She is a magazine faculty member and teaches qualitative methods, magazine scholarship, journalism and democracy and magazine writing. Hinnant earned her PhD in Media, Technology and Society from Northwestern University's School of Communication in 2006. She had previously earned a master's degree in Journalism from the University of Missouri and a bachelor's degree in English from Bates College (Lewiston, Maine). For eight years, Hinnant wrote and edited for *Glamour* magazine, followed by *Real Simple* magazine and its related books.

Katherine Holden is the author of a British Academy funded history of nannies, *Nanny Knows Best: The History of the British Nanny* (2013). Other key publications include, *The Shadow of Marriage: Singleness in England 1914–1960* (2007); *The Family Story: Blood, Contract and Intimacy 1830–1960*, co-authored with Leonore Davidoff, Megan Doolittle and Janet Fink (1999); 'Showing them How': The Cultural Reproduction of Ideas about Spinsterhood in Interwar England,' *Women's History Review* (2011); 'Imaginary Widows: Spinsters, Marriage and the "Lost Generation" in Britain after the Great War,' *Journal of Family History* (2002); 'Other People's Children: Single Women and Residential Childcare in Mid-Twentieth Century England,' *Management & Organizational History* (2010). In 2011 she retired from her post as senior lecturer in history at the University of the West of England (Bristol, UK), where she is now a visiting research fellow. A founder member and co-chair of the West of England and South Wales Women's History Network, Katherine has also served on the steering committee of the National Women's History Network, including a three-year term as convenor from 2007–2010. Her main research interests are in historical perspectives on family, marital status and singleness.

Karla Huebner received her PhD in the History of Art and Architecture from the University of Pittsburgh, Pennsylvania, US, and her MA from American University, Washington, DC, US. She is Associate Professor of

Art History and Women's Studies at Wright State University in Dayton, Ohio, US. Her research areas include the history of gender and sexuality, surrealism, women artists and Czech modernism 1890–1950. Recent publications include 'Prague Flânerie from Neruda to Nezval,' in *The Flâneur Abroad: Historical and International Perspectives* (2014); 'Otherness in First Republic Czechoslovak Representations of Women,' in *Competing Eyes: Visual Encounters with Alterity in Central and Eastern Europe* (2013); 'In Pursuit of Toyen: Feminist Biography in an Art-historical Context,' *Journal of Women's History* 25 (2013); 'Girl, Trampka, or Žába? The Czechoslovak New Woman,' in *The New Woman International: Representations in Photography and Film from the 1870s Through the 1960s* (2011); *The New Woman International* (2011); 'Fire Smoulders in the Veins: Toyen's Queer Desire and its Roots in Prague Surrealism,' *Papers of Surrealism* (2010); 'The Whole World Revolves around It: Sex Education and Sex Reform in First Republic Czech Print Media,' *Aspasia* (2010).

Sarah Jones is a PhD student at the University of Exeter, UK, under the supervision of Professor Kate Fisher. Her current research looks at free love and sex radicalism in Britain and the United States from 1890–1914 and reflects her broad interest in the history of sex reform. She is also interested in the history of medicine and is one of founders of the *Postgraduate Journal of Medical Humanities*. You can follow her on twitter @sljones206.

S. Jay Kleinberg devised and taught one of the first women's history courses in the US while studying economic and social history at the University of Pittsburgh. She worked as a lecturer at the London School of Economics before moving to the West London Institute of Higher Education, where she was Head of American Studies. When WLIHE merged with Brunel, she became Head of the Department of American Studies and History, and then Professor of American History. She also served as Associate Dean of the Faculty of Arts and Social Sciences and edited the *Journal of American Studies*. Her publications include *The Shadow of the Mills: Working-Class Families in Pittsburgh, 1870–1907*, *Widows and Orphans First: The Family Economy and Social Welfare, 1880–1939*, *Women in the United States, 1830–1945* and the co-edited collection *The Practice of US Women's History: Narratives, Intersections, and Dialogues*. Her interest in trans-national American history led to her founding the Society for History of Women in the Americas (SHAW). As Chairperson of SHAW, she is co-convenor of the Gender and History in the Americas seminar at the Institute for Historical Research and editor of *History of Women in the Americas*. She is also Professor Emerita at Brunel University London as well as a Fellow of both the Royal Society of Arts and the Academy of Social Sciences. Her ongoing research on women in the twentieth-century US includes a forthcoming journal article on married women's employment and plans for a book exploring changes in the lives of middle-aged and older women.

Megan Le Masurier lectures in the Department of Media and Communications at the University of Sydney, Australia, where she teaches undergraduate and postgraduate students about feature journalism and magazines. Her research interests are based around magazines (history, practice, theory), popular feminism and journalism studies. She is currently working on Slow Journalism and independent ('indie') magazines.

Tracey Loughran is Senior Lecturer in Modern British History at Cardiff University, UK. She is the author of several articles on medicine and psychiatry in the late nineteenth and early twentieth centuries, as well as the monograph *Shell-Shock and Medical Culture in First World War Britain* (forthcoming, Cambridge University Press). She is also co-editor of a major interdisciplinary collection on *Infertility in History: Approaches, Contexts, Perspectives* (forthcoming, Palgrave Macmillan). Her current research explores women's magazines as spaces for the mediation of selfhood, bodily knowledge and familial relationships, focusing on British women's magazines published between 1960 and 1980. This project probes the ways in which forms of knowledge are transmitted, diffused and mutate as they travel across different forums and are received by different agents. It combines textual and visual analysis with oral history to consider the influence of women's magazines on expectations, behaviour and familial relationships; the mechanisms which mediate between individual subjects (the daughters, wives and mothers who read magazines) and cultural formations (women's magazines, and the perceptions of self, society and family which they reflected and shaped); and how these cultural formations operate in the lived relationships between individuals.

Sinead McEneaney is a lecturer in US history and History Programme Director at St. Mary's University, London, UK, where she teaches around issues of race and gender in nineteenth- and twentieth-century America. She has previously held posts at the University of Essex, Newcastle University and the National University of Ireland, Maynooth, where she received her doctorate in 2004. Her research interests lie in the intersection between gender and protest, especially in the protest movements of the 1960s in France and the US. She is also on the steering committee of the Society for Historians of Women in the Americas and an editor of the society's journal, *History of Women in the Americas*.

Rochelle Pereira-Alvares was awarded her PhD in History at the University of Guelph, Canada, in 2015. Her dissertation investigated the various marketing and advertising strategies of North American whisky distillers

Hiram Walker and Seagram between 1950 and 1969 in North America. Her interests lie in alcohol and drug studies, food and drink advertising, gastronomy and visual representations of gender and race. She has recently published the chapter, 'Distinguished Men: Respectability and Responsibility in Whisky Advertisements for the African American Consumer,' in *Biographies of Drink: A Case Study Approach to our Historical Relationship with Alcohol*, eds. Mark Hailwood and Deborah Toner (Cambridge: Cambridge Scholars Publishing, 2015). She is an independent scholar who lives in Toronto, Canada.

Nicola Phillips is a gender historian. She is Co-Director of the Bedford Centre for the History of Women and for the MA in Public History at Royal Holloway College, University of London. She has written on women's work in the eighteenth and nineteenth century and her first book, *Women in Business, 1700–1850* (Boydell Press, 2006), focused on the experience, representation and legal position of entrepreneurial women. More recently she has published articles on issues of inter-generational conflict, debt and criminal and civil law. She is the author of *The Profligate Son: Or, a True Story of Family Conflict, Fashionable Vice and Financial Ruin in Regency England* (Oxford: OUP and New York: Basic Books, 2013) and is currently working on a case study of litigation pursued by a 'notorious' seventeenth-century woman. She is also the Chair of the Historical Association's Public History Committee and a Convener of the IHR Public History seminar. From September 2015, she has been based at Royal Holloway University of London.

Rachel Ritchie gained her PhD from the University of Manchester in 2011 and since then has been an Associate Research Fellow at Brunel University. Her research focuses on personal appearance (fashion, home-dressmaking, beauty) and the home (domestic consumption, interior design and decor) in women's magazines and women's organisations. She is the author of 'Young Women in *Woman*: Representations of Youthful Femininity in the "World's Greatest Weekly for Women", 1954–1969' in *Women and the Media: Feminism and Femininity in Britain, 1900 to the Present*, edited by Maggie Andrews and Sallie McNamara (Routledge, 2014) and '"Beauty isn't all a matter of Looking Glamorous": Attitudes to Glamour and Beauty in 1950s Women's Magazines,' *Women's History Review* 23 (2014): 723–43. Her latest project is looking at new magazines for women in Britain between 1950 and 2000.

Carina Spaulding completed her PhD in 2013 at the University of Manchester in the UK, where she currently works as a temporary lecturer in American Studies. She is co-editor, with Josephine Metcalf, of *African American Culture and Society After Rodney King: Provocations and Protests, Progression and 'Post-Racialism'* (Ashgate: Aldershot, 2015).

She holds a BA in Journalism and German from the University of Wisconsin-Madison and previously worked professionally as a journalist in Madison and Chicago, editing and writing for women's and hair magazines. She also served as the editor of *US Studies Online*, the official postgraduate journal of the British Association for America Studies (BAAS). Research for her chapter in this volume was supported by a Marcus Cunliffe Award from BAAS.

Penny Tinkler is a senior lecturer in Sociology at the University of Manchester, UK. She has written extensively on the history of girls and young women, popular magazines, the feminisation of smoking, photography and photographic methods. Her books include: *Constructing Girlhood: Popular Magazines for Girls Growing up in England 1920–50* (1995); *Smoke Signals: Women, Smoking and Visual Culture in Britain 1880–1980* (2006); *Using Photographs in Social and Historical Research* (2013).

Bibliography

Abrahamson, David. 'Reflecting and shaping American culture: Magazines since World War II.' http://www.davidabrahamson.com. Research folder/Magazines since World War II Accessed 15 August 2015.

Abrams, Mark. *The Teenage Consumer.* London: London Press Exchange, 1959.

Agnew, Hugh. *The Czechs and the Lands of the Bohemian Crown.* Stanford: Hoover Institution Press, 2004.

Albury, Kath. *Yes Means Yes. Getting Explicit About Heterosex.* Crows Nest, NSW: Allen & Unwin, 2002.

Alexander, Sally. *Becoming a Woman, and Other Essays in 19th and 20th Century Feminist History.* London: Virago, 1994.

Altman, Meryl. 'Beyond trashiness: The sexual language of 1970s feminist fiction.' *Journal of International Women's Studies* 4 (2003): 1–19.

Anderson, Benedict. *Imagined Communities: Reflections on the Origin and Spread of Nationalism.* London: Verso, 1983.

Anderson, Doris. *Rebel Daughter: An Autobiography.* Toronto: Key Porter Books, 1996.

Anderson, Patricia. 'Free love and free thought: *The Adult* 1897–1899.' *Media History* 1 (1993): 179–81.

Andrew, John A. III. *The Other Side of the Sixties: Young Americans for Freedom and the Rise of Conservative Politics.* New Brunswick: Rutgers University Press, 1997.

Ang, Ien and Joke Hermes. 'Gender and/in media consumption.' In *Mass Media and Society*, edited by James Curran and Michael Gurevitch, 307–28. London: Edward Arnold, 1991.

Ardis, Ann and Patrick Collier, eds. *Transatlantic Print Culture, 1880–1940: Emerging Media, Emerging Modernisms.* Basingstoke: Palgrave Macmillan, 2008.

Auerbach, Jeffrey A. 'What they read: Mid-nineteenth century English women's magazines and the emergence of a consumer culture.' *Victorian Periodicals Review* 30 (1997): 121–40.

Aynsley, Jeremy. 'Fashioning graphics in the 1920s: Typefaces, magazines and fashion.' In *Design and the Modern Magazine*, edited by Jeremy Aynsley and Kate Forde, 37–55. Manchester: Manchester University Press, 2007.

Aynsley, Jeremy and Francesca Berry, eds. 'Special Issue: Publishing the modern home: Magazines and the domestic interior 1870–1965.' *Journal of Design History* 18 (2005).

Aynsley, Jeremy and Kate Forde, eds. *Design and the Modern Magazine.* Manchester: Manchester University Press, 2007

Bailey, Jenna. *Can Any Mother Help Me? Fifty Years of Women's Friendship through a Secret Magazine*. London: Faber and Faber, 2007.
Ballaster, Ros, Margaret Beetham, Elizabeth Fraser and Sandra Hebron. *Women's Worlds: Ideology, Femininity and the Woman's Magazine*. Houndmills, Basingstoke: Macmillan, 1991.
Banta, Martha. *Imaging American Women: Idea and Ideals in Cultural History*. New York: Columbia University Press, 1987.
Battan, Jesse F. ' "Sexual selection" and the social revolution: Anarchist eugenics and radical Darwinism in the United States, 1850–1910.' In *Darwin in Atlantic Cultures: Evolutionary Visions of Race, Gender and Sexuality*, edited by Jeannette Eileen Jones and Patrick B. Sharp, 33–52. New York and Abingdon: Routledge, 2010.
Battan, Jesse F. ' "Socialism will cure all but an unhappy marriage": Free love and the American Left, 1850–1910.' In *Meetings and Alcôves: The Left and Sexuality in Europe and the United States since 1850*, edited by Jesse Battan, Thomas Bouchet and Tania Régin, 29–46. Dijon: Editions Universitaires de Dijon, 2004.
Beard, Alice. 'Put in just for pictures: Fashion editorial and the composite image in Nova 1965–1975.' *Fashion Theory: Journal of Dress, Body and Culture* 1 (2002): 247–60.
Beaumont, Caitriona. *Housewives and Citizens: Domesticity and the Women's Movement in England, 1928–1964*. Manchester: Manchester University Press, 2013.
Beddoe, Deirdre. *Back to Home and Duty: Women Between the Wars 1918–1939*. London: Pandora, 1989.
Beetham, Margaret. 'Thinking back through our mother's magazines: Feminism's inheritance from nineteenth-century magazines for mothers.' *Nineteenth-Century Gender Studies* 6 (2010). No page numbers. http://www.ncgsjournal.com/issue62/issue62.htm Accessed 15 August 2015.
Beetham, Margaret. 'The reinvention of the English domestic woman: Class and "race" in the 1890s' woman's magazine.' *Women's Studies International Forum* 21 (1998): 223–33.
Beetham, Margaret. *A Magazine of Her Own?: Domesticity and Desire in the Woman's Magazine, 1800–1914*. London and New York: Routledge, 1996.
Beetham, Margaret and Kay Boardman, eds. *Victorian Women's Magazines: An Anthology*. Manchester: Manchester University Press, 2001.
Benson, Susan Porter. *Counter Cultures: Saleswomen, Managers, and Customers in American Department Stores, 1890–1940*. Urbana: University of Illinois Press, 1986.
Berns, Nancy. ' "My problem and how I solved it": Domestic violence in women's magazines.' *The Sociological Quarterly* 40 (1999): 85–108.
Bland, Lucy. *Banishing the Beast: Feminism, Sex and Morality*. London: Tauris Parke, 2002.
Boardman, Kay. 'The ideology of domesticity: The regulation of the household economy in Victorian women's magazines.' *Victorian Periodicals Review* 33 (2000): 150–64.
Bordo, Susan. 'Material girl: The effacements of postmodern culture.' In *The Female Body: Figures, Styles, Speculations*, edited by Laurence Goldstein, 106–30. Ann Arbor: Michigan University Press, 1991.
Bowallius, Marie-Louise. 'Advertising and the use of colour in Woman's Home Companion, 1923–33.' In *Design and the Modern Magazine*, edited by Jeremy Aynsley and Kate Forde, 18–36. Manchester: Manchester University Press, 2007.

Bowler, Peter. *The Invention of Progress: The Victorians and the Past*. Oxford: Basil Blackwell, 1989.
Braithwaite, Brian. *Women's Magazines: The First 300 Years*. London: Peter Owen, 1995.
Braithwaite, Brian and Joan Barrell. *The Business of Women's Magazines*. Second Edition. London: Kogan Paul, 1988.
Brake, Laurel and Julie F Codell. 'Introduction: Encountering the press.' In *Encounters in the Victorian Press: Editors, Authors, Readers*, edited by Laurel Brake and Julie F. Codell, 1–10. Palgrave MacMillan, 2005.
Braungart, Margaret M. and Richard G. Braungart. 'The life-course development of left- and right-wing youth activist leaders from the 1960s.' *Political Psychology* 11 (1990): 257–65.
Brennan, Mary C. *Wives, Mothers and the Red Menace: Conservative Women and the Crusade Against Communism*. Boulder: University of Colorado Press, 2008.
Breward, Christopher. *Fashioning London: Clothing and the Modern Metropolis*. Oxford: Berg, 2004.
Burkhauser, Jude, ed. *Glasgow Girls: Women in Art and Design 1880–1920*. Edinburgh: Canongate, 1990.
Burnham, John C. *Bad Habits: Drinking, Smoking, Taking Drugs, Gambling, Sexual Misbehavior, and Swearing in American History*. New York: New York University Press, 1993.
Buttrose, Ita. *Early Edition: My First Forty Years*. South Melbourne: Macmillan, 1985.
Cancian, Francesca M. and Steven L. Gordon. 'Changing emotion norms in marriage: Love and anger in U.S. women's magazines since 1900.' *Gender and Society* 2 (1988): 308–42.
Carey, Tanith. *Never Kiss a Man in a Canoe: Words of Wisdom from the Golden Age of Agony Aunts*. London: Boxtree, 2009.
Chambers, Jason. 'Equal in every way: African Americans, consumption and materialism from reconstruction to the Civil Rights movement.' *Advertising & Society Review* 7 (2006). http://muse.jhu.edu/journals/advertising_and_society_review/v007/7.1chambers.html.
Cohen, Lizabeth. *A Consumers' Republic: The Politics of Mass Consumption in Postwar America*. New York: Alfred A. Knopf, 2003.
Cornej, Petr and Jiří Pokorny. *A Brief History of the Czech Lands to 2000*. Prague: Prah Press, 2000.
Corzine, Nathan Michael. 'Right at home: Freedom and domesticity in the language and imagery of beer advertising 1933–1960.' *Journal of Social History* 43 (2010): 843–66.
Creedon, Pamela J. and Judith Cramer. *Women in Mass Communication*. Third Edition.Thousand Oaks, CA and London: Sage Publications, 2007.
Critchlow, Donald T. *Phyllis Schlafly and Grassroots Activism: A Woman's Crusade*. Princeton: Princeton University Press, 2005.
Damon-Moore, Helen. *Magazines for the Millions: Gender and Commerce in the Ladies' Home Journal and the Saturday Evening Post, 1880–1910*. Albany: SUNY Press, 1994.
David, Katherine. 'Czech feminists and nationalism in the late Hapsburg monarchy: "The first in Austria."' *Journal of Women's History* 3 (1991): 26–45.

Davidson, Laura, Lisa McNeill and Shelagh Ferguson. 'Magazine communities: Brand community formation in magazine consumption.' *International Journal of Sociology and Social Policy* 27 (2007): 208–20.

Davis, Flora. *Moving the Mountain*. New York City: Touchstone, 1991.

Delap, Lucy. *The Feminist Avant-Garde: Transatlantic Encounters of the Early Twentieth Century*. Cambridge: Cambridge University Press, 2007.

Dreifus, Claudia, ed. *Seizing Our Bodies*. New York: Vintage Books, 1977.

Edwards, Lee. 'The other sixties: A flag waver's memoir.' *Policy Review* 46 (1988): 58–65.

Ehrenreich, Barbara. *The Hearts of Men: American Dreams and the Flight from Commitment*. New York: Anchor Press, 1983.

Ehrenreich, Barbara and Deirdre English. *Complaints and Disorders: The Sexual Politics of Sickness*. Old Westbury, NY: Feminist Press, 1973.

D'Emilio, John and Estelle B. Freedman, *Intimate Matters: A History of Sexuality in America*. Second Edition. Chicago: University of Chicago Press, 1997.

English, Deirdre, Amber Hollibaugh and Gayle Rubin. 'Talking sex: A conversation on sexuality and feminism.' *Feminist Review* 11 (1982): 40–52.

Entwistle, Joanne. *The Fashioned Body*. Cambridge: Polity Press, 2000.

Fairley, Roma. *A Bomb in the Collection: Fashion with the Lid Off*. London: Clifton Books, 1969.

Farrell, Amy Erdman. *Yours in Sisterhood: Ms Magazine and the Promise of Popular Feminism*. Chapel Hill: University of North Carolina Press, 1998.

Faulder, Carolyn. 'Women's magazines.' In *Is This Your Life? Images of Women in the Media*, edited by Josephine King and Mary Stott, 173–94. London: Virago, 1977.

Feinberg, Melissa. *Elusive Equality: Gender, Citizenship, and the Limits of Democracy in Czechoslovakia, 1918–1950*. Pittsburgh: University of Pittsburgh Press, 2006.

Ferguson, Marjorie. *Forever Feminine. Women's Magazines and the Cult of Femininity*. London: Heinemann, 1983.

Forster, Laurel. 'Printing liberation: The women's movement and magazines in the 1970's.' In *British Culture and Society in the 1970s: The Lost Decade*, edited by Laurel Forster and Sue Harper, 93–106. Cambridge: Cambridge Scholars Publishing, 2010.

Fraser, Hilary, Stephanie Green and Judith Johnson. *Gender and the Victorian Periodical*. Cambridge: Cambridge University Press, 2008.

Freeze, Karen Johnson. 'Medical education for women in Austria: A study in the politics of the Czech women's movement in the 1890s.' In *Women, State and Party in Eastern Europe*, edited by Sharon L. Wolchik and Alfred G. Meyer, 51–63. Durham: Duke University Press, 1985.

Friedan, Betty. *The Feminine Mystique*. Various Editions. First Edition. New York: WW Norton & Co., 1963.

Gardiner, Juliet. *The Thirties: An Intimate History*. London: Harper Press, 2010.

Garver, Bruce M. 'Women in the first Czechoslovak Republic.' In *Women, State and Party in Eastern Europe*, edited by Sharon L. Wolchik and Alfred G. Meyer, 64–81. Durham: Duke University Press, 1985.

Garvey, Ellen Gruber. *The Adman in the Parlor: Magazines and the Gendering of Consumer Culture, 1880s to 1910s*. Oxford: Oxford University Press, 1996.

Gathorne-Hardy, Jonathan. *The Rise and Fall of the British Nanny*. London: Weidenfield and Nicholas, 1993.

Gelber, Steven. *Hobbies: Leisure and the Culture of Work*. New York: Columbia University Press, 1999.

Gerhard, Jane. 'Revisiting "The myth of the vaginal orgasm": The female orgasm in American sexual thought.' *Feminist Studies* 26, no. 2 (2000): 440–76.

Giles, Judy. *Women, Identity and Private Life in Britain, 1900–50*. London: Macmillan Press, 2004.

Glucksmann, Miriam. *Women Assemble: Women Workers and the New Industries in Inter-War Britain*. London: Routledge, 1990.

Gough-Yates, Anna. '"A shock to the system": Feminist interventions in youth subculture—The adventures of shocking pink.' *Contemporary British History* 26 (2012): 375–403.

Gough-Yates, Anna. *Understanding Women's Magazines; Publishing Markets and Readerships*. London: Routledge, 2003.

Graham, Philip. *Susan Isaacs: A Life Freeing the Minds of Children*. London: Karnac Books, 2009.

Green, Barbara. 'The feminist periodical press: Women, periodical studies and modernity.' *Literature Compass* 6 (2009): 191–205.

Gumbs, Alexis Pauline. 'Black (buying) power: The story of *Essence* magazine.' In *The Business of Black Power: Community Development, Capitalism, and Corporate Responsibility in Postwar America*, edited by Laura Warren Hill and Julia Rabig, 95–115. Rochester, NY: University of Rochester Press, 2012.

Hackney, Fiona. *Women's Magazines and the Feminine Imagination: Opening Up a New World for Women in Interwar Britain*. London: I. B. Tauris (in press).

Hackney, Fiona. 'Quiet activism & the new amateur: The Power of home and hobby crafts.' *Design and Culture* 5 (2013): 169–94.

Hackney, Fiona. '"They opened up a whole new world": Feminine modernity and the feminine imagination in women's magazines, 1919–1939.' PhD diss., Goldsmith's College University of London, 2012.

Hackney, Fiona. '"Use your hands for happiness": Home craft and make-do-and-mend in British women's magazines in the 1920s and 1930s.' *Journal of Design History* 19 (2006): 23–38.

Hackney, Fiona. 'Making modern woman, stitch by stitch: Dressmaking in women's magazines in Britain, 1919–1939.' In *The Culture of Sewing: Gender, Consumption and Home Dressmaking*, edited by Barbara Burman, 73–95. Oxford: Berg, 1999.

Haidarali, Laila. 'Polishing brown diamonds: African American women, popular magazines, and the advent of modeling in early postwar America.' *Journal of Women's History* 17 (2005): 10–37.

Hall, Lesley A. *The Life and Times of Stella Browne: Feminist and Free Spirit*. London: I. B. Tauris: 2011.

Hamlett, Jane. *Material Relations: Domestic Interiors and Middle-Class Families 1850–1910*. Manchester: Manchester University Press, 2010.

Hardyment, Christina. *Dream Babies: Childcare from John Locke to Gina Ford*. London: Francis Lincoln Ltd, 2007.

Harrison, Martin. *Appearances: Fashion Photography since 1945*. New York: Rizzoli, 1991.

Hatch, Mary G. and David L. Hatch. 'Problems of married working women as presented by three popular working women's magazines.' *Social Forces* 37 (1958): 148–53.

Hayden, Wendy. *Evolutionary Rhetoric: Sex, Science, and Free Love in Nineteenth-Century Feminism.* Southern Illinois University Press, 2013.

Hermes, Joke. *Reading Women's Magazines: An Analysis of Everyday Media Use.* Cambridge: Polity Press, 1995.

Heron, Craig. *Booze: A Distilled History.* Toronto: Between the Lines, 2003.

Hochschild, Arlie R. 'Love and gold.' In *Global Woman: Nannies, Maids and Sex Workers in the New Economy,* edited by Barbara Ehrenreich and Arlie R. Hochschild, 15–30. London: Granta Books, 2002.

Holden, Katherine. *Nanny Knows Best: The History of the British Nanny.* Stroud: The History Press, 2013.

Holden, Katherine. *The Shadow of Marriage: Singleness in England 1914–1960.* Manchester: Manchester University Press, 2007.

Holloway, Gerry. *Women and Work in Britain since 1840.* London: Routledge, 2005.

Hollows, Joanne and Rachel Moseley. 'Introduction.' In *Feminism in Popular Culture,* edited by Joanne Hollows and Rachel Moseley, 1–24. Oxford and New York: Berg, 2006.

Horowitz, Daniel. *Betty Friedan and the Making of the Feminine Mystique: The American Left, the Cold War, and Modern Feminism.* Amherst: University of Massachusetts Press, 1998.

Huebner, Karla. 'Otherness in First Republic Czechoslovak representations of women.' In *Competing Eyes: Visual Encounters with Alterity in Central and Eastern Europe,* edited by Dagnosław Demski, Ildikó Sz. Kristóf and Kamila Baraniecka-Olszewska, 438–60. Budapest: L'Harmattan, 2013.

Huebner, Karla. 'Girl, trampka, or žába? The Czechoslovak new woman.' In *The New Woman International: Representations in Photography and Film from the 1870s Through the 1960s,* edited by Elizabeth Otto and Vanessa Rocco, 231–51. Ann Arbor: University of Michigan Press, 2011.

Huebner, Todd. 'The Multinational "Nation-State": The origins and the paradox of Czechoslovakia, 1914–1920.' Ph.D. diss., Columbia University, 1993.

Humpherys, Anne. 'The journals that did: Writing about sex in the late 1890s.' *19: Interdisciplinary Studies in the Long Nineteenth Century* 3 (2006). www.19.bbk.ac.uk Accessed 15 August 2015.

Humpherys, Anne. 'The journal that did: Form and content in *The Adult* (1897–1899).' *Media History* 9 (2003): 63–78.

Isaacs, Susan. *Children and Parents: Their Problems and Difficulties.* London: Routledge and Kegan Paul, 1968.

Joannou, Maroula. *"Ladies, Please Don't' Smash These Windows": Women's Writing, Feminist Consciousness and Social Change 1918–38.* Oxford: Berg, 1995.

Johnson, Sammye. 'Why should they care?' *Journalism Studies* 8 (2007): 525.

Johnson, Sammye and Patricia Prijatel. *The Magazine from Cover to Cover.* Third Edition. Oxford and New York: Oxford University Press, 2012.

Jusová, Iveta. 'Fin-de-siècle feminisms: The development of feminist narratives within the discourses of British imperialism and Czech nationalism.' Ph.D. diss., Miami University, 2000.

Keller, Kathryn. 'Nurture and work in the middle class: Imagery from women's magazines.' *International Journal of Politics, Culture, and Society* 5 (1992): 577–600.

Kelley, Robin D.G. 'Nap Time: Historicizing the Afro.' *Fashion Theory* 1 (1997): 339–51.

Kent, Robin. *Aunt Agony Advises: Problem Pages Through the Ages*. London: W.H. Allen, 1979.
King, M. Truby. *Mothercraft*. London: Simkin, Marshall Ltd. 1934.
Kirkham, Pat. 'Women and the inter-war handicrafts revival.' In *A View from the Interior, Women and Design*, edited by Judy Attfield and Pat Kirkham, 174–83. London: The Women's Press, 1989.
Kirschbaum, Stanislav J. *A History of Slovakia: The Struggle for Survival*. New York: St. Martin's Griffin, 1995.
Kitch, Carolyn L. *Pages from the Past: History and Memory in American Magazines*. Chapel Hill: University of North Carolina Press, 2005.
Kitch, Carolyn L. *The Girl on the Magazine Cover: The Origins of Visual Stereotypes in American Mass Media*. Chapel Hill, NC: University of North Carolina Press, 2001.
Klatch, Rebecca E. *A Generation Divided: The New Left, the New Right and the 1960s*. Berkeley: University of California Press, 1999.
Klatch, Rebecca E. *Women of the New Right*. Philadelphia: Temple University Press, 1987.
Kline, Barbara. *White House Nannies: True Tales from the Other Department of Homeland Security*. New York: Tarcher/Penguin Group, 2006.
Koedt, Anne. 'The myth of the vaginal orgasm.' In *Radical Feminism*, edited by Anne Koedt, Ellen Levine and Anita Rapone, 198–207. New York: Quadrangle Books, 1973 [1970].
Korinek, Valerie J. *Roughing It in the Suburbs: Reading Chatelaine Magazine in the Fifties and Sixties*. Toronto: University of Toronto Press, 2000.
Langhamer, Claire. *Women's Leisure in England 1920–1960*. Manchester: Manchester University Press, 2000.
Le Masurier, Megan. 'My other, my self.' *Australian Feminist Studies* 22 (2007): 191–211.
Lewis, Jane, ed. *Labour and Love, Women's Experience of Home and Family, 1850–1940*. Oxford: Blackwell, 1986.
Lewis, Jane. *Women in England, 1870–1950: Sexual Division and Social Change*. London: Harvester Wheatsheaf, 1984.
Light, Alison. *Mrs Woolf and Her Servants*. London: Penguin, 2007.
Littauer, Amanda H. 'The B-Girl evil: Bureaucracy, sexuality, and the menace of Barroom Vice in postwar California.' *Journal of the History of Sexuality* 12 (2003): 171–204.
Long, Vicky and Hilary Marland. 'From danger and motherhood to health and beauty: Health advice for the factory girl in early twentieth-century Britain.' *Twentieth Century British History* 20 (2009): 454–81.
Looser, Devoney. *Women Writers and Old Age in Great Britain, 1750–1850*. Baltimore, MD: Johns Hopkins University Press, 2008.
Lupton, Mary Jane. ' "Ladies" entrance: Women and bars.' *Feminist Studies* 5 (1979): 571–88.
Lyons, Paul. *New Left, New Right and the Legacy of the Sixties*. Philadelphia: Temple University Press, 1996.
Macdonald, Cameron L. *Shadow Mothers, Nannies, Au Pairs, and the Micropolitics of Mothering*. Berkeley, CA: University of California Press, 2011.
Magocsi, Paul Robert. *The Shaping of a National Identity: Subcarpathian Rus', 1848–1948*. Cambridge: Harvard University Press, 1978.

Malečková, Jitka. 'The emancipation of women for the benefit of the nation: The Czech women's movement.' In *Women's Emancipation Movements in the Nineteeth Century: A European Perspective*, edited by Bianka Petrow-Ennker and Sylvia Paletschek, 167–88. Stanford: Stanford University Press, 2004.

Mankiller, Wilma P., Gwendolyn Mink, Marysa Navarro, Gloria Steinem and Barbara Smith. *The Reader's Companion to US Women's History*. New York: Houghton Mifflin Harcourt, 1999.

Marcellus, Jane. *Business Girls & Two-Job Wives: Emerging Media Stereotypes of Employed Women*. Cresskill, NJ: The Hampton Press, 2011.

Marchand, Roland. *Advertising the American Dream: Making Way for Modernity, 1920–1940*. Berkeley: University of California Press, 1985.

Matthews, Jill Julius. *Sex in Public. Australian Sexual Cultures*. St Leonards, NSW: Allen & Unwin, 1997.

McClellan, Michelle. '"Lady Tipplers": Gendering the modern alcoholism paradigm, 1933–1960.' In *Altering American Consciousness: The History of Alcohol and Drug Use in the United States, 1800–2000*, edited by Sarah Tracy and Carol Ackerman, 267–97. Amherst and Boston: University of Massachusetts Press, 2004.

McCracken, Ellen. *Decoding Women's Magazines: From Mademoiselle to Ms*. London: MacMillan Press, 1993.

McGirr, Lisa. *Suburban Warriors*. Princeton: Princeton University Press, 2001.

McMillian, John. *Smoking Typewriters: The Sixties Underground Press and the Rise of Alternative Media in America*. New York: Oxford University Press, 2011.

McPherson, James Brian. *The Conservative Resurgence and the Press: The Media's Role in the Rise of the Right*. Evanston: Northwestern University Press, 2008.

McRobbie, Angela. *Feminism and Youth Culture: From Jackie to Just Seventeen*. Second Edition. Basingstoke: Macmillan, 2000.

McRobbie, Angela. *In the Culture Society: Art, Fashion, and Popular Music*. New York: Routledge, 1999.

McRobbie, Angela. '*More!*: New sexualities in girls' and women's magazines.' In *Back to Reality? Social Experience and Cultural Studies*, edited by Angela McRobbie, 190–209. Manchester: Manchester University Press, 1997.

McRobbie, Angela. '*Jackie* magazine: Romantic individualism and the teenage girl.' In *Feminism and Youth Culture*, edited by Angela McRobbie, 81–134. London: Macmillan, 1991.

Mendes, Kaitlynn. 'Reading *Chatelaine*: Dr Marion Hilliard and 1950s women's health advice.' *Canadian Journal of Communication* 35 (2010): 515–31.

Menon, Elizabeth K. *Evil by Design: The Creation and Marketing of the Femme Fatale*. Chicago: University of Illinois Press, 2006.

Meyerowitz, Joanne. 'Beyond *The Feminine Mystique*: A reassessment of postwar mass culture, 1946–1958.' *Journal of American History* 79 (1993): 1455–82.

Millum, Trevor. *Images of Woman: Advertising in Women's Magazines*. London: Chatto and Windus, 1975.

Morrison, Mark S. *The Public Face of Modernism: Little Magazines, Audiences, and Reception 1905–1920*. Wisconsin: University of Wisconsin Press, 2001.

Moruzi, Kristine. *Constructing Girlhood through the Periodical Press, 1850–1915*. Farnham: Ashgate, 2012.

Moscucci, Ornella. *The Science of Woman: Gynaecology and Gender in England, 1800–1929*. Cambridge: Cambridge University Press, 1993.

Mott, Frank Luther. *A History of American Magazines: 1885–1915*, Vol. 4. Cambridge, MA: Harvard University Press, 1957.
Muellner, Beth. 'The photographic enactment of the early new woman in 1890s German women's bicycling magazines.' *Women in German Yearbook* 22 (2006): 167–88.
Murdock, Catherine Gilbert. *Domesticating Drink: Women, Men, and Alcohol in America, 1870–1940*. Baltimore and London: Johns Hopkins University Press, 1998.
Murphy, Mary. 'Bootlegging mothers and drinking daughters: Gender and prohibition in Butte, Montana.' *American Quarterly* 46 (1994): 174–94.
Nash, George. *The Conservative Intellectual Movement in America since 1945*. New York: Basic Books, 1976.
Neudorfl, Marie. 'Masaryk and the women's question.' In *Thinker and Politician*. Vol. 1 of T. G. Masaryk (1850–1937), edited by Stanley B. Winters, 258–82. New York: St. Martin's, 1990.
Nicholson, Virginia. *Singled Out: How Two Million Women Survived Without Men after the First World War*. London: Penguin, 2007.
Nickerson, Michelle. *Mothers of Conservatism: Women and the Postwar Right*. Princeton: Princeton University Press, 2012.
Olewniczak, Timothy. 'Giggle water on the mighty Niagara: Rum-runners, homebrewers, redistillers, and the changing social fabric of drinking culture during alcohol prohibition in Buffalo, N.Y., 1920–1933.' *Pennsylvania History: A Journal of Mid-Atlantic Studies* 78 (2011): 33–61.
Oliver, Hermia. *The International Anarchist Movement in Late Victorian London*. London and New York: St. Martin's Press, 1983.
Osgerby, William. *Youth in Britain since 1945*. London: Wiley-Blackwell, 1997.
Passet, Joanne. *Sex Radicals and the Quest for Women's Equality*. Chicago: University of Illinois Press, 2003.
Patterson, Martha H. ed. *The American New Woman Revisited: A Reader, 1894–1930*. New Brunswick, NJ: Rutgers University Press, 2008.
Patton, Tracey Owens. 'Hey girl, am I more than my hair?: African American women and their struggles with beauty, body, and hair.' *National Women's Studies Association Journal* 18 (2006): 24–51.
Peck, Abe. *The Life and Times of the Underground Press*. New York: Pantheon Books, 1985.
Pederson, Joyce Senders. 'The reform of women's secondary and higher education: Institutional change and social values in mid and late Victorian England.' *History of Education Quarterly* 19 (1979): 61–91.
Peiss, Kathy. *Hope in a Jar: The Making of America's Beauty Culture*. New York: Henry Holt, 1998.
Pendergast, Tom. *Creating the Modern Man: American Magazines and Consumer Culture, 1900–1950*. Columbia: University of Missouri Press, 2000.
Pennock, Pamela E. *Advertising Sin and Sickness: The Politics of Alcohol and Tobacco Marketing, 1950–1990*. DeKalb: Northern Illinois University Press, 2007.
Pennock, Pamela E. 'The evolution of U.S. temperance movements since repeal: A comparison of two campaigns to control alcoholic beverage marketing, 1950s and 1980s.' *The History of Drugs and Alcohol* 20 (2005): 14–65.
Peterson, Theodore. *Magazines in the Twentieth Century*. Urbana: University of Illinois Press, 1964.

Phipps, Pauline. 'Faith, desire, and sexual identity: Constance Maynard's atonement for passion.' *Journal of the History of Sexuality* 18 (2009): 265–86.
Pistorius, Georges. *Destin de la Culture Française dans une Démocratie Populaire: La Présence Française en Tchécoslovaquie*. Paris: Les Isles d'Or, 1957.
Powers, Madelon. 'Women and public drinking, 1890–1920.' *History Today* 45 (1995): 46–52.
Prentice, Alison, Paula Bourne, Gail Cuthbert Brandt, Beth Light, Wendy Mitchinson and Naomi Black. *Canadian Women: A History*. Second Edition. Toronto, ON: Harcourt Brace, 1996.
Radner, Hilary. 'On the move: Fashion, photography and the single girl in 1960s.' In *Fashion Cultures: Theory, Exploration and Analysis*, edited by Stella Bruzzi, 128–42. London: Routledge, 2000.
Radway, Janice. *Reading the Romance*. London: Verso, 1984.
Richardson, Angelique. 'Eugenics and freedom at the Fin de Siècle.' In *Culture and Science in the Nineteenth-Century Media*, edited by Louise Henson, Geoffrey Cantor, Gowan Dawson, Richard Noakes, Sally Shuttleworth and Jonathan Topham, 275–86. Farnham: Ashgate, 2004.
Richardson, Angelique. *Love and Eugenics in the Late Nineteenth Century: Rational Reproduction and the New Woman*. Oxford: Oxford University Press, 2003.
Richardson, Peter. *A Bomb in Every Issue*. New York: The New Press, 2009.
Ritchie, Rachel. '"Beauty isn't all a matter of looking glamorous": Attitudes to glamour and beauty in 1950s women's magazines.' *Women's History Review* 23 (2014): 723–43.
Ritchie, Rachel. 'Women and Woman: Representations of youthful femininity in the 'World's Greatest Weekly for Women', 1954–1969.' In *Women and the Media: Feminism and Femininity in Britain, 1900 to the Present*, edited by Maggie Andrews and Sallie McNamara, 143–55. Routledge: London, 2014.
Roach Pierson, Ruth. *'They're Still Women After All': The Second World War and Canadian Womanhood*. Toronto: McClelland & Stewart, 1986.
Robb, George. 'Race motherhood: Moral eugenics vs. progressive eugenics, 1880–1920.' In *Maternal Instincts: Visions of Motherhood and Sexuality in Britain, 1875–1925*, edited by Claudia Nelson and Ann Sumner Holmes, 58–75. London: MacMillan, 1997.
Robb, George. 'The way of all flesh: Degeneration, eugenics and the gospel of free love.' *Journal of the History of Sexuality* 4 (1996): 589–603.
Roberts, James C. *The Conservative Decade: Emerging Leaders of the 1980s*. Westport, CT: Arlington House, 1980.
Rooks, Noliwe M. *Ladies' Pages: African American Women's Magazines and the Culture That Made Them*. New Brunswick: Rutgers University Press, 2004.
Rosen, Ruth. *The World Split Open*. New York City: Viking, 2000.
Rotskoff, Lori. *Love on the Rocks: Men, Women, and Alcohol in Post-World War II America*. Chapel Hill: University of North Carolina Press, 2002.
Rowbotham, Sheila. *Dreamers of a New Day: Women Who Invented the Twentieth Century*. London: Verso, 2010.
Rowold, Katharina. *The Educated Woman: Minds, Bodies and Women's Higher Education in Britain, Germany and Spain, 1865–1914*. New York: Routledge, 2010.
Royle, Edward. *Radicals, Secularists and Republicans: Popular Freethought in Britain, 1866–1915*. Manchester: Manchester University Press, 1980.

Rudinsky, Norma. *Incipient Feminists: Women Writers in the Slovak National Revival.* Columbus, OH: Slavica, 1991.
Russet, Cynthia Eagle. *Sexual Science: The Victorian Construction of Motherhood.* Cambridge, MA: Harvard University Press, 1989.
Ruzek, Sheryl Burt. *The Women's Health Movement.* New York City: Praeger Publishers, 1978.
Sangster, Joan. *Transforming Labour: Women and Work in Post-war Canada.* Toronto: University of Toronto Press, 2010.
Sangster, Joan. 'Doing two jobs: The wage-earning mother, 1945–1970.' In *A Diversity of Women: Ontario, 1945–1980*, edited by Joy Parr, 98–132. Toronto: University of Toronto Press, 1995.
Sayer, Derek. *The Coasts of Bohemia: A Czech History.* Princeton, NJ: Princeton University Press, 1998.
Scanlon, Jennifer. *Bad Girls Go Everywhere. The Life of Helen Gurley Brown.* Oxford and New York: Oxford University Press, 2009.
Scanlon, Jennifer. *Inarticulate Longings. The Ladies' Home Journal, Gender, and the Promises of Consumer Culture.* London and New York: Routledge, 1995.
Schneider, Gregory. *Cadres for Conservatism.* New York: New York University Press, 1999.
Schoenwald, Jonathan M. *A Time for Choosing: The Rise of Modern American Conservatism.* New York: Oxford University Press, 2001.
Schreiber, Ronnee. *Righting Feminism: Conservative Women and American Politics.* New York: Oxford University Press, 2008.
Schudson, Michael. *The Sociology of News.* New York: W.W. Norton & Company, 2003.
Sears, Hal. *The Sex Radicals: Free Love in High Victorian America.* Kansas: Regents Press, 1977.
Segal, Lynne. *Straight Sex. The Politics of Pleasure.* London: Virago, 1994.
Shapiro, Laura. *Something from the Oven: Reinventing Dinner in 1950's America.* New York: Viking, 2004.
Shepherd, John. *George Lansbury: At the Heart of Old Labour.* Oxford: Oxford University Press: 2004.
Sheridan, Susan, Susan Magarey and Sandra Lilburn. 'Feminism in the news.' In *Feminism in Popular Culture,* edited by Joanne Hollows and Rachel Moseley, 25–40. Oxford and New York: Berg, 2006.
Shevelow, Kathryn. *Women and Print Culture: The Construction of Femininity in the Early Periodical.* London: Routledge, 1989.
Siegel, Carol. *New Millennial Sexstyles.* Bloomington, IN: Indiana University Press, 2000.
Smart, Carol. 'Collusion, collaboration and confession: On moving beyond the heterosexuality debate.' In *Theorising Heterosexuality. Telling it Straight*, edited by Diane Richardson, 161–78. Buckingham and Philadelphia: Open University Press, 1996.
Smith, Michelle. 'Fiction and the nation: The construction of Canadian identity in *Chatelaine* and *Canadian Home Journal* during the 1930s and 1940s.' *British Journal of Canadian Studies* 27 (2014): 37–53.
Sochen, June. *Enduring Values: Women in Popular Culture.* New York: Praeger, 1987.
Steedman, Carolyn. *Landscape for a Good Woman.* London: Virago, 1986.

Steinberg, Salme Harju. *Reformer in the Marketplace: Edward W. Bok and the Ladies' Home Journal*. Baton Rouge: Louisiana State University Press, 1979.

Stephen, Jennifer A. *Pick One Intelligent Girl: Employability, Domesticity and the Gendering of Canada's Welfare State, 1939–1947*. Toronto: Toronto University Press, 2007.

Strauss, David. *Setting the Table for Julia Child: Gourmet Dining in America, 1934–1961*. Baltimore: Johns Hopkins University Press, 2011.

Strong-Boag, Veronica. 'Canada's wage-earning wives and the construction of the middle-class, 1945–1960.' *Journal of Canadian Studies* 29 (1994): 5–25.

Summers, Anne. *The End of Equality*. Milsons Point, NSW: Random House, 2003.

Tamboukou, Maria. 'Of other spaces: Women's colleges at the turn of the nineteenth century in the UK.' *Gender, Place and Culture* 7 (2000): 247–63.

Tebbel, John William and Mary Ellen Zuckerman, *The Magazine in America: 1741–1990*. New York: Oxford University Press, 1991.

Thorburn, Wayne. *A Generation Awakes: Young Americans for Freedom and the Creation of the Conservative Movement*. Ottawa, IL: Jameson Books, 2010.

Tinkler, Penny. ' "Are you really living?" If not, "GET WITH IT!" The teenage self and lifestyle in young women's magazines, Britain 1957–70.' *Cultural and Social History* 11 (2014): 597–619.

Tinkler, Penny. ' "Red tips for hot lips": Advertising cigarettes for young women in Britain, 1920–70.' *Women's History Review* 10 (2001): 249–72.

Tinkler, Penny. ' "A material girl?" Adolescent girls and their magazines, 1920–58.' In *All the World and Her Husband. Women in Twentieth-century Consumer Culture*, edited by Maggie Andrews and Mary M. Talbot, 97–112. London: Cassell, 2000.

Tinkler, Penny. *Constructing Girlhood: Popular Magazines for Girls Growing up in England 1920–50*. London: Taylor & Francis, 1995.

Tinkler, Penny. 'Women and popular literature.' In *Women's History: Britain, 1850–1950*, edited by June Purvis, 132–56. London: UCL Press, 1995.

Tinkler, Penny. 'Learning through Leisure: Feminine Ideology in Girls' Magazines, 1920–50.' In *Lessons for Life: The Schooling of Girls and Women*, edited by Felicity Hunt, 60–79. Oxford: Basil Blackwell, 1987.

Todd, Selina. 'Poverty and aspiration: Young women's entry to employment in interwar England.' *Twentieth Century British History* 15 (2004): 122.

Toma, Peter A. and Dušan Kováč. *Slovakia from Samo to Dzurinda*. Stanford: Hoover Institution Press, 2001.

Vicinus, Martha. *Independent Women: Work and Community for Single Women, 1850–1920*. Chicago: University of Chicago Press, 1985.

Viguerie, Richard A. and David Franke. *America's Right Turn: How Conservatives Used New and Alternative Media to Take Power*. Los Angeles: Bonus Books, 2004.

Walker, Susannah. *Style & Status: Selling Beauty to African American Women, 1920–1975*. Lexington: University Press of Kentucky, 2007.

Walker, Susannah. 'Black is profitable: The commodification of the Afro, 1960–1975.' In *Beauty and Business: Commerce, Gender, and Culture in Modern America*, edited by Philip Scranton, 254–77. New York: Routledge, 2001.

Walkerdine, Valerie. *Schoolgirl Fictions*. London: Verso, 1990.

Warner, Michael. *The Trouble with Normal: Sex, Politics, and the Ethics of Queer Life*. Cambridge, MA: Harvard University Press, 2000.

Warsh, Cheryl Krasnick. 'Smoke and mirrors: Gender representation in North American alcohol and tobacco advertisements before 1950.' *Histoire Sociale/ Social History* 62 (1998): 183–222.

Webb, Alisa. 'Constructing the gendered body: Girls, health, beauty, advice, and the Girls' Best Friend, 1898–1899.' *Women's History Review* 15 (2006): 253–75.

Weber, Nora. 'Feminism, patriarchy, nationalism, and women in '*Fin-de-Siecle*' Slovakia.' *Nationalities Papers* 25 (1997): 35–65.

Welter, Barbara. *Dimity Convictions: The American Woman in the Nineteenth Century*. Athens, OH: Ohio University Press, 1976.

Welter, Barbara. 'The cult of true womanhood: 1820–1860.' *American Quarterly* 18 (1966): 151–74.

White, Cynthia. *Women's Magazines 1693–1968*. London: Michael Joseph, 1970.

Winship, Janice. ' "A girl needs to get street-wise": Magazines for the 1980s.' *Feminist Review* 20 (1987): 25–46.

Winship, Janice. *Inside Women's Magazines*. London and New York: Pandora, 1987.

Wolf, Naomi. *The Beauty Myth: How Images of Beauty Are Used Against Women*. London: Vintage, 1991.

Zuckerman, Mary Ellen. *A History of Popular Women's Magazines in the United States, 1792–1995*. Westport, CT: Greenwood Publishing Group, 1998.

Index

abortion 108, 204, 222–3
Abrams, Mark 31, 185, 187
The Adult 10, 55–9
advertisers 2, 10, 25–6, 31, 35, 81–90, 110, 183–4, 186, 228–31, 234, 236–7
advertising/advertisement 11, 12, 18, 27, 29–33, 35, 75–6, 110–11, 143–5, 183–4, 228, 237; of alcohol 11, 81–91, 83, *86, 88;* and Black hair industry 228–34, 236–7; as a career 110–11; of contraception 191; group buying 17, 186; relationship with editorial content 17, 110, 183; targeting of 230–2, 234; of tobacco 35
advice columns 2, 12, 42, 48–9, 96–8, 138, 152, 167, 107–20, 177–8, 205–11; *see also* doctor's advice; Eyles, Leonora; Home, Evelyn
African American women 14, 228–31, 233, 236–7, 240; magazines for 6, 237; *see also* beauty culture and Black hair
Afro/Natural *see* Black hair
agency: of nannies 149; political 94; of readers 46, 49, 108, 111, 118, 183, 214, 222
agony aunt *see* advice columns
alcohol: consumption of by women 81–3; 89; *see also* advertising; Hiram Walker Distillery
American Girl 165–82, *168;* Anglo-Saxon 168, 170, 172; as archetype 165–6; Mr Gibson's 165, 167–9, 179n1
anarchist eugenics 56, 58–61

Anderson, Doris (editor of *Chatelaine*) 140–1, 144
Australian women's magazines 201–11

'bachelor girl' 97, 108
The Beatles 189
Beauty: Black 228, 230–1; contest 98, 232–3; culture 230–1; industry 229, 230–3; standards of 230–1; *see also* magazines; hair and beauty
The Beauty Myth 47
Beauty Trade 228–37
Beetham, Margaret 4, 6
Biba 191
birth control *see* contraception; the Pill
birth rate: in Australia 204; declining 149, 173, 175
Black hair 228–37; Afro 233–7; magazines 6, 27, 228–37; natural 233–7
Black Power Movement 16, 220, 228, 232
Black press 229–30
Black women *see* African American women
Bok, Edward W. (editor of *Ladies Home Journal*) 14, 18, 165–8, 174–8
Bowlby, John 154
Bowlby, Ursula 154–5
brand/branding 83, 90; in *Beauty Trade* 231; extension 187; in *Honey* 183, 185–91; loyalty 193
Brown, Helen Gurley 96–7, 201
Burgess, Anthony 42
'business girl' 13, 110; *see also* 'bachelor girl'
business girls' magazines *see* magazines

Calvin, Bernice (editor and publisher *Beauty Trade*) 232
Campbell, J. W. 132
Canadian women's magazines 137–47
Careers for Women 108, 114–17, 119
Carter, Angela 47–8
Chambers, Jason 229, 231
Chatelaine 137–47
childbirth 223
childcare magazines *see* magazines
children 72, 74; health 13, 58, 61; responsibility for 55, 57; slavish 60; unwanted 60–1; working class 50; working with 148; *see also* nannies
Christian/ Christianity 107, 113, 117, 129–31, 133; *see also* Quakers/ Religious Society of Friends
Christie, Julie 43
Civil Rights Movement 10, 16, 96, 232
class 28–31, 33, 40–51, 68, 111, 118–19, 148, 57, 159, 195n20, 211, 216; barriers 157–8; conflict 157–8; middle 28, 29, 30–1, 33, 44, 45, 49, 51, 68–9, 77, 81–7, 108, 110, 112–17, 119, 138–40, 148, 150, 154, 165–6, 173, 184–6, 202, 216–17; upper 33, 81–4, 110, 148–50; working 28, 29, 40–1, 43–51, 83, 108, 111–13, 117, 118, 119, 138, 184, 202, 211; *see also* nannies
Cleo magazine 201–11
composite form of magazines 32, 37
consciousness raising 12, 16, 111, 113–14, 118, 202, 204, 215–16, 225
conservative/ism: as political movement in the US 92–100; women's magazines in Canada 144
consumer/s: advocacy 219, 222; Black women as 228, 229–30, 231, 233–4, 236; culture 30, 46, 66–80, 183–4, 187, 217; groups 299–30; magazines 11, 25, 27, 29–31, 38, 60–76, 108, 110, 228, 230, 231, 235, 236; markets 15, 144, 184, 237; power 29; teenage 30–1, 185–7, 192; women as 81, 84–90, 215, 217, 219, 222, 224–5
consumerism 9, 43–5, 140
Contemporary Review 127

contraception 121n28, 191, 202, 204, 219, 220–2
contradiction (within magazines) 5, 26, 31, 33, 35–6, 95–6
cookery/cooking advice 75, 83–7, 90
cordials *see* alcohol
correspondence columns/pages 6, 13, 18, 96, 107–8, 110–14, 116, 138, 142, 149–52, *151*, 206–10; *see also* letters
Cosmopolitan 3, 5, 201–2
covers, magazine *see* magazine covers
cultural: imagination 42; studies 9, 41, 45–8
Czechoslovakia: feminism in 66, 68–9; First Republic 66–9, 76; New Woman 68; women's magazines in 66–80

Darling 43
Darwin's theory of evolution and free love 59, 61
Dawson (Bauman), Carol 93, 95
Degeneration/degradation of society 56, 61; *see also* racial decline
Distilled Spirits Institute (DSI) 81, 83, 86
doctor's advice 140, 202, 205, 209–10, 219–23
domestic/domesticity 45, 75, 87, 89–90, 115–17, 137, 139, 144–5, 217
domestic service *see* women and work

Ebony 81–2, 229, 231
editors/editorial 84, 111, 139–41, 183–4, 189, 191; and advertising 32, 82, 110, 183, 185, 237; policy 31, 72, 93, 113, 167–8, 183, 186, 193, 202–4, 231–3; for specific editors *see* individual entries
education 50, 66, 75, 202, 211; health 215–16, 221, 224; higher 50, 66, 125–6; high school 202; reform 130; status 51; *see also* sex education
employment, women's *see* working women
Essence 228, 229–30, 236–7
eugenics 171; and evolution 170, 174–5; *see also* anarchist eugenics; free love
exercise, physical 72, 75, 174–5
Eyles, Leonora 12, 107–8, *109*, 111, 113, 119–20

Index

fashion 40, 66, 69, 71–5, 86–9; 167, 177, 183, 186, 189, 191–3, 235
The Female Eunuch 48, 207
female sexual choice *see* sex and relationships
The Feminine Mystique see Betty Friedan
feminism 95, 100, 108, 111, 118; in Czechoslovakia (*see* Czechoslovakia); liberal 202, 216–17, 219, 223, 224; popular 203–4, 211; radical 202, 216–17, 224; second wave 45–50, 95, 100, 201–11, 214, 215–18, 219, 220, 222, 223–5; therapeutic 223–5
fiction in magazines 4, 28, 33–4; cautionary 144; romantic 4, 29, 96, 177, 185
First World War 127–33
Fisher, Harrison 167, 178
food/food industry 75, 83–7, 89–90
free love 55–65, 65n45; American 59, 61; and eugenics 59, 61; and female sexual choice 55, 58–9; feminists and 55, 58–9, 61; and monogamous marriage 55–65; and patriarchy 59; politics of 55–7, 59, 61–2; and reproduction 55–9; system 57–9, 61; *see also* Harman, Lillian
Friedan, Betty 3, 5, 7, 15, 137, 202, 217–18
friendship 32, 157–8, 178
front covers *see* magazine covers

gender 36, 41, 59, 61–2, 67–8, 193; equality 95, 201, 203, 211; ideology 56; and reproduction 56; roles 69, 82–5, 87, 89, 95–6, 143, 157, 159
Gibson, Charles Dana *see* American Girl
Gibson Girl *see* American Girl
Girls' Favourite 33, 35–7, 36
Girl's Own Paper 28
Girton College 125
Good Housekeeping 113, 119, 139, 167
Greer, Germaine 48–9

hair care industry 228–37
Harman, Lillian 56, 58–61
Harper's Bazaar 43
health: mental 174; physical 174; women's 140, 173, 175, 202, 214; *see also* women's health movement
Heiress 29
heterosexuality 28–9, 34, 36, 98, 125–6, 138, 203–11; *see also* homosexuality
The Hibbert 125, 127–9, 130–3; 'Love which is not fulfilling of the law' 125, 130–3
Hilliard, Marion 137, 140, 142
Hiram Walker Distillery 81–90, *86*, *88*
home crafts 116–17
Home, Evelyn 48–9, 114
homemaking 140–1
homosexuality 208–9; *see also* sexuality
Honey 183–97; Boutiques 187, 189, 193
Hospitality/hostess 83–7, 89–90
housewife/housewifery 11–12, 45, 81, 84–6, 108, 110, 113, 115–19, 139–40, 142–3, 159, 186
Howard, Chandler Christy 167–8, 170

identity: Bourdieu, Patrick on 169; magazines as promoters of, 11, 13, 30, 75–7, 112, 166, 172, 178
image/imagery 7, 26, 27, 31–3, 36–7, 47, 74–5, 77, 87, 186, 192–3, 234; aesthetics of 36, 177, 187; of Black women 228, 233; of women 67–9, 76, 86, 88, 89, 98–9, 144–5, 183, 209; *see also* American Girl; magazine covers
Inside Mr Enderby 42
IPC (International Publishing Corporation) 185
Isaacs, Susan *see* Wise, Ursula

Johnson, George/Johnson Products 231

A Kind of Loving 43–4, 48
King, Frederick Truby 152, 154–5

The Labour Party 111–12, 115, 121n28
Ladies' Home Journal 165–82, 214, 217–25
lady nurses 13, 157–9
Landscape for a Good Woman 40–1, 50–1
Lansbury's Labour Weekly 108, 111–15, 117, 119
The Legitimation League 55, 59–60; *see also The Adult*
leisure 83, 89, 116, 184–5, 193

Lessing, Doris 45
letters 42, 45, 48, 116–17, 122n47, 139, 148, 153–5, 202, 205; *see also* correspondence columns/pages
Life 81–2, 85, 87, 89
liqueurs *see* alcohol
love 42, 69, 117, 131–2, 176–7, 209; and marriage 69, 176; *see also* nannies; romance
love comics 187
love-play 207
Lucifer the Light-Bearer 59–60

magazine covers 35–6, 70, 71, 73, 101n12, 111, 165, 167, *168*, 169–70, 192, 172, 174, 177–8, 187, *188*, 189
magazine design 7, 25–6, 31, 33, 34, 37, 41, 69
magazine publishers 28–30, 72, 76, 113, 126, 128, 183–5, 228–30, 232, 236–7
magazines: and academic scholarship 2–7, 41–51, 66, 94–5; business girls' 28, 31, 33, 35–6; childcare 148–61; fashion 48, 68–9, 76, 183; general interest 68–9, 84, 166, 230, 234; hair and beauty 228–37; in the late nineteenth century 55–65; political content in 93–103, 108, 114, 118, 167–8, 170, 201–2, 206, 217–19, 232, 234; schoolgirl 28; as taste-creators 166; for teens 29, 30–1, 183–97; trade 84–5, 87, 184, 228–40; for working girls 28–30, 33; for young women 27–30, 33; 69, 95, 98, 165, 167, 183–4, 201–2; *see also* individual titles
The Magic Toyshop 47–8
male: contributors 12, 33, 37, 82, 125, 130, 133; readers 82, 205
Manion, Marilyn 95, 96–100
Margaret Protests 108, 119
mass culture 41, 46–7, 50–1, 167, 172, 176–7
masturbation 206, 207, 210
maternity *see* mothers/motherhood
Mayfair 29, 31
Maynard, Constance 125–33
McInlay, Jean (editor of *Honey*) 187–9, 196n36

middle class *see* class
Miss America 98
Miss Modern 28–30
Miss YAF 94, 95, 97–100
Modern Girl *see* Moderní dívka
Moderní dívka 69, 70, 71, 74, 75
Modern Woman 108, 110, 113–17, 119
modern woman/ modernity 33, 34–5, 67, 68, 72, 76–7, 107–24, 192, 208
motherhood 117, 125, 128, 137, 149, 176, 204

nannies 148–61; and class 148, 150, 157–8; and housework 149; and loneliness 151; nanny/child relationship 149, 151, 155, *156*, 157; nanny/mother relationship 148–51, 153–4, 158–9; trained 13, 149, 150, 152; in the US 150
nanny loss 155
National Review 92–4
nativism/nativist 171
The New Guard 92–100
The New Look 40–1
New Woman 68, 168, 175–6
Nineteenth Century 127–9
Norland Quarterly 150–3
nursery training colleges 152–3
Nursery World 148, 150–8, *156*

orgasm 16, 204–5, 207–11
Our Bodies, Ourselves 215, 219, 223

pacifism 130–3
Peg's Paper 46
Peiss, Kathy 229–30
photos/photography 33, 48, 68–9, 72, 74–5, 82, 98, 187, 189–92, 232–4
physical exercise *see* exercise, physical
The Pill 204, 219, 220
'Pin-up(s)' 48, 94–5, 97–100, 182n58, 190
politics: The Left/left wing 92–6, 98, 100, 108, 113; Republicanism/Republican politics 92, 93, 98–100; The Right/right wing 91–100; socialism/socialist 107, 108, 111–12, 114–16, 118–19; *see also* free love; race/racial
pornographic magazines 43–4, 48

Quakers/Religious Society of Friends 125–6, 128–30
Quant, Mary 191

race/racial 56, 84–5, 172, 192, 229–31, 234, 237; American 169–71, 173–4, 177–8; citizenship and 172, constructs of 165; decline 59, 61–2, 170, 173, 175; equality 16, 228–9, 232–3; improvement of 61–2, 174; politics 231–2, 233–7 (*see also* Black Power Movement; Civil Rights Movement); pride 232; solidarity 231, 233; *see also* African American women; white/whiteness
race suicide 173, 175
racial degeneration *see* racial decline
racism 232–3
radicalism, *see* sex radicalism
readers 25, 26, 27–31, 32–8, 82, 95–6, 108, 110–17, 119, 138–43, 151–2, 186–7, 189–90, 217, 205–11, 230–7; competitions 112, 186; enquiry services 186; letters (*see* correspondence pages; letters)
research practices: contextual 25–7, 34; digitisation 26; fragmentary 26–7, 37–8; holistic approach 7, 26, 31–8; lateral mapping 26–9, 31, 37–8; longitudinal mapping 26–7; methods/methodology 25–6, 31, 37–8, 42; semiotics 25, 31, 34; textual analysis 26, 31–7; visual analysis 26, 27, 31, 32–4, 36–7
respectable/respectability 81, 83, 85, 90, 114, 117, 157, 176, 205
rhetoric in magazines 55, 58, 61, 191–2, 218, 225, 234
romance 29, 30, 34, 69, 167, 177; *see also* love
romantic fiction, *see* fiction
Roosevelt, Alice 173
Roosevelt, Theodore 173, 175

Sanders, Byrne Hope (editor of *Chatelaine*) 139–40
schoolgirl magazines *see* magazines
sex/sexual: choice 61; education 177, 204–6; equality 55, 57–8, 216; freedom 56, 58–9, 62, 201; health 178; inequality 56–7; liberation 3, 201, 203, 205–6, 208; morality 171, 173; pleasure 204, 208–10 (*see also* orgasm); radicalism 10, 55–7, 59; and relationships 10, 60, 175, 177, 190–1; 203–11; shops 208; transmitted diseases 202
Sex and the Single Girl 96–7
sexism 15, 95, 97, 100, 121n22, 144, 202, 214, 216–19, 223, 225
sexology/sexologists 114, 173, 177, 209
sexuality 44, 59–62, 83, 165–8, 177, 204, 206–9; *see also* heterosexuality; homosexuality
single girls/women 12–14, 96–8, 108–10, 118, 148, 183–5, 191–3
Slaughter, Audrey 17, 189–91, 196n37
smoking 9, 31, 33–7, 35
socialism 12, 46, 107–8, 111–2, 114–16, 118–19
Spencer, Herbert 175
Sports Illustrated 81, 82, 84–5, 88–9
Steedman, Carolyn 40–1, 50–1
Students for a Democratic Society (SDS) 94–5, 98–9
subjectivity, female 47, 49–50, 96
suffrage 67, 69, 108, 111, 113, 173, 175–6, 217–18
Sundial Cottage 127, 128, 133
surgery, gynaecological 218, 222

The Teenage Consumer 31, 183–4; *see also* Abrams, Mark
teen magazines *see* magazines
teen/teenager 27, 46, 29–31, 173, 183, 193, 204; as consumers 31, 183–5, 187, 193
tone *see* voice(s)
trade magazines *see* magazines

The Uses of Literacy 4, 46–8

Valentine 29, 185
vibrator 206, 208
visuals 110–11, 168, 172, 187, 191–2
Vogue 1, 3, 17, 33, 43, 186–7, 191
voice(s) 32–3, 37, 56, 58–9, 94, 97, 100, 113, 130, 152, 159, 167, 202, 209, 211

Walker, Hiram *see* Hiram Walker Distillery
Westfield College 125–9, 132–3

white/whiteness 11, 81, 84–5, 98, 138, 165, 170–5, 178, 229–30, 232–3
Wise, Ursula 155
Woman 48, 114, 185, 187, 191
women and work *see* working women; working wives/mothers
women, biological nature of 56–8, 62, 174–5, 215
The Woman in the Little House 110, 113, 118
women's health 72, 75, 110, 167, 174–5; *see also* doctor's advice; women's health movement
women's health movement 214–25
women's liberation 100, 193, 201–3, 211, 215, 218, 225
The Women's Liberation Movement 201–3, 211, 215
women's magazines *see* magazines
Woman's Own 12, 43, 119, 185, 187, 191
Woman's Weekly 1, 114

working wives/mothers 12–13, 17, 29, 112, 114–19, 137–45; and family 126, 140–1; marriage bar 110, 138
working women 3, 12–13, 72, 74–5, 108, 110, 112, 116, 185, 192, 202, 219; and class 28, 119, 138–9; clerical/office 13, 28, 108–9, 114, 184; domestic service 28, 108–9, 114–16, 224–6, 248; and equal pay 115, 117; paid 6, 28–30, 118, 137–8, 140–5; professional work 113–17, 119, 122n55, 125–6, 128, 140, 148, 149; retail/shop 28, 114; *see also* housewife/housewifery
World War One *see* First World War

Young Americans for Freedom (YAF) 92–100
youth movements 92, 96, 98